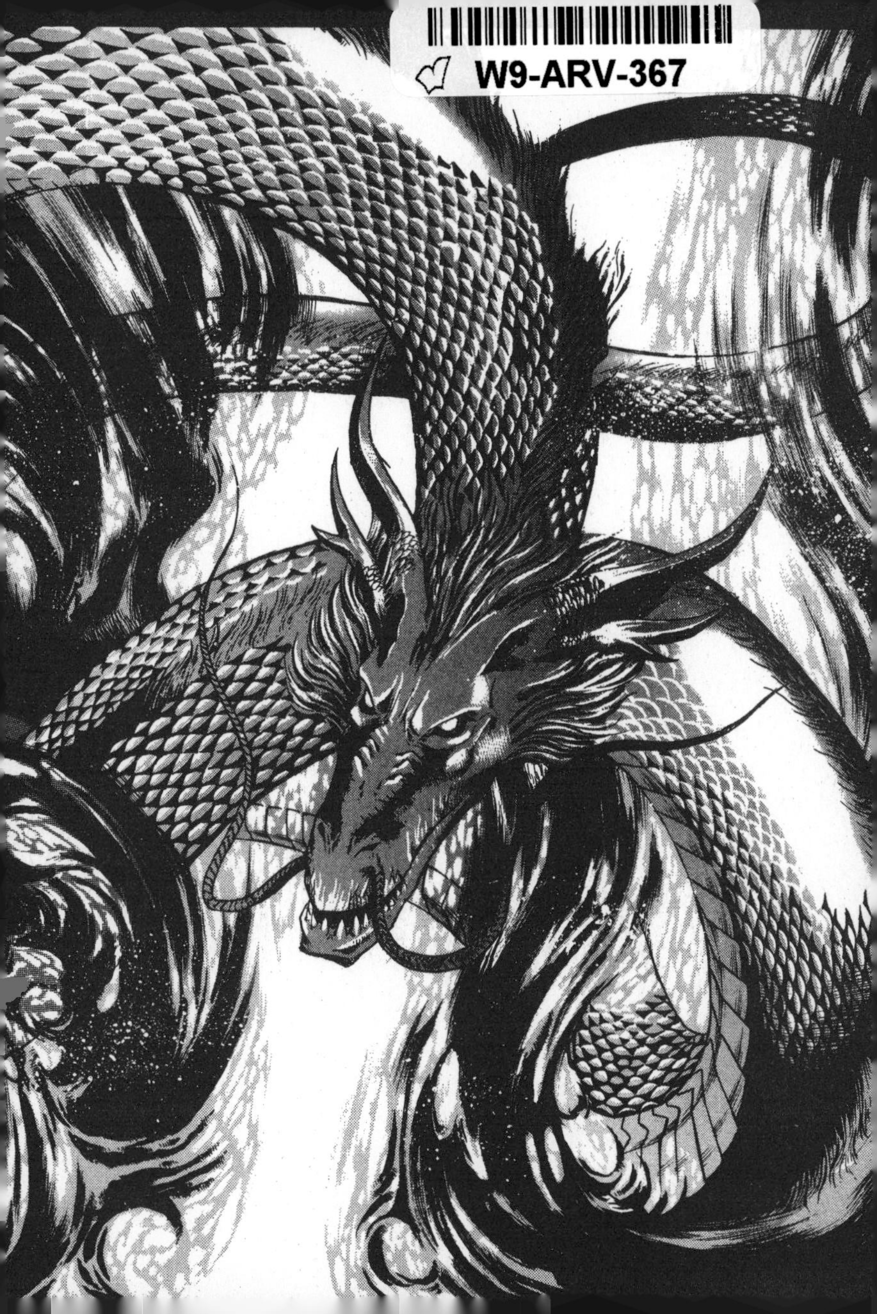

CHRONICLES OF THE CURSED SWORD

Volume 5

Story by
YEO BEOP-RYONG
Art by
PARK HUI-JIN

TOKYOPOP®

Los Angeles • Tokyo • London

Translation - Yongju Ryu
English Adaptation - Matt Varosky
Graphic Designer - Monalisa de Asis
Copy Editor - Chrissy Schilling
Retouch & Lettering - Steven Redd
Cover Design - Gary Shum

Editor - Paul Morrissey
Managing Editor - Jill Freshney
Production Coordinator - Antonio DePietro
Production Managers - Jennifer Miller, Mutsumi Miyazaki
Art Director - Matt Alford
Director of Editorial - Jeremy Ross
VP of Production - Ron Klamert
President & C.O.O. - John Parker
Publisher & C.E.O. - Stuart Levy

Email: editor@TOKYOPOP.com
Come visit us online at www.TOKYOPOP.com

A  Manga

TOKYOPOP Inc.
5900 Wilshire Blvd. Suite 2000
Los Angeles, CA 90036

Chronicles of the Cursed Sword Vol. 5
©2001 YEO BEOP-RYONG and PARK HUI-JIN.
First printed in Korea in 2001 by Daiwon C.I. Inc. English translation rights in
North America, UK, NZ and Australia arranged by Daiwon C.I. Inc.

English text copyright ©2004 TOKYOPOP Inc.

ISBN: 1-59182-422-2

First TOKYOPOP printing: March 2004

10 9 8 7 6 5 4 3 2 1
Printed in the USA

Chronicles

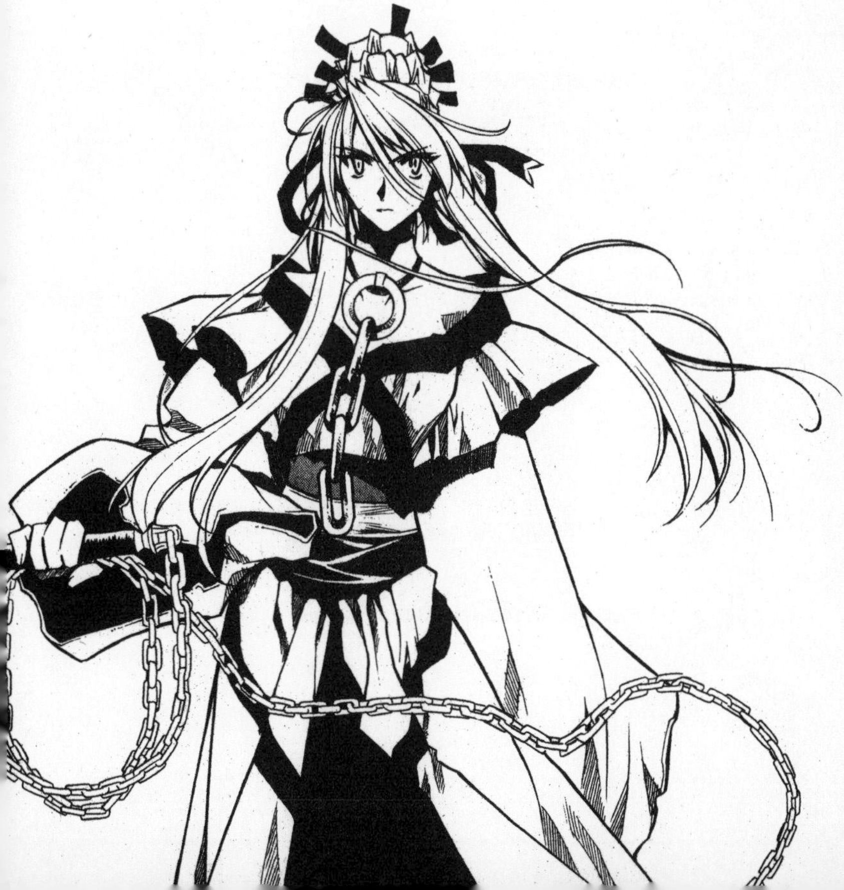

CHRONICLES OF THE CURSED SWORD

the cast of characters

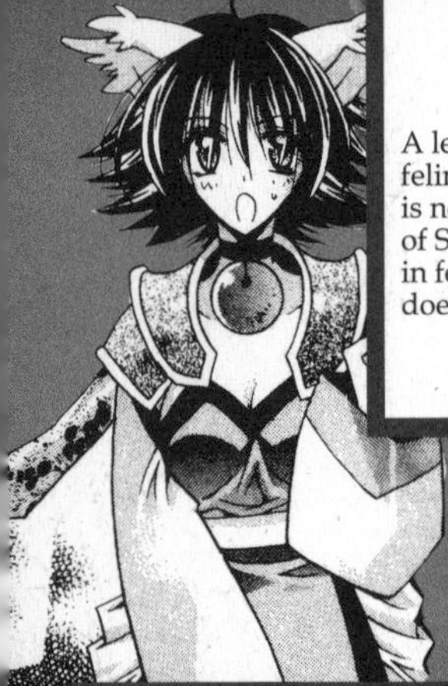

MINGLING

A lesser demon with feline qualities, Mingling is now the loyal follower of Shyao Lin. She lives in fear of Rey who still doesn't trust her.

THE PASA SWORD

A living sword that hungers for demon blood. It grants its user incredible power, but at a great cost—it can take over the user's body and, in time, his soul.

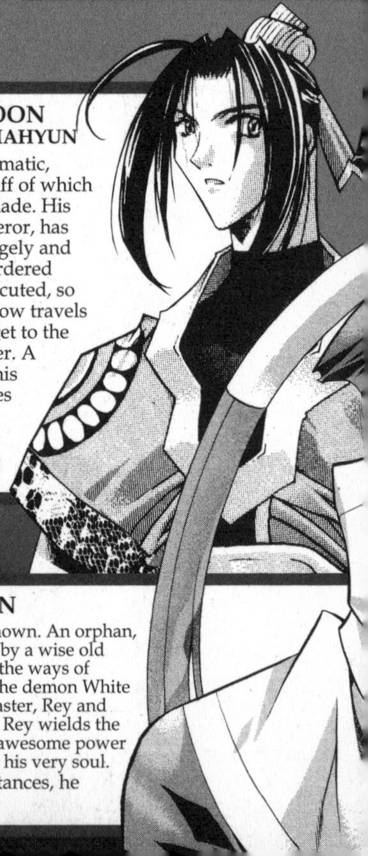

JARYOON
KING OF HAHYUN

Noble and charismatic, Jaryoon is the stuff of which great kings are made. His brother, the emperor, has been acting strangely and apparently has ordered Jaryoon to be executed, so the young king now travels to the capital to get to the heart of the matter. A great warrior in his own right, he does not have magical abilities and is unaccustomed to battling demons.

SHYAO LIN

A sorceress and Rey Yan's traveling companion. Shyao grew fond of Rey during their five years of study together with their master, and thinks of him as her little brother. She's Rey's conscience—his sole tie to humanity. She also seems quite enamored with the handsome Jaryoon.

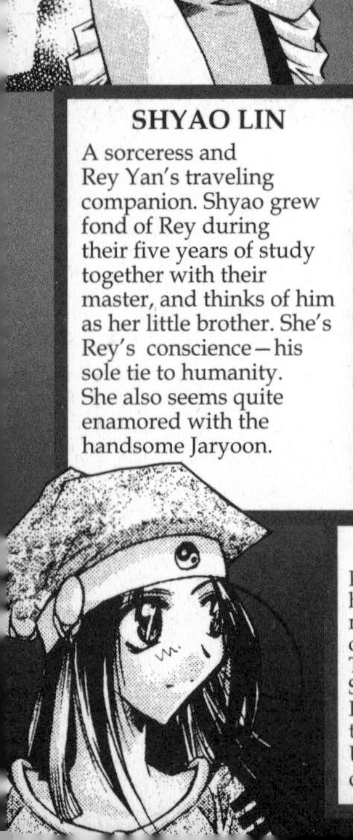

REY YAN

Rey's origins remain unknown. An orphan, he and Shyao were raised by a wise old man who trained them in the ways of combat and magic. After the demon White Tiger slaughtered their master, Rey and Shyao became wanderers. Rey wields the PaSa sword, a weapon of awesome power that threatens to take over his very soul. Under the right circumstances, he could be a hero.

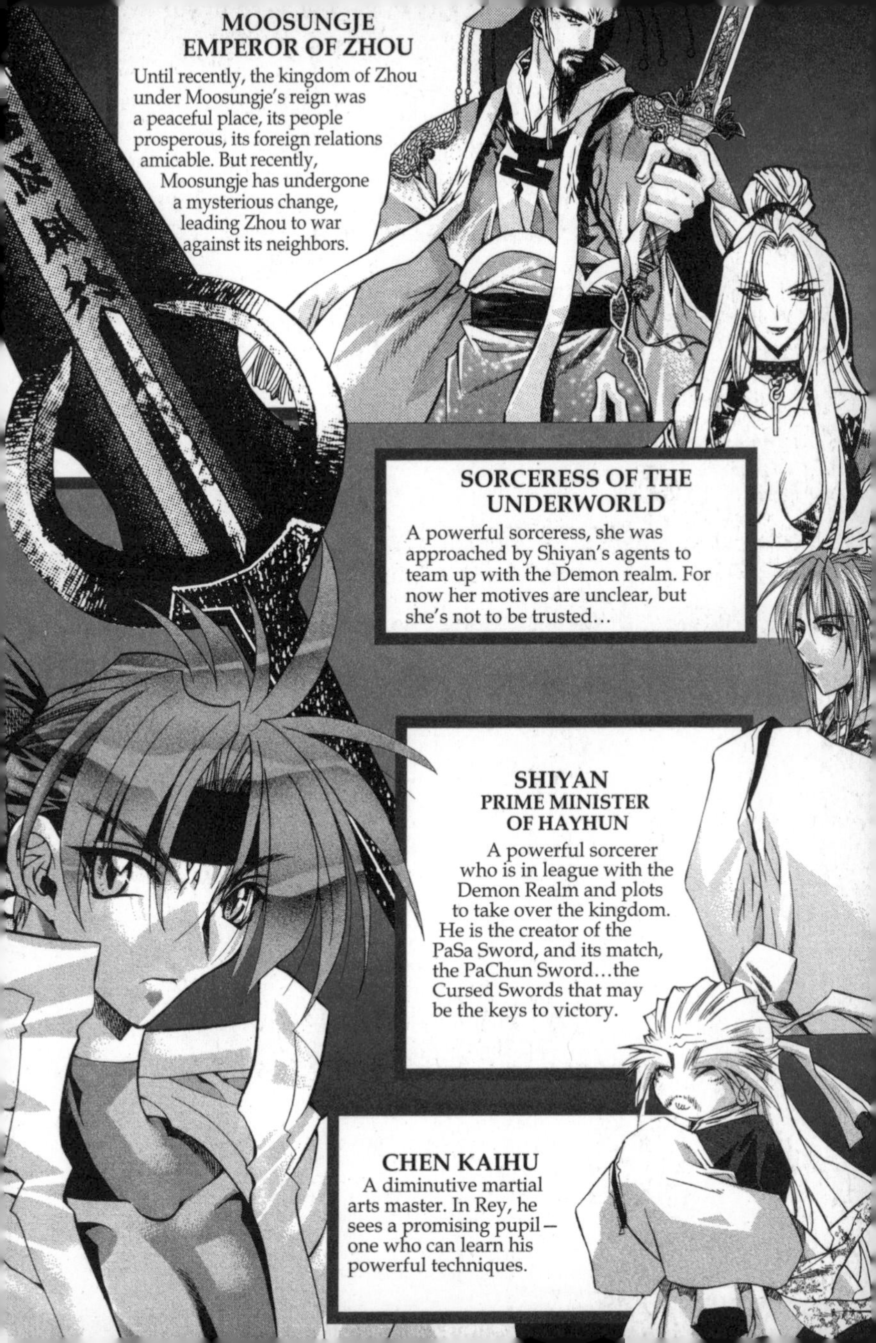
MOOSUNGJE
EMPEROR OF ZHOU
Until recently, the kingdom of Zhou under Moosungje's reign was a peaceful place, its people prosperous, its foreign relations amicable. But recently, Moosungje has undergone a mysterious change, leading Zhou to war against its neighbors.
SORCERESS OF THE UNDERWORLD
A powerful sorceress, she was approached by Shiyan's agents to team up with the Demon realm. For now her motives are unclear, but she's not to be trusted…
SHIYAN
PRIME MINISTER OF HAYHUN
A powerful sorcerer who is in league with the Demon Realm and plots to take over the kingdom. He is the creator of the PaSa Sword, and its match, the PaChun Sword…the Cursed Swords that may be the keys to victory.
CHEN KAIHU
A diminutive martial arts master. In Rey, he sees a promising pupil—one who can learn his powerful techniques.

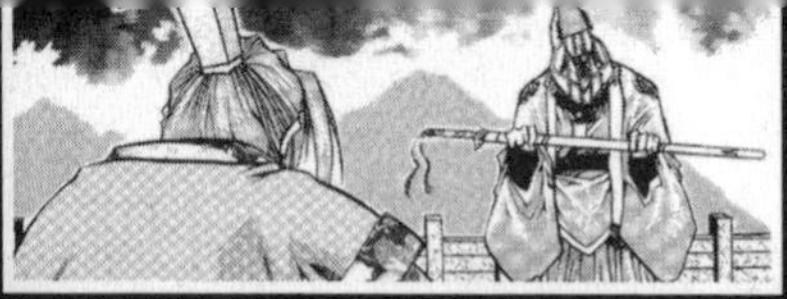

Prime Minister Shiyan presented the Emperor Moosungje with the magical PaChun sword, after which the formerly peaceful Moosungje attacked his neighboring kingdoms.

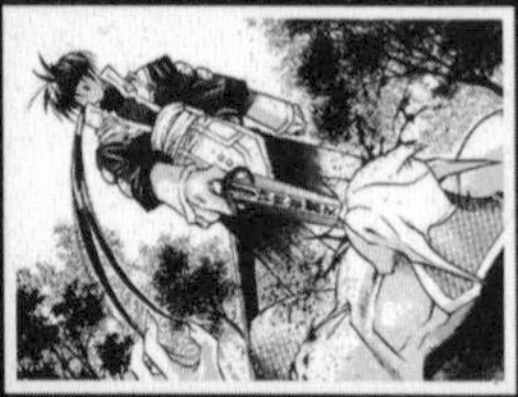

Rey Yan and Shyao Lin rescued Jaryoon using Rey's cursed PaSa sword.

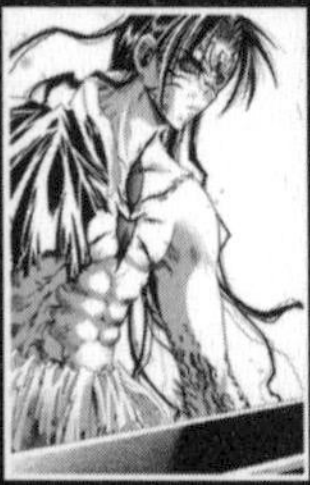

During his confrontation with the Sorceress of the Underworld, Rey transforms into his "true" demon form...

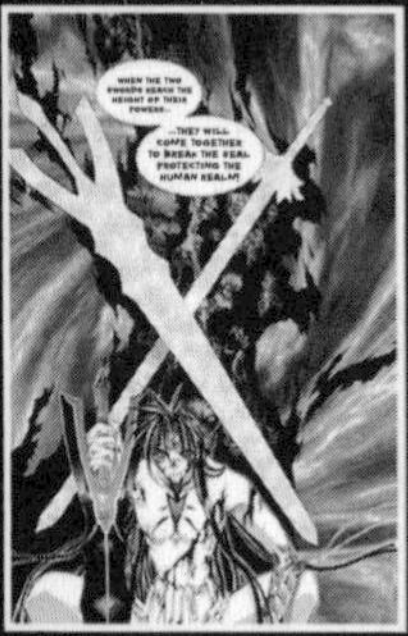
WHEN THE TWO SWORDS REACH THE HEIGHT OF THEIR POWERS...
...THEY WILL COME TOGETHER TO BREAK THE SEAL PROTECTING THE HUMAN REALM!

The demon possessing Rey conspires with the Sorceress to summon the Demon Emperor by combining the powers of the PaSa and PaChun swords.

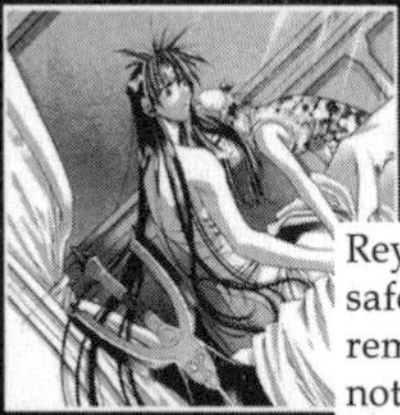

Rey awakens safely with Shyao, remembering nothing of his "demon form."

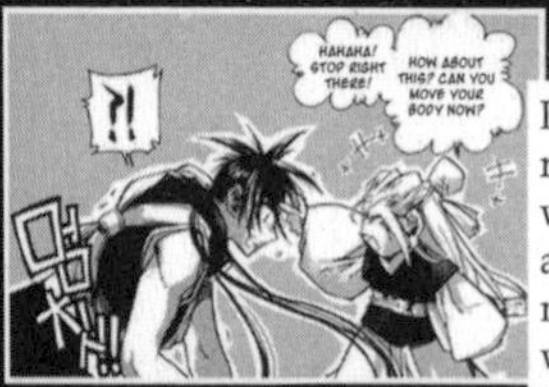
HAHAHA! STOP RIGHT THERE!
HOW ABOUT THIS? CAN YOU MOVE YOUR BODY NOW?
?!

Rey begins rigorous training with chen Kaihu—a diminuitive martial arts master with powerful techniques

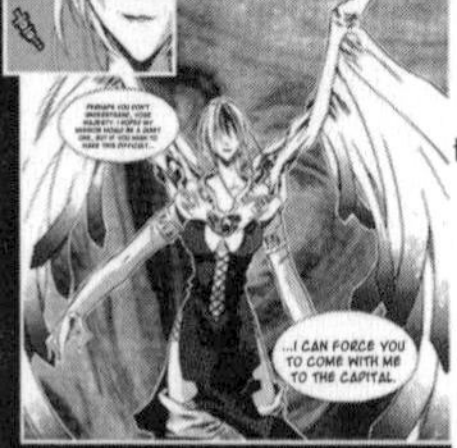
...I CAN FORCE YOU TO COME WITH ME TO THE CAPITAL.

Timura Oshu is sent by the sinister Shiyar to bring Jaryoo back to the capital. Shiyar has plans for Jaryoon—as th new wielder of the PaChun sword!

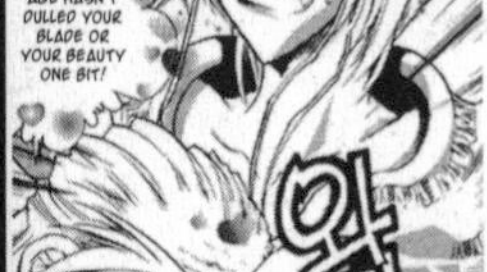
AGE HASN'T DULLED YOUR BLADE OR YOUR BEAUTY ONE BIT!

Chen Kaihu mistakes Timura Oshu for Lady Hwaren, his long-lost love. Could they be one and the same?

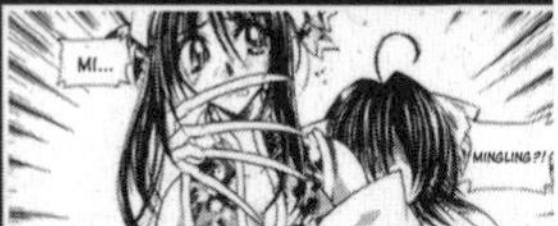
MI...
MINGLING?!

Timura Oshu possesses Mingling using her to threaten Shyao's lif Given no choice, Jaryoon reluctantly accompanies Timu to the capital...

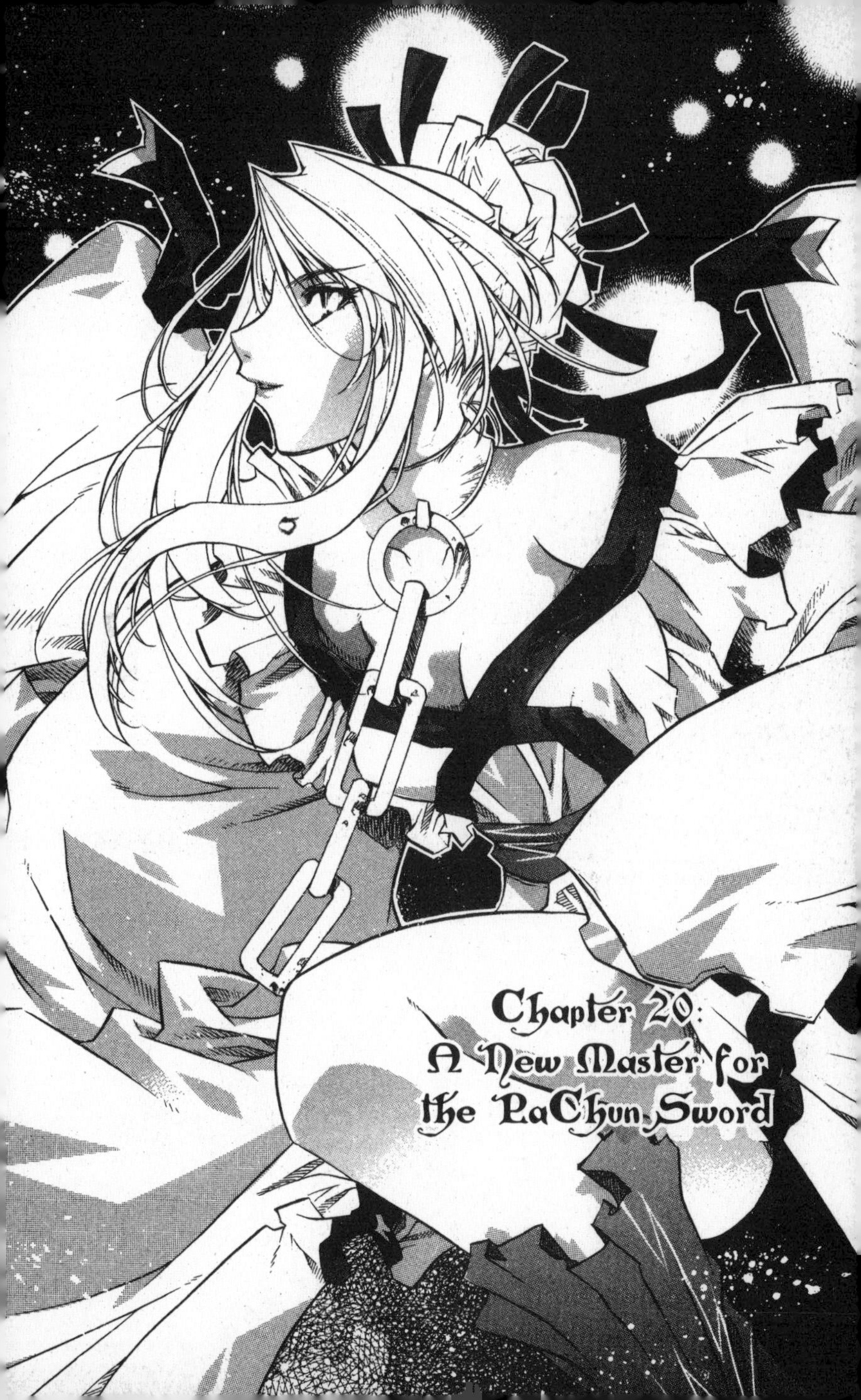
Chapter 20:
A New Master for
the LaChun Sword

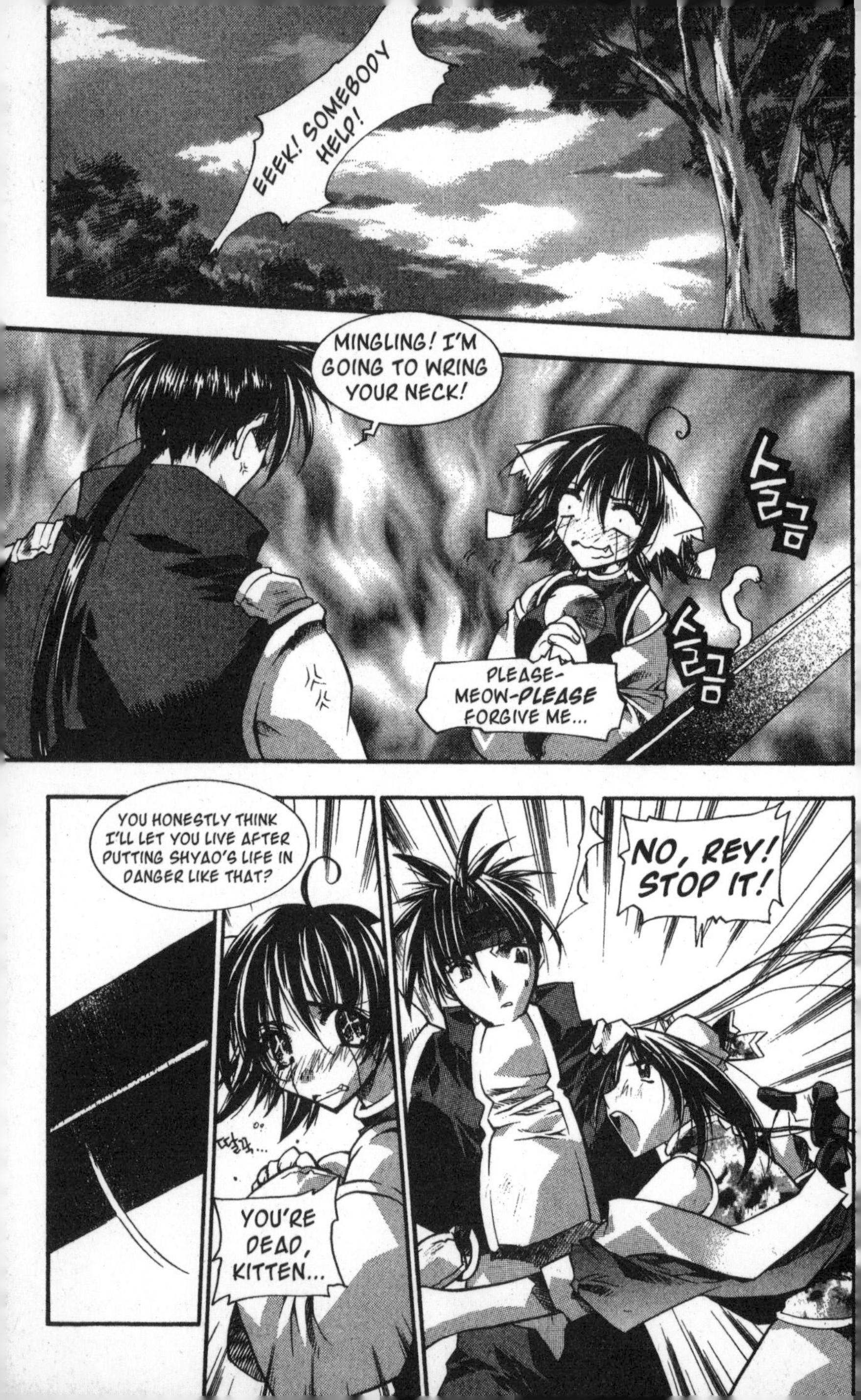
EEEK! SOMEBODY HELP!
MINGLING! I'M GOING TO WRING YOUR NECK!
PLEASE-MEOW-PLEASE FORGIVE ME...
YOU HONESTLY THINK I'LL LET YOU LIVE AFTER PUTTING SHYAO'S LIFE IN DANGER LIKE THAT?
YOU'RE DEAD, KITTEN...
NO, REY! STOP IT!

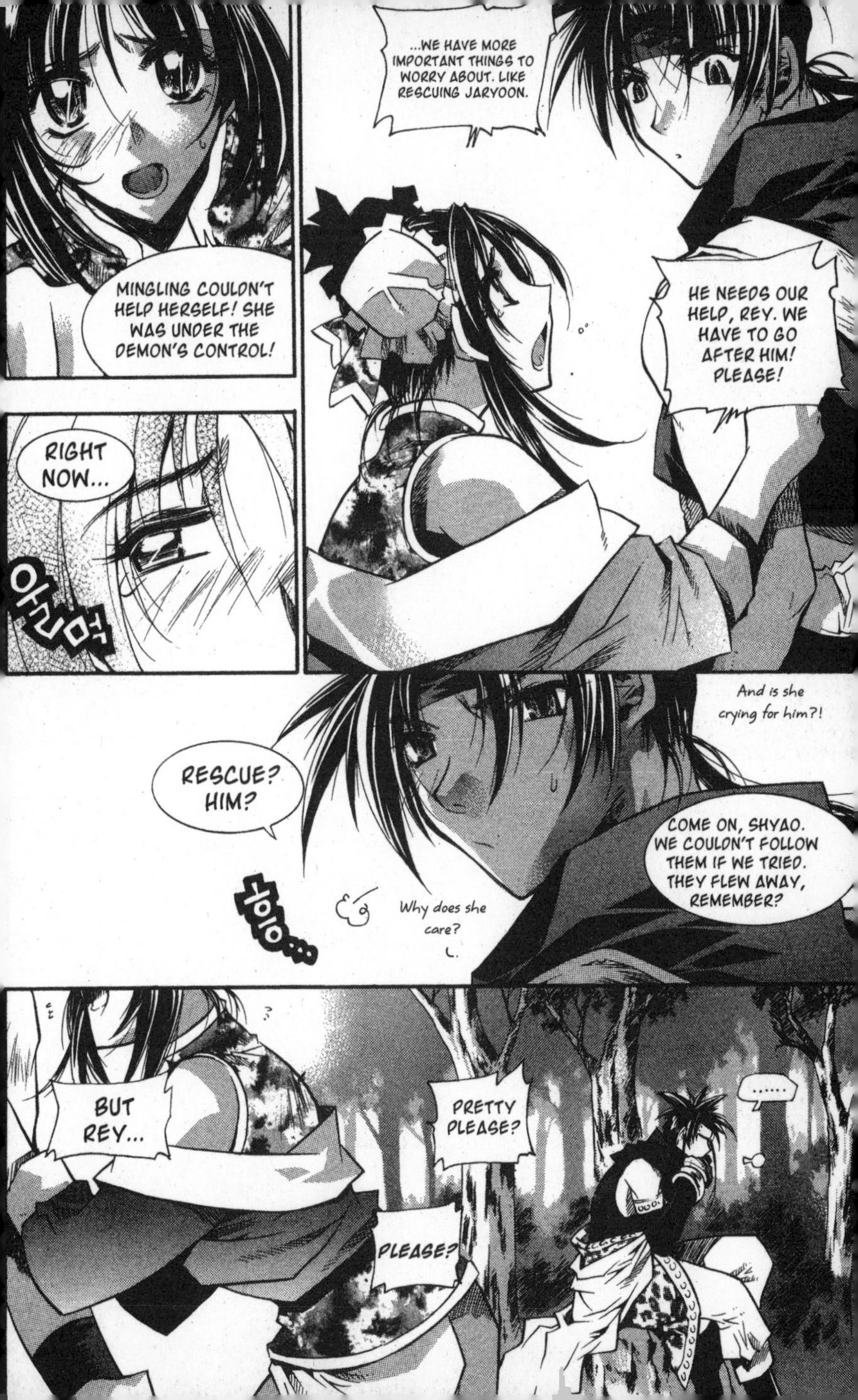
MINGLING COULDN'T HELP HERSELF! SHE WAS UNDER THE DEMON'S CONTROL!
RIGHT NOW...
...WE HAVE MORE IMPORTANT THINGS TO WORRY ABOUT. LIKE RESCUING JARYOON.
HE NEEDS OUR HELP, REY. WE HAVE TO GO AFTER HIM! PLEASE!
RESCUE? HIM?
Why does she care?
And is she crying for him?!
COME ON, SHYAO. WE COULDN'T FOLLOW THEM IF WE TRIED. THEY FLEW AWAY, REMEMBER?
BUT REY...
PRETTY PLEASE?
PLEASE?
......

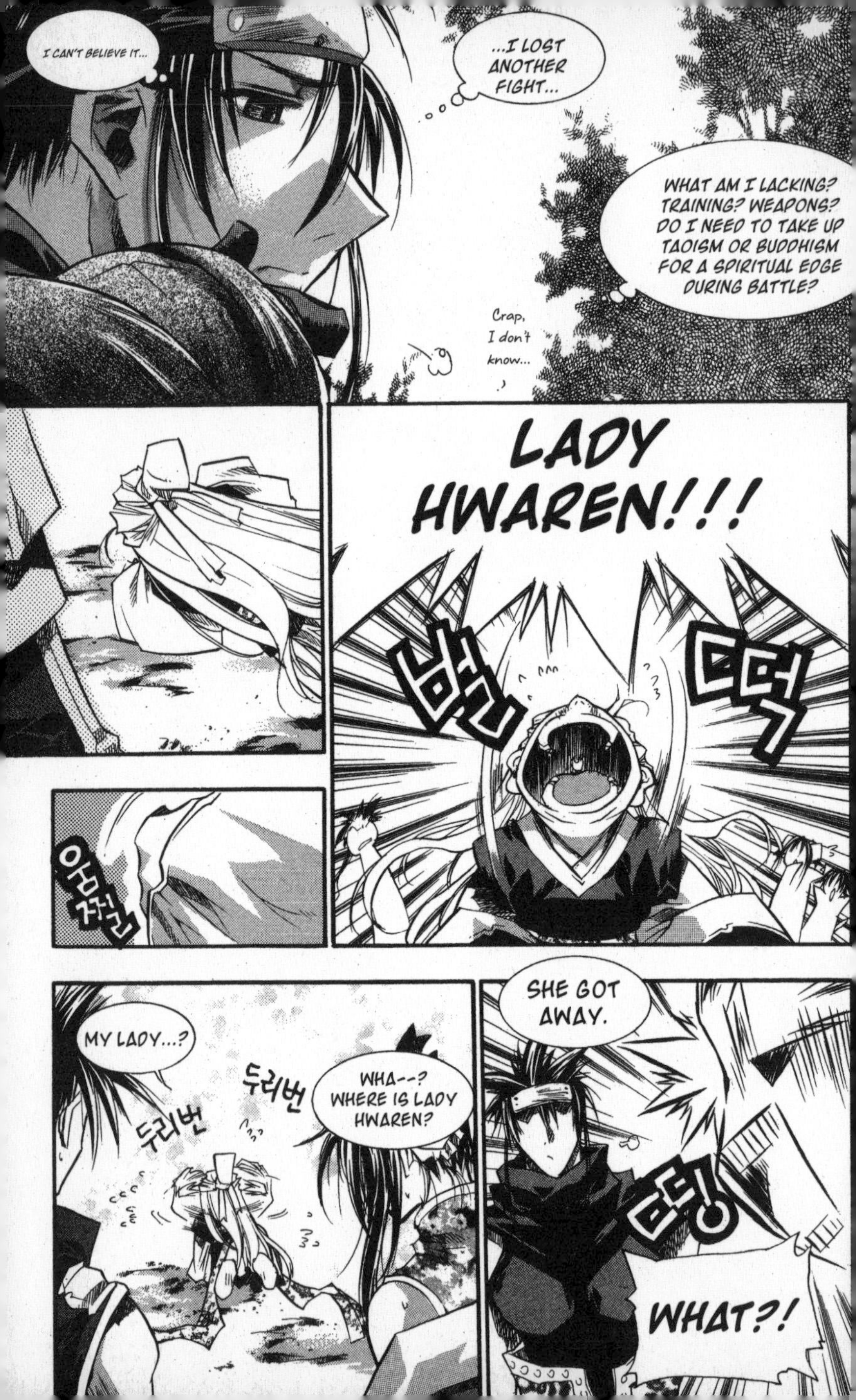
I CAN'T BELIEVE IT...
...I LOST ANOTHER FIGHT...
WHAT AM I LACKING? TRAINING? WEAPONS? DO I NEED TO TAKE UP TAOISM OR BUDDHISM FOR A SPIRITUAL EDGE DURING BATTLE?
Crap, I don't know...
LADY HWAREN!!!
MY LADY...?
두리번
두리번
WHA--? WHERE IS LADY HWAREN?
SHE GOT AWAY.
WHAT?!

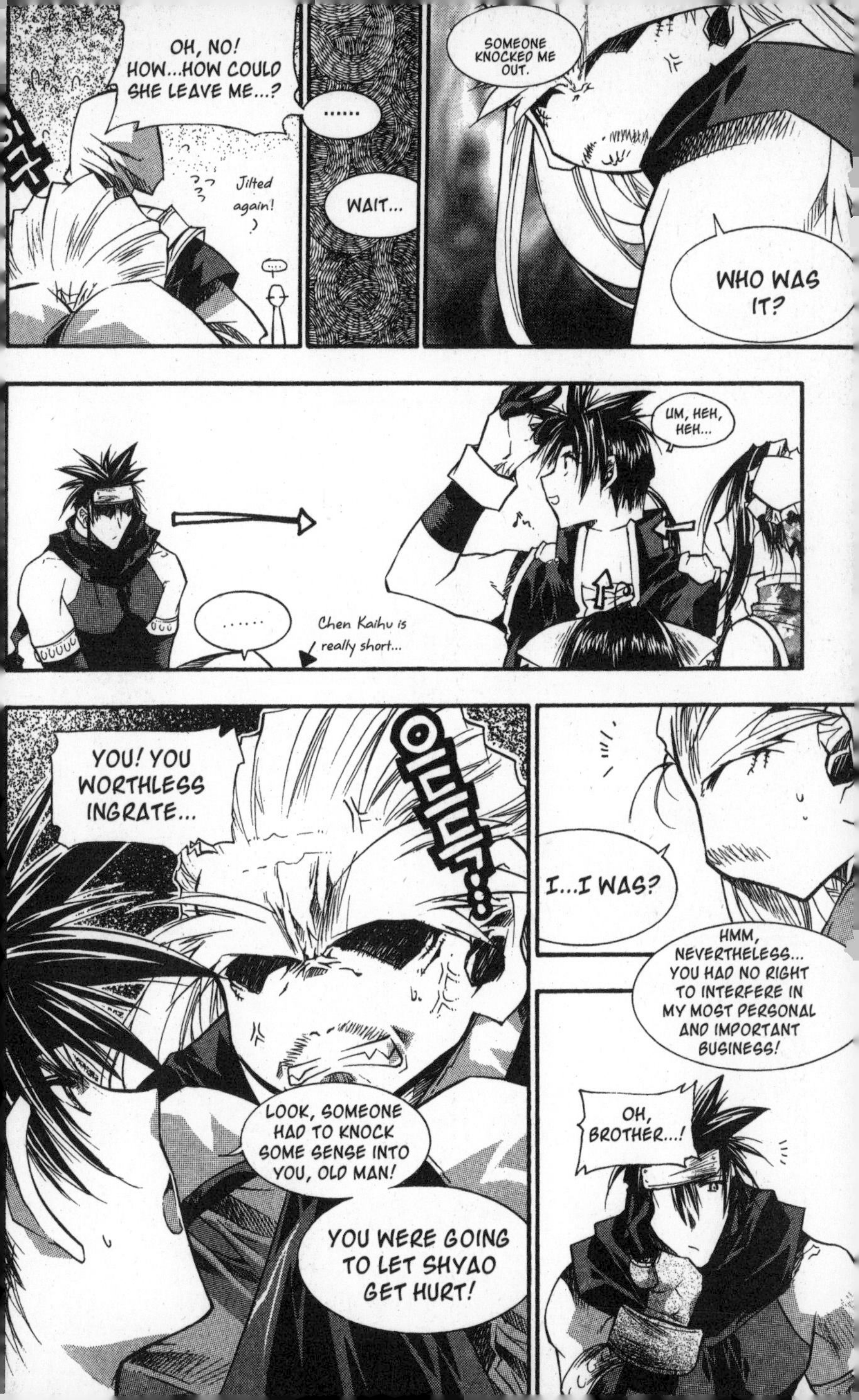
OH, NO! HOW...HOW COULD SHE LEAVE ME...?
Jilted again!
......
WAIT...
SOMEONE KNOCKED ME OUT.
WHO WAS IT?
......
Chen Kaihu is really short...
UM, HEH, HEH...
YOU! YOU WORTHLESS INGRATE...
LOOK, SOMEONE HAD TO KNOCK SOME SENSE INTO YOU, OLD MAN!
YOU WERE GOING TO LET SHYAO GET HURT!
I...I WAS?
HMM, NEVERTHELESS... YOU HAD NO RIGHT TO INTERFERE IN MY MOST PERSONAL AND IMPORTANT BUSINESS!
OH, BROTHER...!

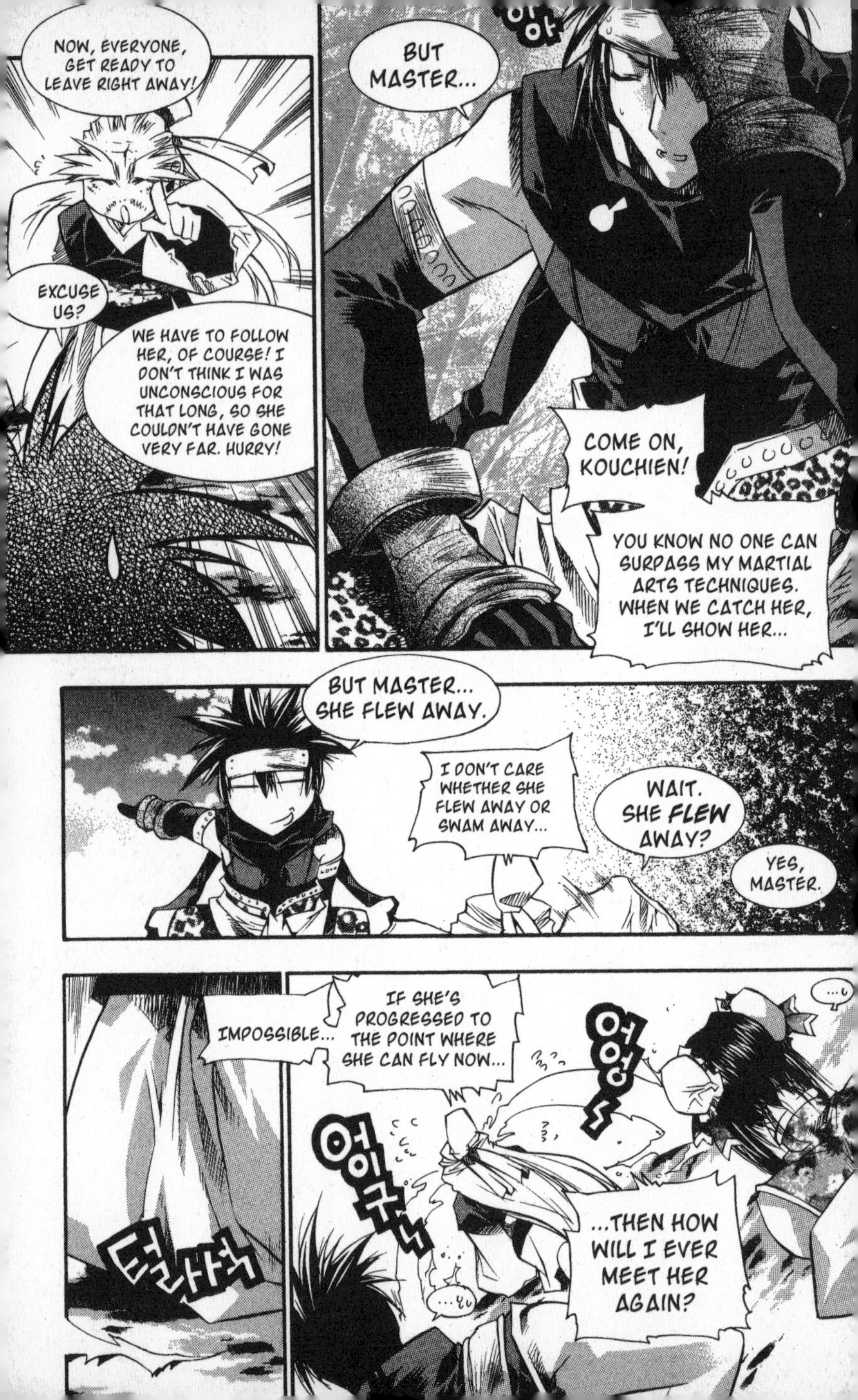

NOW, EVERYONE, GET READY TO LEAVE RIGHT AWAY!
EXCUSE US?
WE HAVE TO FOLLOW HER, OF COURSE! I DON'T THINK I WAS UNCONSCIOUS FOR THAT LONG, SO SHE COULDN'T HAVE GONE VERY FAR. HURRY!
BUT MASTER...
COME ON, KOUCHIEN!
YOU KNOW NO ONE CAN SURPASS MY MARTIAL ARTS TECHNIQUES. WHEN WE CATCH HER, I'LL SHOW HER...
BUT MASTER... SHE FLEW AWAY.
I DON'T CARE WHETHER SHE FLEW AWAY OR SWAM AWAY...
WAIT. SHE *FLEW* AWAY?
YES, MASTER.
IMPOSSIBLE...
IF SHE'S PROGRESSED TO THE POINT WHERE SHE CAN FLY NOW...
...THEN HOW WILL I EVER MEET HER AGAIN?

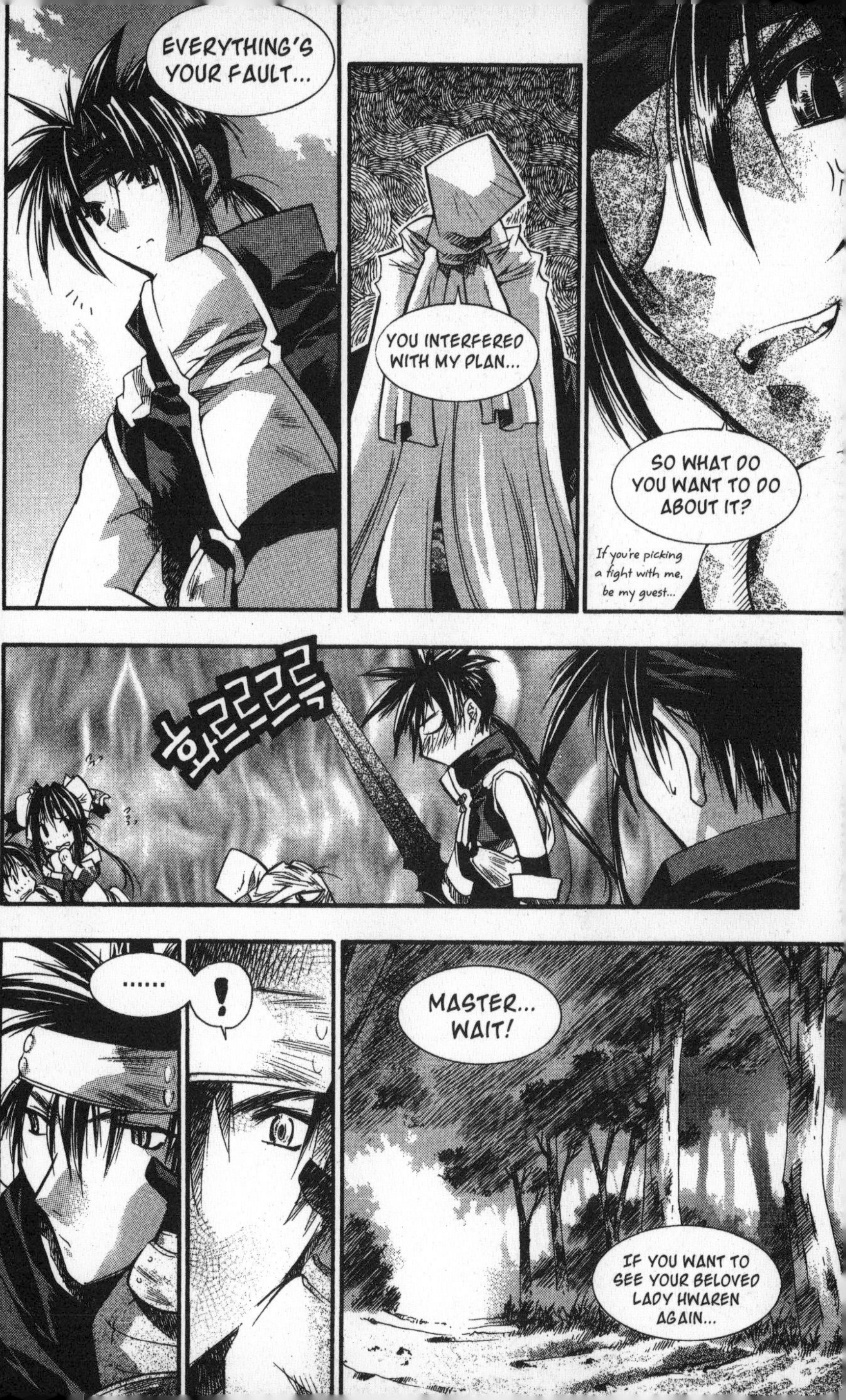
EVERYTHING'S YOUR FAULT...
YOU INTERFERED WITH MY PLAN...
SO WHAT DO YOU WANT TO DO ABOUT IT?
If you're picking a fight with me, be my guest...
화르르르륵
......
!
MASTER... WAIT!
IF YOU WANT TO SEE YOUR BELOVED LADY HWAREN AGAIN...

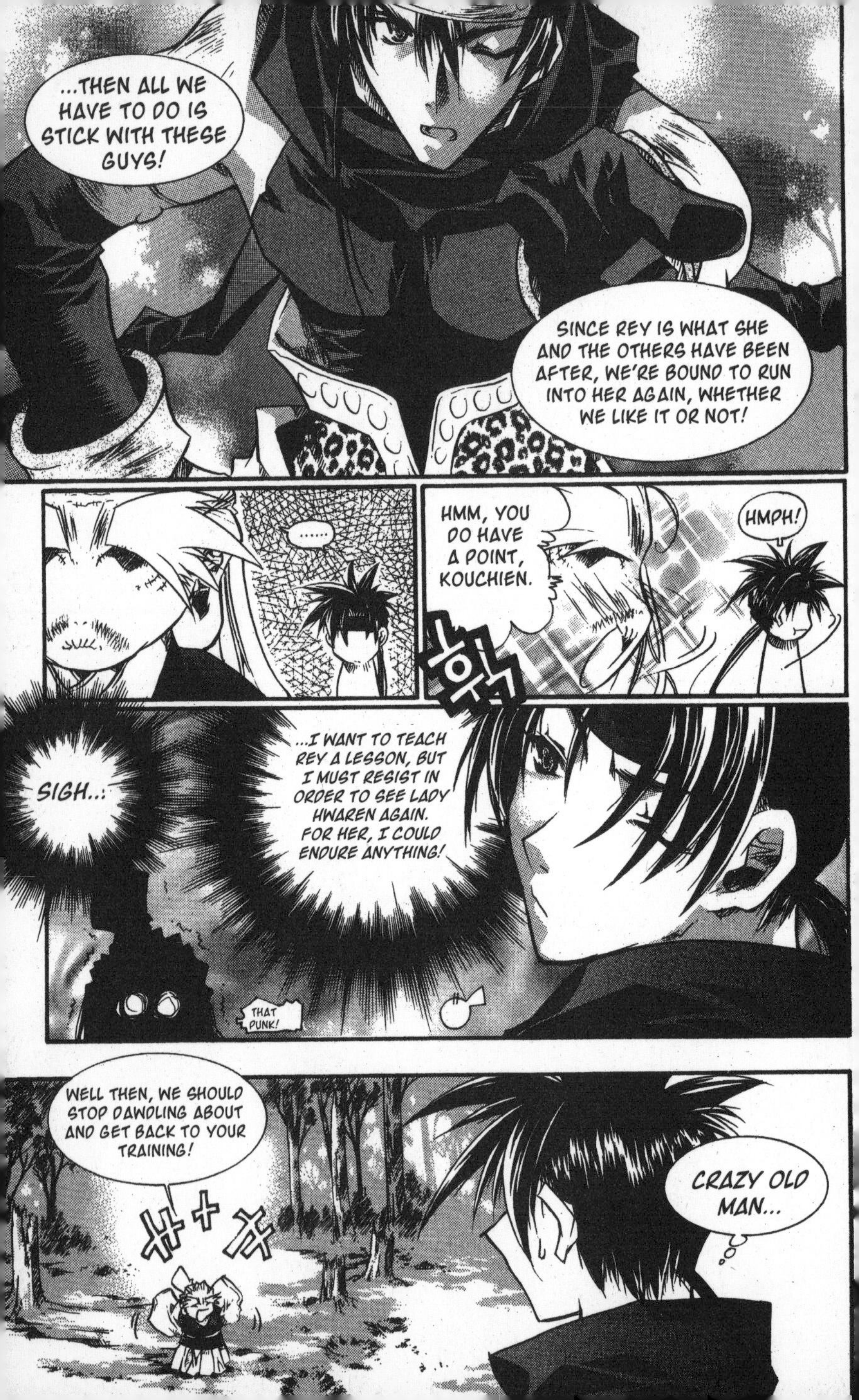
...THEN ALL WE HAVE TO DO IS STICK WITH THESE GUYS!
SINCE REY IS WHAT SHE AND THE OTHERS HAVE BEEN AFTER, WE'RE BOUND TO RUN INTO HER AGAIN, WHETHER WE LIKE IT OR NOT!
....
HMM, YOU DO HAVE A POINT, KOUCHIEN.
HMPH!
SIGH...
...I WANT TO TEACH REY A LESSON, BUT I MUST RESIST IN ORDER TO SEE LADY HWAREN AGAIN. FOR HER, I COULD ENDURE ANYTHING!
THAT PUNK!
WELL THEN, WE SHOULD STOP DAWDLING ABOUT AND GET BACK TO YOUR TRAINING!
CRAZY OLD MAN...

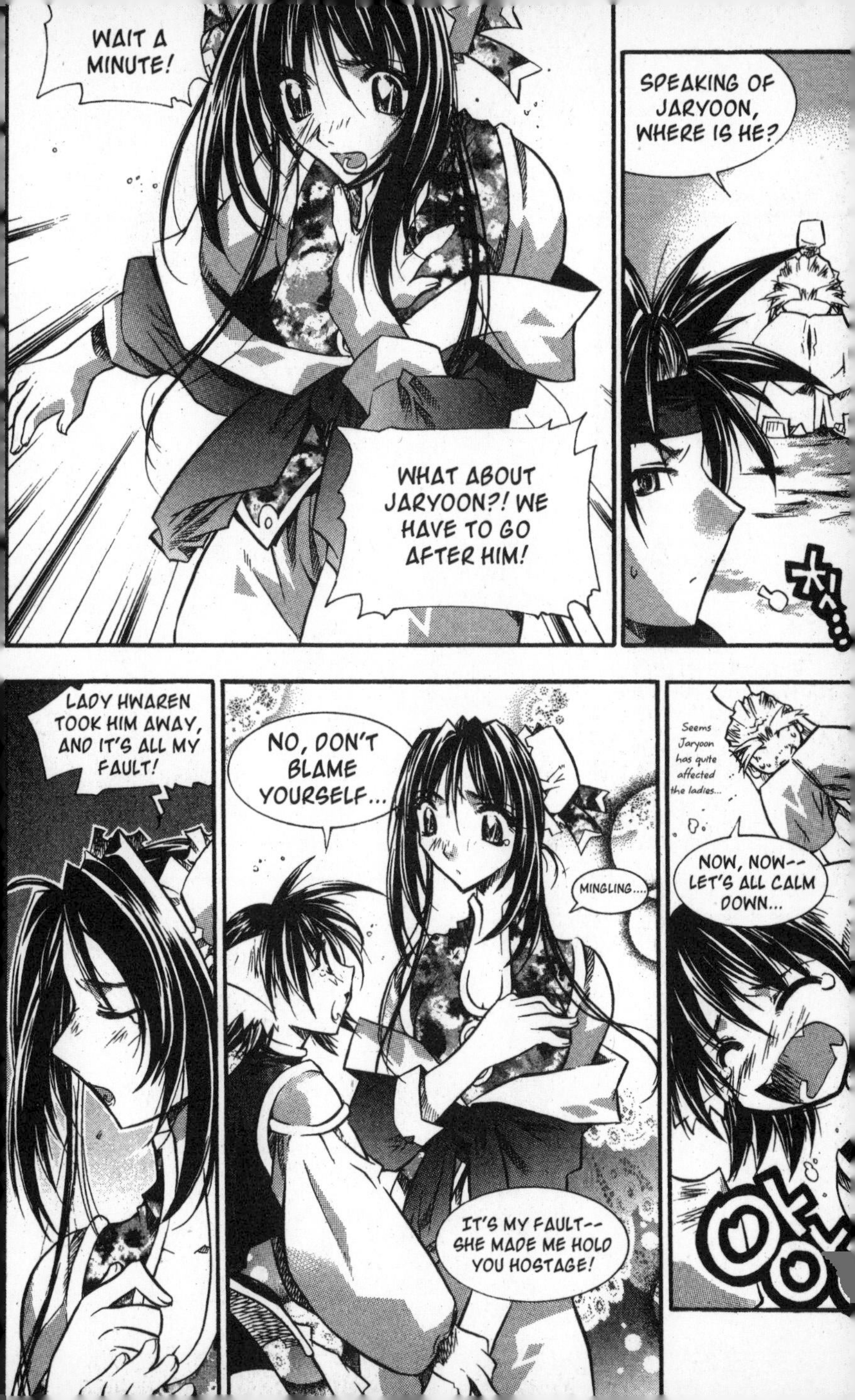
WAIT A MINUTE!
WHAT ABOUT JARYOON?! WE HAVE TO GO AFTER HIM!
SPEAKING OF JARYOON, WHERE IS HE?
LADY HWAREN TOOK HIM AWAY, AND IT'S ALL MY FAULT!
NO, DON'T BLAME YOURSELF...
MINGLING....
IT'S MY FAULT-- SHE MADE ME HOLD YOU HOSTAGE!
Seems Jaryoon has quite affected the ladies...
NOW, NOW-- LET'S ALL CALM DOWN...

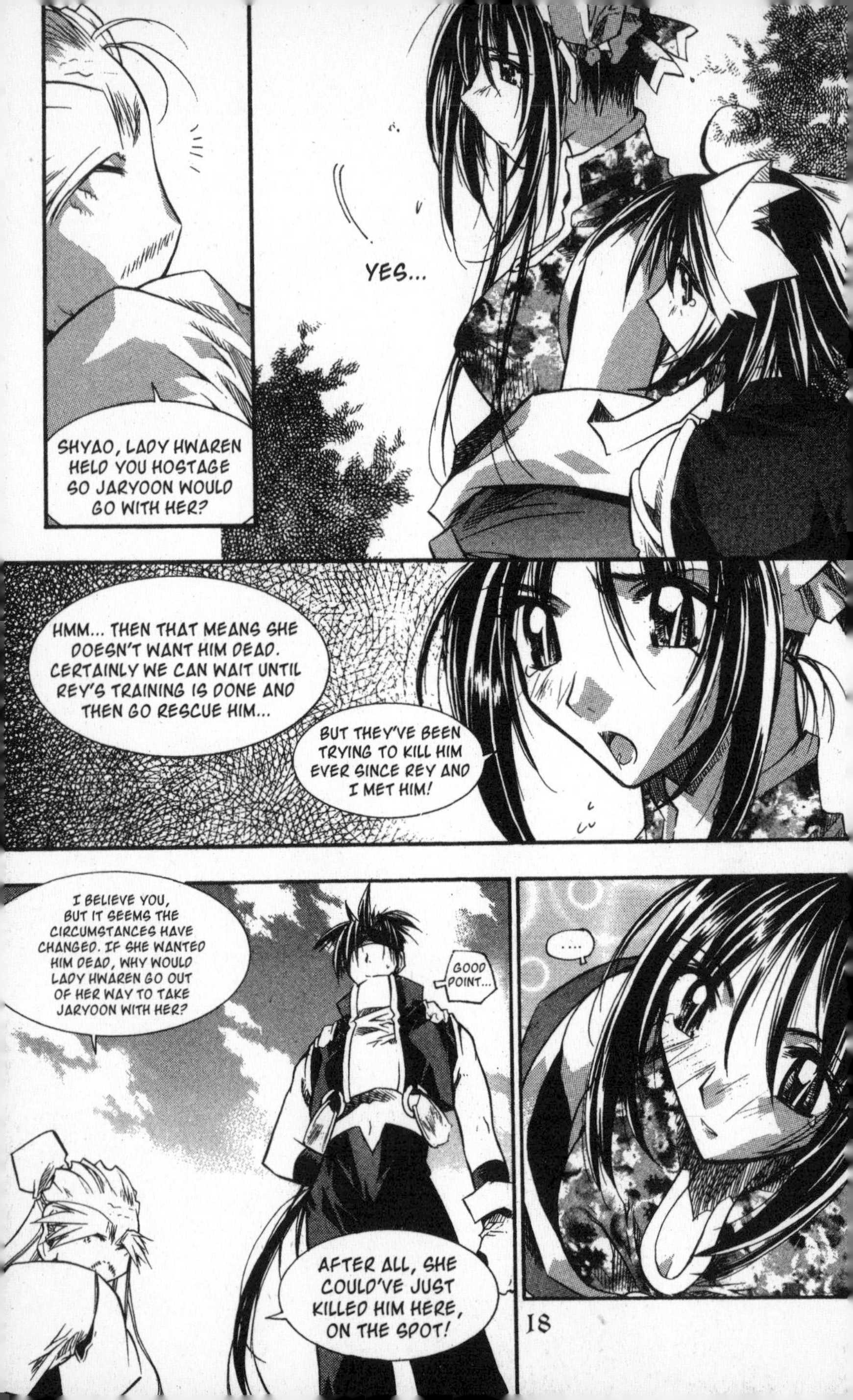
SHYAO, LADY HWAREN HELD YOU HOSTAGE SO JARYOON WOULD GO WITH HER?
YES...
HMM... THEN THAT MEANS SHE DOESN'T WANT HIM DEAD. CERTAINLY WE CAN WAIT UNTIL REY'S TRAINING IS DONE AND THEN GO RESCUE HIM...
BUT THEY'VE BEEN TRYING TO KILL HIM EVER SINCE REY AND I MET HIM!
I BELIEVE YOU, BUT IT SEEMS THE CIRCUMSTANCES HAVE CHANGED. IF SHE WANTED HIM DEAD, WHY WOULD LADY HWAREN GO OUT OF HER WAY TO TAKE JARYOON WITH HER?
GOOD POINT...
AFTER ALL, SHE COULD'VE JUST KILLED HIM HERE, ON THE SPOT!
....

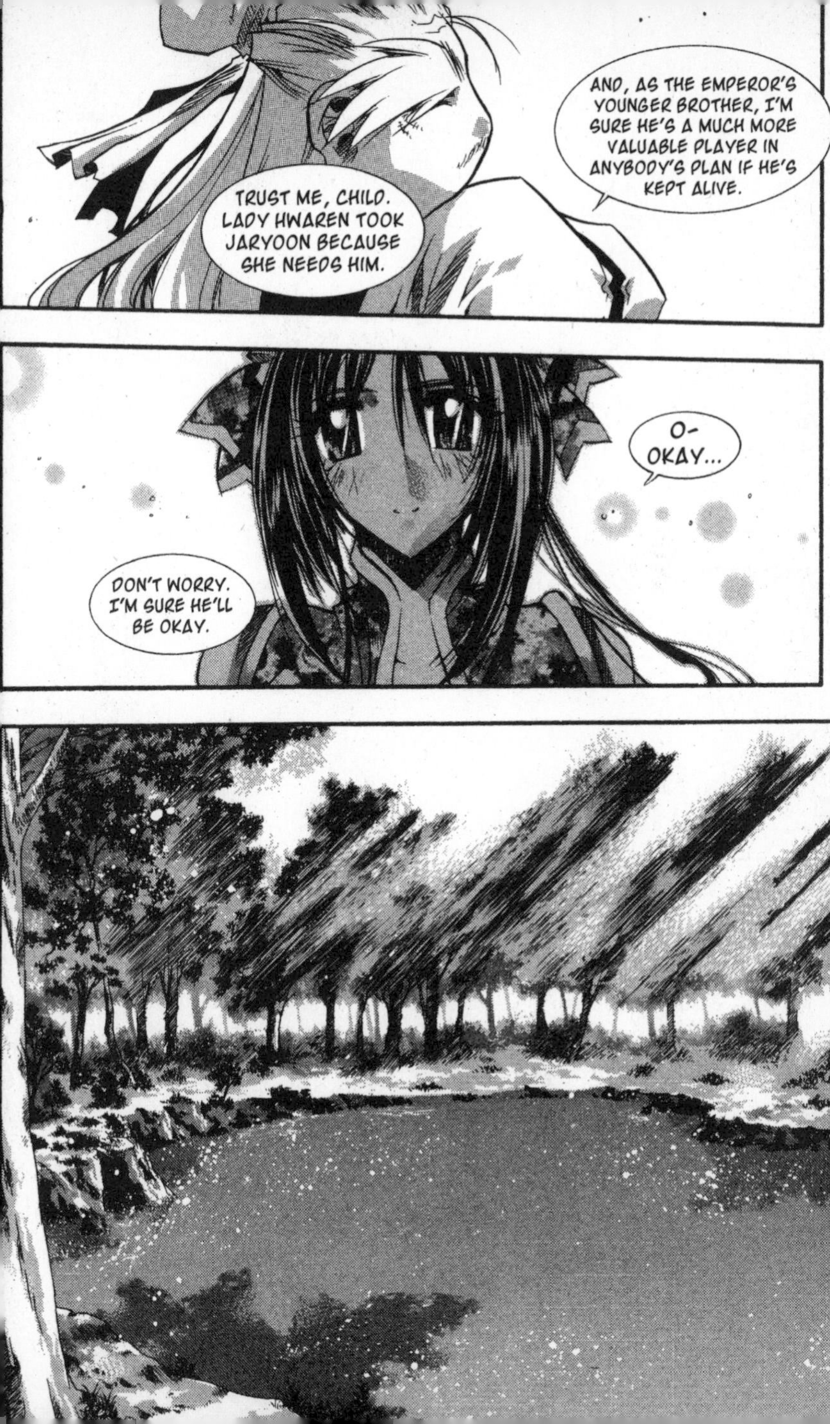
TRUST ME, CHILD. LADY HWAREN TOOK JARYOON BECAUSE SHE NEEDS HIM.
AND, AS THE EMPEROR'S YOUNGER BROTHER, I'M SURE HE'S A MUCH MORE VALUABLE PLAYER IN ANYBODY'S PLAN IF HE'S KEPT ALIVE.
DON'T WORRY. I'M SURE HE'LL BE OKAY.
O-OKAY...

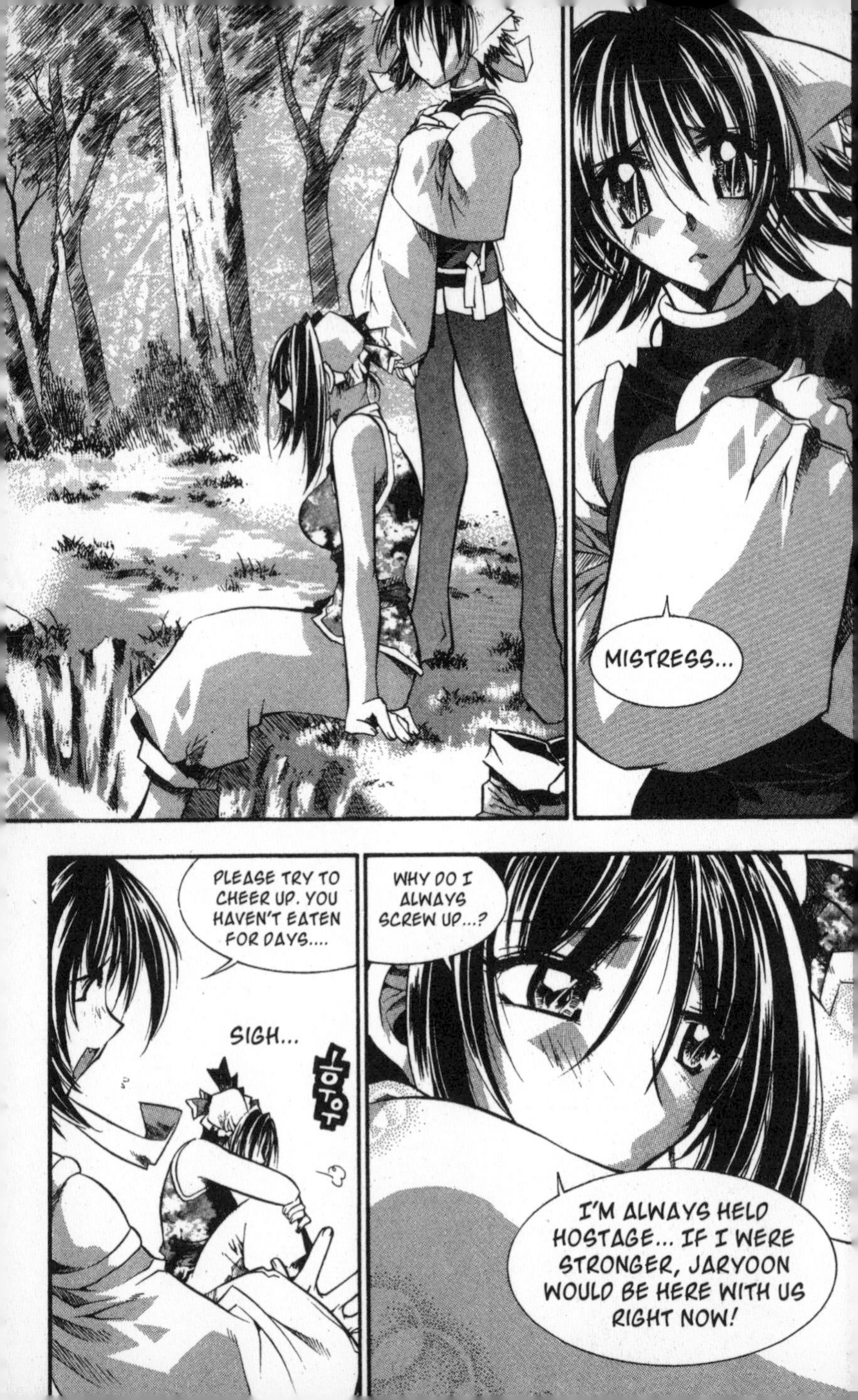
MISTRESS...
PLEASE TRY TO CHEER UP. YOU HAVEN'T EATEN FOR DAYS....
SIGH...
WHY DO I ALWAYS SCREW UP...?
I'M ALWAYS HELD HOSTAGE... IF I WERE STRONGER, JARYOON WOULD BE HERE WITH US RIGHT NOW!

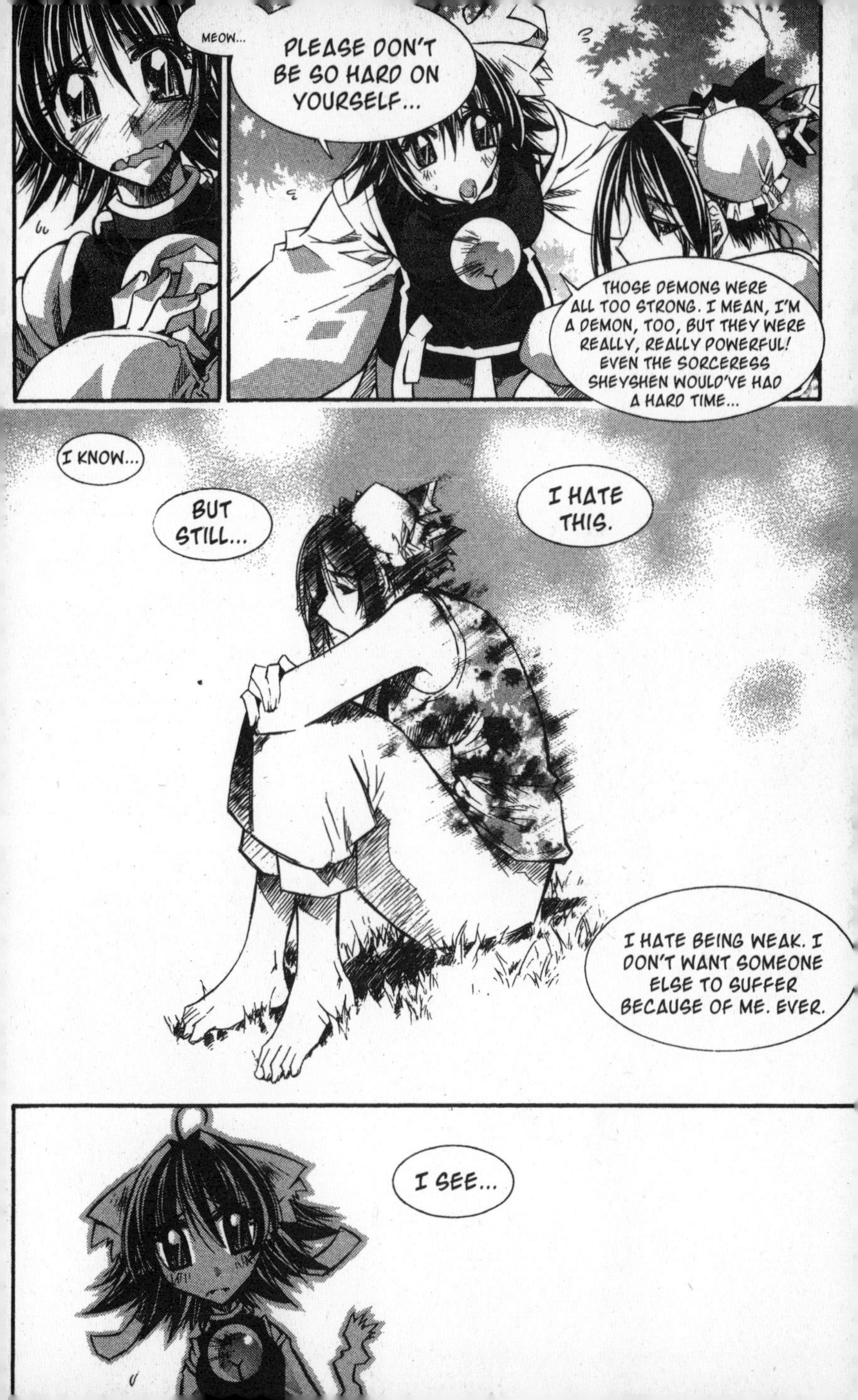
MEOW...
PLEASE DON'T BE SO HARD ON YOURSELF...
THOSE DEMONS WERE ALL TOO STRONG. I MEAN, I'M A DEMON, TOO, BUT THEY WERE REALLY, REALLY POWERFUL! EVEN THE SORCERESS SHEYSHEN WOULD'VE HAD A HARD TIME...
I KNOW...
BUT STILL...
I HATE THIS.
I HATE BEING WEAK. I DON'T WANT SOMEONE ELSE TO SUFFER BECAUSE OF ME. EVER.
I SEE...

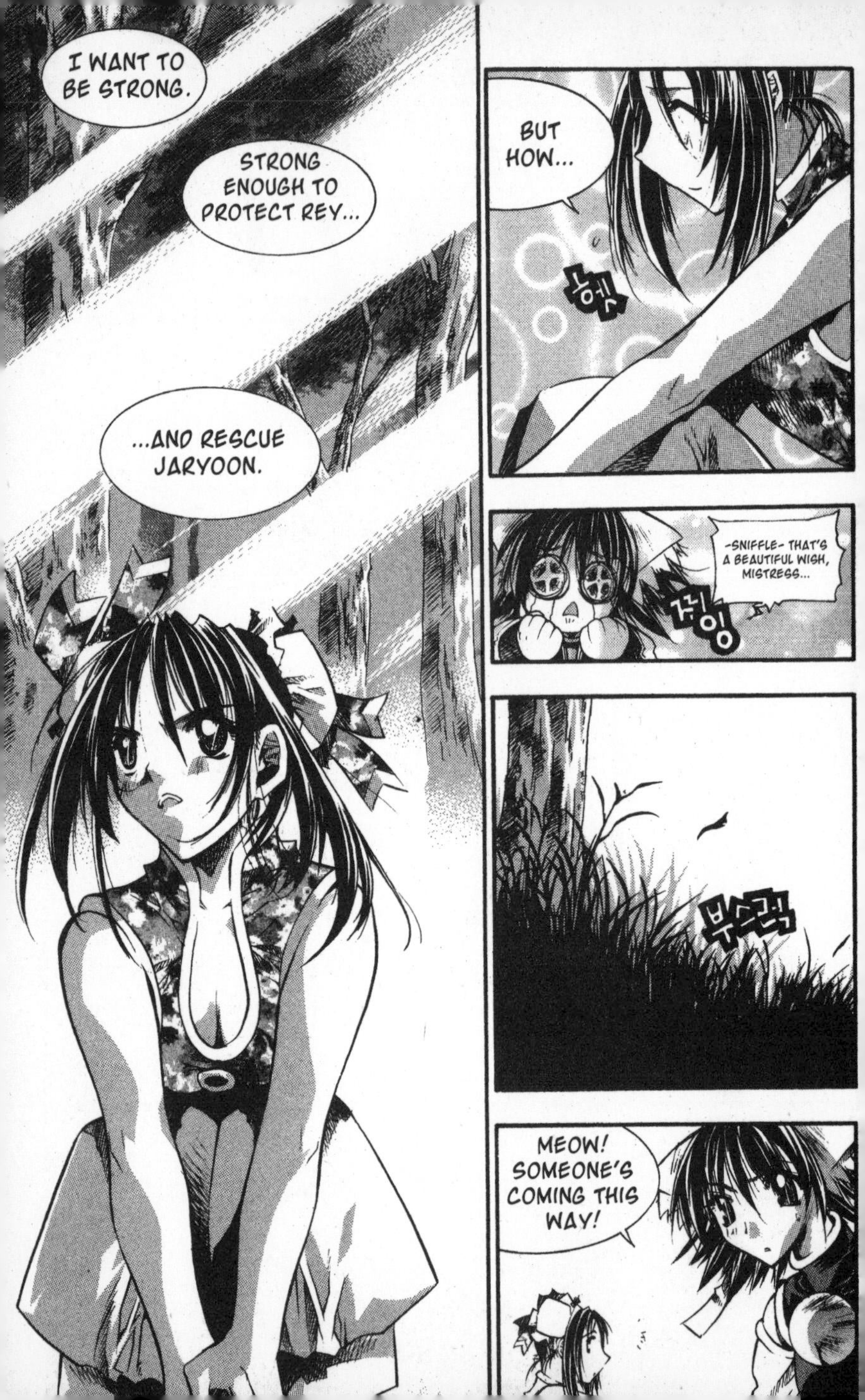
I WANT TO BE STRONG.
STRONG ENOUGH TO PROTECT REY...
...AND RESCUE JARYOON.
BUT HOW...
-SNIFFLE- THAT'S A BEAUTIFUL WISH, MISTRESS...
부스럭
MEOW! SOMEONE'S COMING THIS WAY!

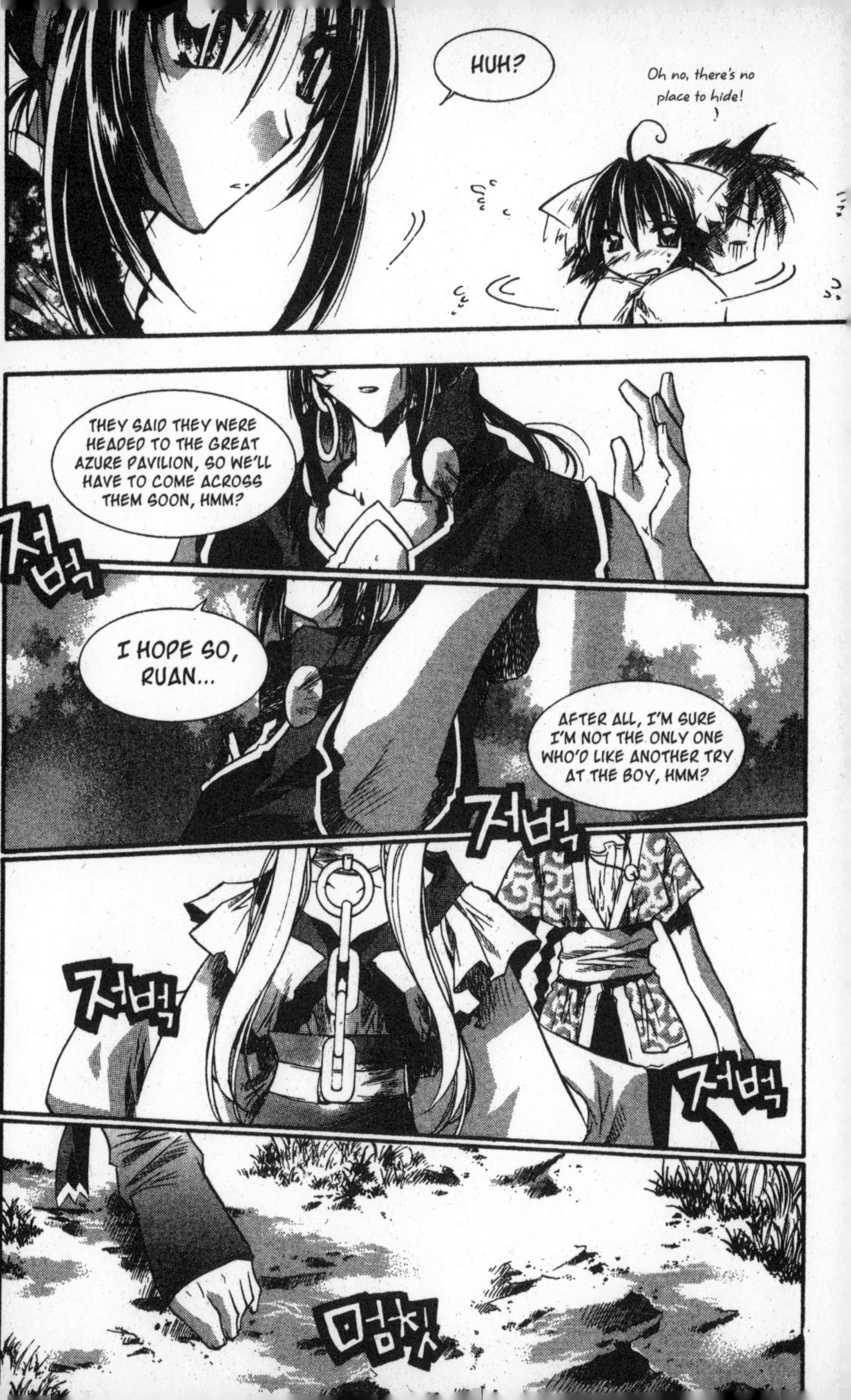
HUH?
Oh no, there's no place to hide!
THEY SAID THEY WERE HEADED TO THE GREAT AZURE PAVILION, SO WE'LL HAVE TO COME ACROSS THEM SOON, HMM?
저벅
I HOPE SO, RUAN...
AFTER ALL, I'M SURE I'M NOT THE ONLY ONE WHO'D LIKE ANOTHER TRY AT THE BOY, HMM?
저벅
저벅
저벅
멈칫

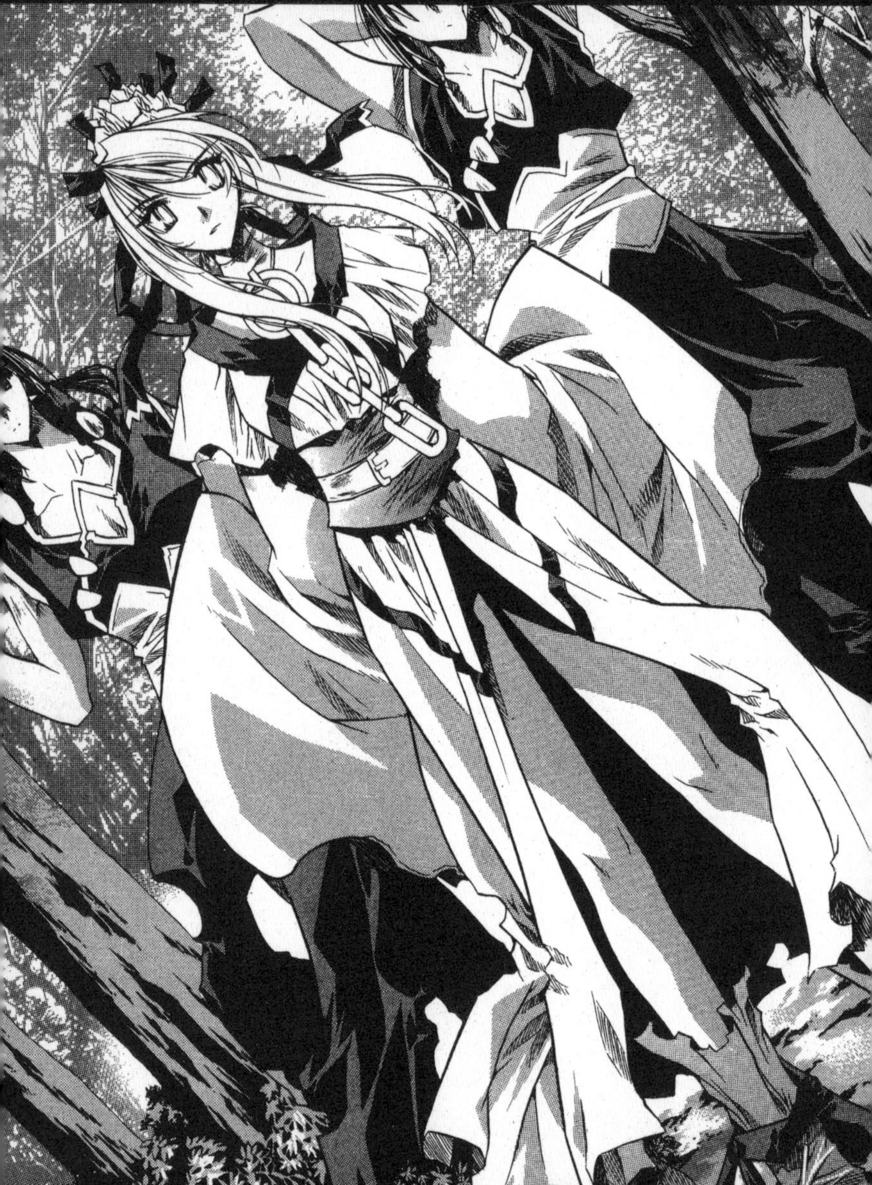

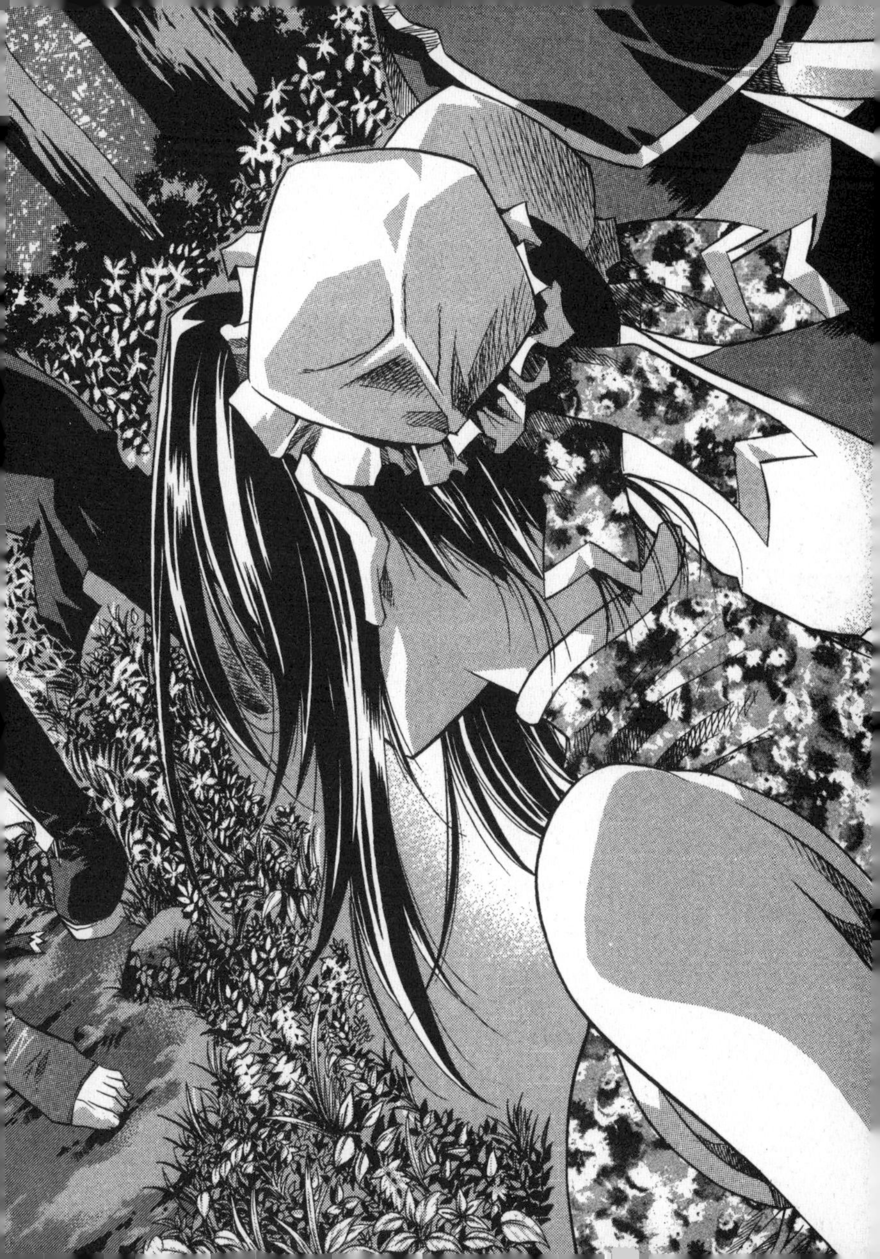

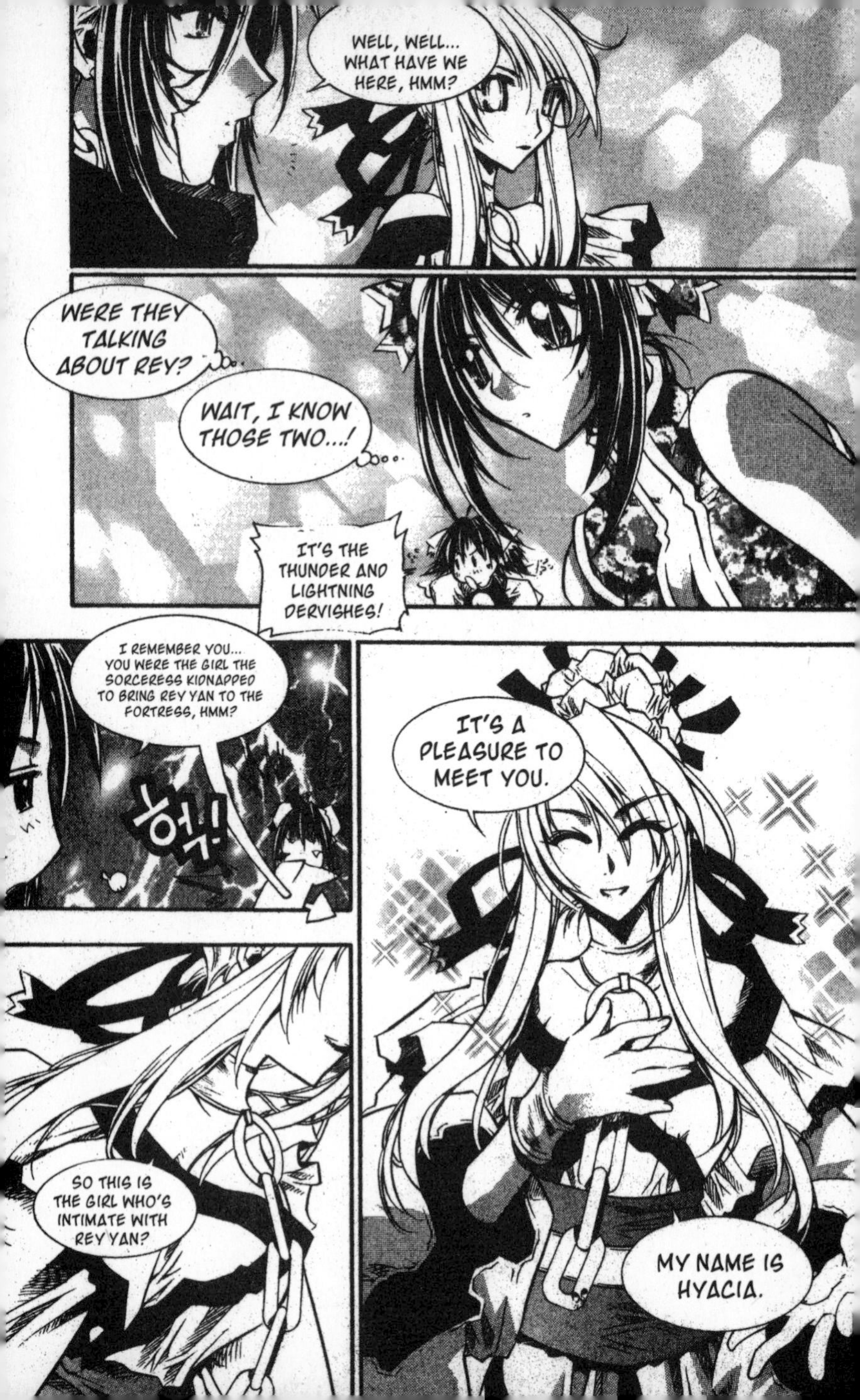
WELL, WELL... WHAT HAVE WE HERE, HMM?
WERE THEY TALKING ABOUT REY?
WAIT, I KNOW THOSE TWO...!
IT'S THE THUNDER AND LIGHTNING DERVISHES!
I REMEMBER YOU... YOU WERE THE GIRL THE SORCERESS KIDNAPPED TO BRING REY YAN TO THE FORTRESS, HMM?
헉!
SO THIS IS THE GIRL WHO'S INTIMATE WITH REY YAN?
IT'S A PLEASURE TO MEET YOU.
MY NAME IS HYACIA.

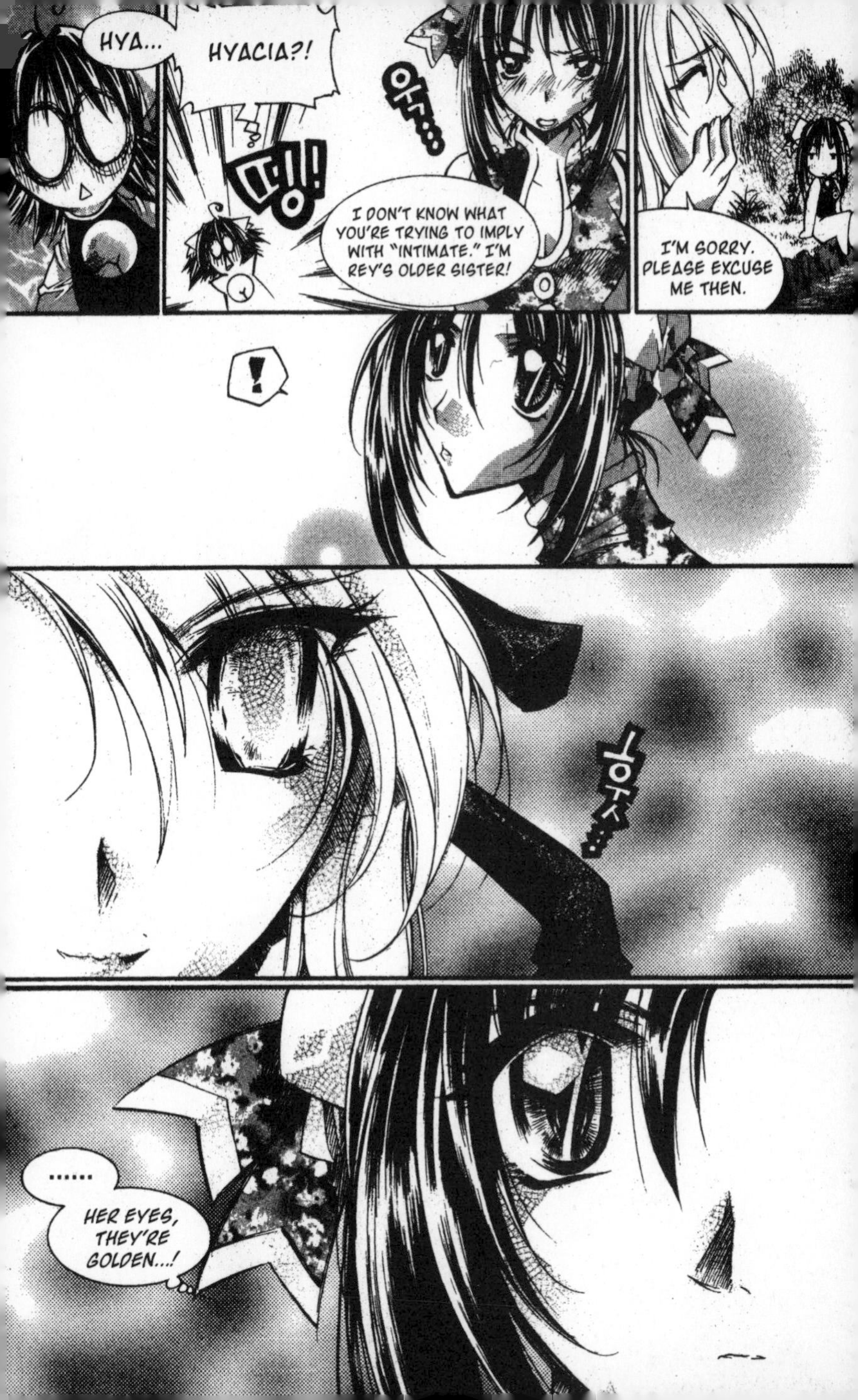
HYA...
HYACIA?!
I DON'T KNOW WHAT YOU'RE TRYING TO IMPLY WITH "INTIMATE." I'M REY'S OLDER SISTER!
I'M SORRY. PLEASE EXCUSE ME THEN.
!
......
HER EYES, THEY'RE GOLDEN...!

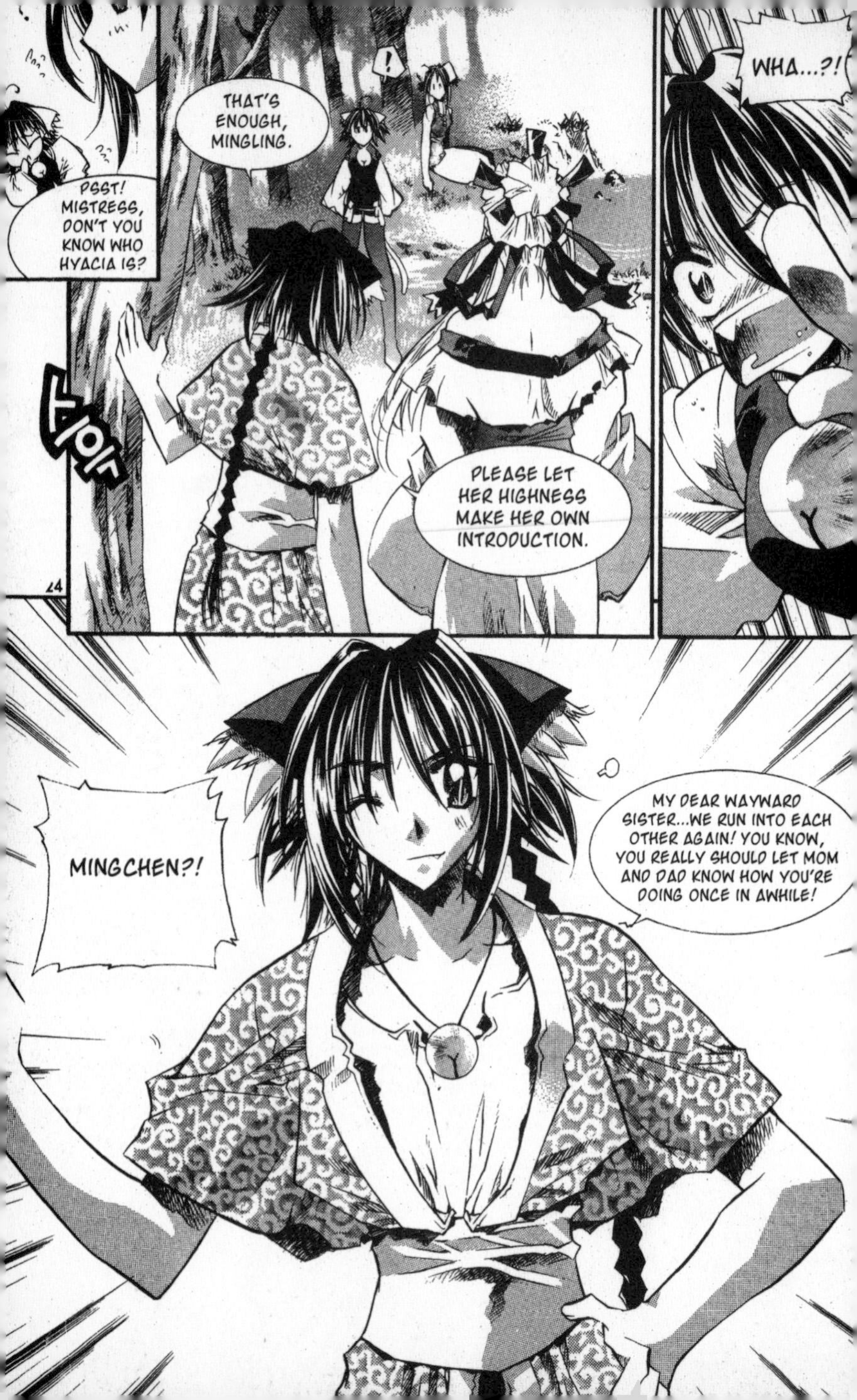
PSST! MISTRESS, DON'T YOU KNOW WHO HYACIA IS?
!
THAT'S ENOUGH, MINGLING.
PLEASE LET HER HIGHNESS MAKE HER OWN INTRODUCTION.
WHA...?!
MINGCHEN?!
MY DEAR WAYWARD SISTER...WE RUN INTO EACH OTHER AGAIN! YOU KNOW, YOU REALLY SHOULD LET MOM AND DAD KNOW HOW YOU'RE DOING ONCE IN AWHILE!

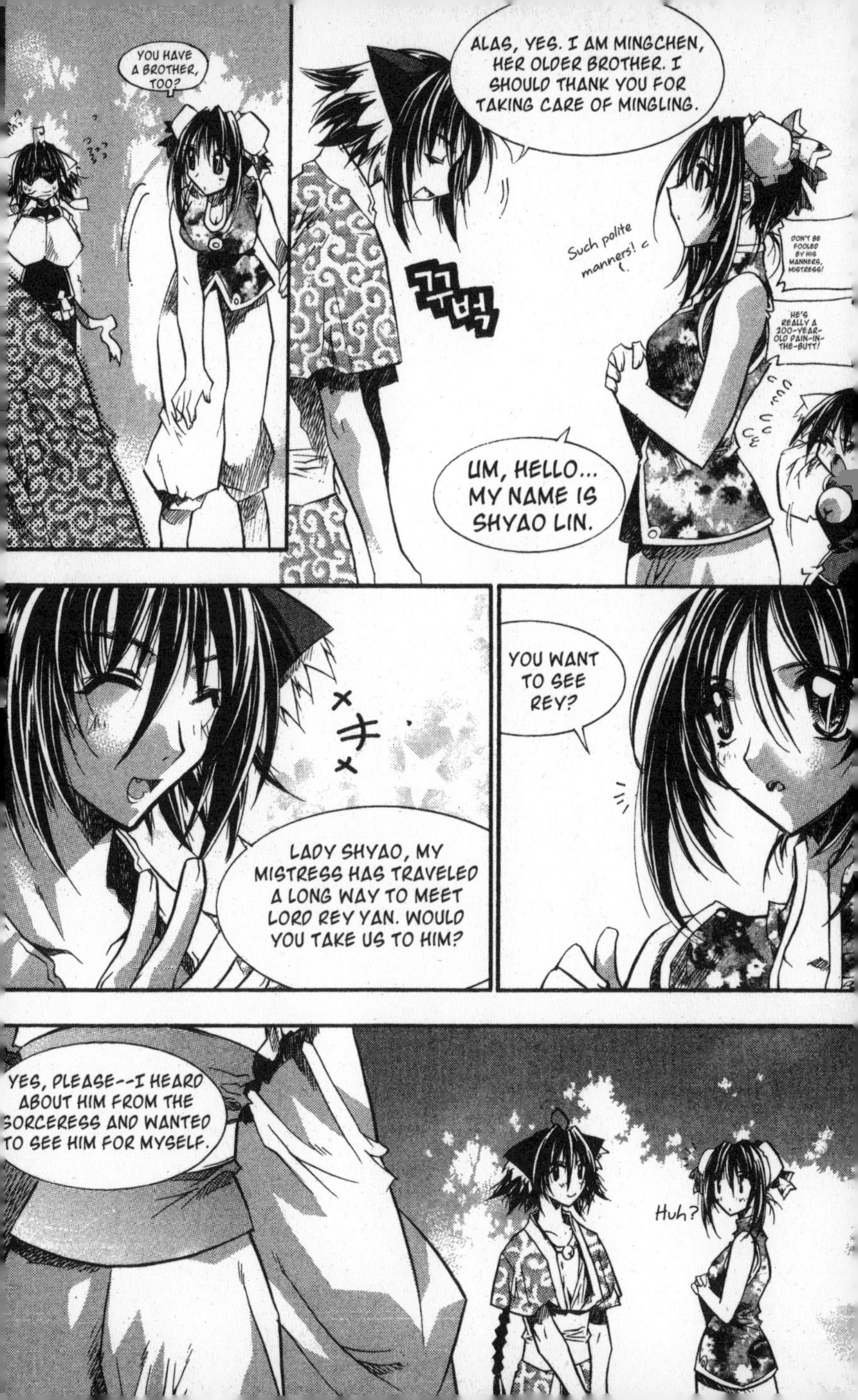
YOU HAVE A BROTHER, TOO?
ALAS, YES. I AM MINGCHEN, HER OLDER BROTHER. I SHOULD THANK YOU FOR TAKING CARE OF MINGLING.
꾸벅
Such polite manners!
DON'T BE FOOLED BY HIS MANNERS, MISTRESS!
HE'S REALLY A 200-YEAR-OLD PAIN-IN-THE-BUTT!
UM, HELLO... MY NAME IS SHYAO LIN.
LADY SHYAO, MY MISTRESS HAS TRAVELED A LONG WAY TO MEET LORD REY YAN. WOULD YOU TAKE US TO HIM?
YOU WANT TO SEE REY?
YES, PLEASE--I HEARD ABOUT HIM FROM THE SORCERESS AND WANTED TO SEE HIM FOR MYSELF.
Huh?

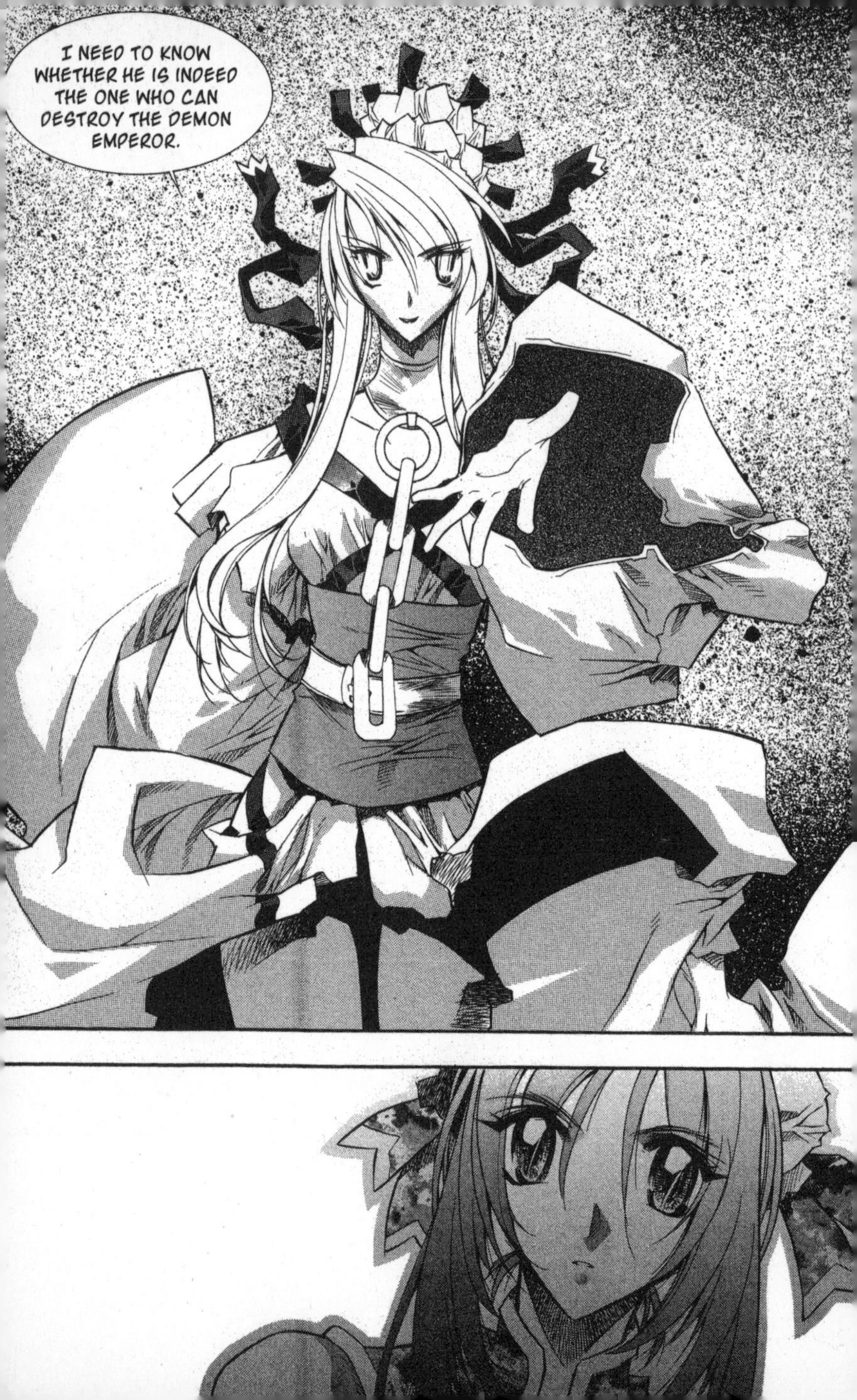
I NEED TO KNOW WHETHER HE IS INDEED THE ONE WHO CAN DESTROY THE DEMON EMPEROR.

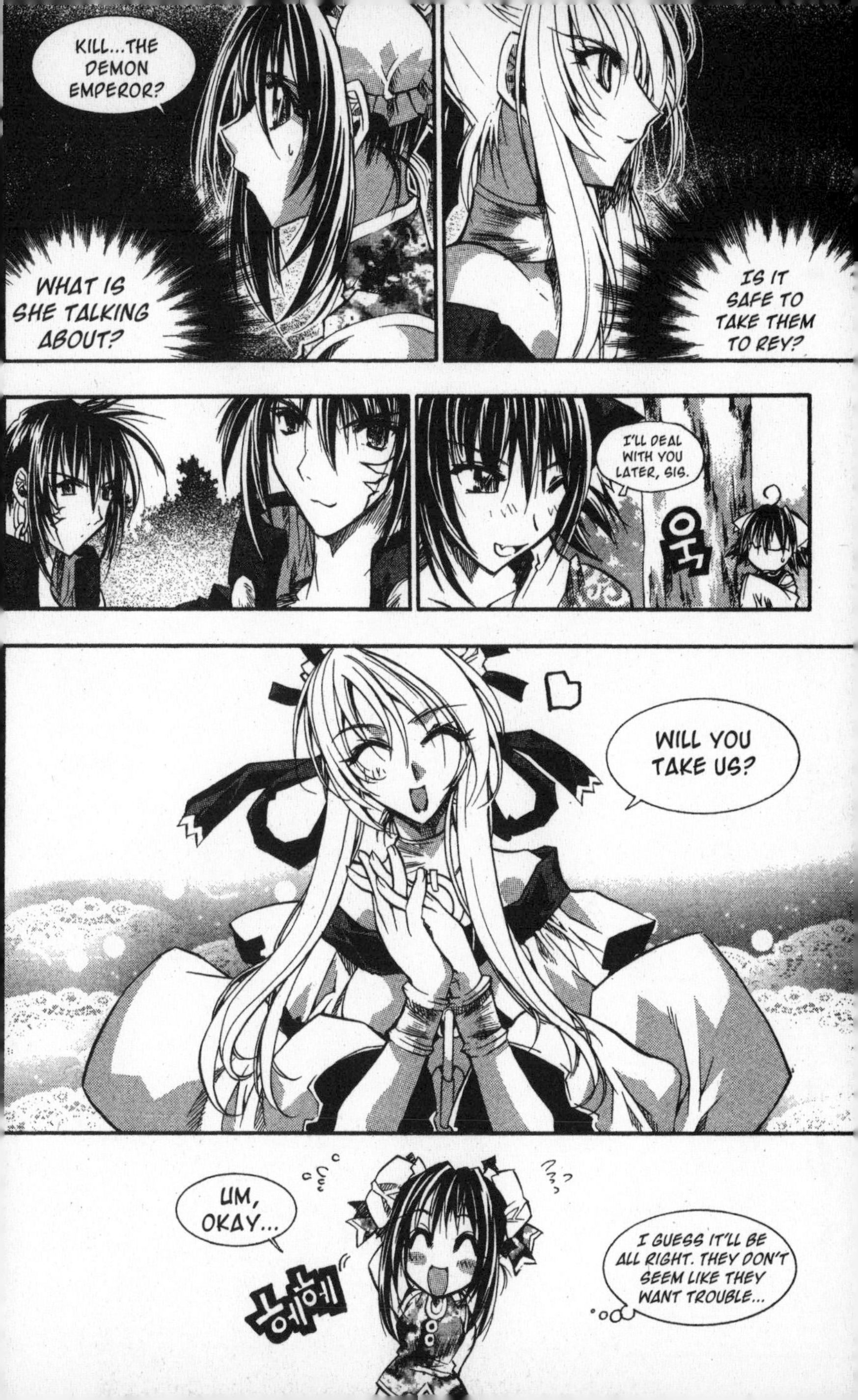
KILL...THE DEMON EMPEROR?
WHAT IS SHE TALKING ABOUT?
IS IT SAFE TO TAKE THEM TO REY?
I'LL DEAL WITH YOU LATER, SIS.
욱
WILL YOU TAKE US?
UM, OKAY...
헤헤
I GUESS IT'LL BE ALL RIGHT. THEY DON'T SEEM LIKE THEY WANT TROUBLE...

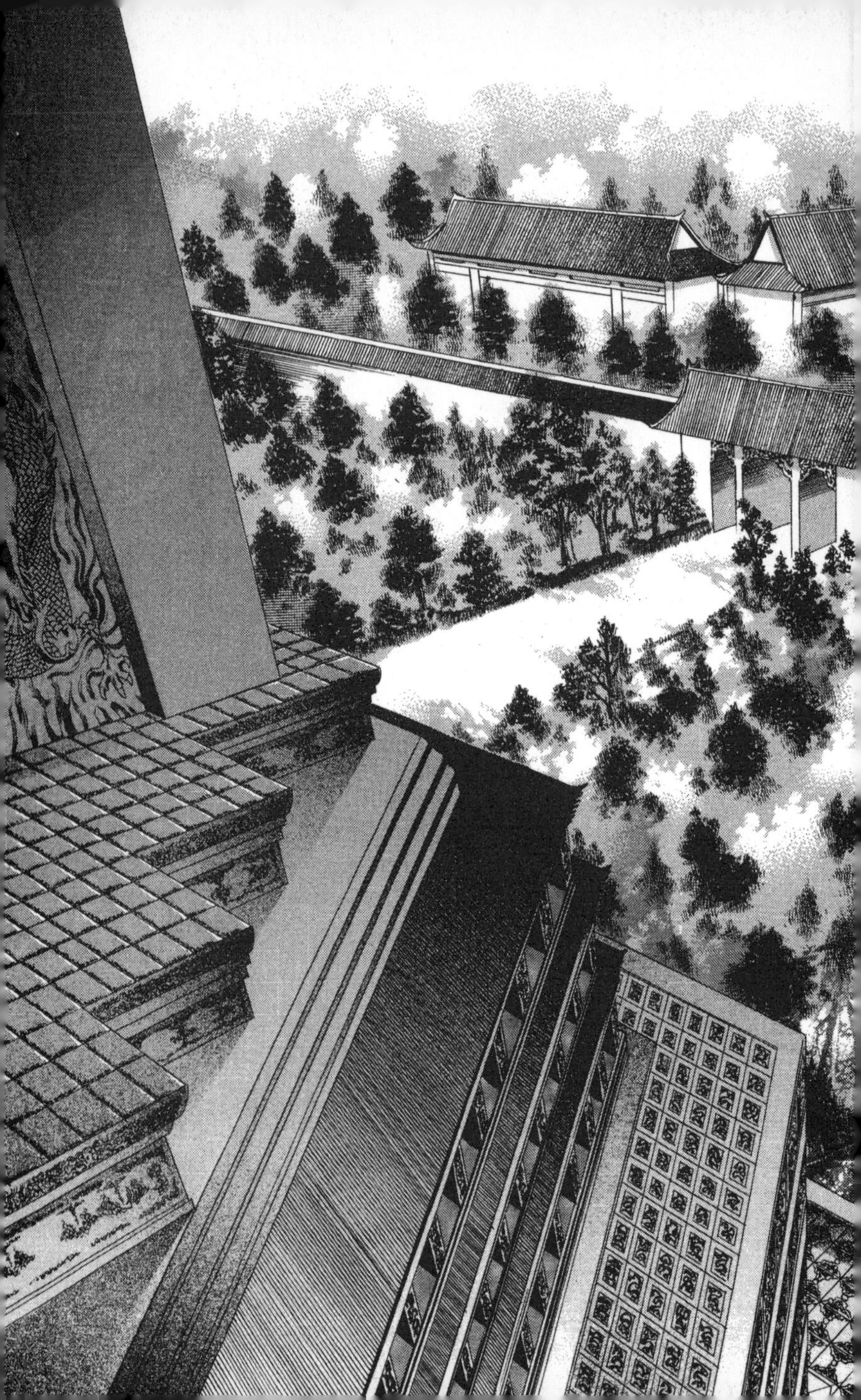

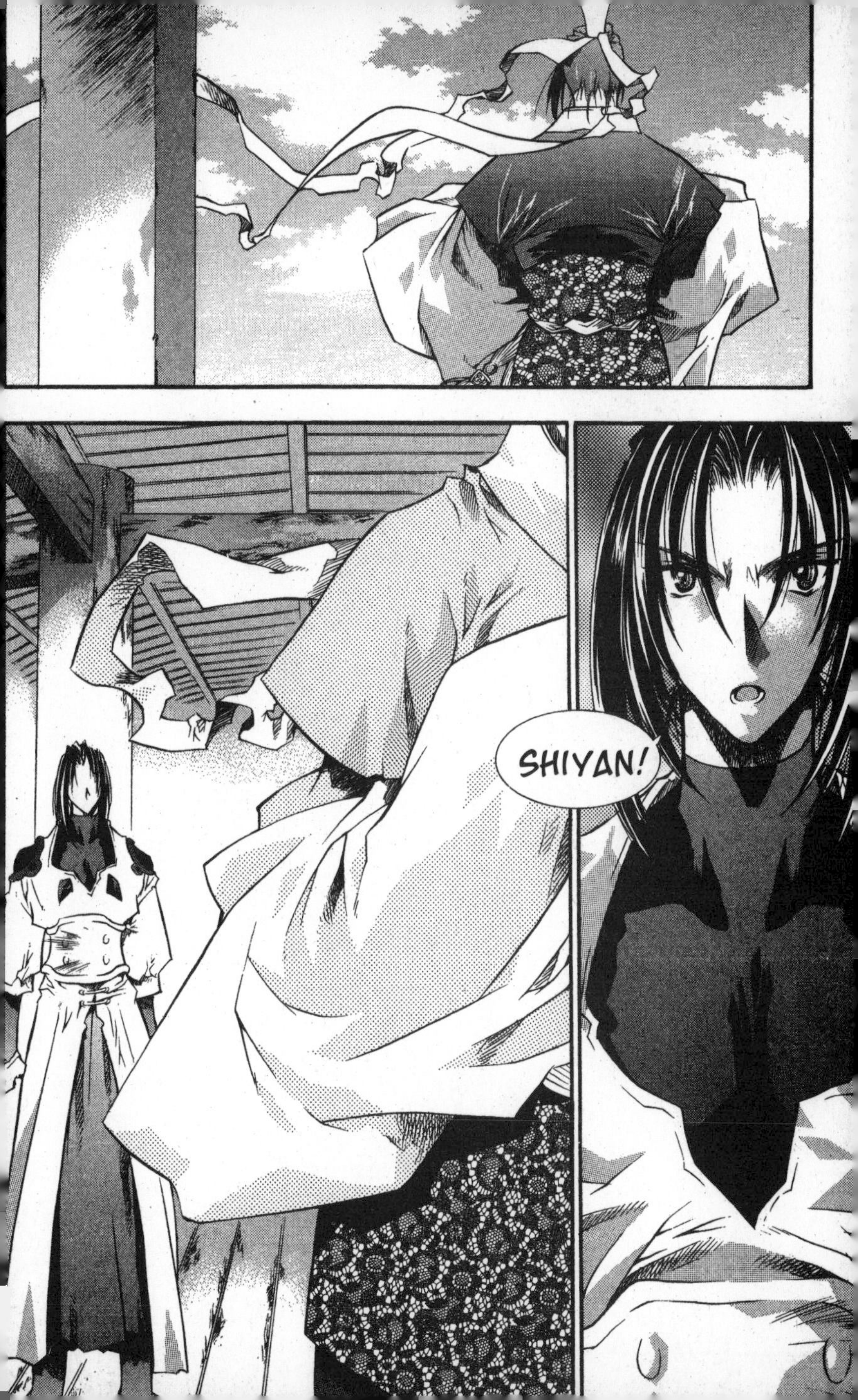
SHIYAN!

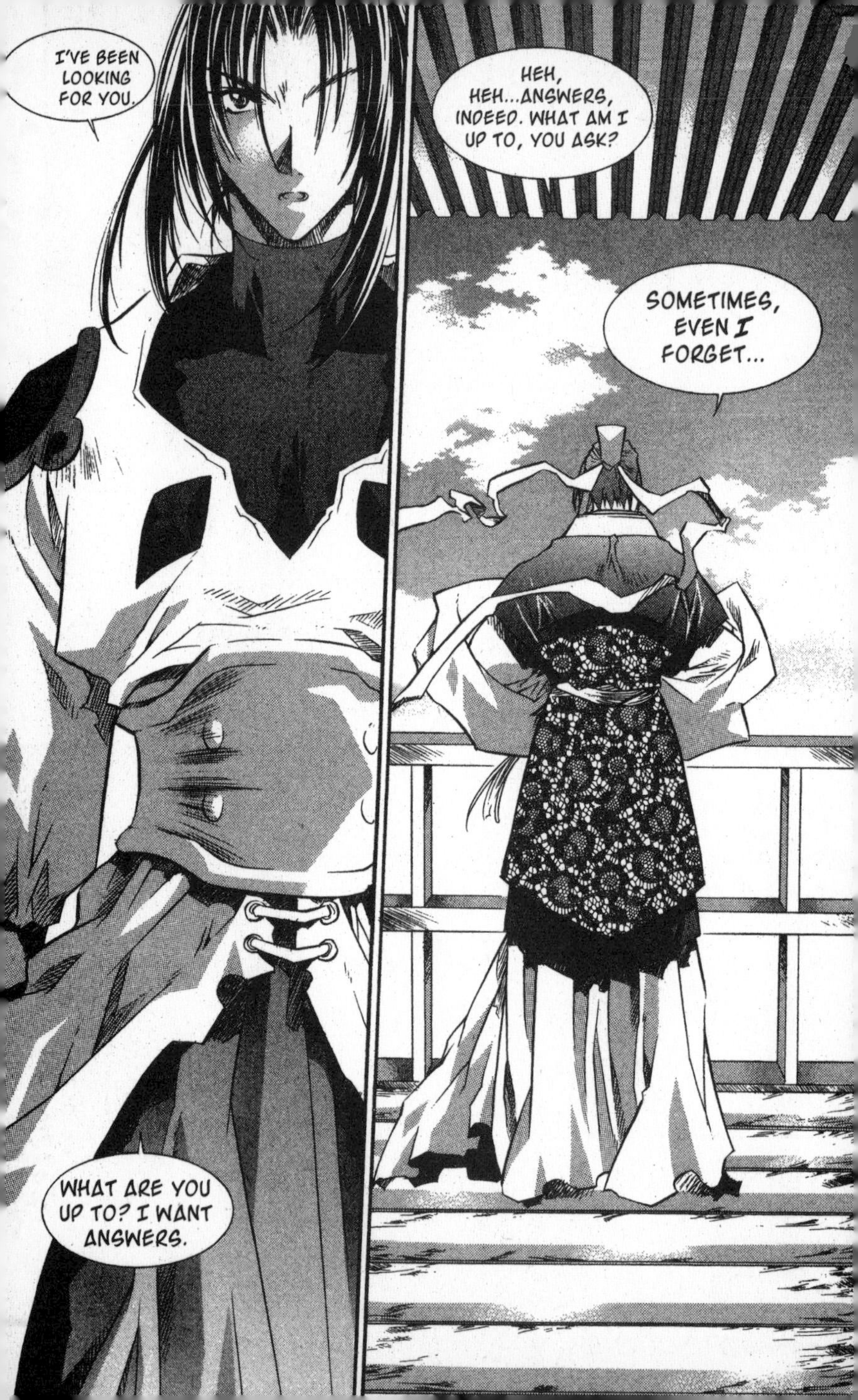
I'VE BEEN LOOKING FOR YOU.
WHAT ARE YOU UP TO? I WANT ANSWERS.
HEH, HEH...ANSWERS, INDEED. WHAT AM I UP TO, YOU ASK?
SOMETIMES, EVEN I FORGET...

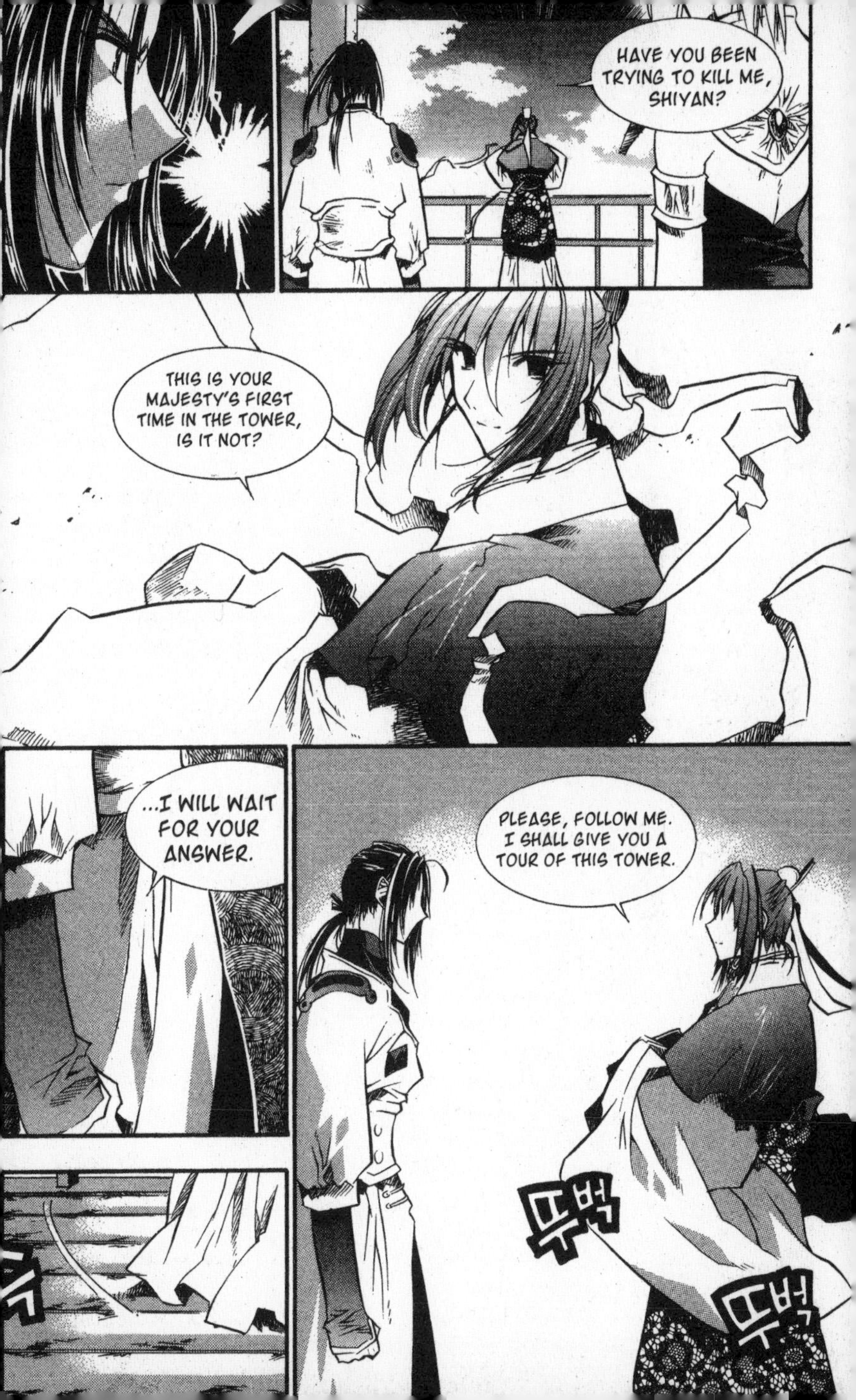
HAVE YOU BEEN TRYING TO KILL ME, SHIYAN?
THIS IS YOUR MAJESTY'S FIRST TIME IN THE TOWER, IS IT NOT?
...I WILL WAIT FOR YOUR ANSWER.
PLEASE, FOLLOW ME. I SHALL GIVE YOU A TOUR OF THIS TOWER.
뚜벅
뚜벅

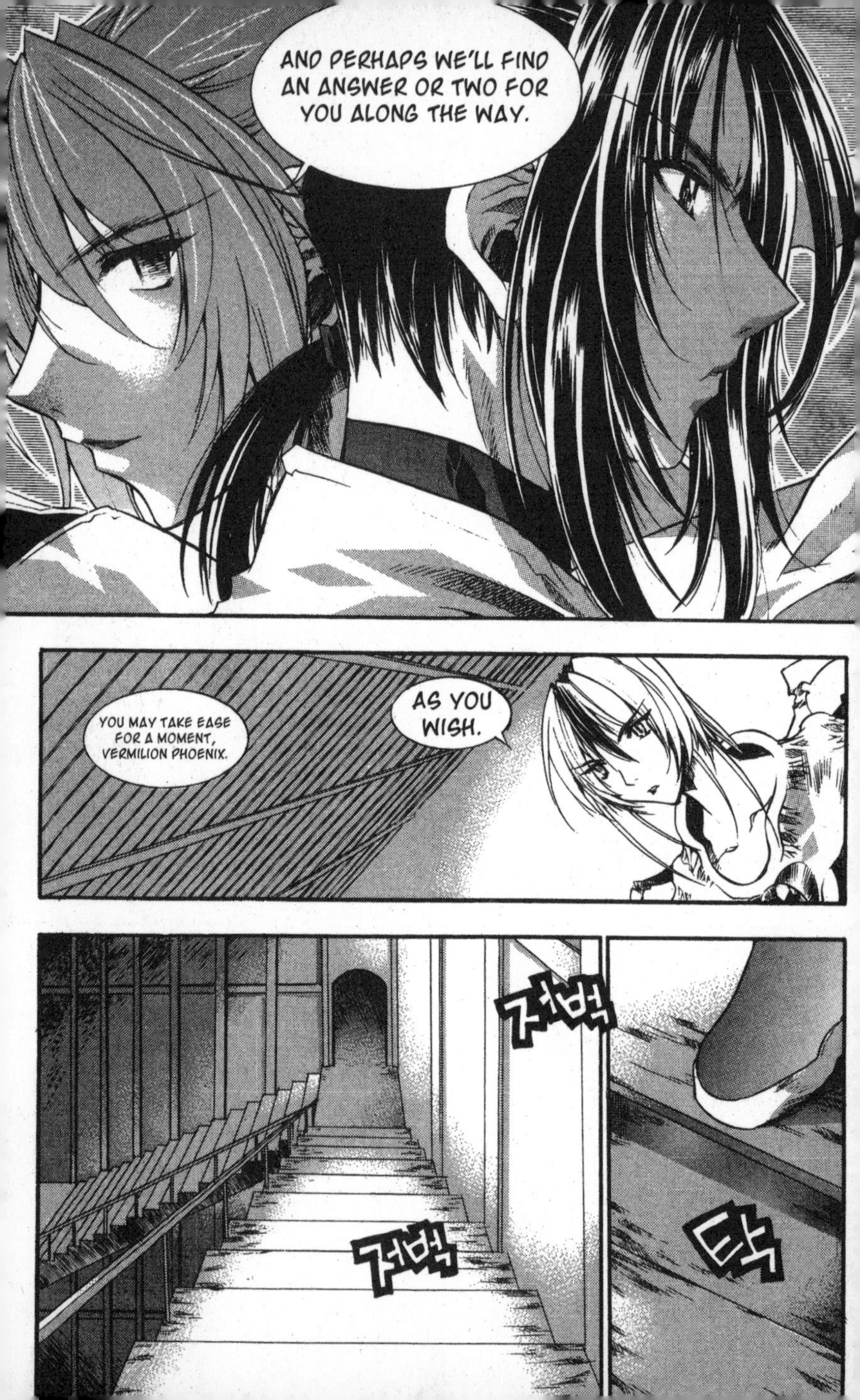
AND PERHAPS WE'LL FIND AN ANSWER OR TWO FOR YOU ALONG THE WAY.
YOU MAY TAKE EASE FOR A MOMENT, VERMILION PHOENIX.
AS YOU WISH.
저벅
저벅
탁

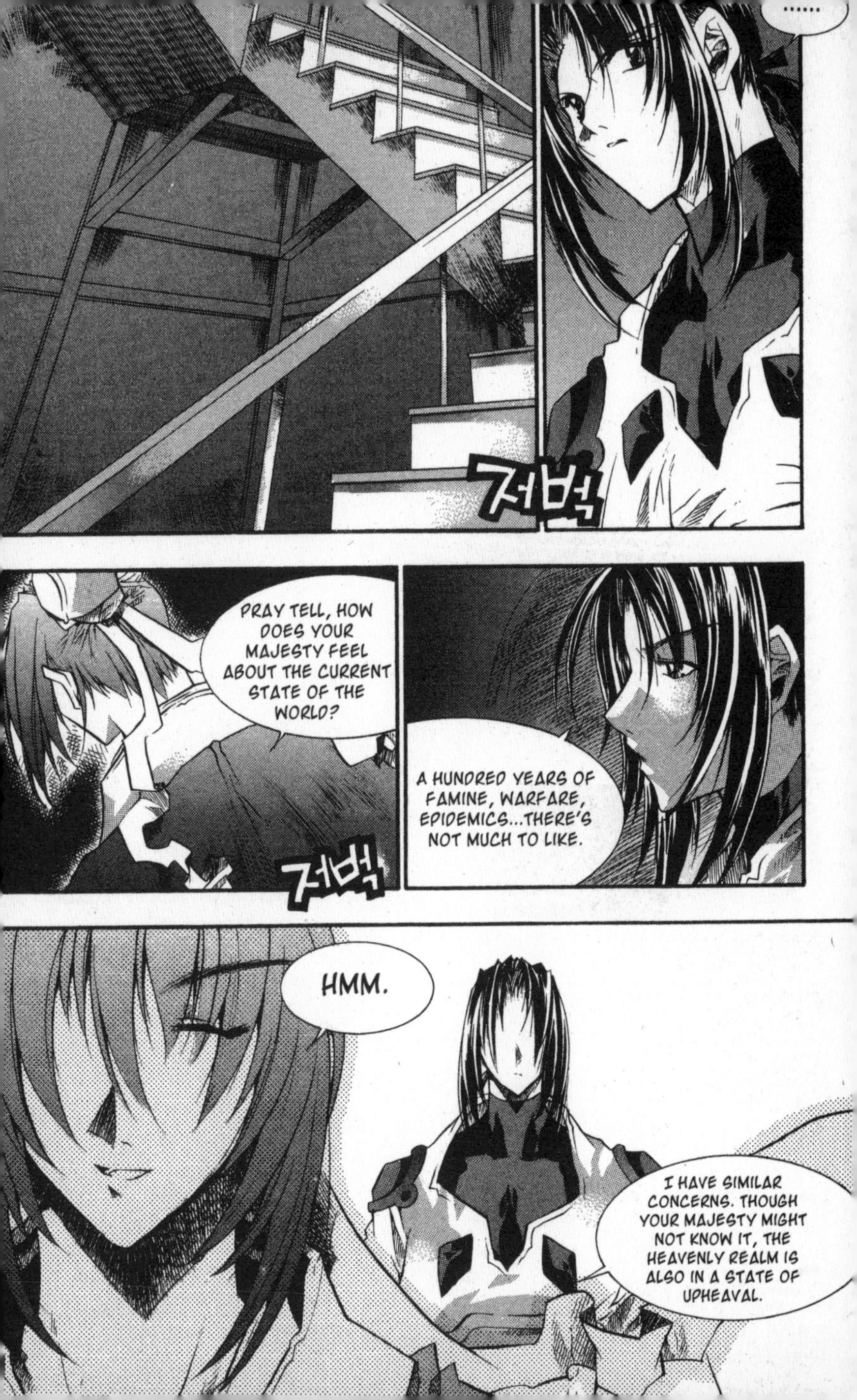

저벅
......
PRAY TELL, HOW DOES YOUR MAJESTY FEEL ABOUT THE CURRENT STATE OF THE WORLD?
저벅
A HUNDRED YEARS OF FAMINE, WARFARE, EPIDEMICS...THERE'S NOT MUCH TO LIKE.
HMM.
I HAVE SIMILAR CONCERNS. THOUGH YOUR MAJESTY MIGHT NOT KNOW IT, THE HEAVENLY REALM IS ALSO IN A STATE OF UPHEAVAL.

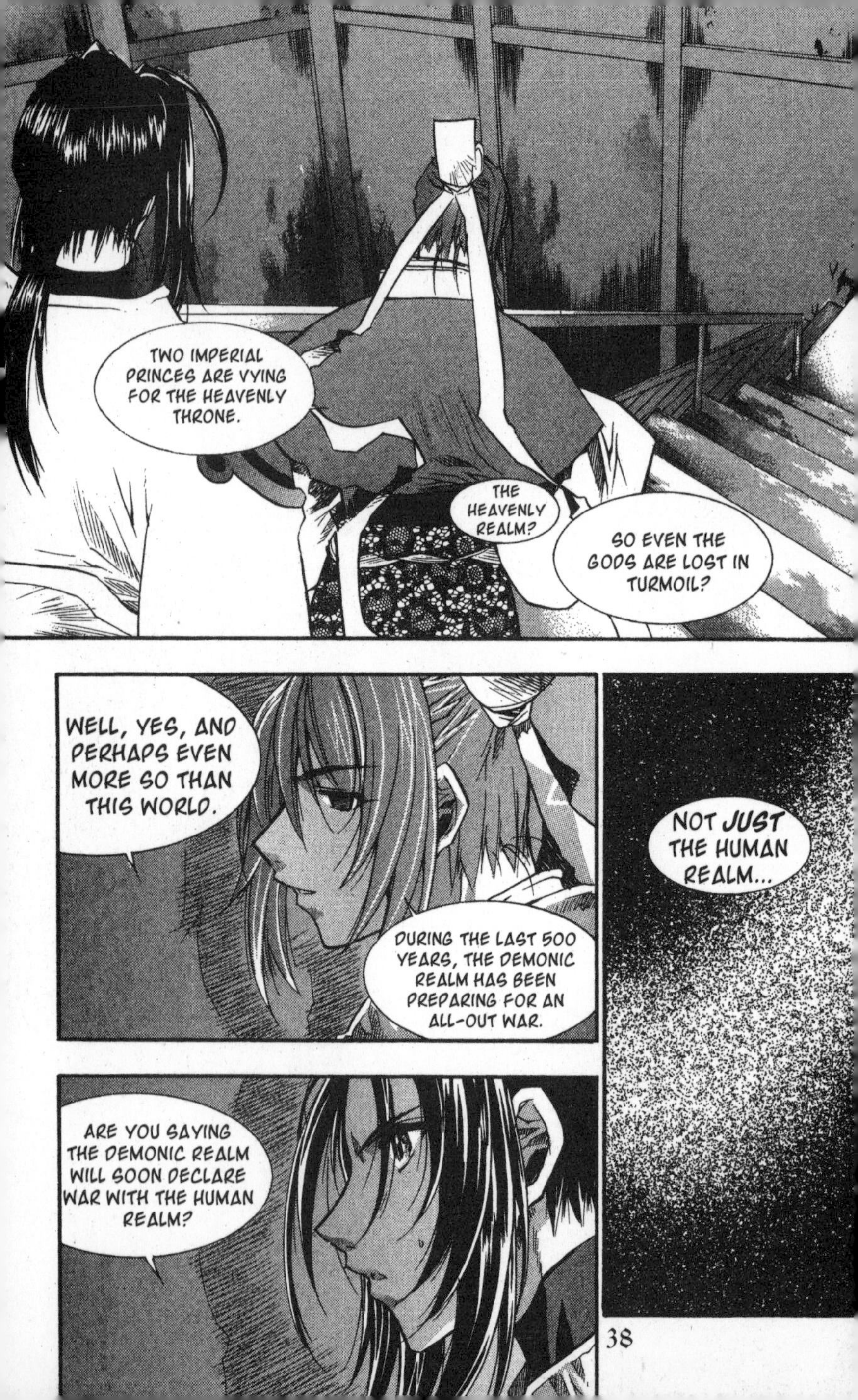
TWO IMPERIAL PRINCES ARE VYING FOR THE HEAVENLY THRONE.
THE HEAVENLY REALM?
SO EVEN THE GODS ARE LOST IN TURMOIL?
WELL, YES, AND PERHAPS EVEN MORE SO THAN THIS WORLD.
DURING THE LAST 500 YEARS, THE DEMONIC REALM HAS BEEN PREPARING FOR AN ALL-OUT WAR.
NOT JUST THE HUMAN REALM...
ARE YOU SAYING THE DEMONIC REALM WILL SOON DECLARE WAR WITH THE HUMAN REALM?

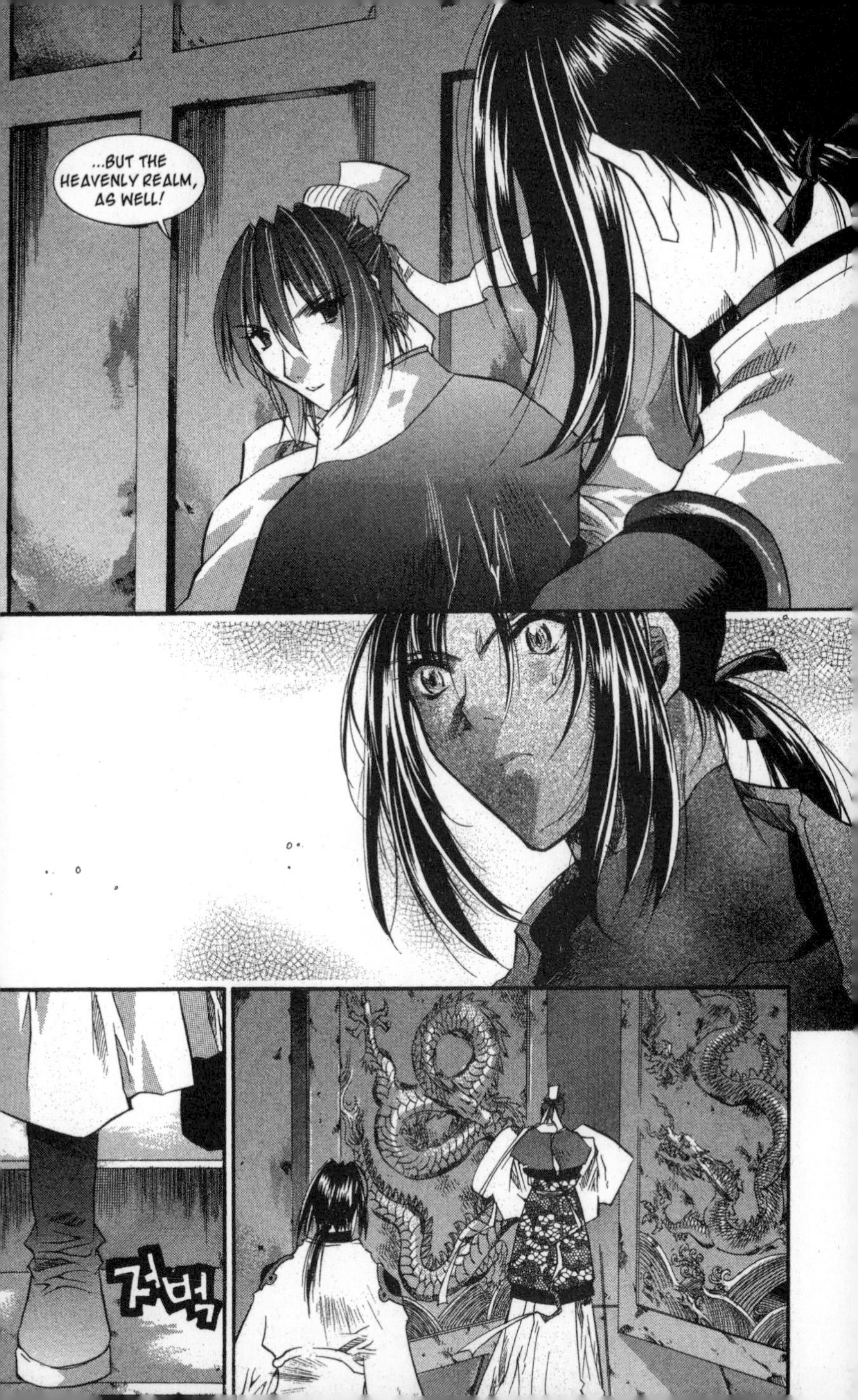
...BUT THE HEAVENLY REALM, AS WELL!
저벅

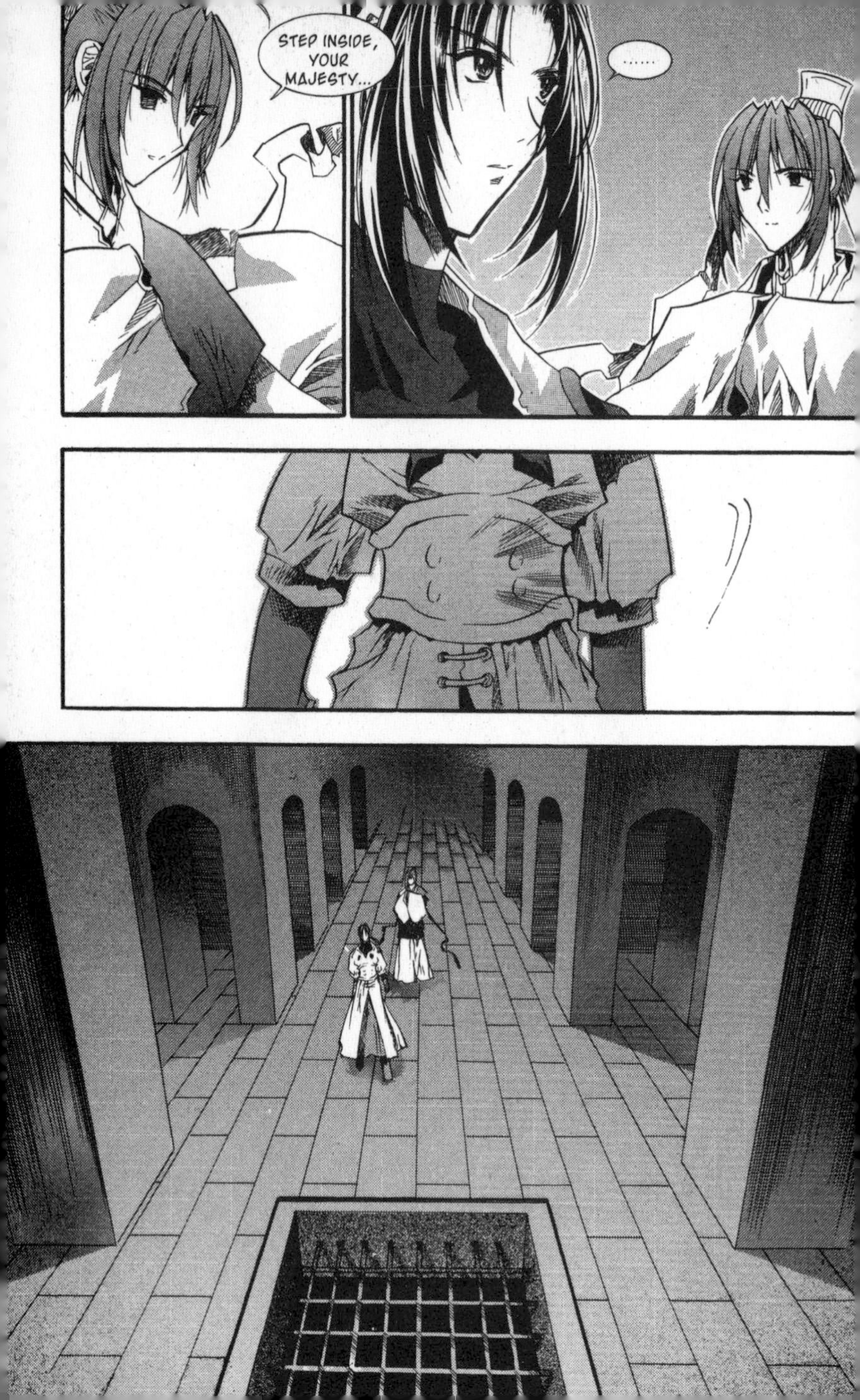
STEP INSIDE, YOUR MAJESTY...
......

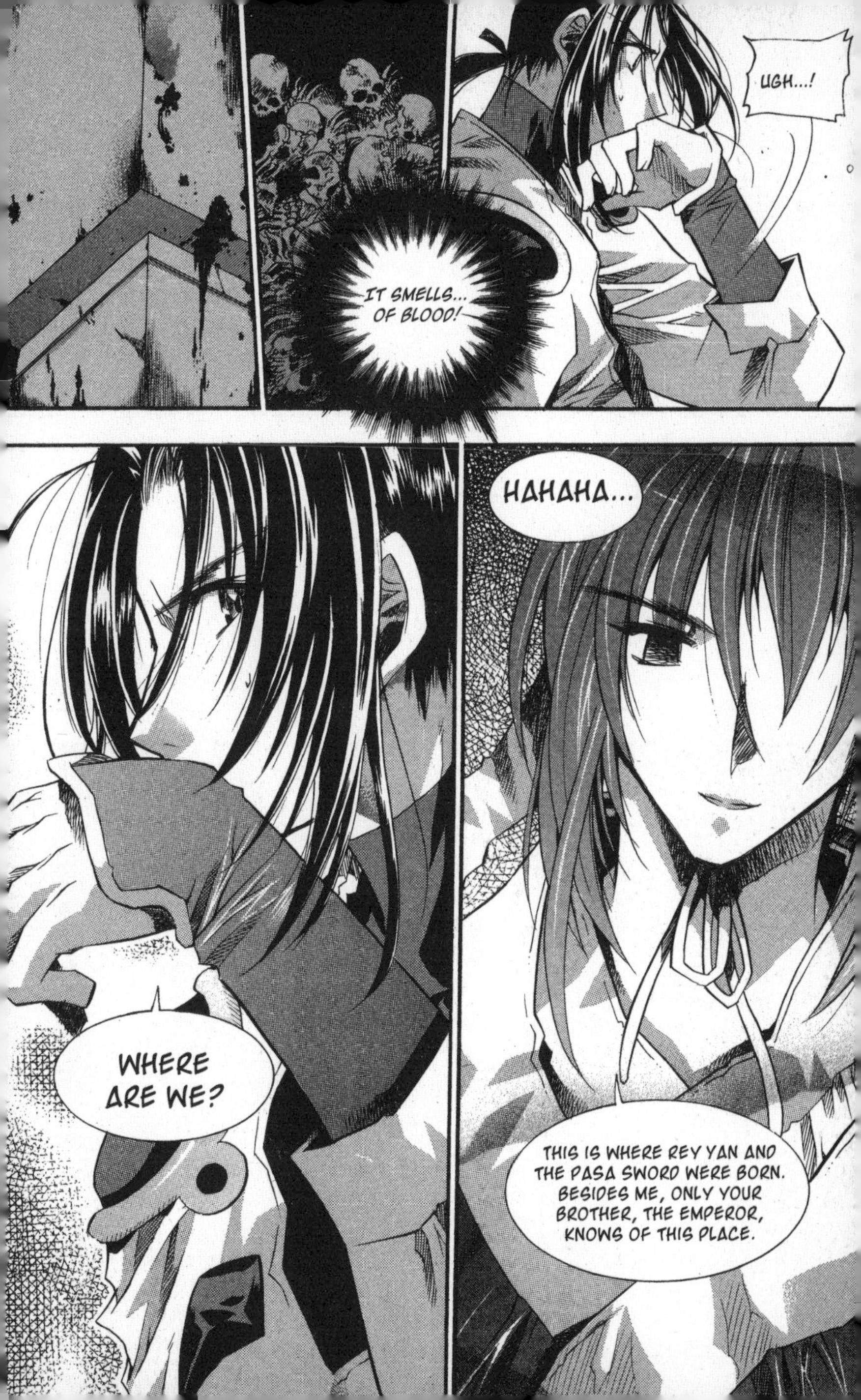
IT SMELLS... OF BLOOD!
UGH...!
WHERE ARE WE?
HAHAHA...
THIS IS WHERE REY YAN AND THE PASA SWORD WERE BORN. BESIDES ME, ONLY YOUR BROTHER, THE EMPEROR, KNOWS OF THIS PLACE.

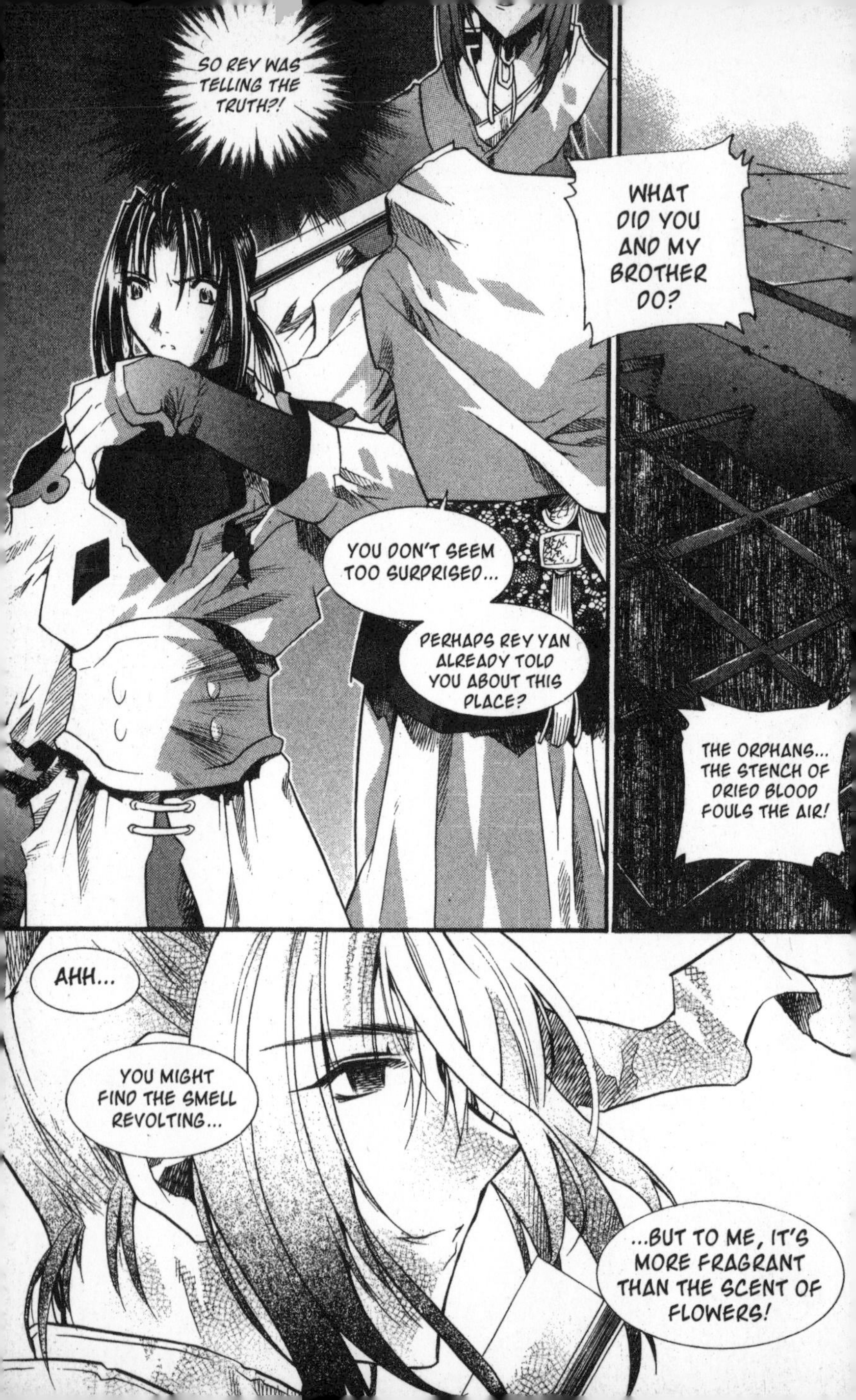
SO REY WAS TELLING THE TRUTH?!
WHAT DID YOU AND MY BROTHER DO?
YOU DON'T SEEM TOO SURPRISED...
PERHAPS REY YAN ALREADY TOLD YOU ABOUT THIS PLACE?
THE ORPHANS... THE STENCH OF DRIED BLOOD FOULS THE AIR!
AHH...
YOU MIGHT FIND THE SMELL REVOLTING...
...BUT TO ME, IT'S MORE FRAGRANT THAN THE SCENT OF FLOWERS!

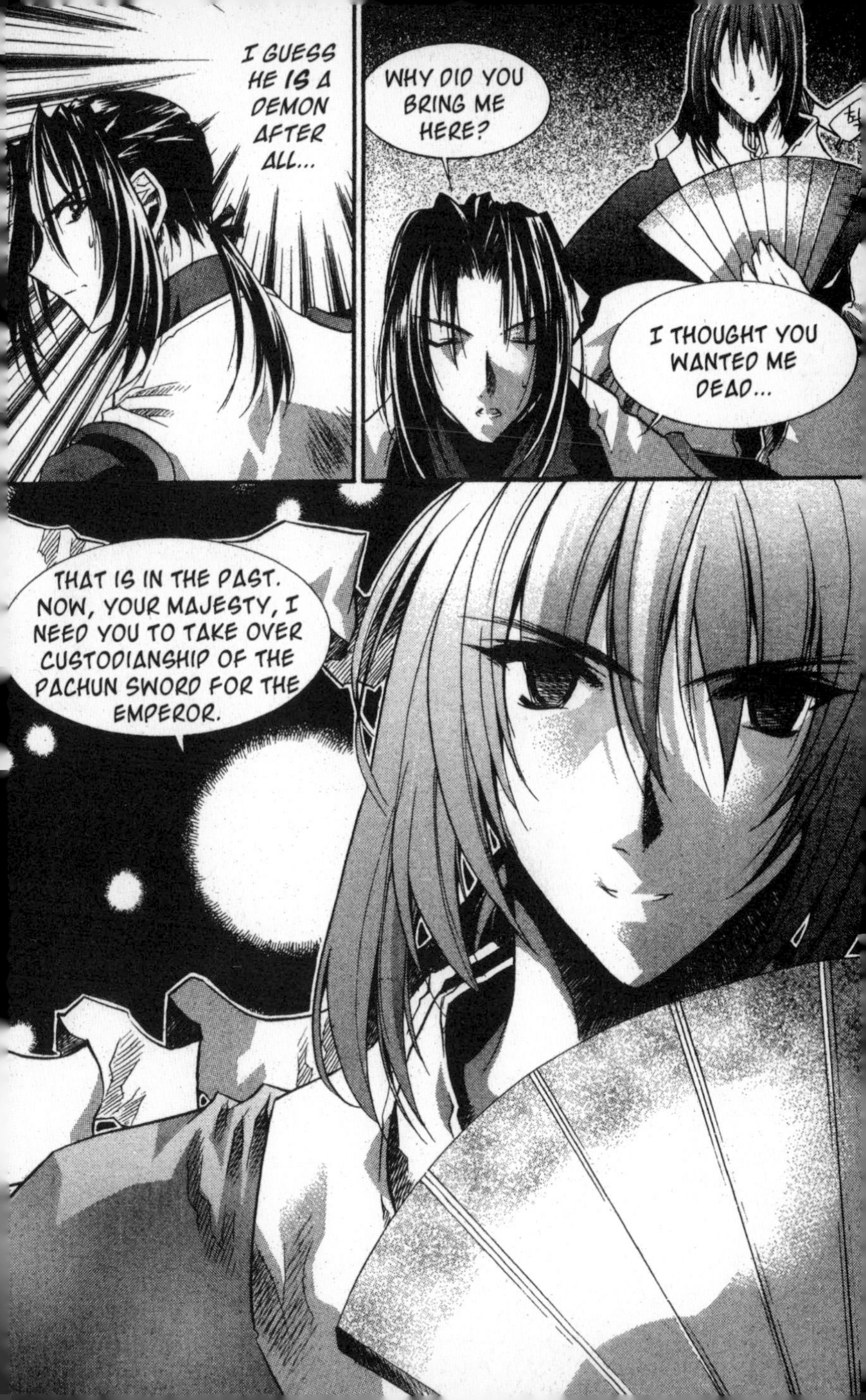
I GUESS HE IS A DEMON AFTER ALL...
WHY DID YOU BRING ME HERE?
I THOUGHT YOU WANTED ME DEAD...
THAT IS IN THE PAST. NOW, YOUR MAJESTY, I NEED YOU TO TAKE OVER CUSTODIANSHIP OF THE PACHUN SWORD FOR THE EMPEROR.

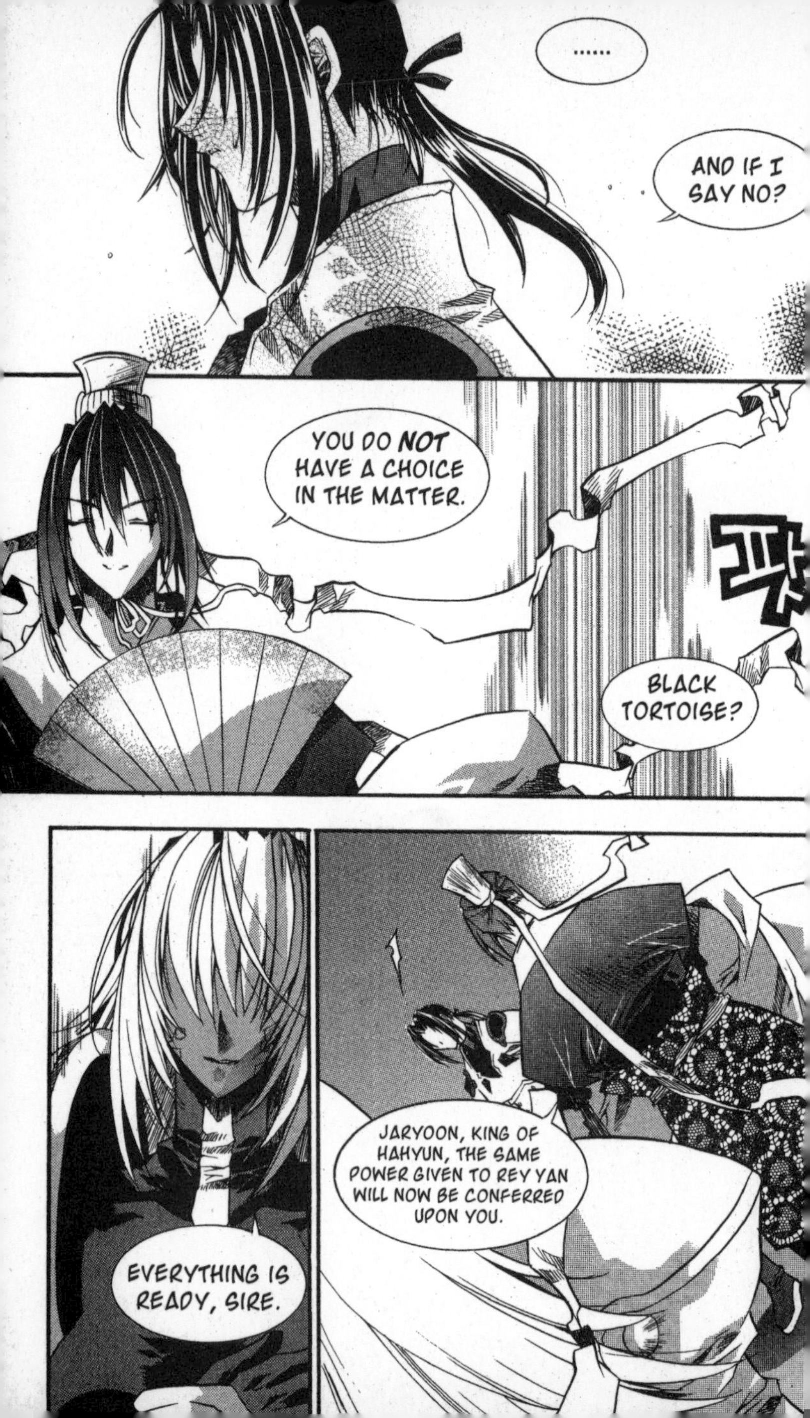
......
AND IF I SAY NO?
YOU DO **NOT** HAVE A CHOICE IN THE MATTER.
BLACK TORTOISE?
EVERYTHING IS READY, SIRE.
JARYOON, KING OF HAHYUN, THE SAME POWER GIVEN TO REY YAN WILL NOW BE CONFERRED UPON YOU.

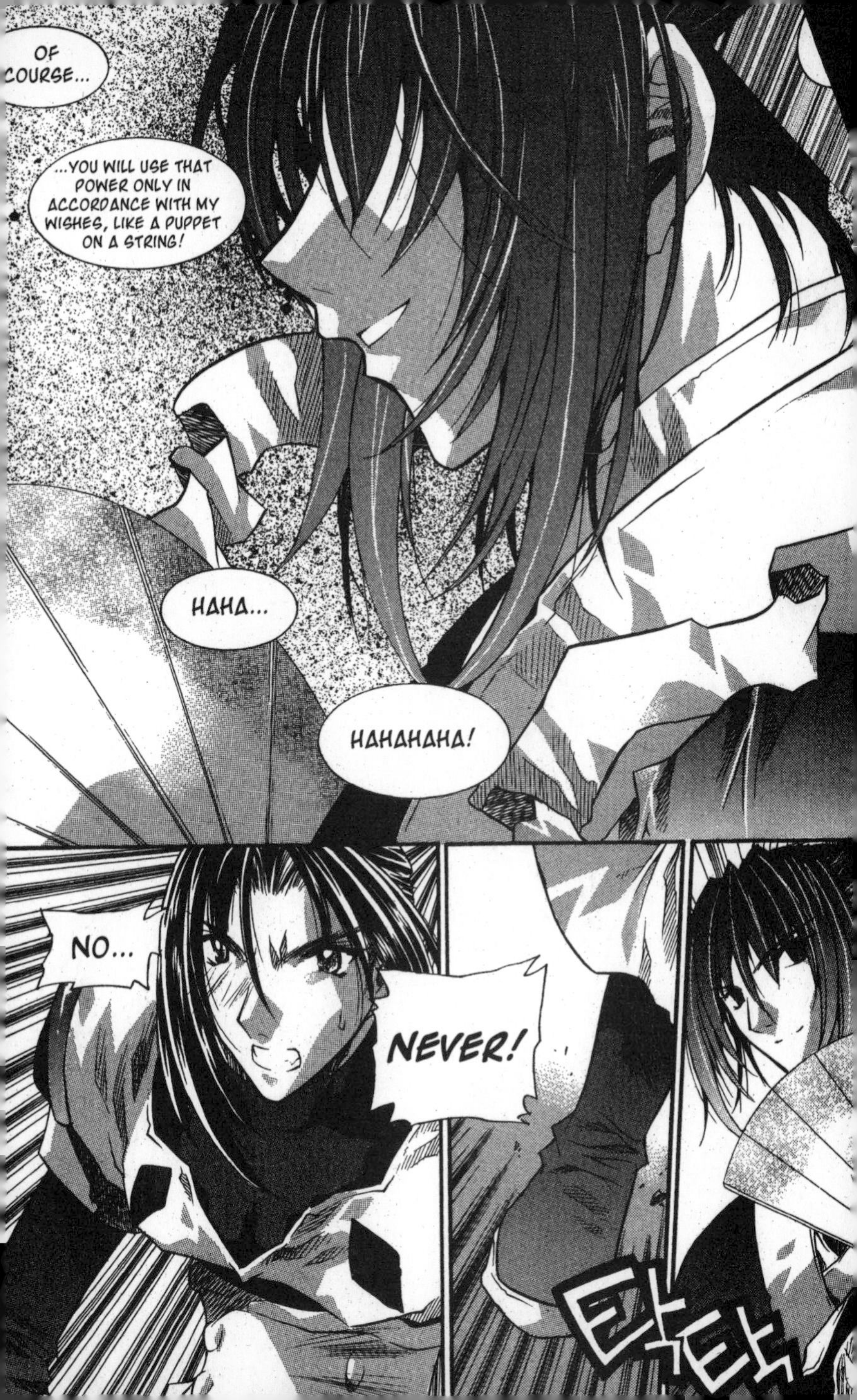
OF COURSE...
...YOU WILL USE THAT POWER ONLY IN ACCORDANCE WITH MY WISHES, LIKE A PUPPET ON A STRING!
HAHA...
HAHAHAHA!
NO...
NEVER!

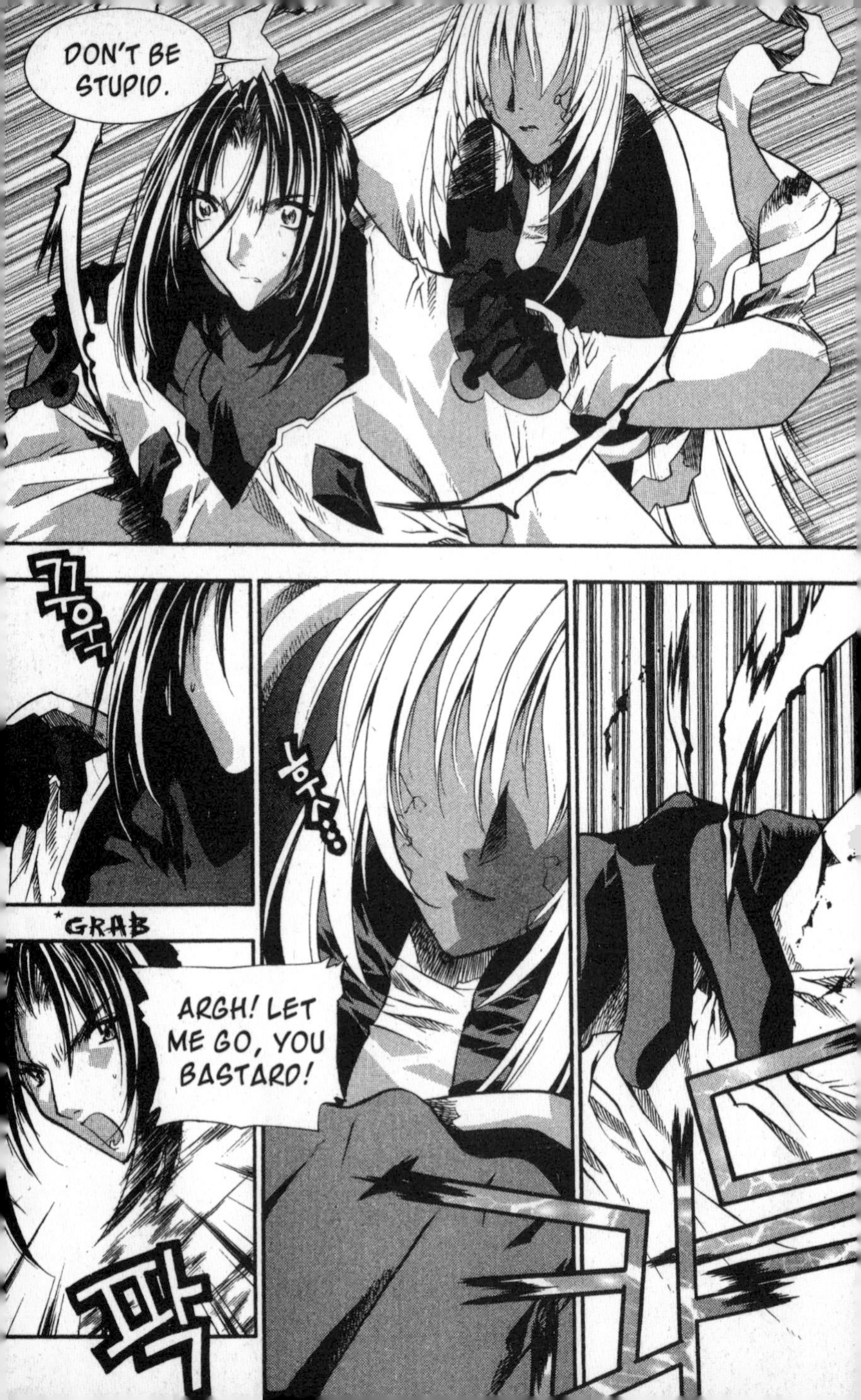
DON'T BE STUPID.
*GRAB
ARGH! LET ME GO, YOU BASTARD!

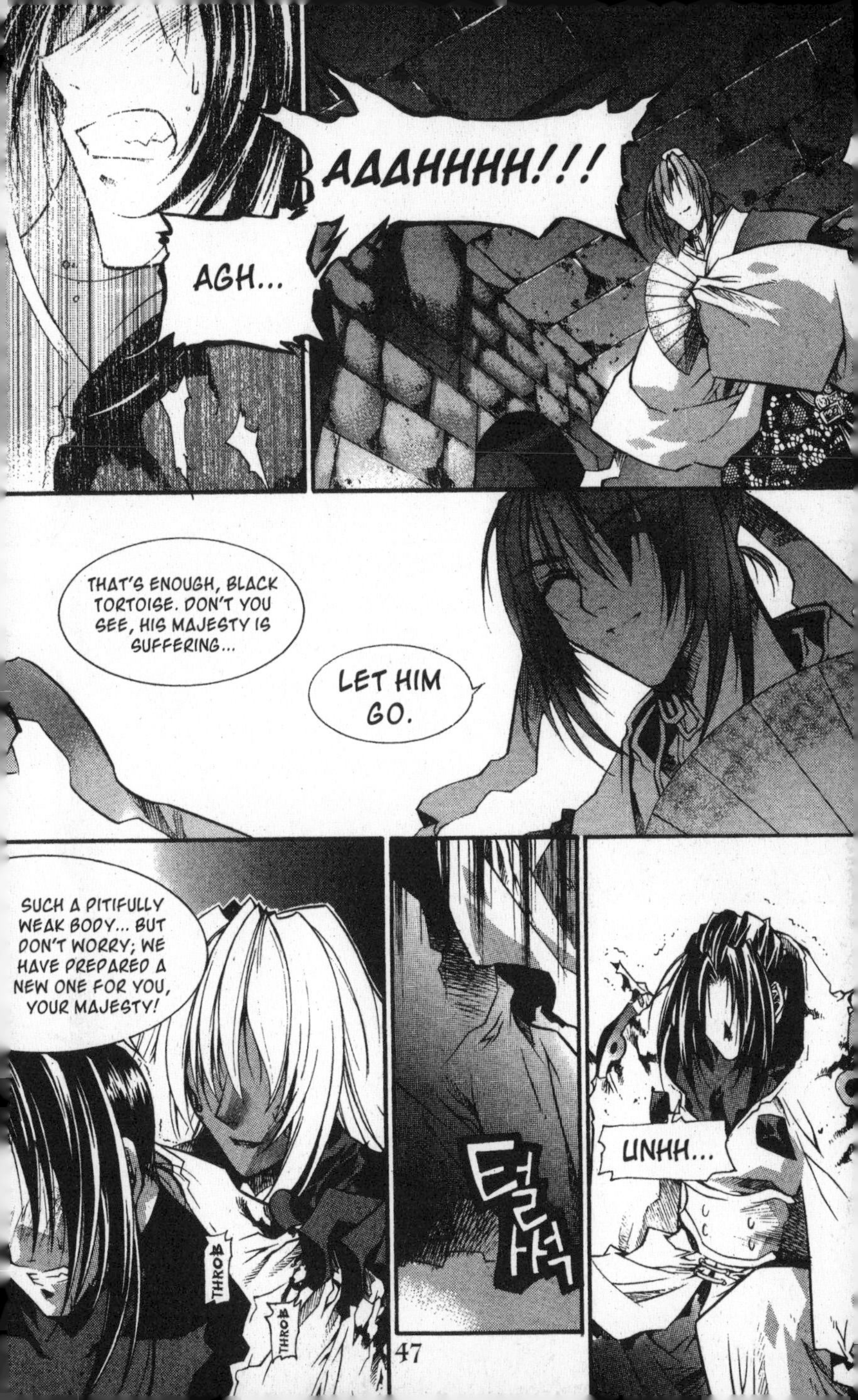
AGH...
AAAHHHH!!!
THAT'S ENOUGH, BLACK TORTOISE. DON'T YOU SEE, HIS MAJESTY IS SUFFERING...
LET HIM GO.
SUCH A PITIFULLY WEAK BODY... BUT DON'T WORRY; WE HAVE PREPARED A NEW ONE FOR YOU, YOUR MAJESTY!
THROB
THROB
UNHH...

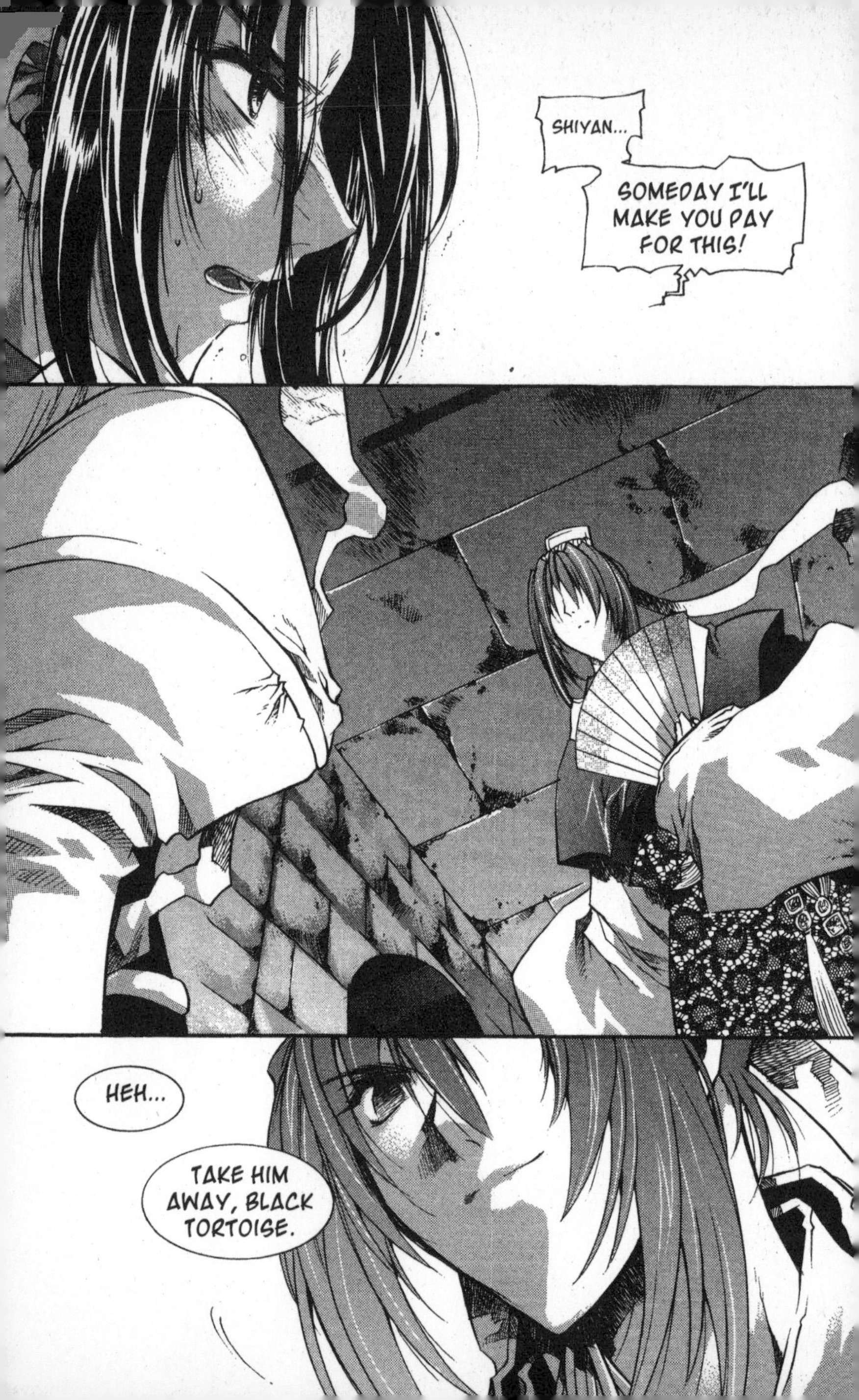
SHIYAN...
SOMEDAY I'LL MAKE YOU PAY FOR THIS!
HEH...
TAKE HIM AWAY, BLACK TORTOISE.

CHAPTER 21: Shyao's Resolution

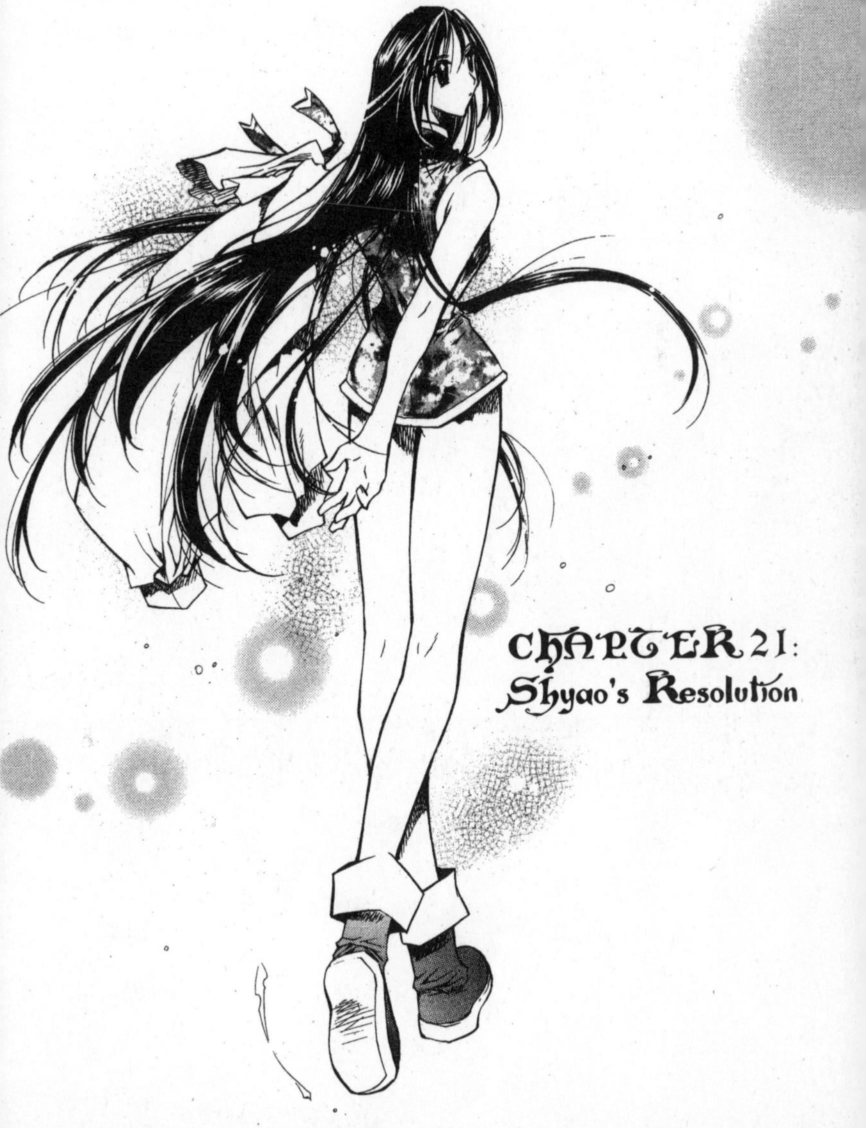

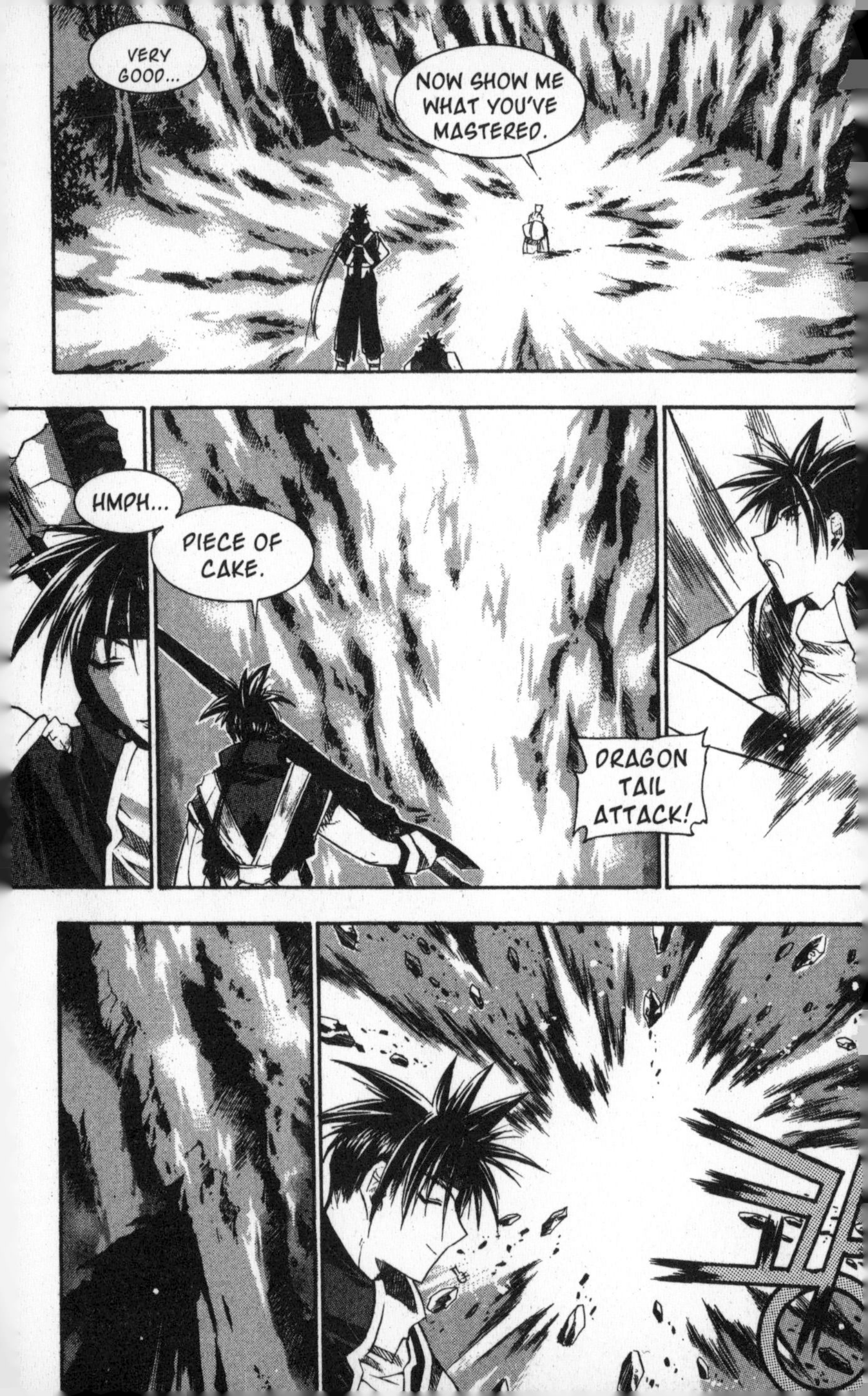

VERY GOOD...
NOW SHOW ME WHAT YOU'VE MASTERED.
HMPH...
PIECE OF CAKE.
DRAGON TAIL ATTACK!

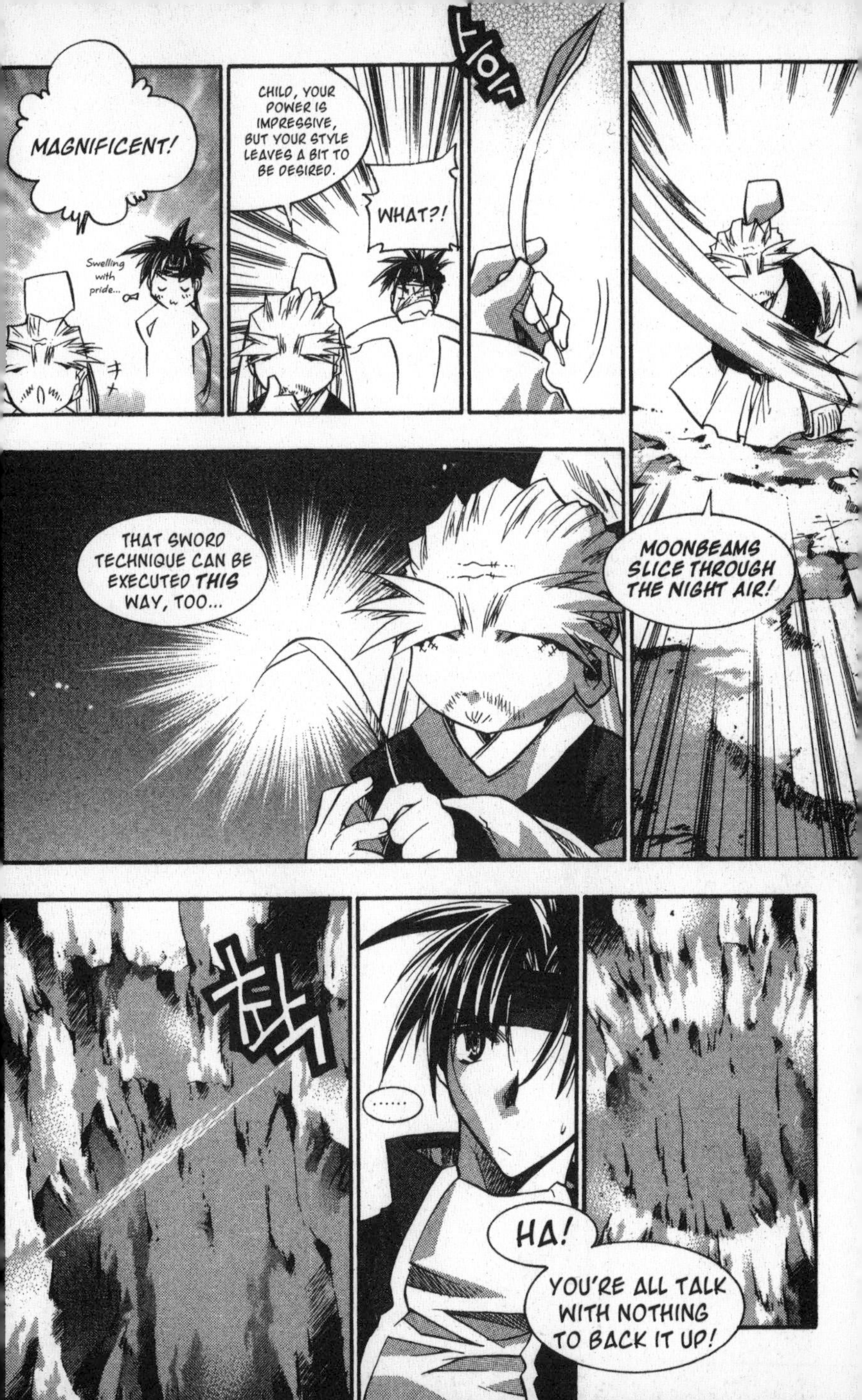
MAGNIFICENT!
Swelling with pride...
CHILD, YOUR POWER IS IMPRESSIVE, BUT YOUR STYLE LEAVES A BIT TO BE DESIRED.
WHAT?!
THAT SWORD TECHNIQUE CAN BE EXECUTED THIS WAY, TOO...
MOONBEAMS SLICE THROUGH THE NIGHT AIR!
......
HA!
YOU'RE ALL TALK WITH NOTHING TO BACK IT UP!

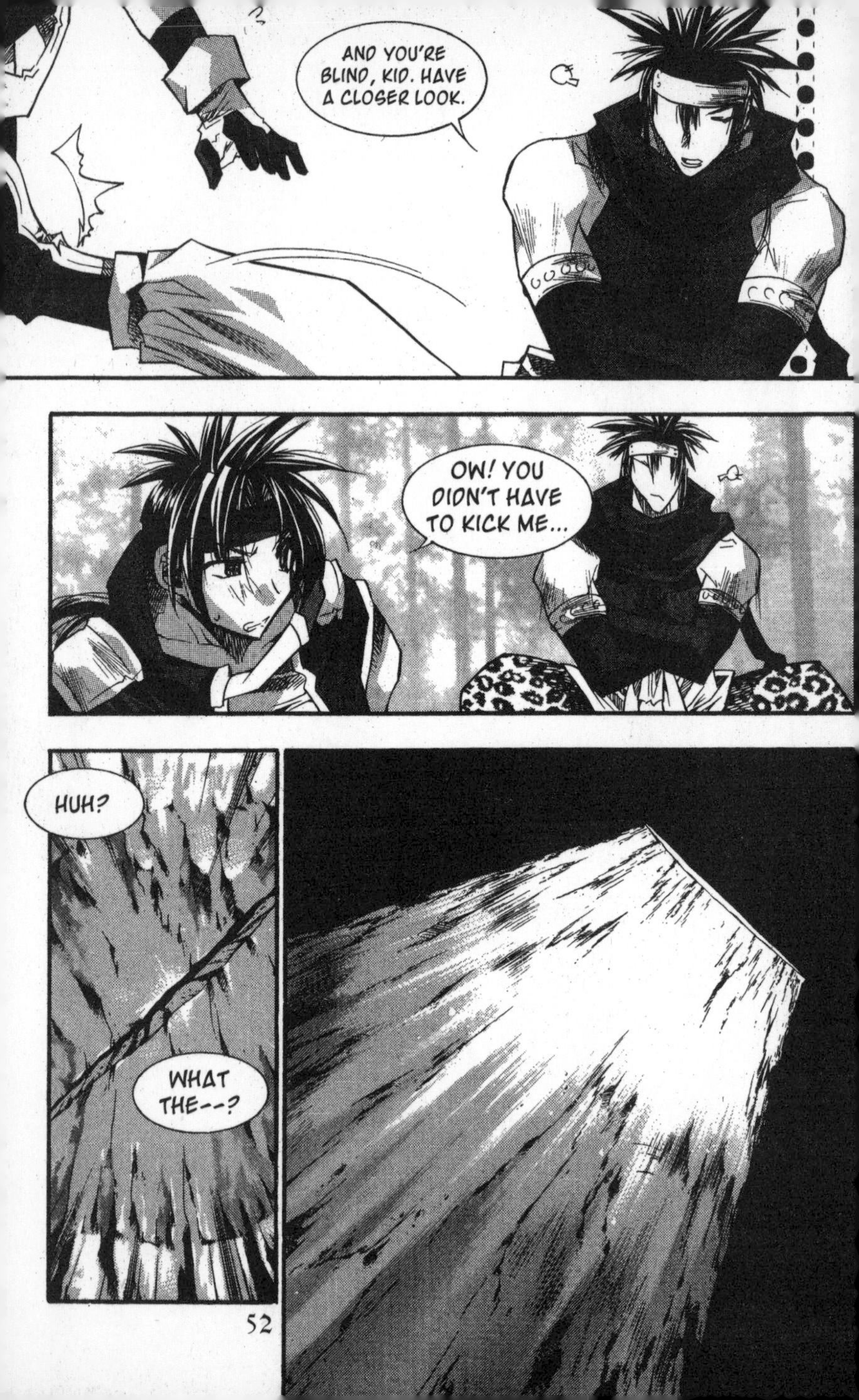
AND YOU'RE BLIND, KID. HAVE A CLOSER LOOK.
OW! YOU DIDN'T HAVE TO KICK ME...
HUH?
WHAT THE--?

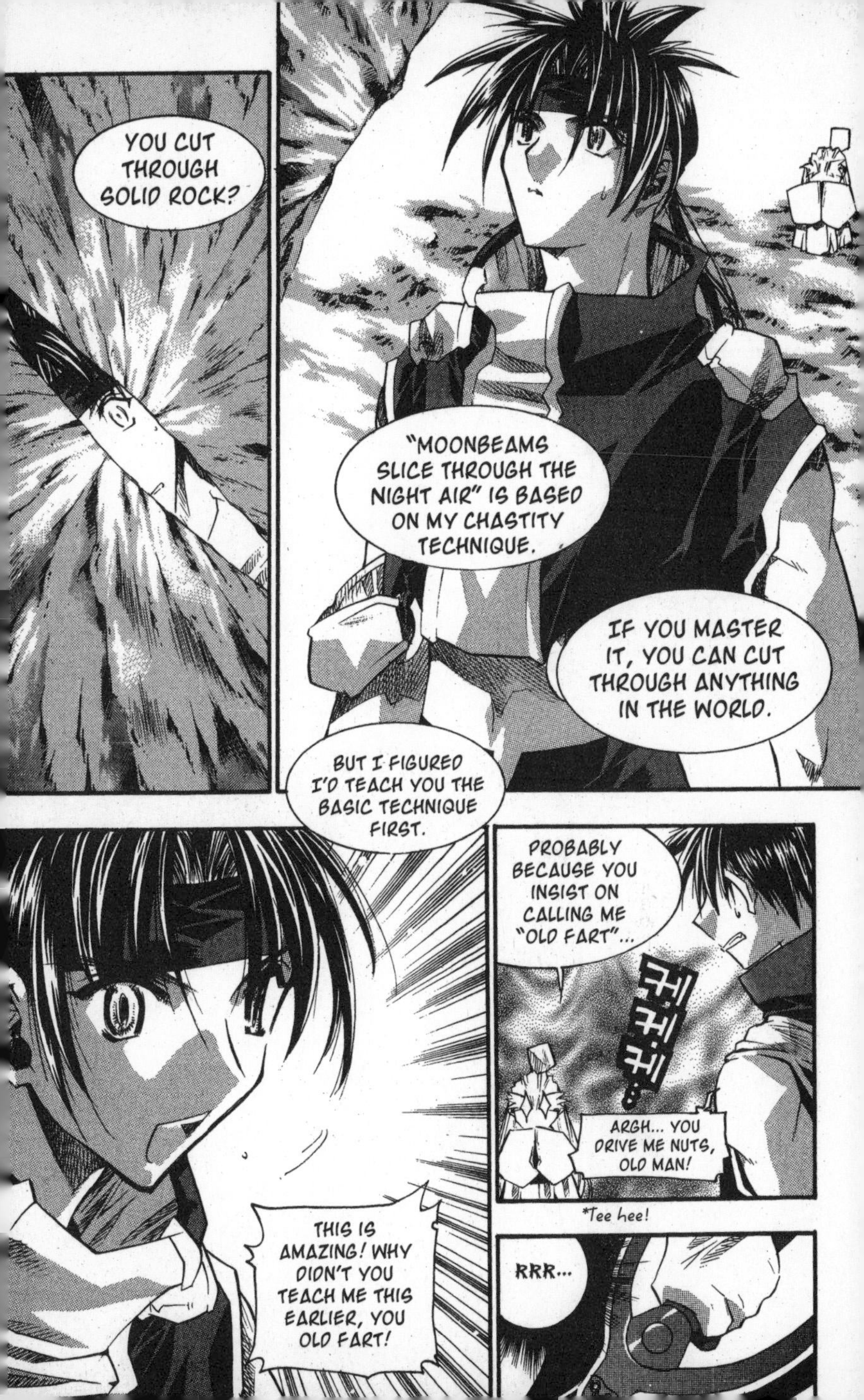
YOU CUT THROUGH SOLID ROCK?
"MOONBEAMS SLICE THROUGH THE NIGHT AIR" IS BASED ON MY CHASTITY TECHNIQUE.
IF YOU MASTER IT, YOU CAN CUT THROUGH ANYTHING IN THE WORLD.
BUT I FIGURED I'D TEACH YOU THE BASIC TECHNIQUE FIRST.
THIS IS AMAZING! WHY DIDN'T YOU TEACH ME THIS EARLIER, YOU OLD FART!
PROBABLY BECAUSE YOU INSIST ON CALLING ME "OLD FART"...
ARGH... YOU DRIVE ME NUTS, OLD MAN!
*Tee hee!
RRR...

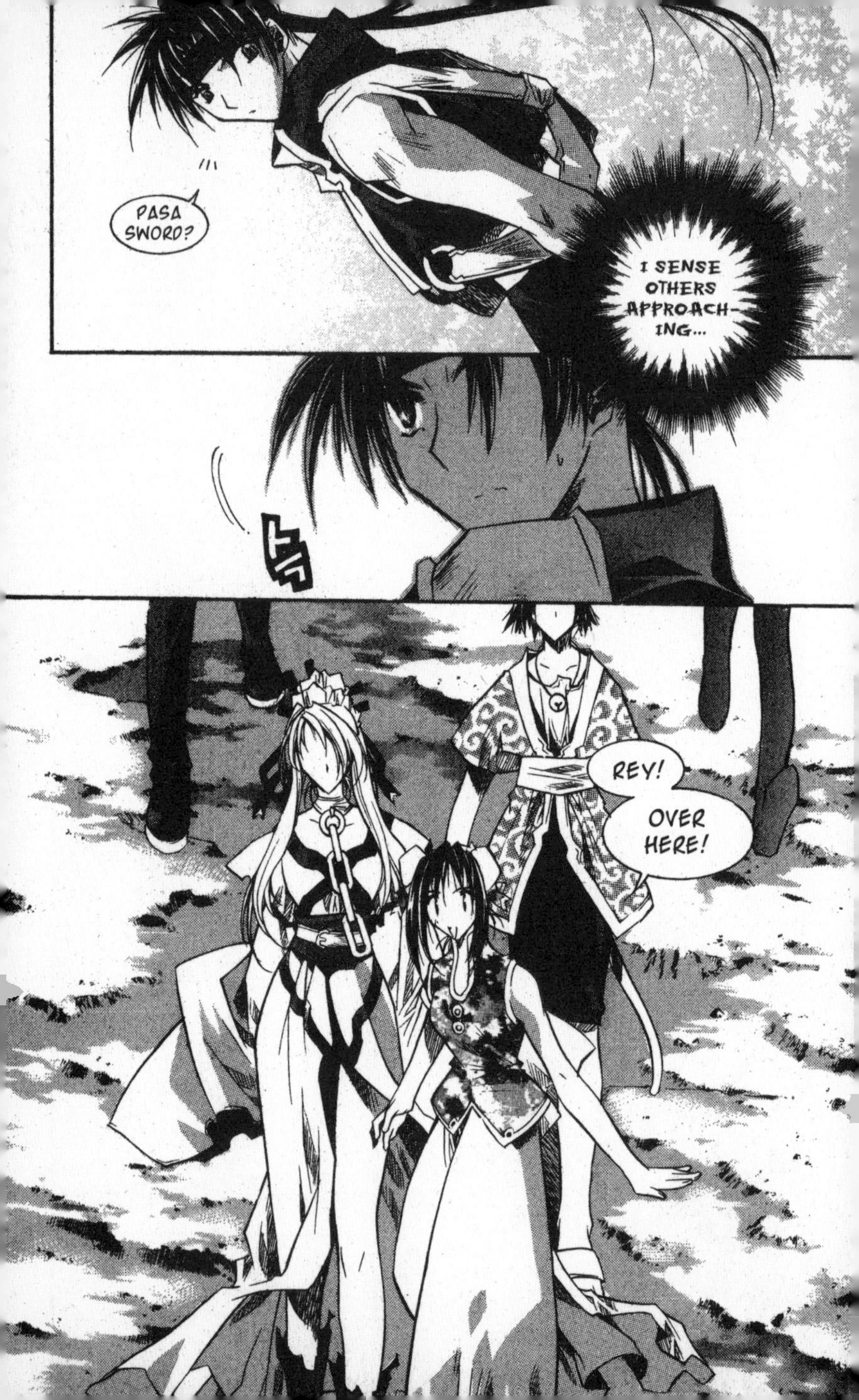
PASA SWORD?
I SENSE OTHERS APPROACHING...
REY!
OVER HERE!

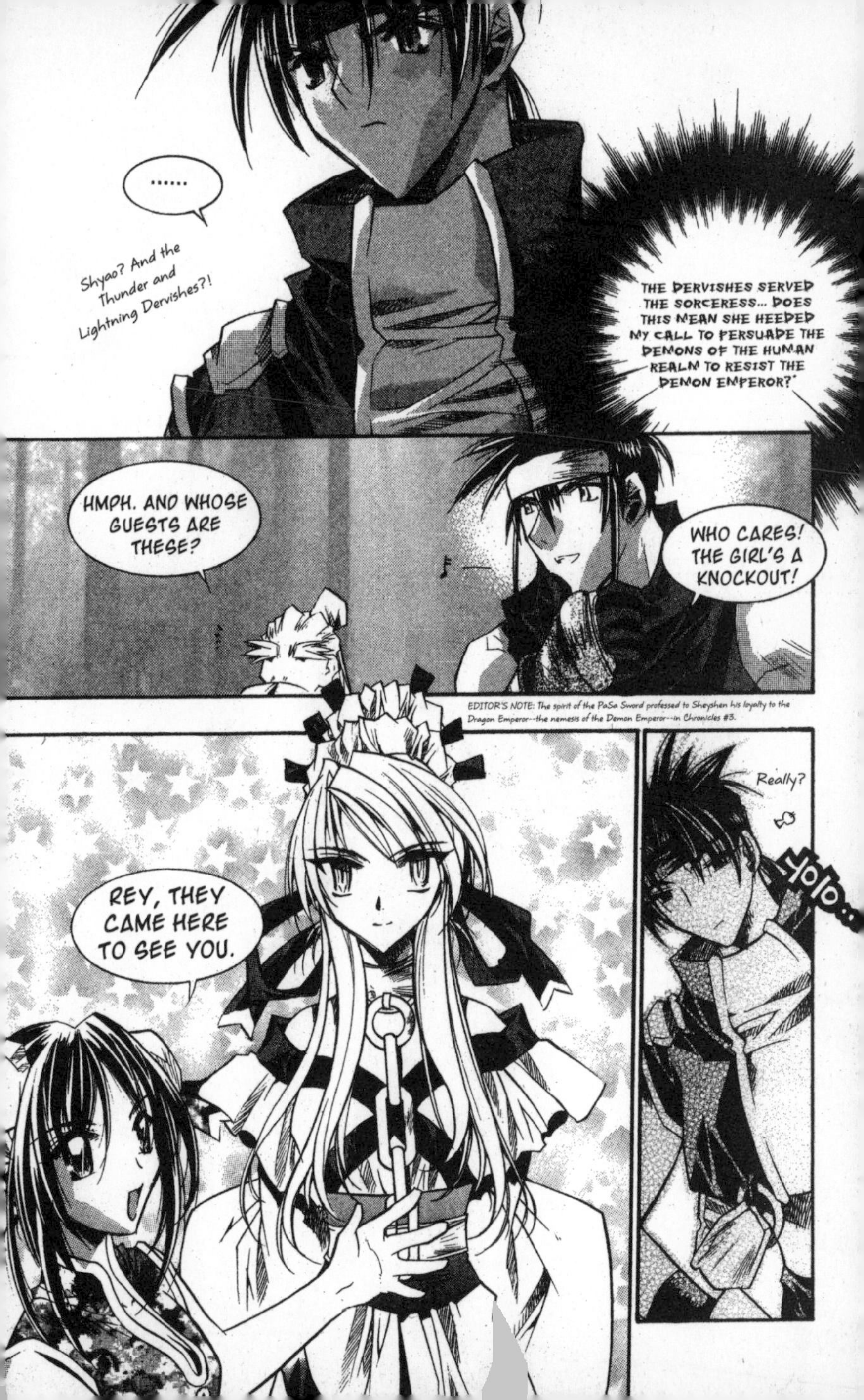
......
Shyao? And the Thunder and Lightning Dervishes?!
THE DERVISHES SERVED THE SORCERESS... DOES THIS MEAN SHE HEEDED MY CALL TO PERSUADE THE DEMONS OF THE HUMAN REALM TO RESIST THE DEMON EMPEROR?*
HMPH. AND WHOSE GUESTS ARE THESE?
WHO CARES! THE GIRL'S A KNOCKOUT!
EDITOR'S NOTE: The spirit of the PaSa Sword professed to Sheyshen his loyalty to the Dragon Emperor--the nemesis of the Demon Emperor--in Chronicles #3.
REY, THEY CAME HERE TO SEE YOU.
Really?
YOLO...

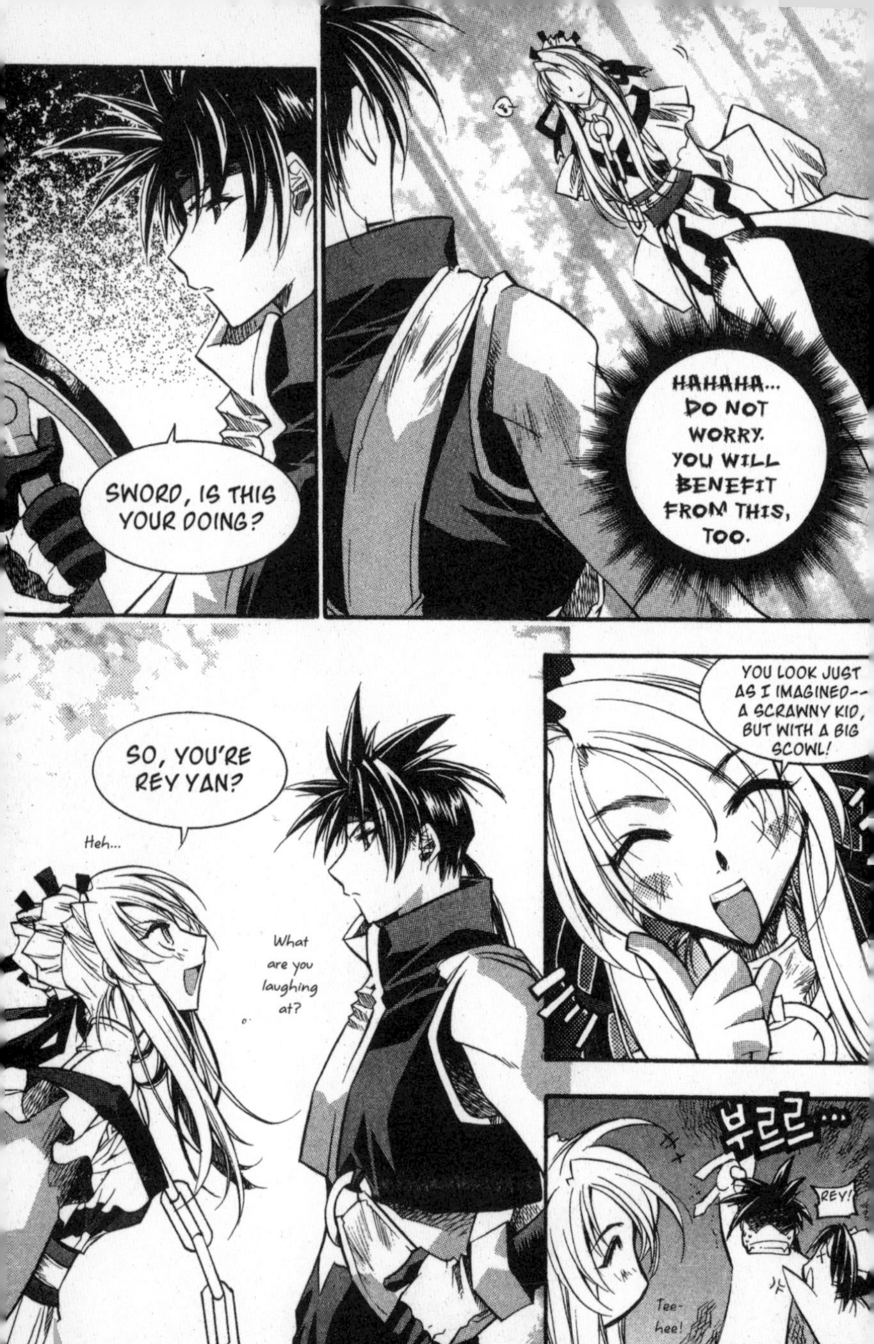
SWORD, IS THIS YOUR DOING?
HAHAHA... DO NOT WORRY. YOU WILL BENEFIT FROM THIS, TOO.
SO, YOU'RE REY YAN?
Heh...
What are you laughing at?
YOU LOOK JUST AS I IMAGINED-- A SCRAWNY KID, BUT WITH A BIG SCOWL!
부르르...
REY!
Tee-hee!

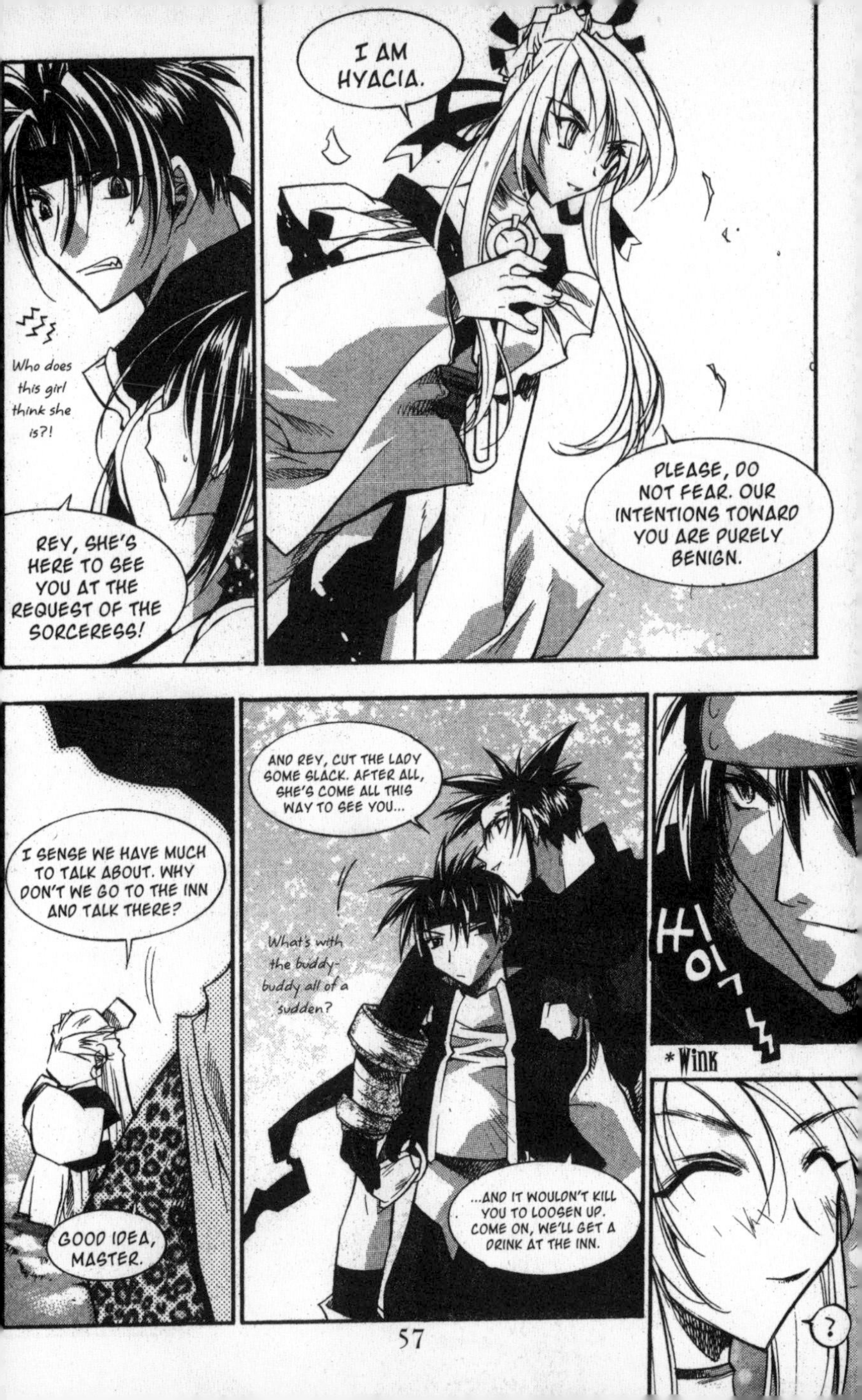
Who does this girl think she is?!
REY, SHE'S HERE TO SEE YOU AT THE REQUEST OF THE SORCERESS!
I AM HYACIA.
PLEASE, DO NOT FEAR. OUR INTENTIONS TOWARD YOU ARE PURELY BENIGN.
I SENSE WE HAVE MUCH TO TALK ABOUT. WHY DON'T WE GO TO THE INN AND TALK THERE?
GOOD IDEA, MASTER.
AND REY, CUT THE LADY SOME SLACK. AFTER ALL, SHE'S COME ALL THIS WAY TO SEE YOU...
What's with the buddy-buddy all of a sudden?
...AND IT WOULDN'T KILL YOU TO LOOSEN UP. COME ON, WE'LL GET A DRINK AT THE INN.
*WINK
?

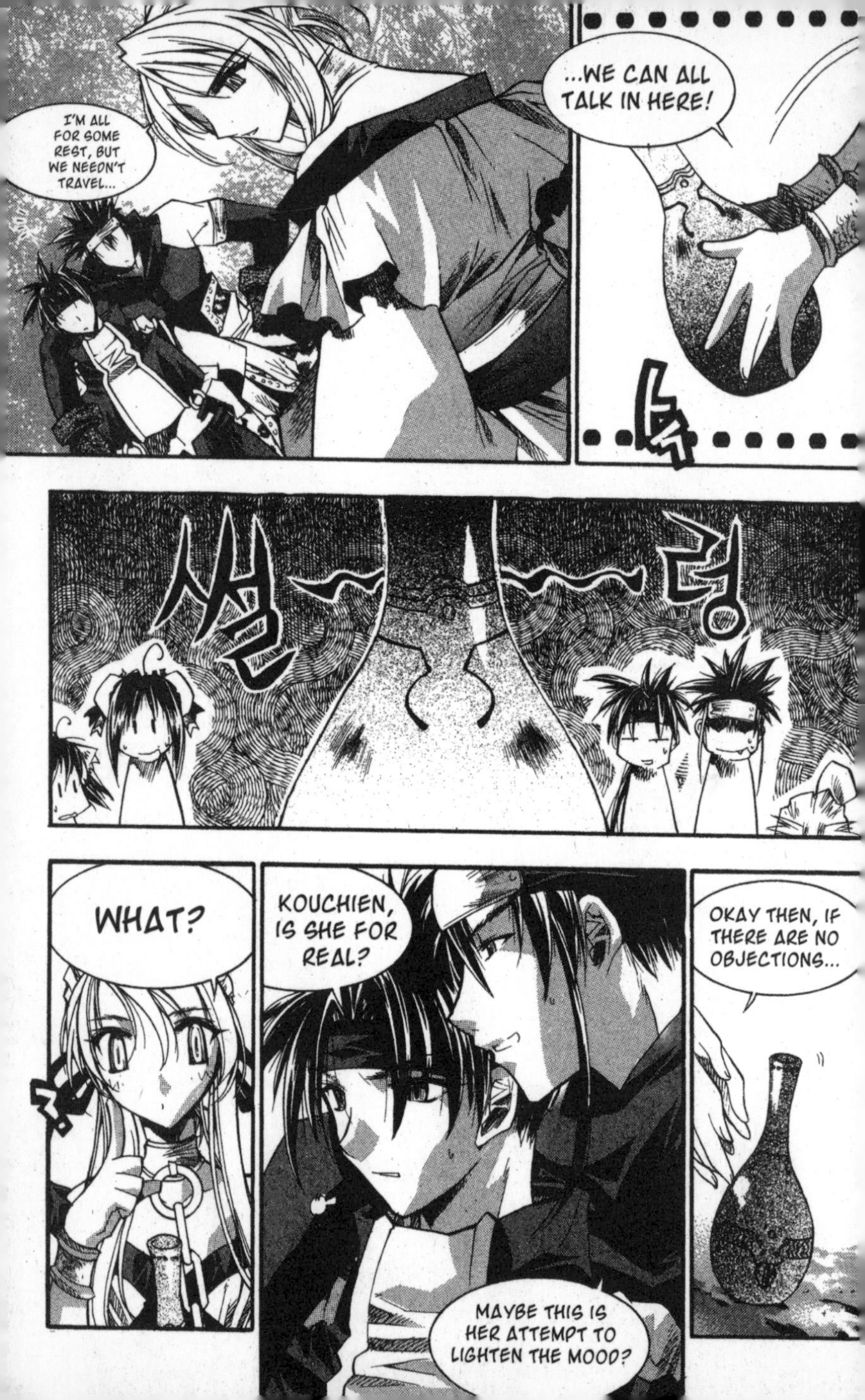
I'M ALL FOR SOME REST, BUT WE NEEDN'T TRAVEL...
...WE CAN ALL TALK IN HERE!
썰~~렁
WHAT?
KOUCHIEN, IS SHE FOR REAL?
MAYBE THIS IS HER ATTEMPT TO LIGHTEN THE MOOD?
OKAY THEN, IF THERE ARE NO OBJECTIONS...

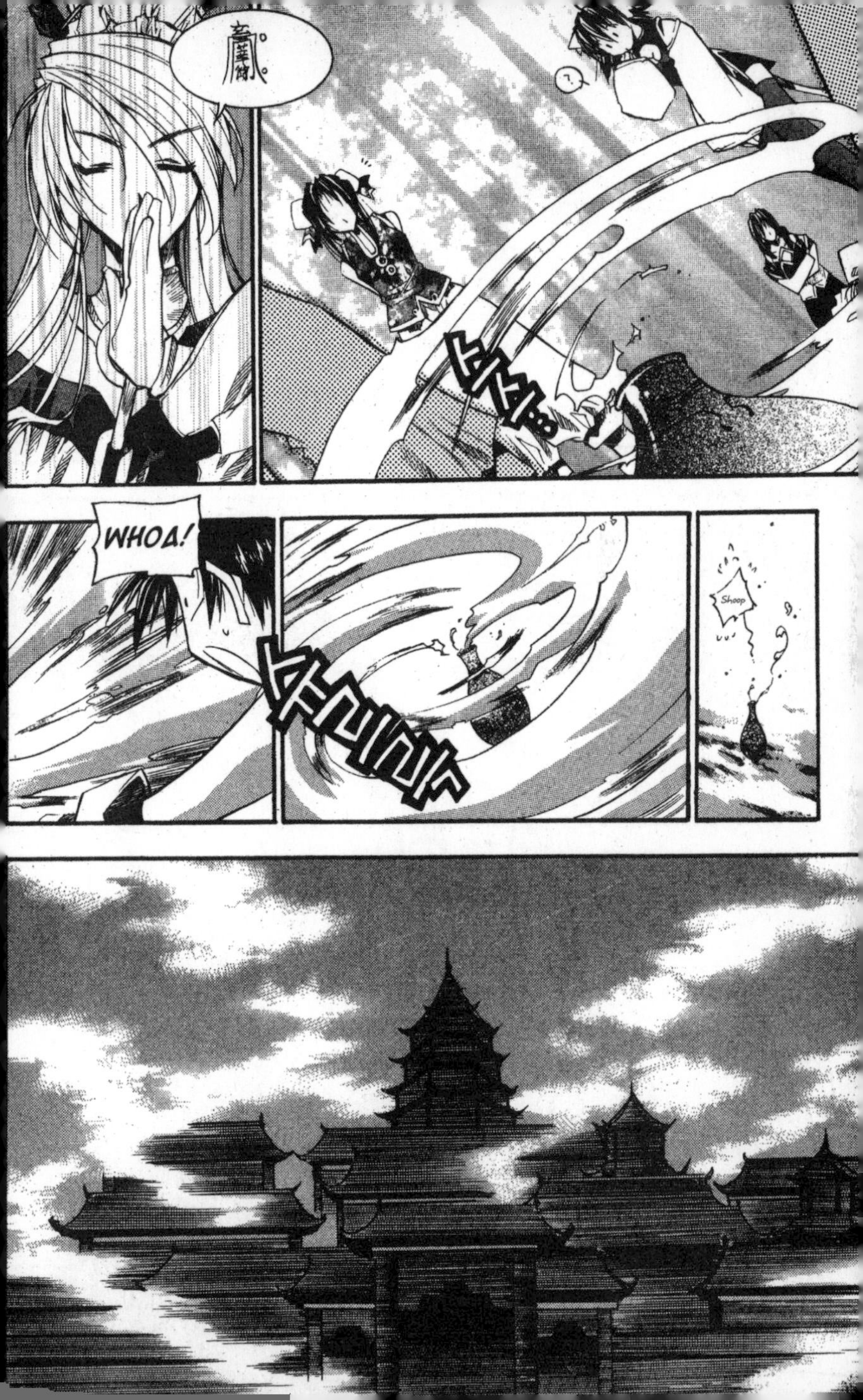
WHOA!
Shoop

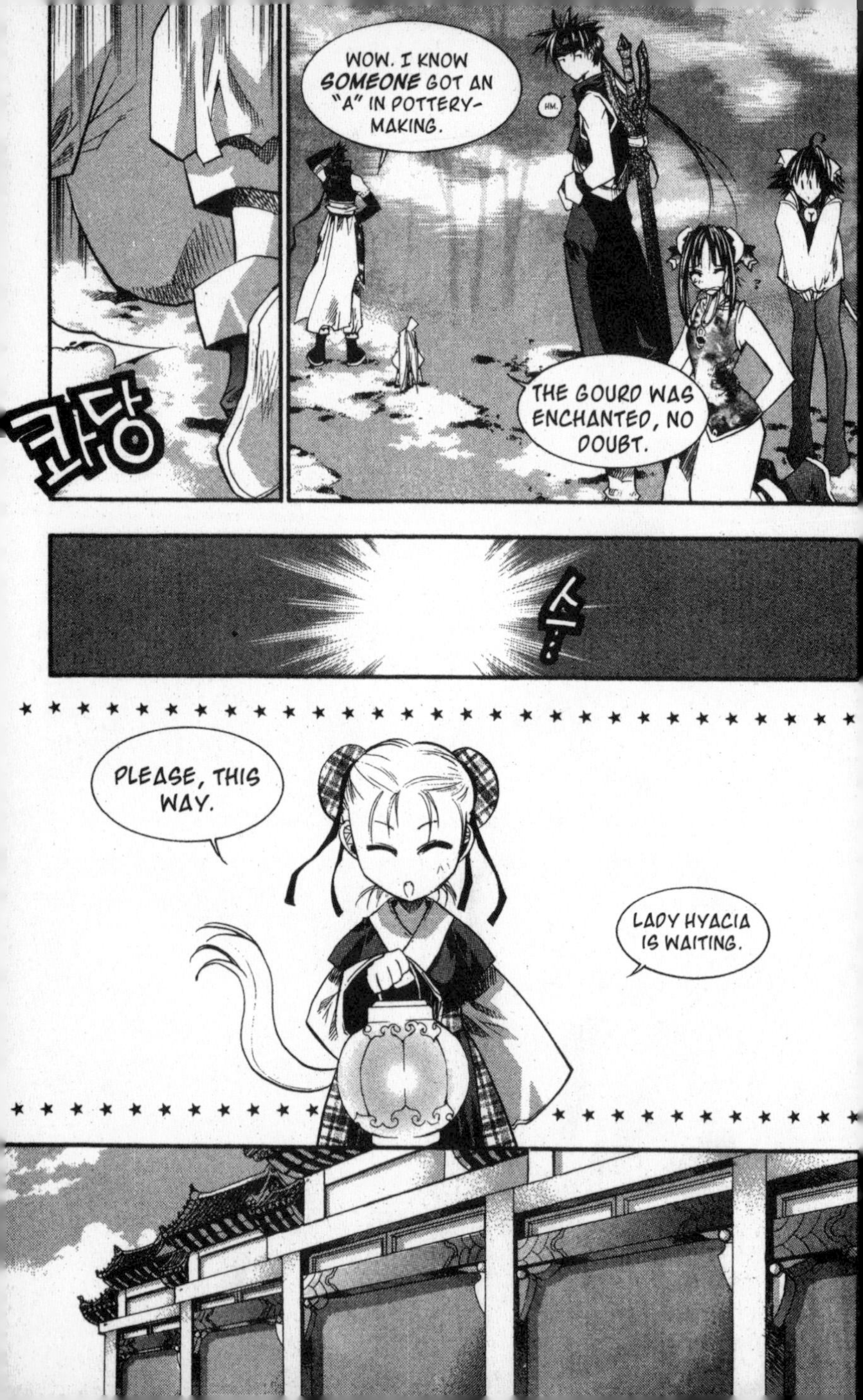
콰당
WOW. I KNOW SOMEONE GOT AN "A" IN POTTERY-MAKING.
HM.
THE GOURD WAS ENCHANTED, NO DOUBT.
스
PLEASE, THIS WAY.
LADY HYACIA IS WAITING.

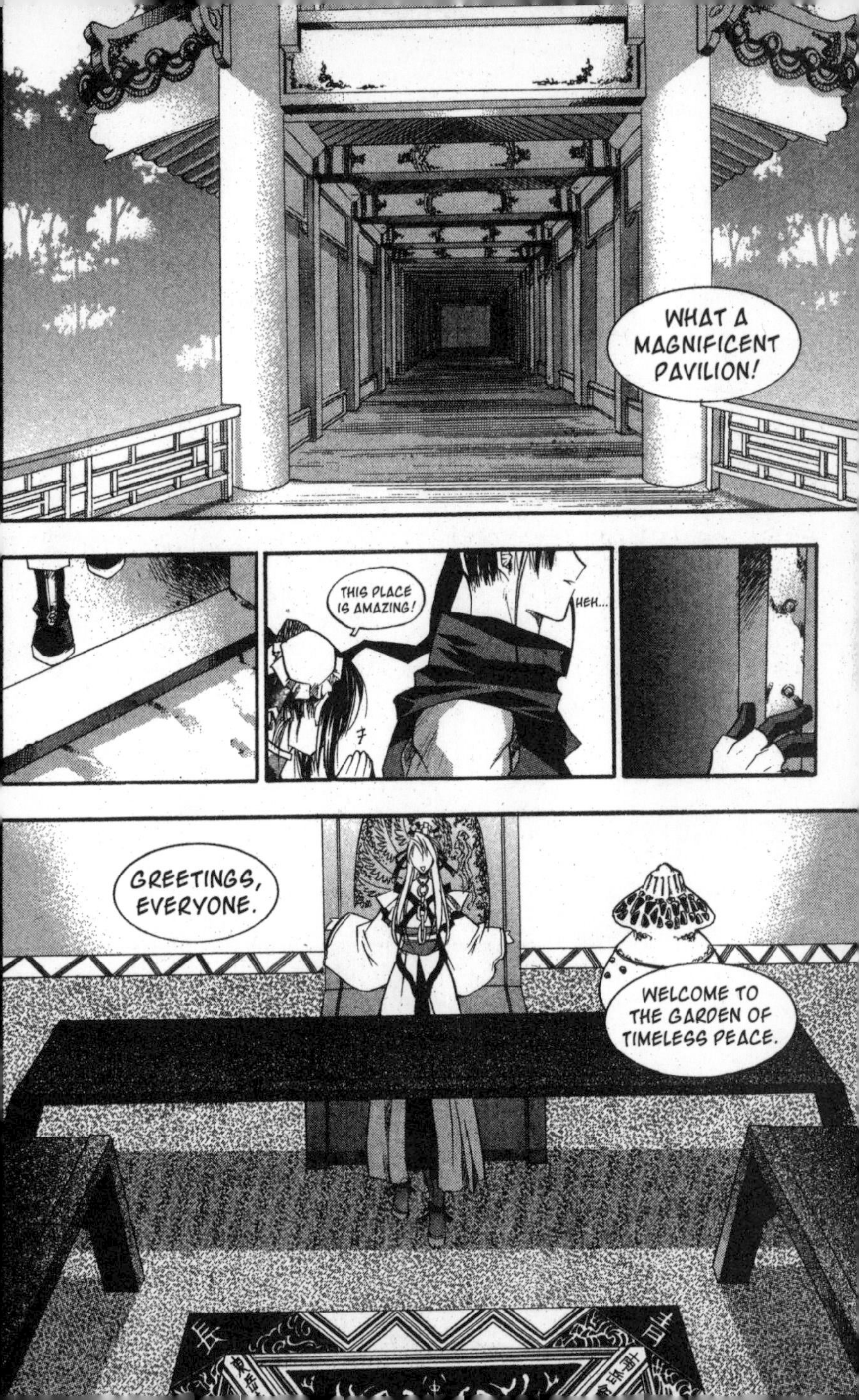
WHAT A MAGNIFICENT PAVILION!
THIS PLACE IS AMAZING!
HEH...
GREETINGS, EVERYONE.
WELCOME TO THE GARDEN OF TIMELESS PEACE.

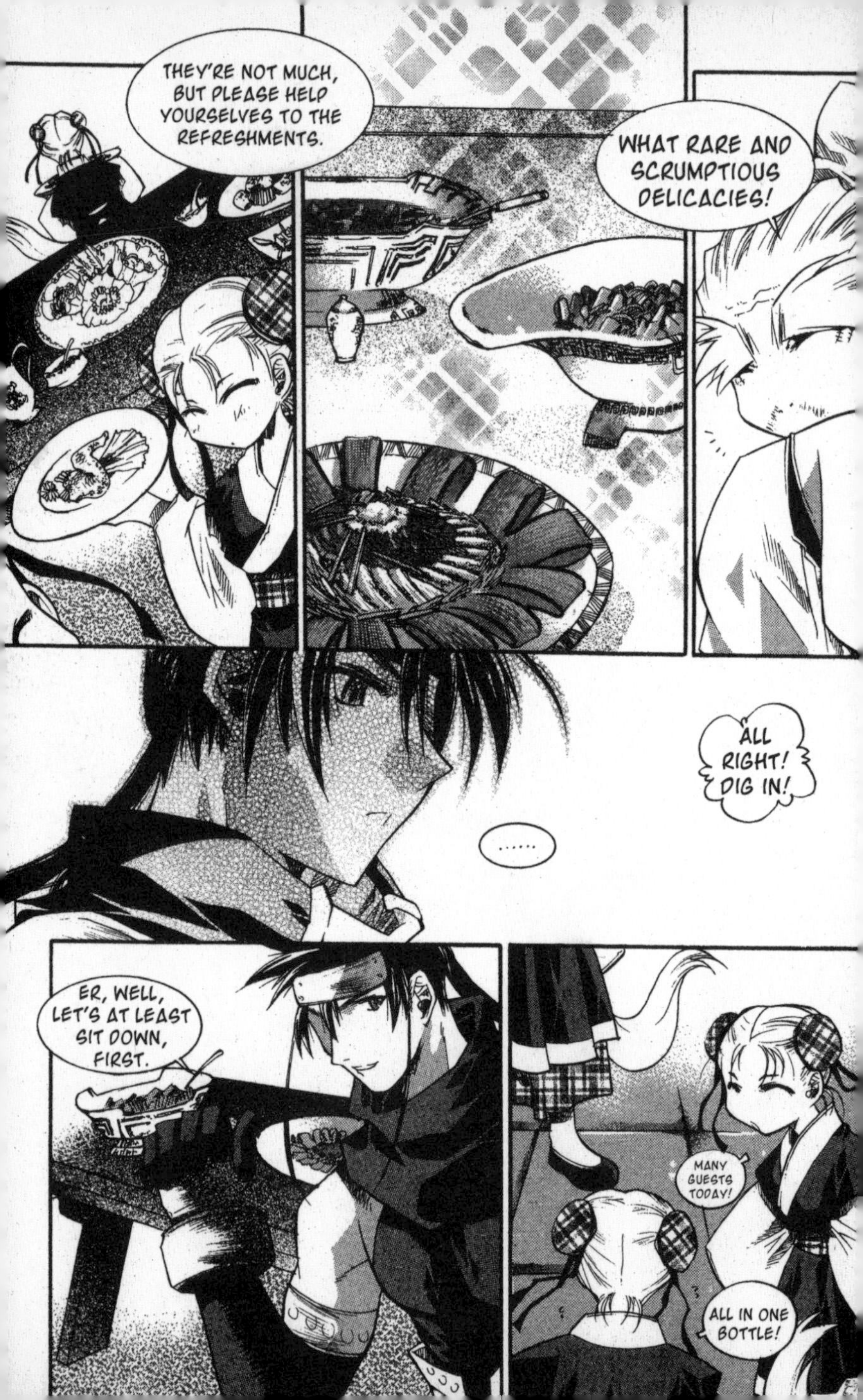
THEY'RE NOT MUCH, BUT PLEASE HELP YOURSELVES TO THE REFRESHMENTS.
WHAT RARE AND SCRUMPTIOUS DELICACIES!
......
ALL RIGHT! DIG IN!
ER, WELL, LET'S AT LEAST SIT DOWN, FIRST.
MANY GUESTS TODAY!
ALL IN ONE BOTTLE!

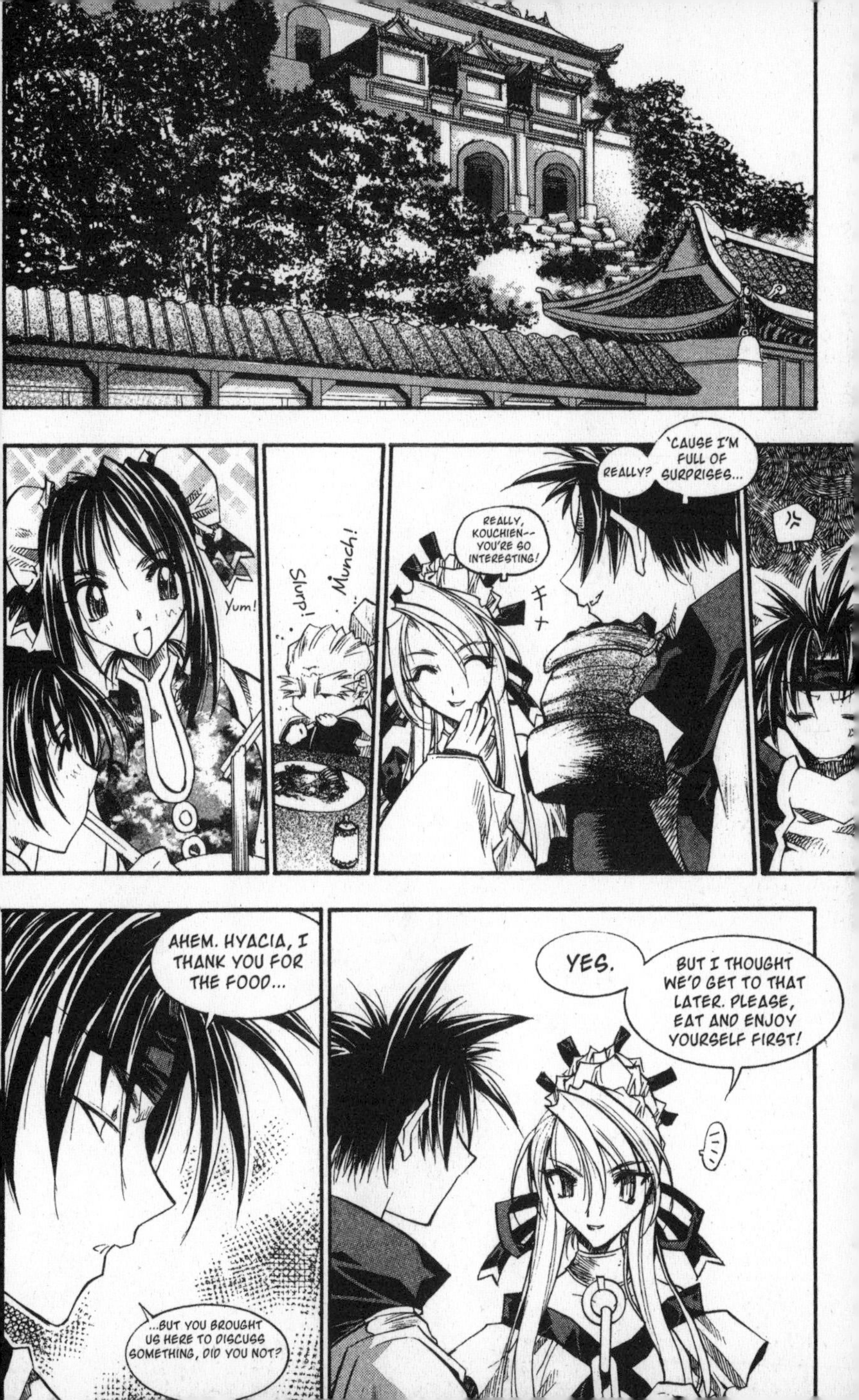
Yum!
Slurp!
Munch!
REALLY, KOUCHIEN-- YOU'RE SO INTERESTING!
REALLY?
`CAUSE I'M FULL OF SURPRISES...
AHEM. HYACIA, I THANK YOU FOR THE FOOD...
...BUT YOU BROUGHT US HERE TO DISCUSS SOMETHING, DID YOU NOT?
YES.
BUT I THOUGHT WE'D GET TO THAT LATER. PLEASE, EAT AND ENJOY YOURSELF FIRST!

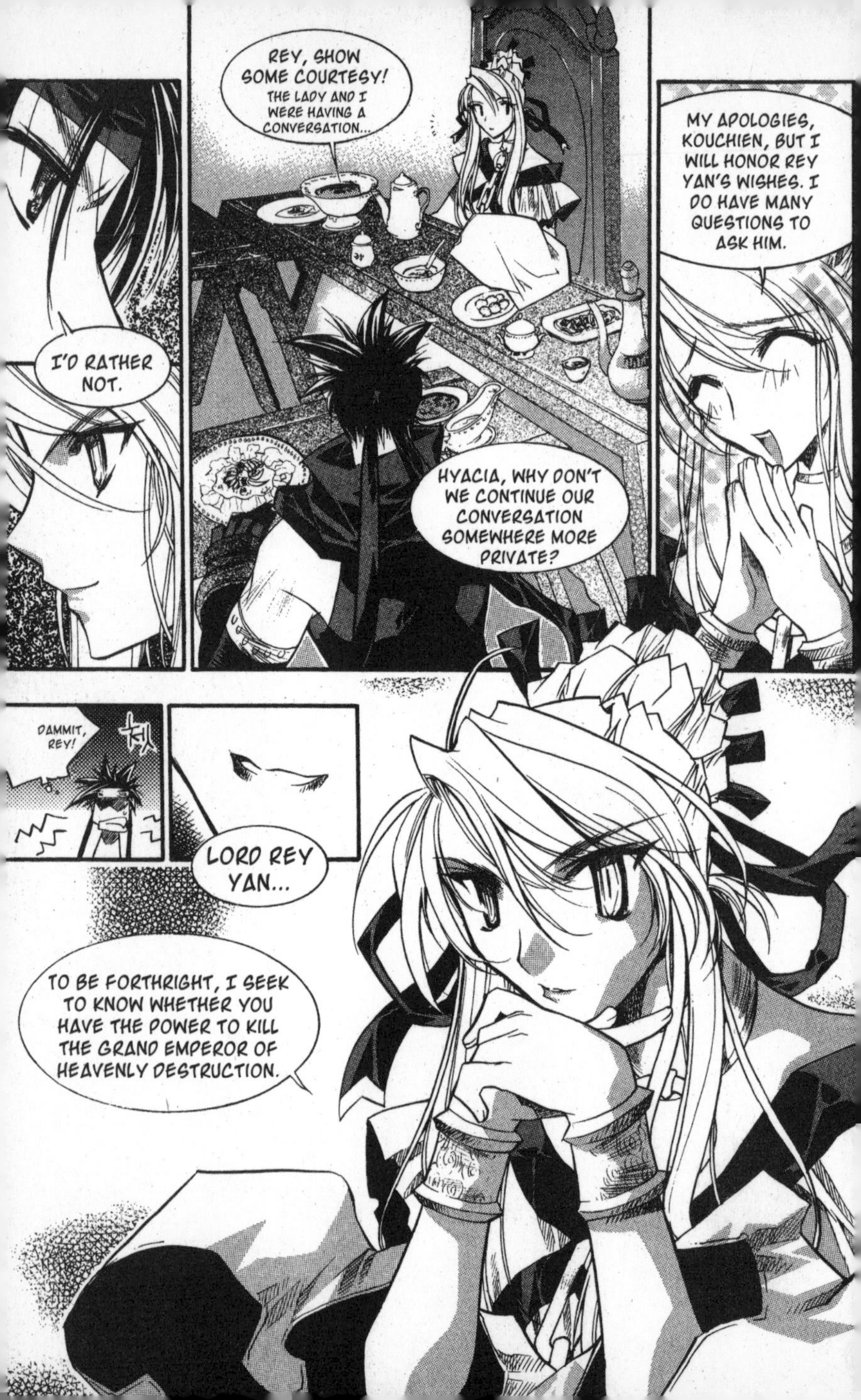
I'D RATHER NOT.
REY, SHOW SOME COURTESY! THE LADY AND I WERE HAVING A CONVERSATION...
HYACIA, WHY DON'T WE CONTINUE OUR CONVERSATION SOMEWHERE MORE PRIVATE?
MY APOLOGIES, KOUCHIEN, BUT I WILL HONOR REY YAN'S WISHES. I DO HAVE MANY QUESTIONS TO ASK HIM.
DAMMIT, REY!
LORD REY YAN...
TO BE FORTHRIGHT, I SEEK TO KNOW WHETHER YOU HAVE THE POWER TO KILL THE GRAND EMPEROR OF HEAVENLY DESTRUCTION.

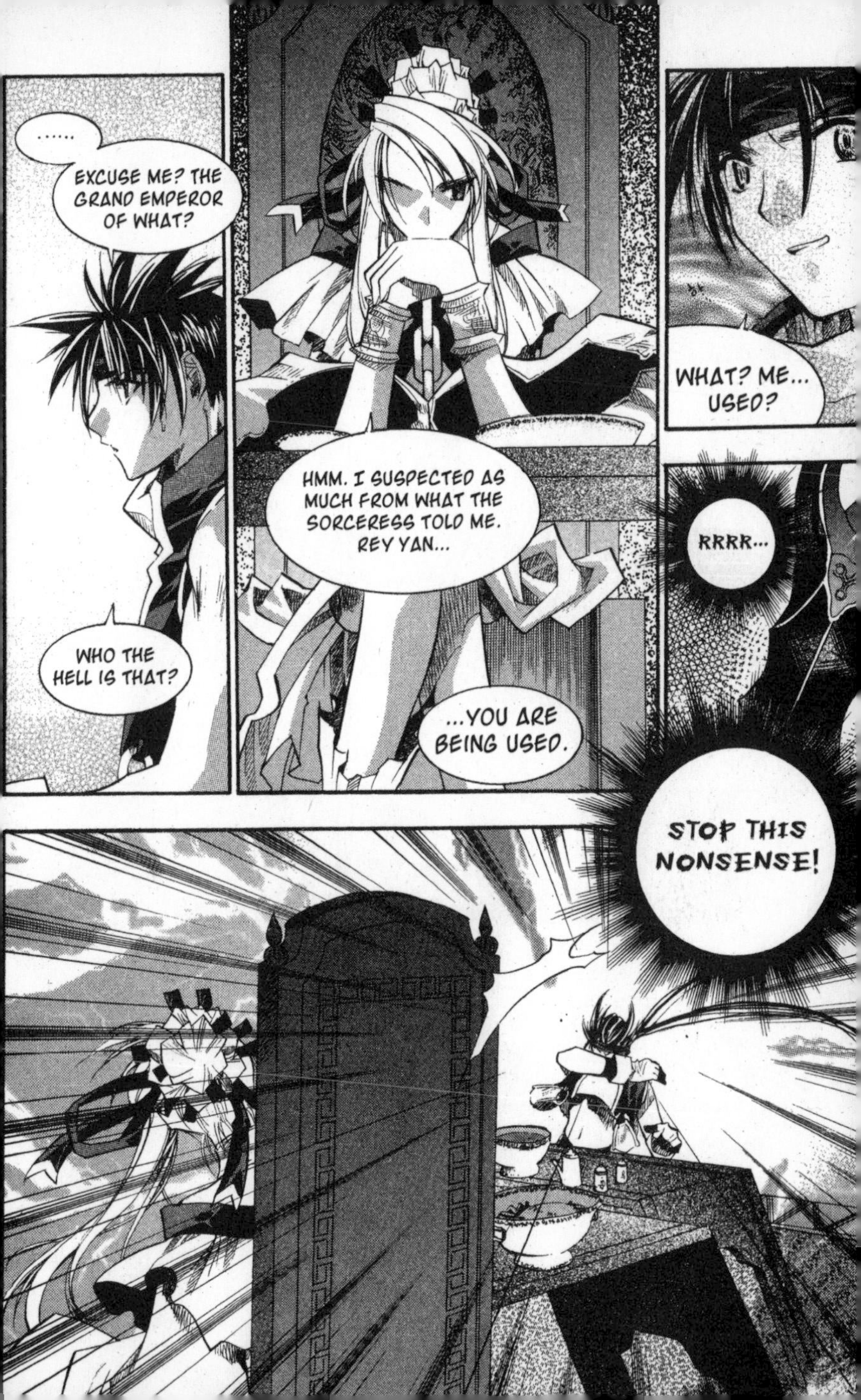
......
EXCUSE ME? THE GRAND EMPEROR OF WHAT?
WHO THE HELL IS THAT?
HMM. I SUSPECTED AS MUCH FROM WHAT THE SORCERESS TOLD ME. REY YAN...
...YOU ARE BEING USED.
WHAT? ME... USED?
RRRR...
STOP THIS NONSENSE!

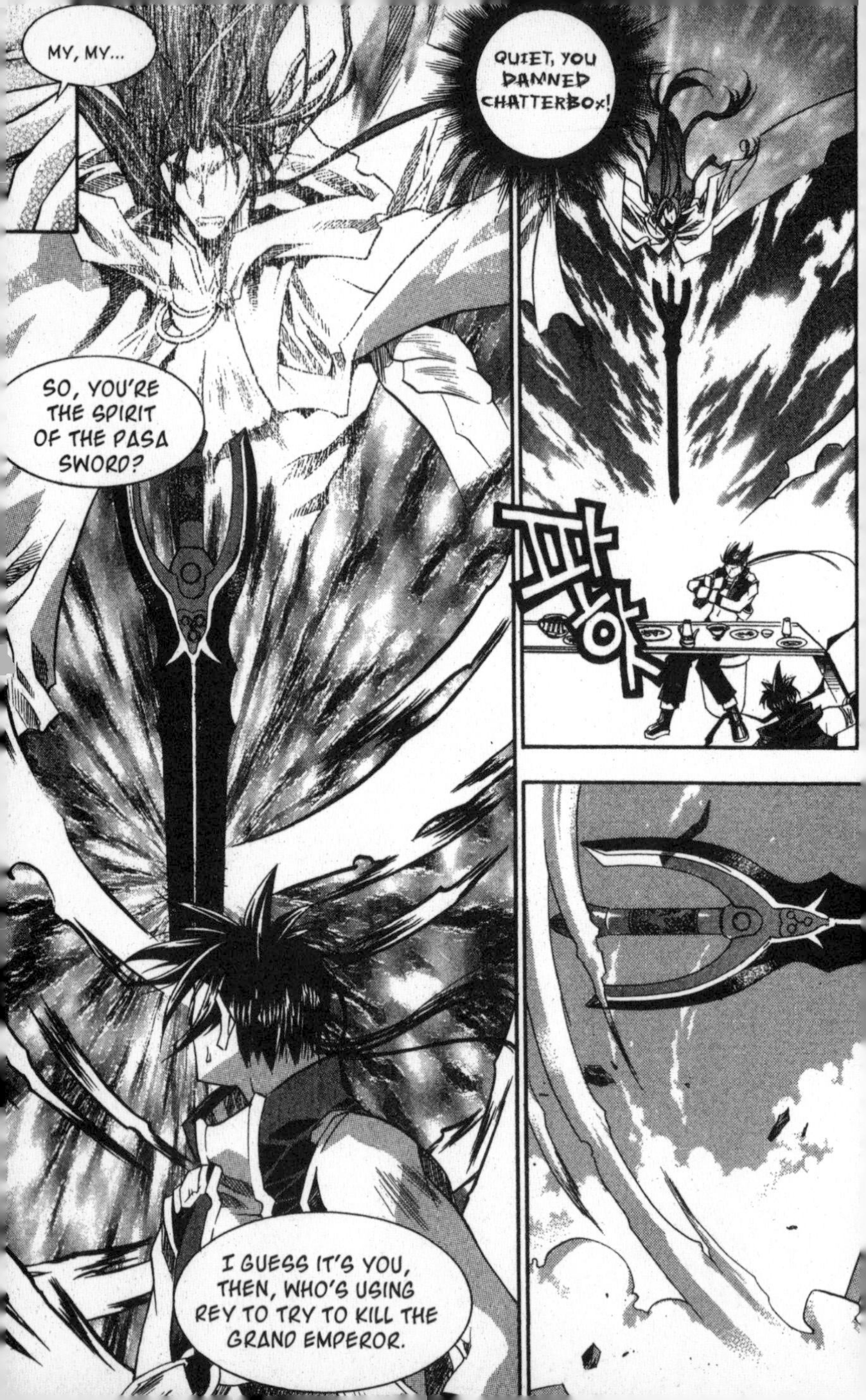
MY, MY...
SO, YOU'RE THE SPIRIT OF THE PASA SWORD?
I GUESS IT'S YOU, THEN, WHO'S USING REY TO TRY TO KILL THE GRAND EMPEROR.
QUIET, YOU DAMNED CHATTERBOX!

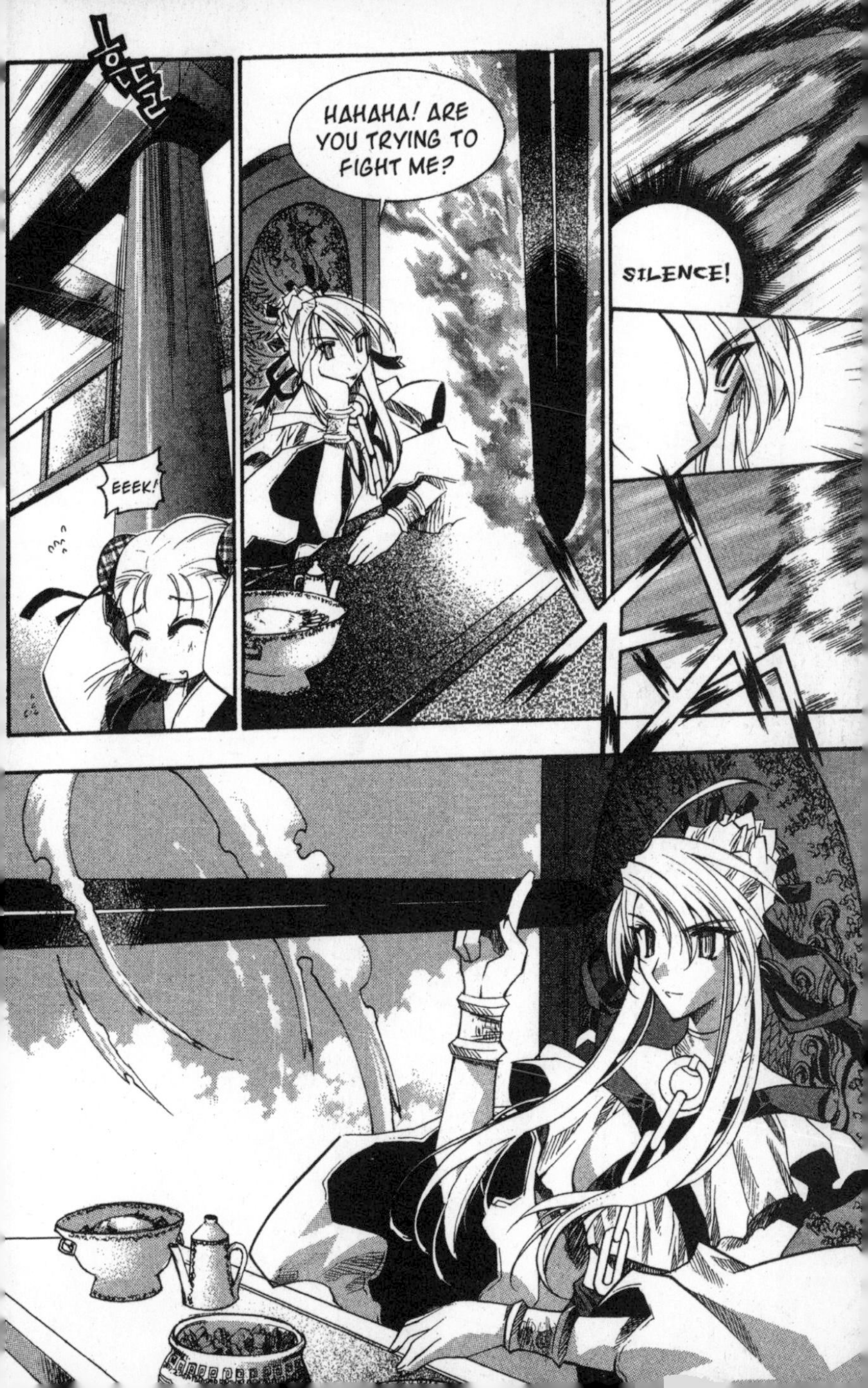
EEEK!
HAHAHA! ARE YOU TRYING TO FIGHT ME?
SILENCE!

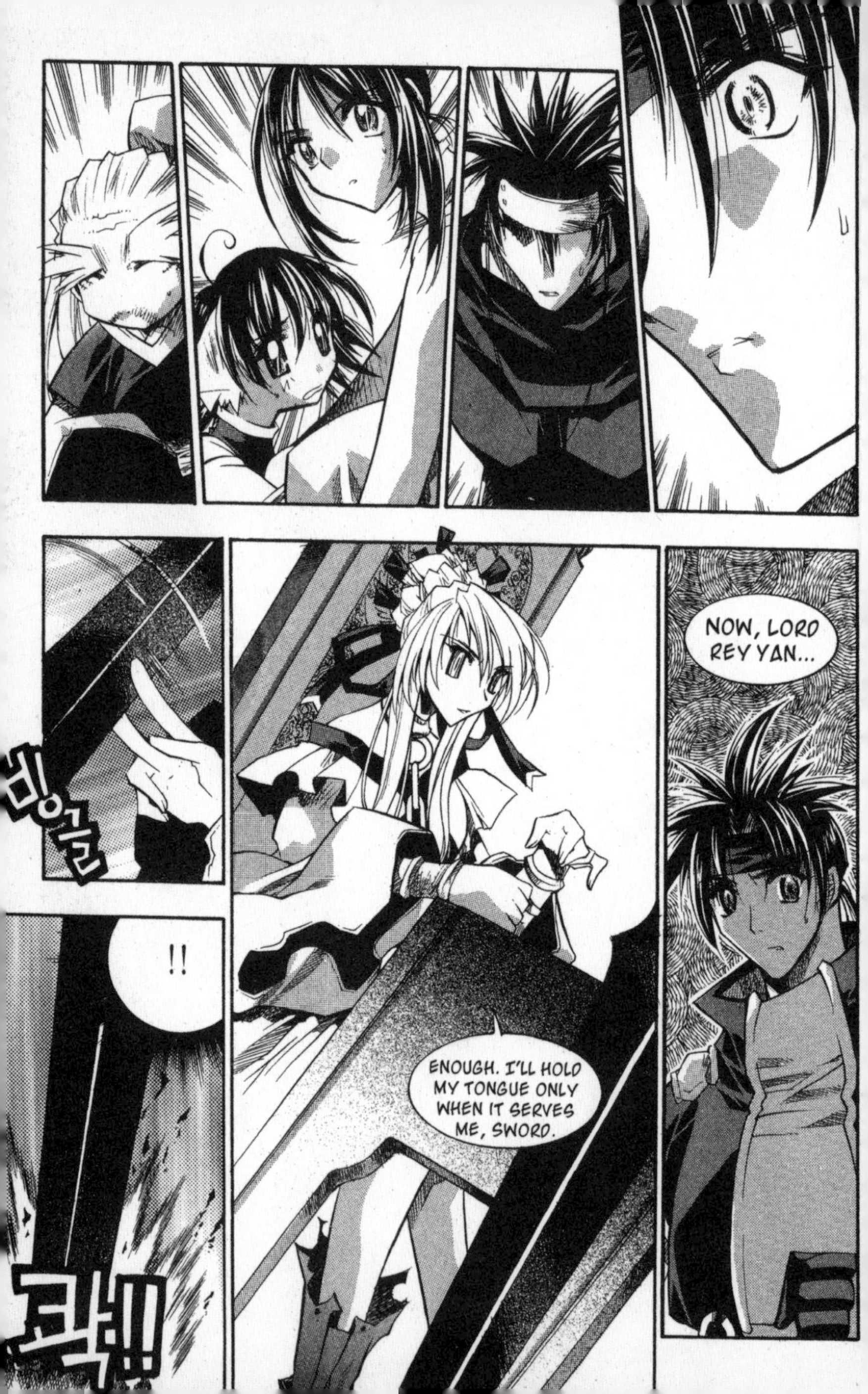
!!
ENOUGH. I'LL HOLD MY TONGUE ONLY WHEN IT SERVES ME, SWORD.
NOW, LORD REY YAN...

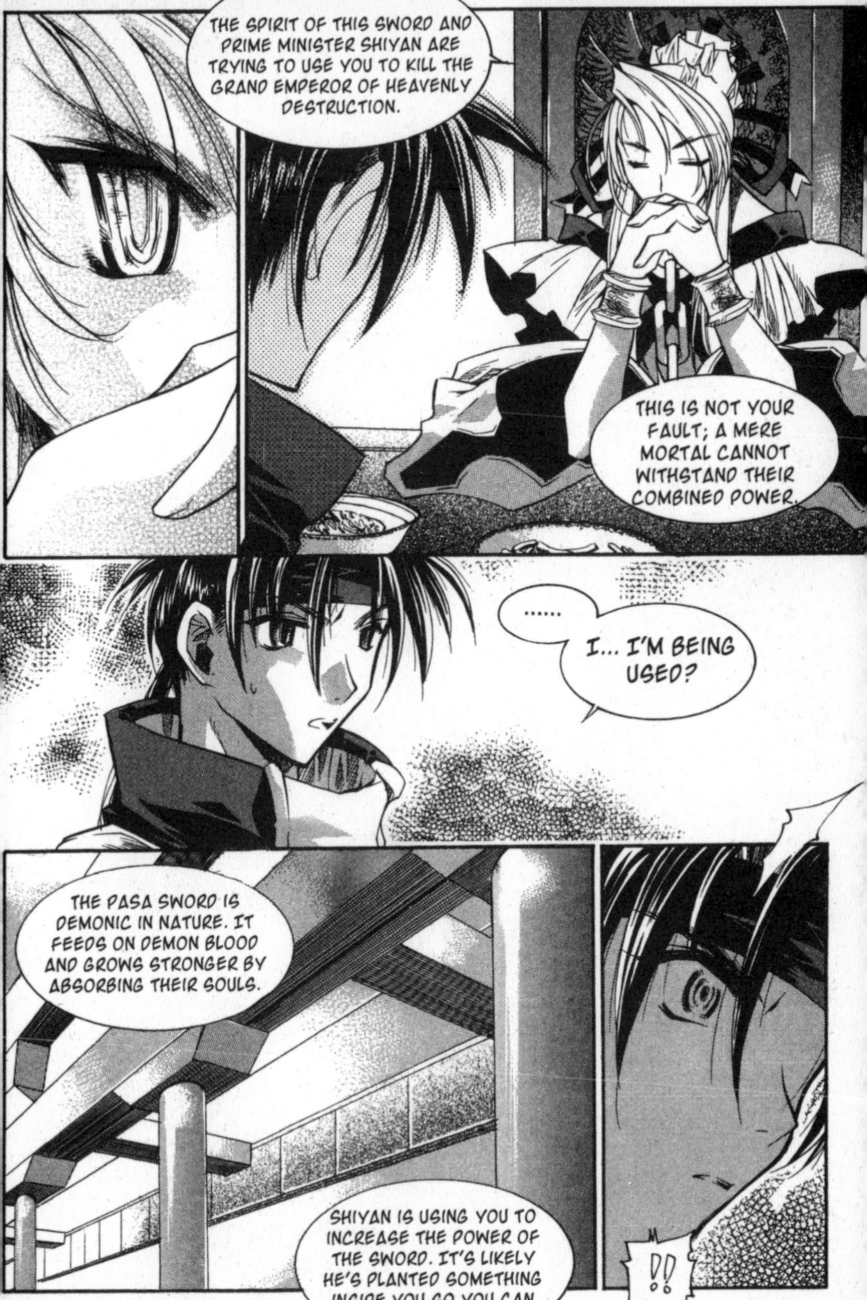
THE SPIRIT OF THIS SWORD AND PRIME MINISTER SHIYAN ARE TRYING TO USE YOU TO KILL THE GRAND EMPEROR OF HEAVENLY DESTRUCTION.
THIS IS NOT YOUR FAULT; A MERE MORTAL CANNOT WITHSTAND THEIR COMBINED POWER.
......
I... I'M BEING USED?
THE PASA SWORD IS DEMONIC IN NATURE. IT FEEDS ON DEMON BLOOD AND GROWS STRONGER BY ABSORBING THEIR SOULS.
SHIYAN IS USING YOU TO INCREASE THE POWER OF THE SWORD. IT'S LIKELY HE'S PLANTED SOMETHING INSIDE YOU SO YOU CAN BE MANIPULATED.
!!

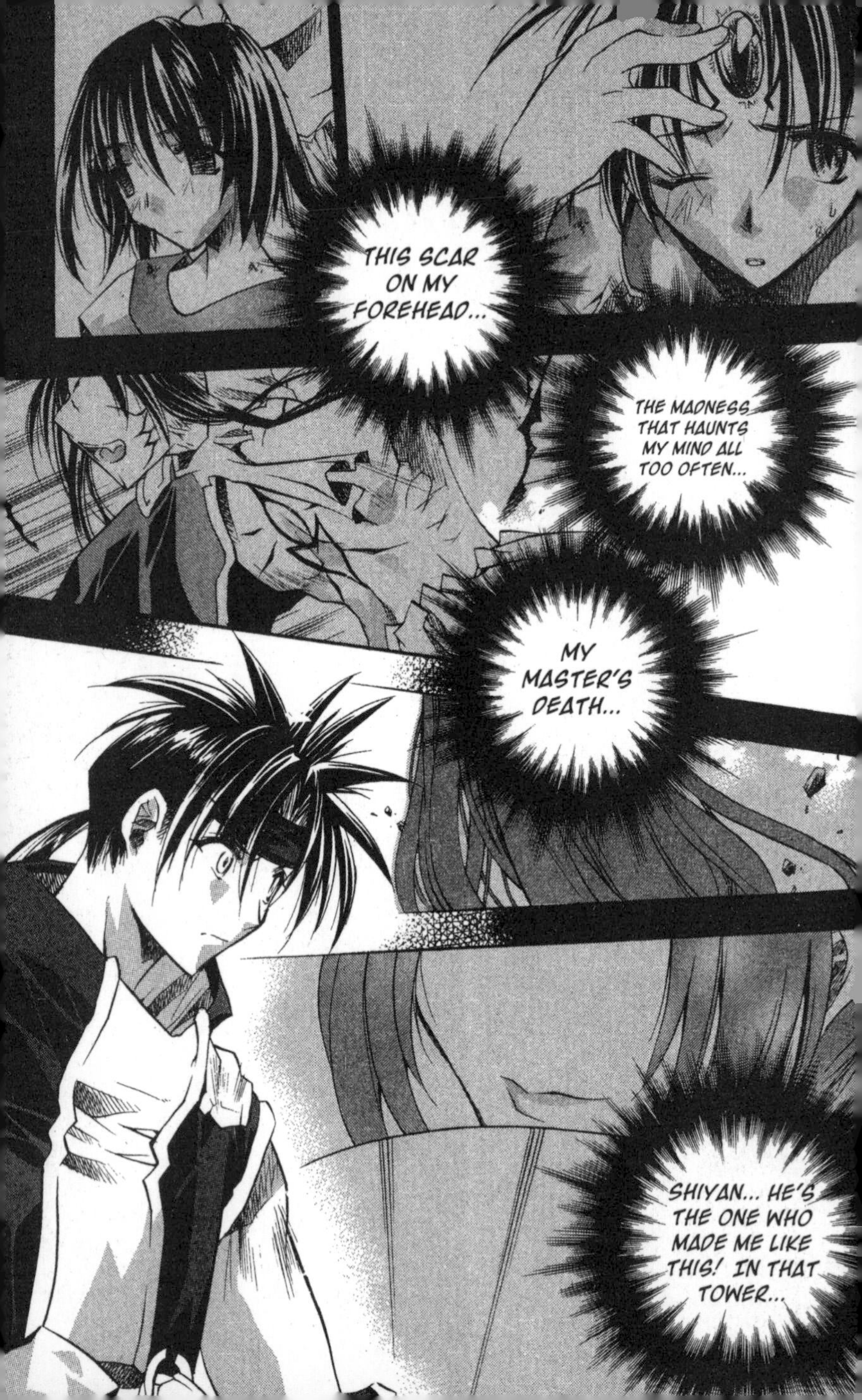
THIS SCAR ON MY FOREHEAD...
THE MADNESS THAT HAUNTS MY MIND ALL TOO OFTEN...
MY MASTER'S DEATH...
SHIYAN... HE'S THE ONE WHO MADE ME LIKE THIS! IN THAT TOWER...

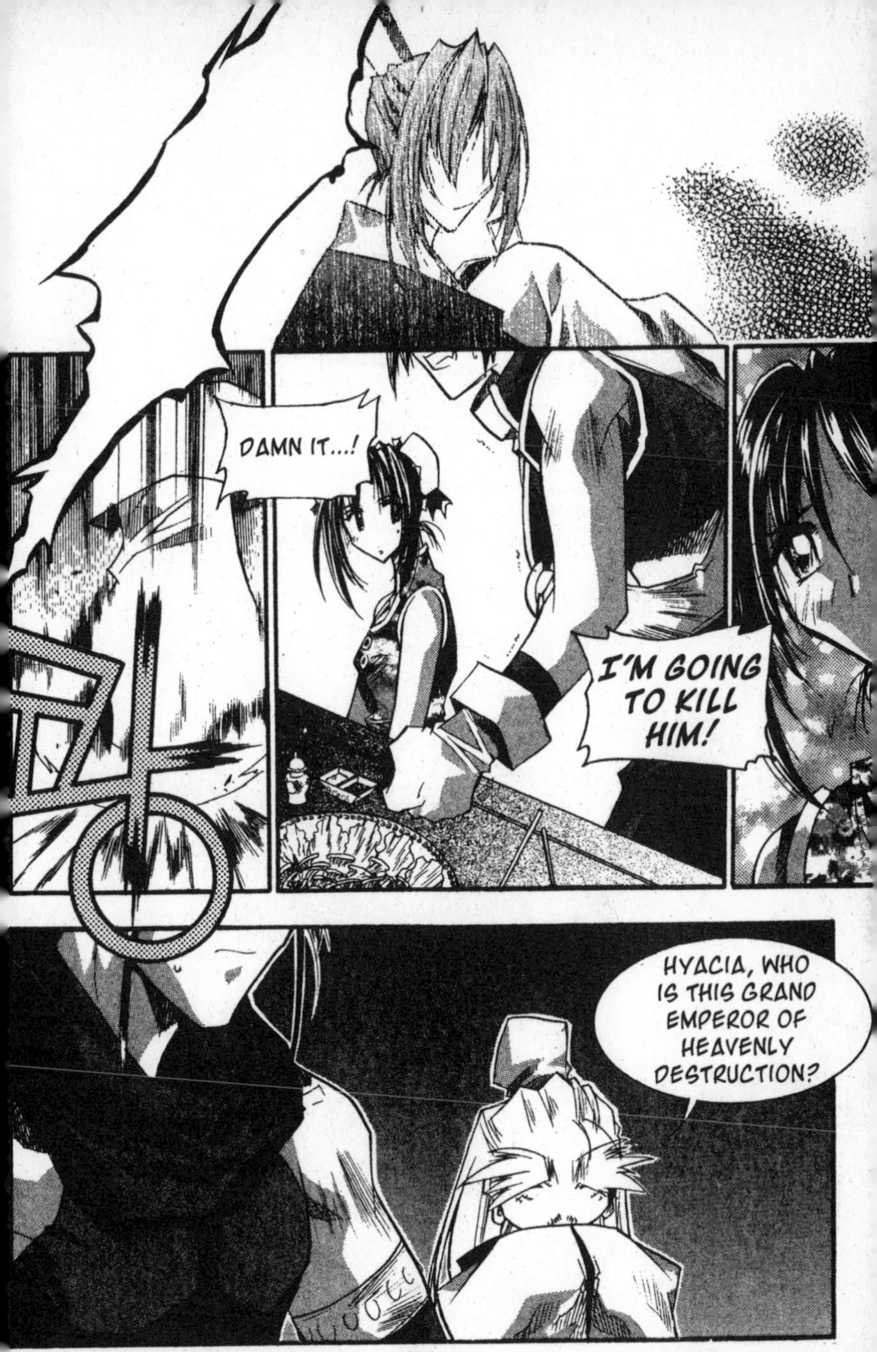
DAMN IT...!
I'M GOING TO KILL HIM!
HYACIA, WHO IS THIS GRAND EMPEROR OF HEAVENLY DESTRUCTION?

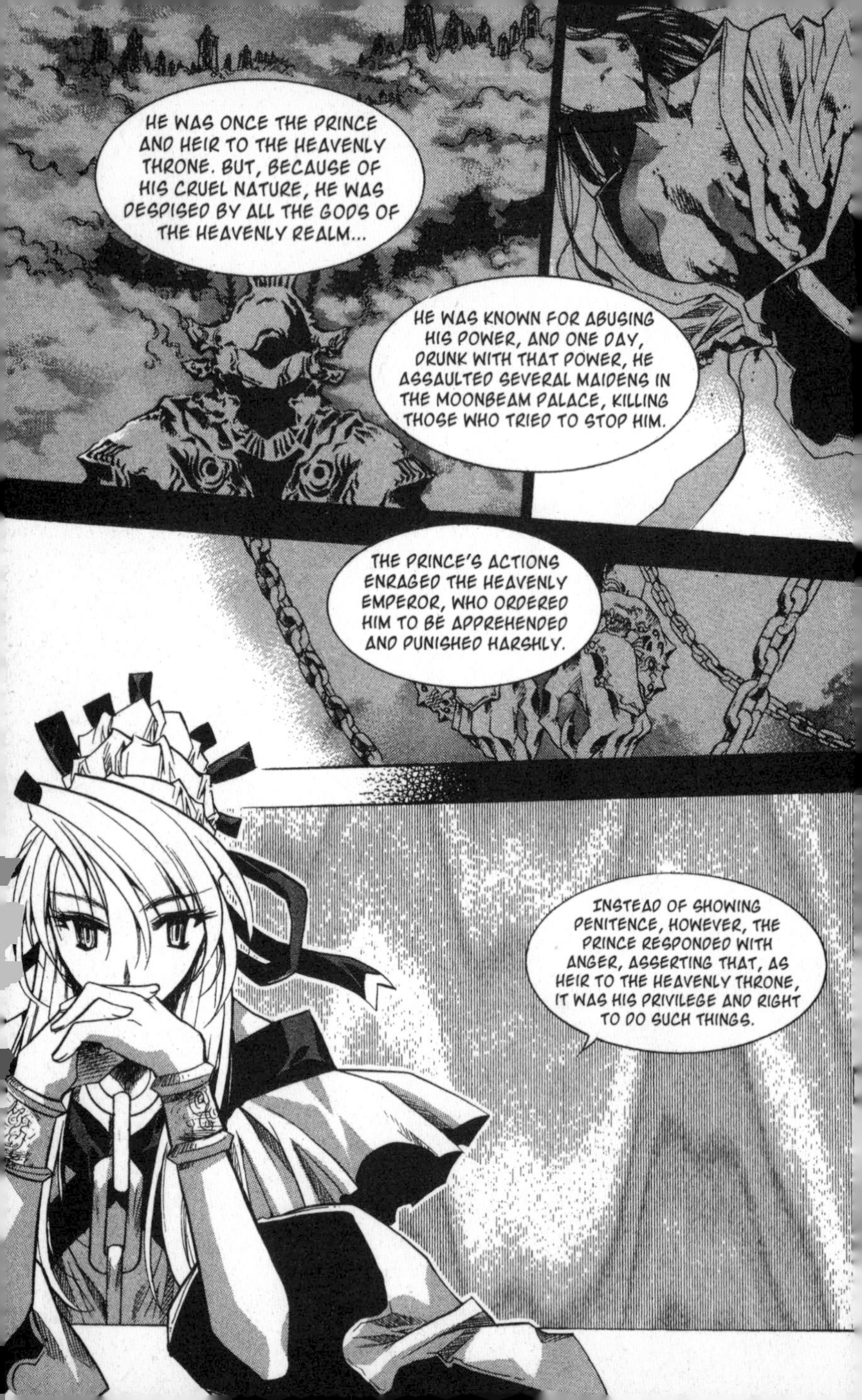
HE WAS ONCE THE PRINCE AND HEIR TO THE HEAVENLY THRONE. BUT, BECAUSE OF HIS CRUEL NATURE, HE WAS DESPISED BY ALL THE GODS OF THE HEAVENLY REALM...
HE WAS KNOWN FOR ABUSING HIS POWER, AND ONE DAY, DRUNK WITH THAT POWER, HE ASSAULTED SEVERAL MAIDENS IN THE MOONBEAM PALACE, KILLING THOSE WHO TRIED TO STOP HIM.
THE PRINCE'S ACTIONS ENRAGED THE HEAVENLY EMPEROR, WHO ORDERED HIM TO BE APPREHENDED AND PUNISHED HARSHLY.
INSTEAD OF SHOWING PENITENCE, HOWEVER, THE PRINCE RESPONDED WITH ANGER, ASSERTING THAT, AS HEIR TO THE HEAVENLY THRONE, IT WAS HIS PRIVILEGE AND RIGHT TO DO SUCH THINGS.

THE HEAVENLY EMPEROR, WORRIED THAT THE HEAVENLY REALM WOULD BE PLUNGED INTO CHAOS IF THE AMORAL PRINCE WERE TO ASCEND THE THRONE...
EXILED THE ERRANT PRINCE FROM THE HEAVENLY REALM.
IN HIS FALL, THE PRINCE DESCENDED UPON THE HUMAN REALM, AND THEN PLUNGED FURTHER INTO THE DEMON REALM, CURSING THE HEAVENLY EMPEROR AND THE GODS ALL THE WHILE...
THE GODS, MEANWHILE, WERE RELIEVED AND DELIGHTED WITH HIS BANISHMENT.
BUT LESS THAN TWO CENTURIES LATER, DREADFUL NEWS REACHED THEIR EARS...

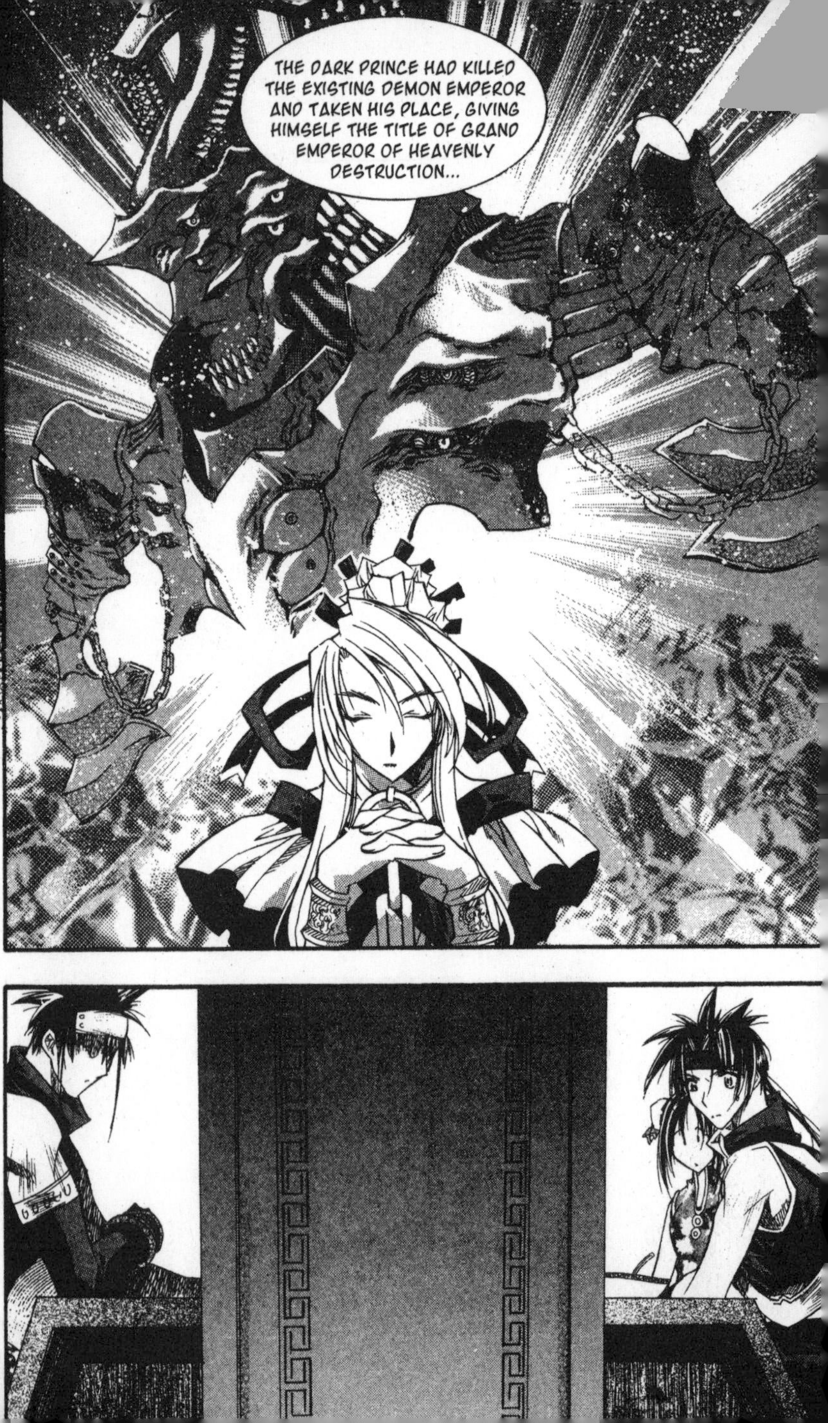
THE DARK PRINCE HAD KILLED THE EXISTING DEMON EMPEROR AND TAKEN HIS PLACE, GIVING HIMSELF THE TITLE OF GRAND EMPEROR OF HEAVENLY DESTRUCTION...

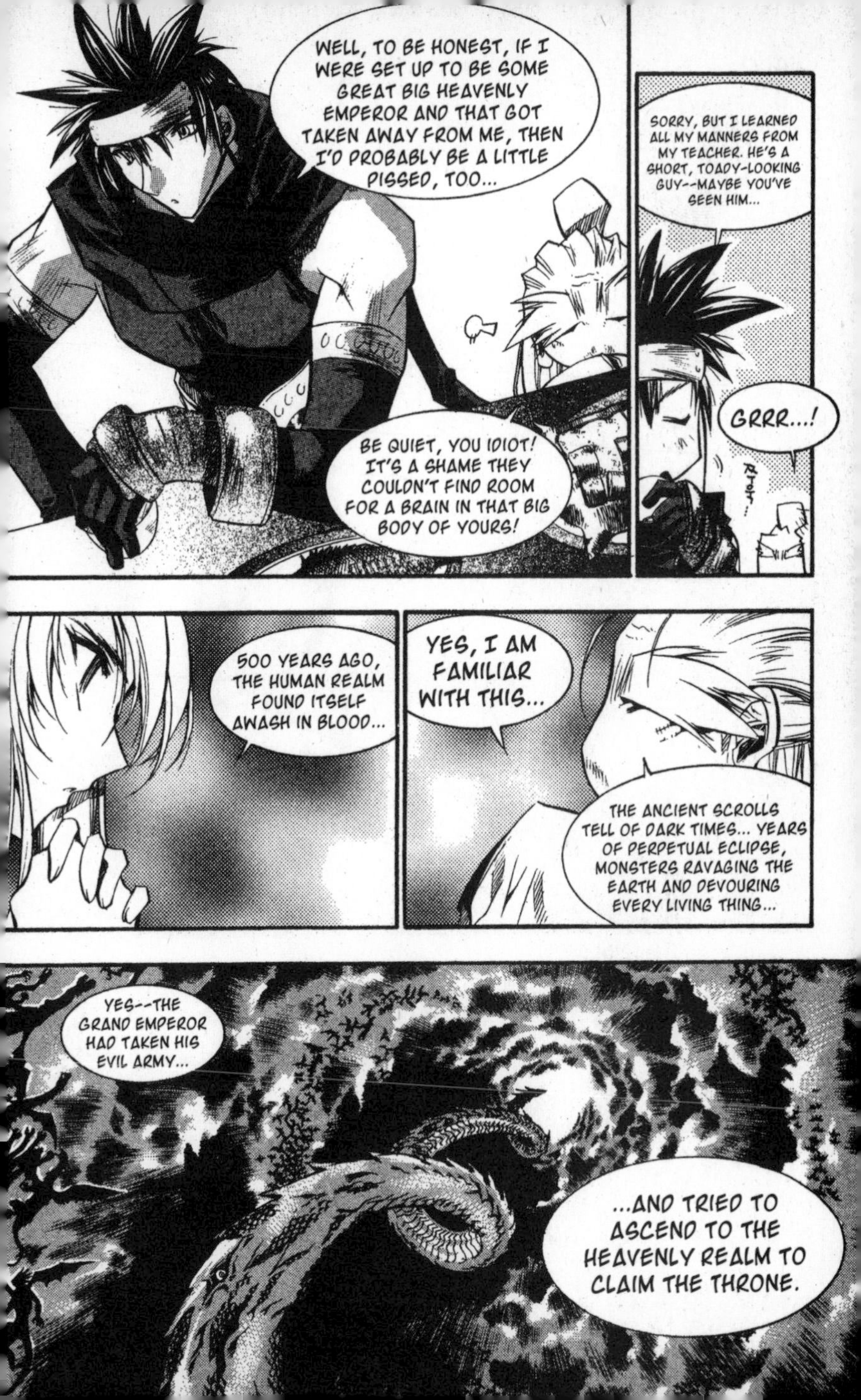
WELL, TO BE HONEST, IF I WERE SET UP TO BE SOME GREAT BIG HEAVENLY EMPEROR AND THAT GOT TAKEN AWAY FROM ME, THEN I'D PROBABLY BE A LITTLE PISSED, TOO...
BE QUIET, YOU IDIOT! IT'S A SHAME THEY COULDN'T FIND ROOM FOR A BRAIN IN THAT BIG BODY OF YOURS!
SORRY, BUT I LEARNED ALL MY MANNERS FROM MY TEACHER. HE'S A SHORT, TOADY-LOOKING GUY--MAYBE YOU'VE SEEN HIM...
GRRR...!
500 YEARS AGO, THE HUMAN REALM FOUND ITSELF AWASH IN BLOOD...
YES, I AM FAMILIAR WITH THIS...
THE ANCIENT SCROLLS TELL OF DARK TIMES... YEARS OF PERPETUAL ECLIPSE, MONSTERS RAVAGING THE EARTH AND DEVOURING EVERY LIVING THING...
YES--THE GRAND EMPEROR HAD TAKEN HIS EVIL ARMY...
...AND TRIED TO ASCEND TO THE HEAVENLY REALM TO CLAIM THE THRONE.

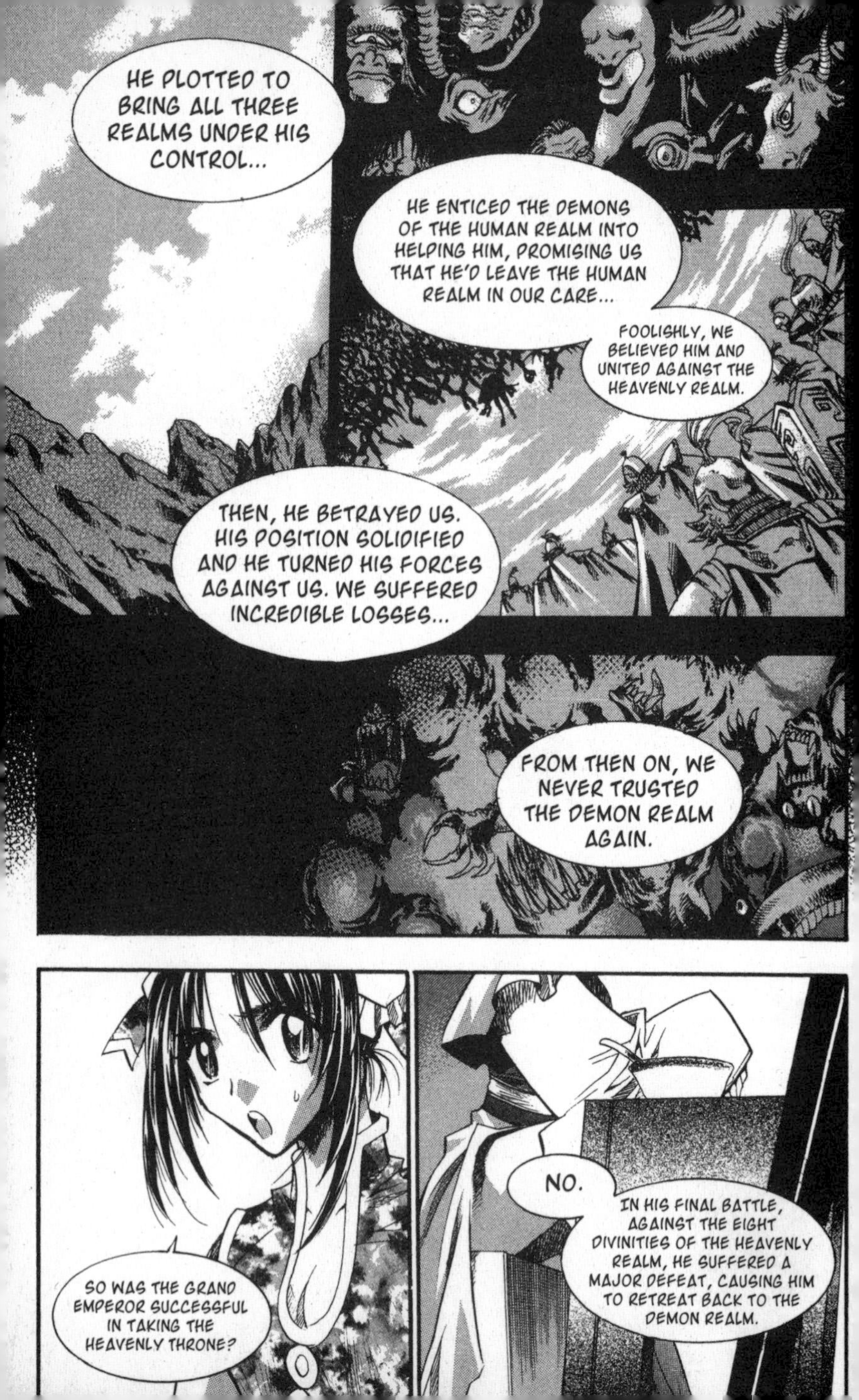

HE PLOTTED TO BRING ALL THREE REALMS UNDER HIS CONTROL...
HE ENTICED THE DEMONS OF THE HUMAN REALM INTO HELPING HIM, PROMISING US THAT HE'D LEAVE THE HUMAN REALM IN OUR CARE...
FOOLISHLY, WE BELIEVED HIM AND UNITED AGAINST THE HEAVENLY REALM.
THEN, HE BETRAYED US. HIS POSITION SOLIDIFIED AND HE TURNED HIS FORCES AGAINST US. WE SUFFERED INCREDIBLE LOSSES...
FROM THEN ON, WE NEVER TRUSTED THE DEMON REALM AGAIN.
SO WAS THE GRAND EMPEROR SUCCESSFUL IN TAKING THE HEAVENLY THRONE?
NO.
IN HIS FINAL BATTLE, AGAINST THE EIGHT DIVINITIES OF THE HEAVENLY REALM, HE SUFFERED A MAJOR DEFEAT, CAUSING HIM TO RETREAT BACK TO THE DEMON REALM.

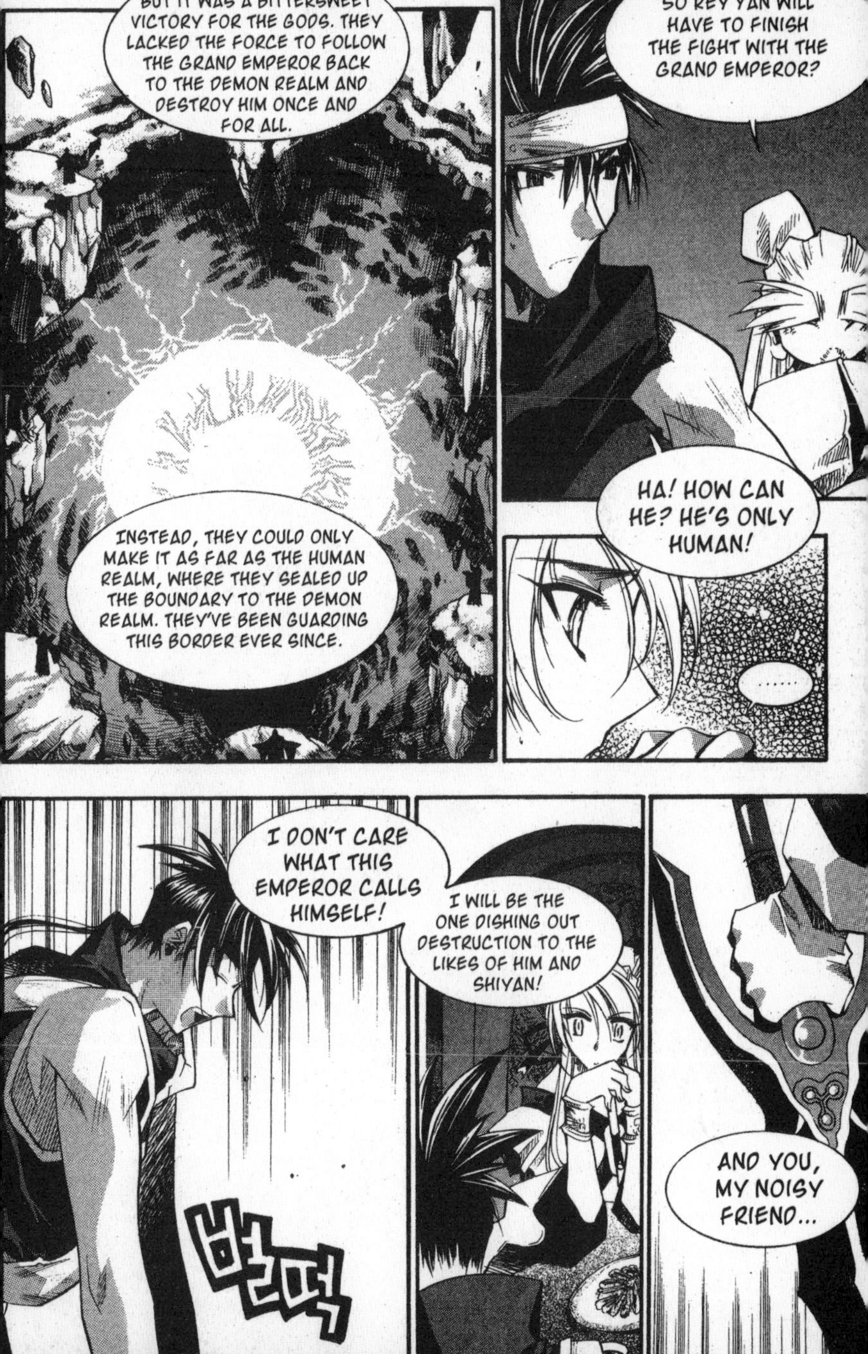
BUT IT WAS A BITTERSWEET VICTORY FOR THE GODS. THEY LACKED THE FORCE TO FOLLOW THE GRAND EMPEROR BACK TO THE DEMON REALM AND DESTROY HIM ONCE AND FOR ALL.
INSTEAD, THEY COULD ONLY MAKE IT AS FAR AS THE HUMAN REALM, WHERE THEY SEALED UP THE BOUNDARY TO THE DEMON REALM. THEY'VE BEEN GUARDING THIS BORDER EVER SINCE.
SO REY YAN WILL HAVE TO FINISH THE FIGHT WITH THE GRAND EMPEROR?
HA! HOW CAN HE? HE'S ONLY HUMAN!
......
I DON'T CARE WHAT THIS EMPEROR CALLS HIMSELF!
벌떡
I WILL BE THE ONE DISHING OUT DESTRUCTION TO THE LIKES OF HIM AND SHIYAN!
AND YOU, MY NOISY FRIEND...

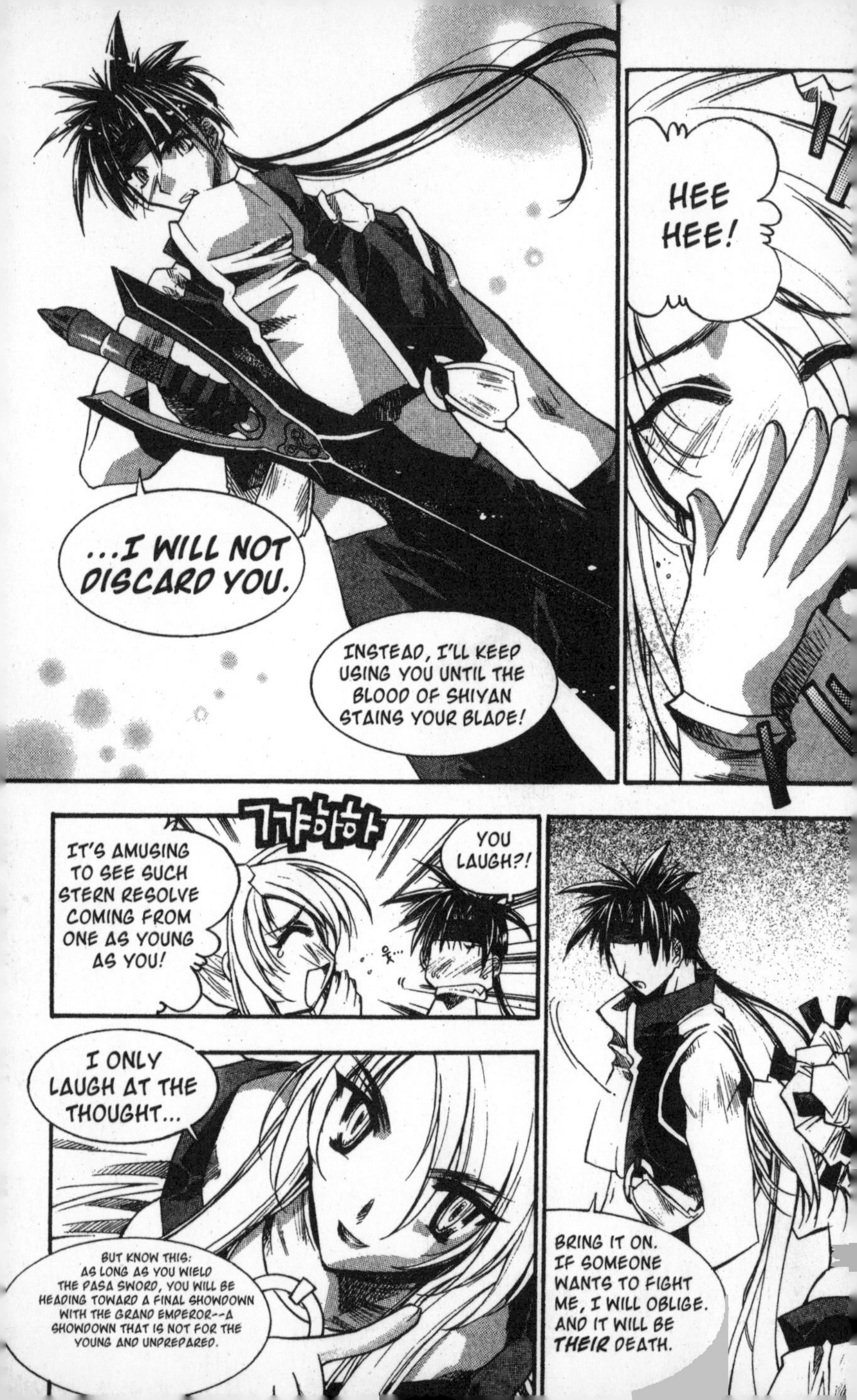
...I WILL NOT DISCARD YOU.
INSTEAD, I'LL KEEP USING YOU UNTIL THE BLOOD OF SHIYAN STAINS YOUR BLADE!
HEE HEE!
꺄하하
IT'S AMUSING TO SEE SUCH STERN RESOLVE COMING FROM ONE AS YOUNG AS YOU!
YOU LAUGH?!
I ONLY LAUGH AT THE THOUGHT...
BUT KNOW THIS: AS LONG AS YOU WIELD THE PASA SWORD, YOU WILL BE HEADING TOWARD A FINAL SHOWDOWN WITH THE GRAND EMPEROR--A SHOWDOWN THAT IS NOT FOR THE YOUNG AND UNPREPARED.
BRING IT ON. IF SOMEONE WANTS TO FIGHT ME, I WILL OBLIGE. AND IT WILL BE THEIR DEATH.

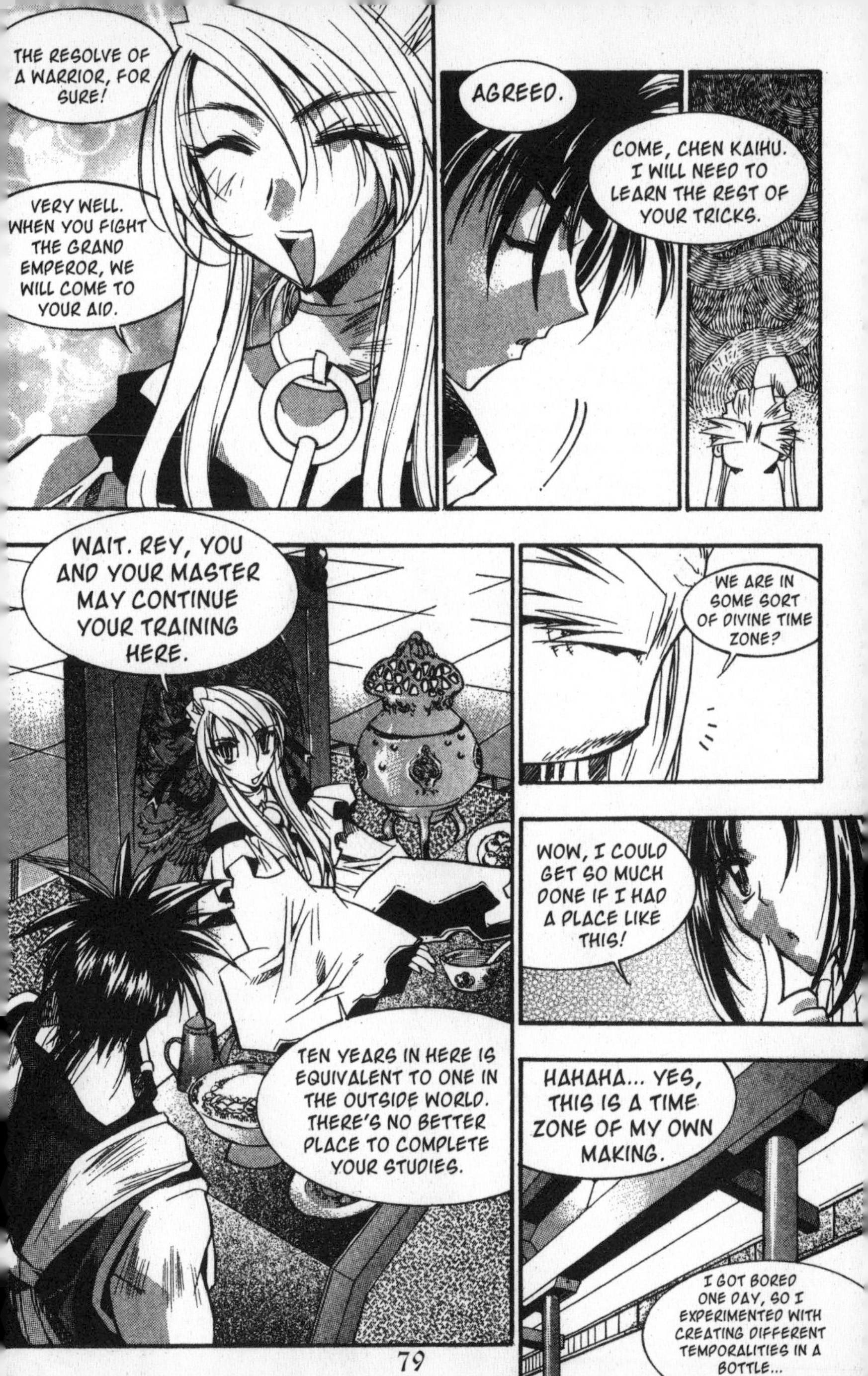
THE RESOLVE OF A WARRIOR, FOR SURE!
VERY WELL. WHEN YOU FIGHT THE GRAND EMPEROR, WE WILL COME TO YOUR AID.
AGREED.
COME, CHEN KAIHU. I WILL NEED TO LEARN THE REST OF YOUR TRICKS.
WAIT. REY, YOU AND YOUR MASTER MAY CONTINUE YOUR TRAINING HERE.
TEN YEARS IN HERE IS EQUIVALENT TO ONE IN THE OUTSIDE WORLD. THERE'S NO BETTER PLACE TO COMPLETE YOUR STUDIES.
WE ARE IN SOME SORT OF DIVINE TIME ZONE?
WOW, I COULD GET SO MUCH DONE IF I HAD A PLACE LIKE THIS!
HAHAHA... YES, THIS IS A TIME ZONE OF MY OWN MAKING.
I GOT BORED ONE DAY, SO I EXPERIMENTED WITH CREATING DIFFERENT TEMPORALITIES IN A BOTTLE...

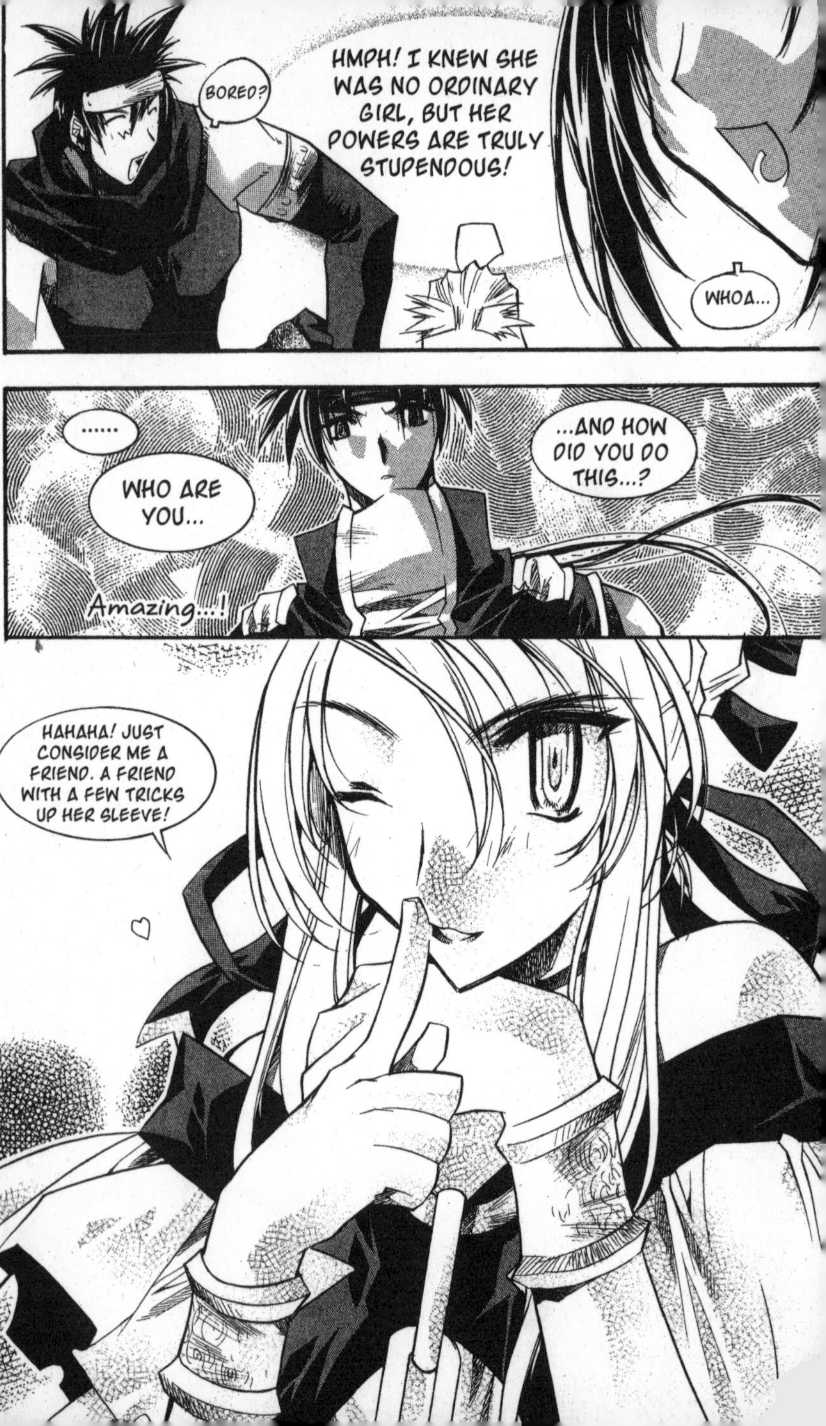
BORED?
HMPH! I KNEW SHE WAS NO ORDINARY GIRL, BUT HER POWERS ARE TRULY STUPENDOUS!
WHOA...
......
WHO ARE YOU...
...AND HOW DID YOU DO THIS...?
Amazing...!
HAHAHA! JUST CONSIDER ME A FRIEND. A FRIEND WITH A FEW TRICKS UP HER SLEEVE!

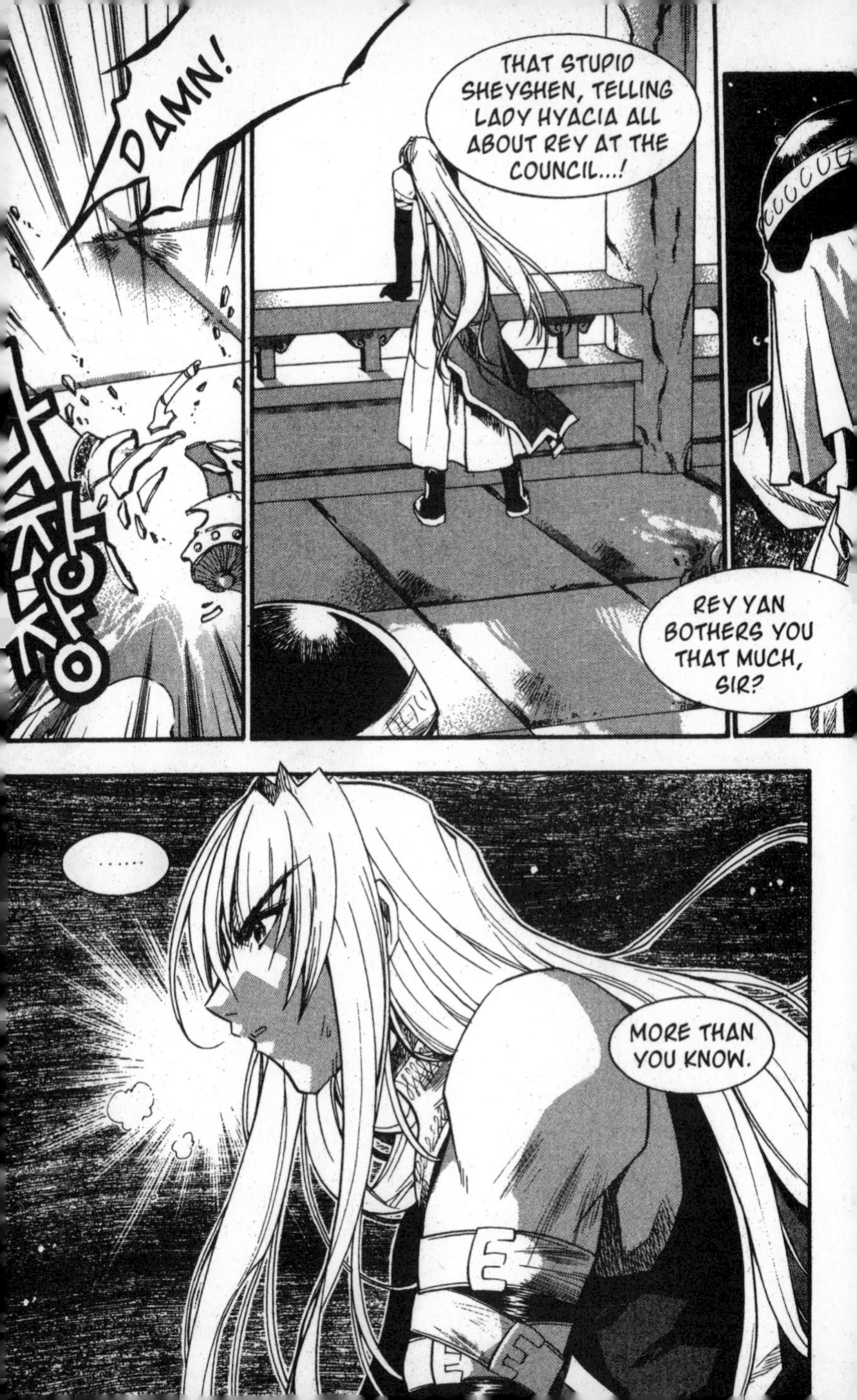
DAMN!
THAT STUPID SHEYSHEN, TELLING LADY HYACIA ALL ABOUT REY AT THE COUNCIL...!
REY YAN BOTHERS YOU THAT MUCH, SIR?
......
MORE THAN YOU KNOW.

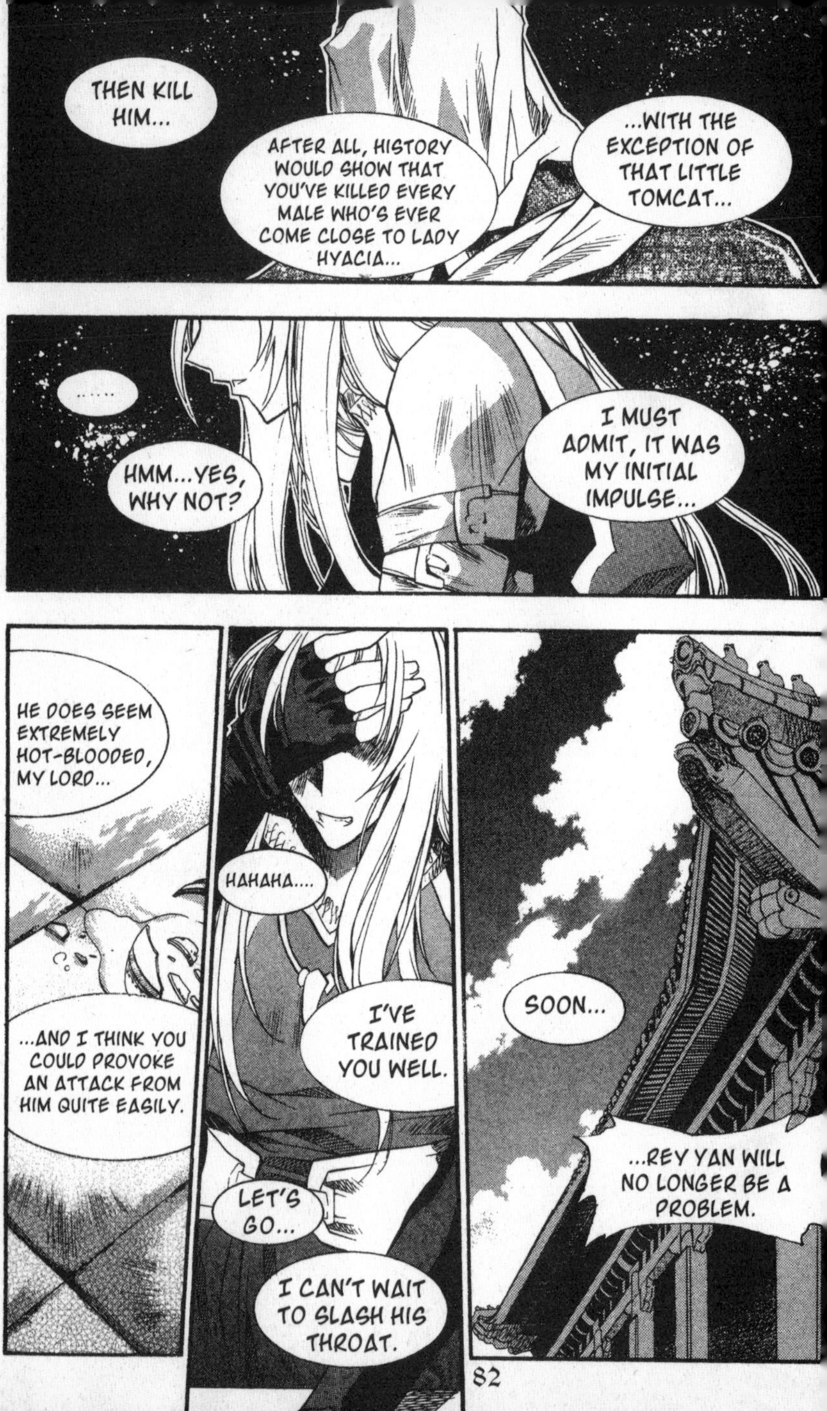
THEN KILL HIM...
AFTER ALL, HISTORY WOULD SHOW THAT YOU'VE KILLED EVERY MALE WHO'S EVER COME CLOSE TO LADY HYACIA...
...WITH THE EXCEPTION OF THAT LITTLE TOMCAT...
......
HMM...YES, WHY NOT?
I MUST ADMIT, IT WAS MY INITIAL IMPULSE...
HE DOES SEEM EXTREMELY HOT-BLOODED, MY LORD...
...AND I THINK YOU COULD PROVOKE AN ATTACK FROM HIM QUITE EASILY.
HAHAHA....
I'VE TRAINED YOU WELL.
LET'S GO...
I CAN'T WAIT TO SLASH HIS THROAT.
SOON...
...REY YAN WILL NO LONGER BE A PROBLEM.

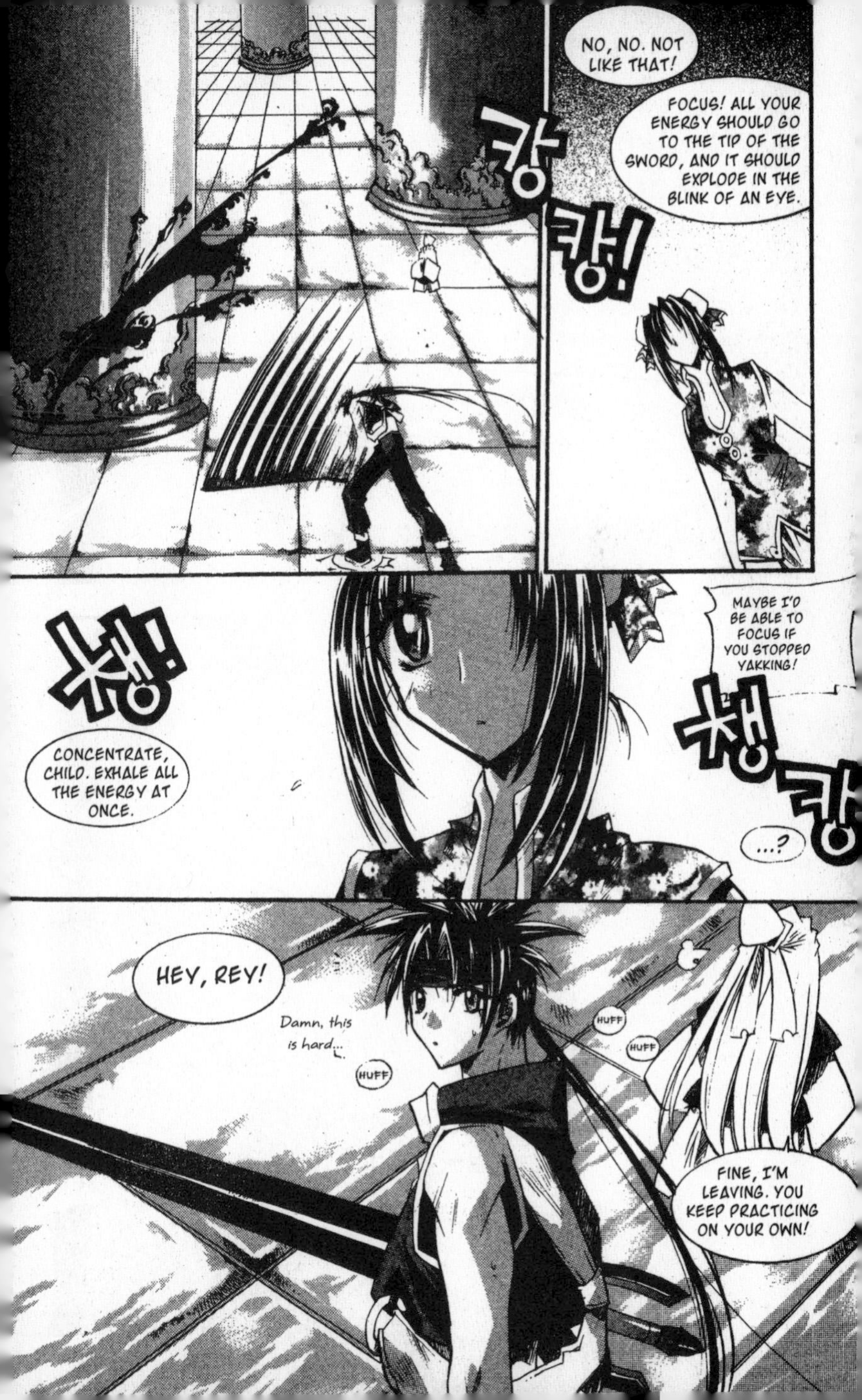
NO, NO. NOT LIKE THAT!
FOCUS! ALL YOUR ENERGY SHOULD GO TO THE TIP OF THE SWORD, AND IT SHOULD EXPLODE IN THE BLINK OF AN EYE.
캉
캉!
챙!
CONCENTRATE, CHILD. EXHALE ALL THE ENERGY AT ONCE.
MAYBE I'D BE ABLE TO FOCUS IF YOU STOPPED YAKKING!
챙
캉
...?
HEY, REY!
Damn, this is hard...
HUFF
HUFF
HUFF
FINE, I'M LEAVING. YOU KEEP PRACTICING ON YOUR OWN!

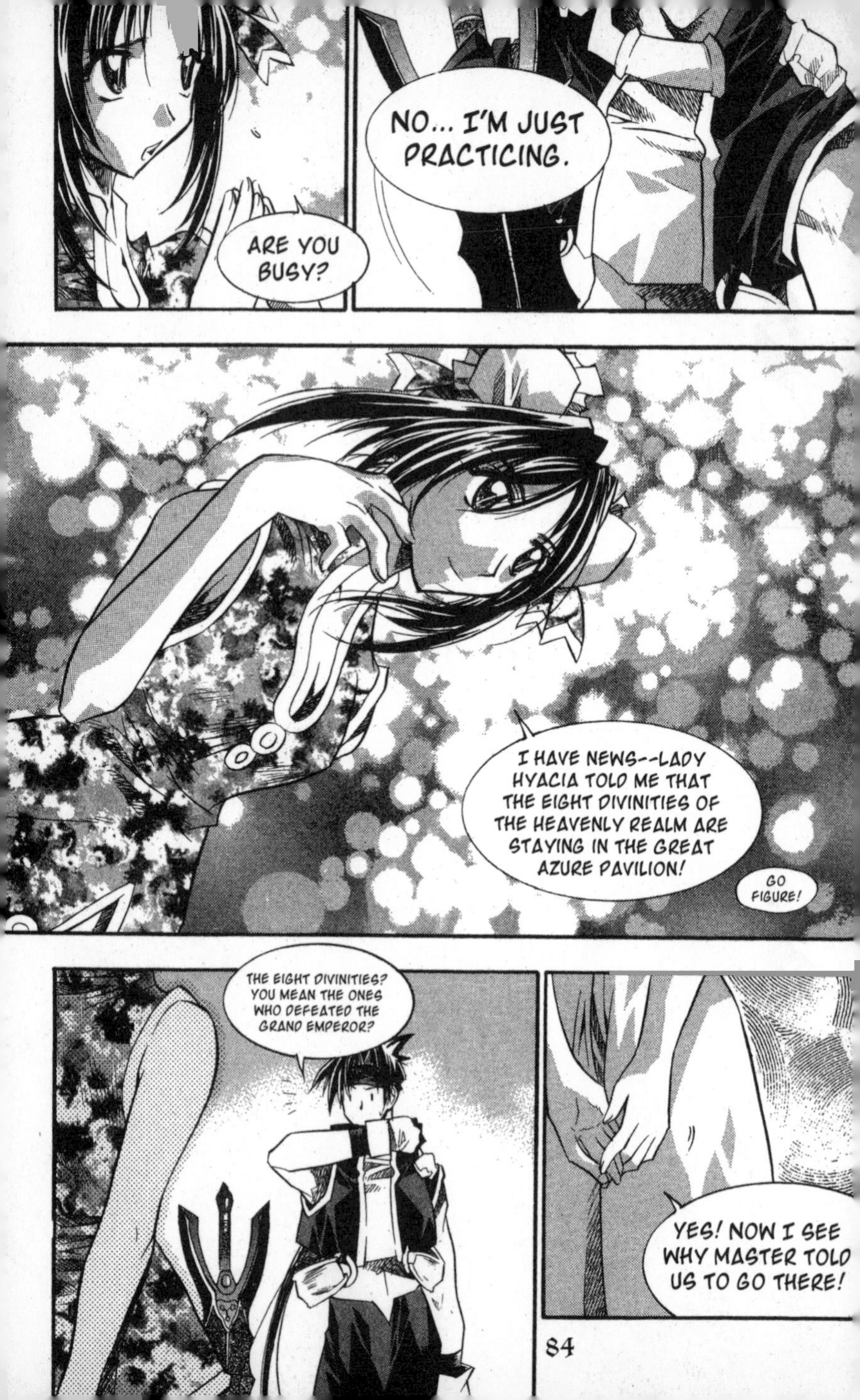
ARE YOU BUSY?
NO... I'M JUST PRACTICING.
I HAVE NEWS--LADY HYACIA TOLD ME THAT THE EIGHT DIVINITIES OF THE HEAVENLY REALM ARE STAYING IN THE GREAT AZURE PAVILION!
GO FIGURE!
THE EIGHT DIVINITIES? YOU MEAN THE ONES WHO DEFEATED THE GRAND EMPEROR?
YES! NOW I SEE WHY MASTER TOLD US TO GO THERE!

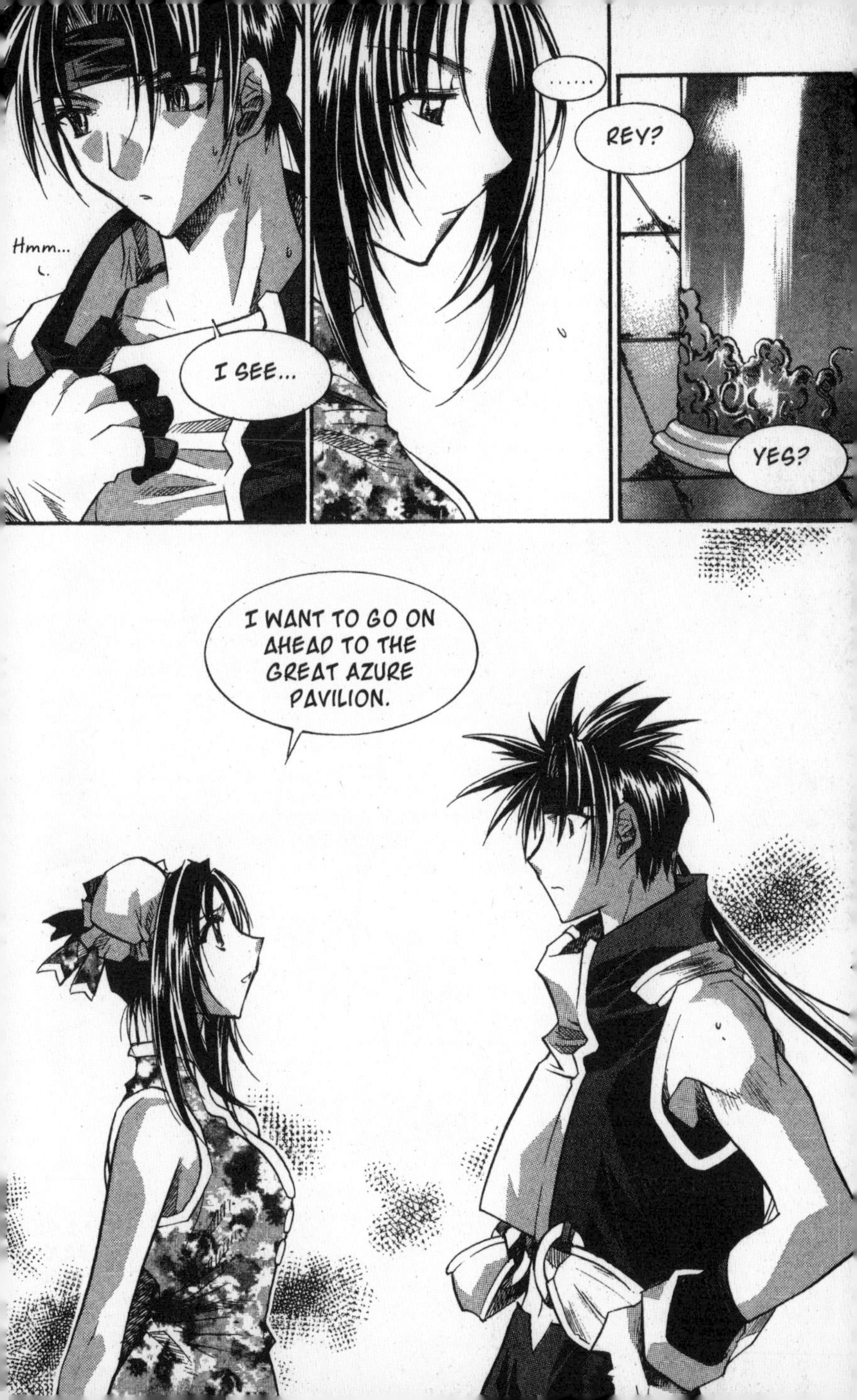
Hmm...
I SEE...
......
REY?
YES?
I WANT TO GO ON AHEAD TO THE GREAT AZURE PAVILION.

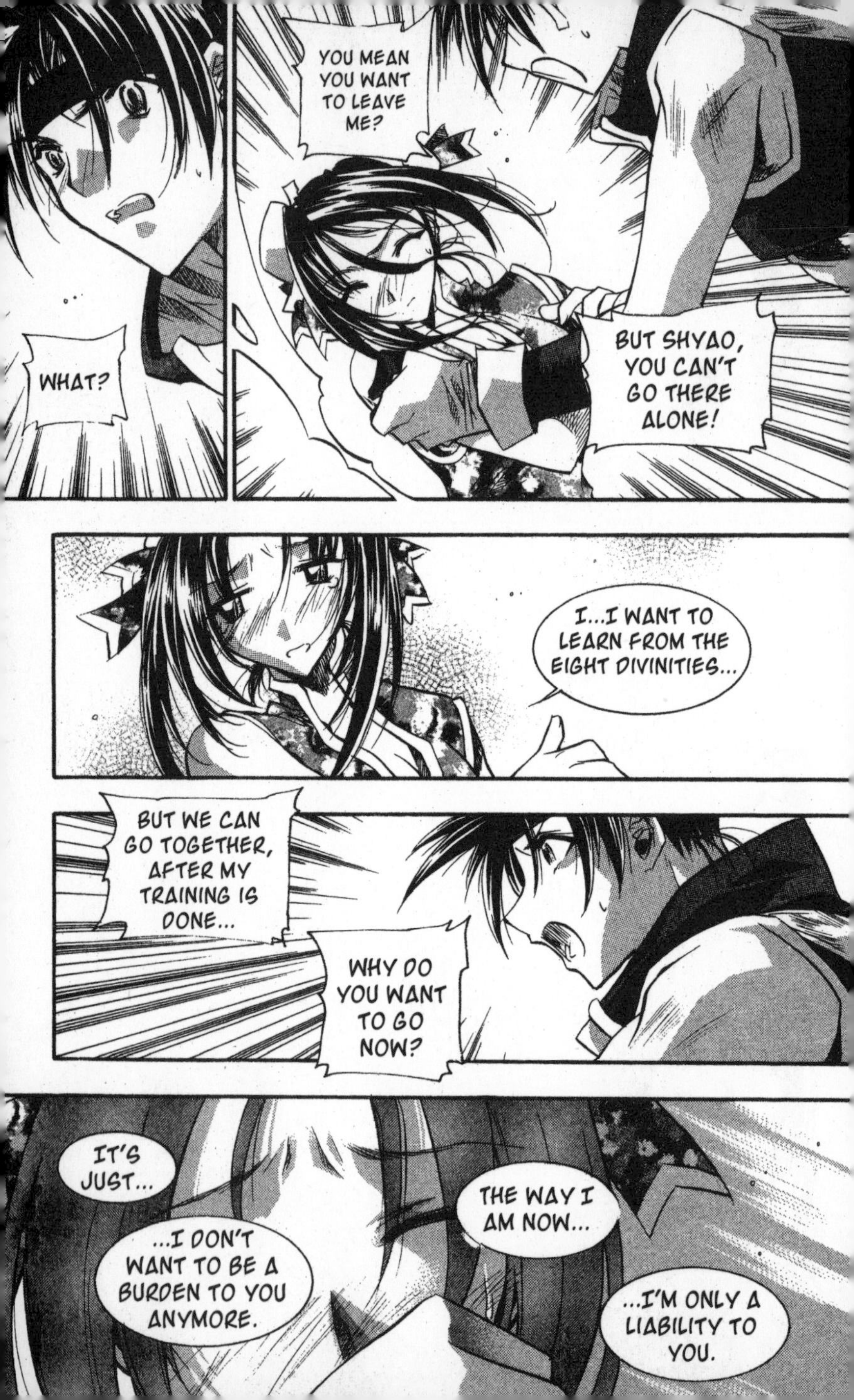
WHAT?
YOU MEAN YOU WANT TO LEAVE ME?
BUT SHYAO, YOU CAN'T GO THERE ALONE!
I...I WANT TO LEARN FROM THE EIGHT DIVINITIES...
BUT WE CAN GO TOGETHER, AFTER MY TRAINING IS DONE...
WHY DO YOU WANT TO GO NOW?
IT'S JUST...
...I DON'T WANT TO BE A BURDEN TO YOU ANYMORE.
THE WAY I AM NOW...
...I'M ONLY A LIABILITY TO YOU.

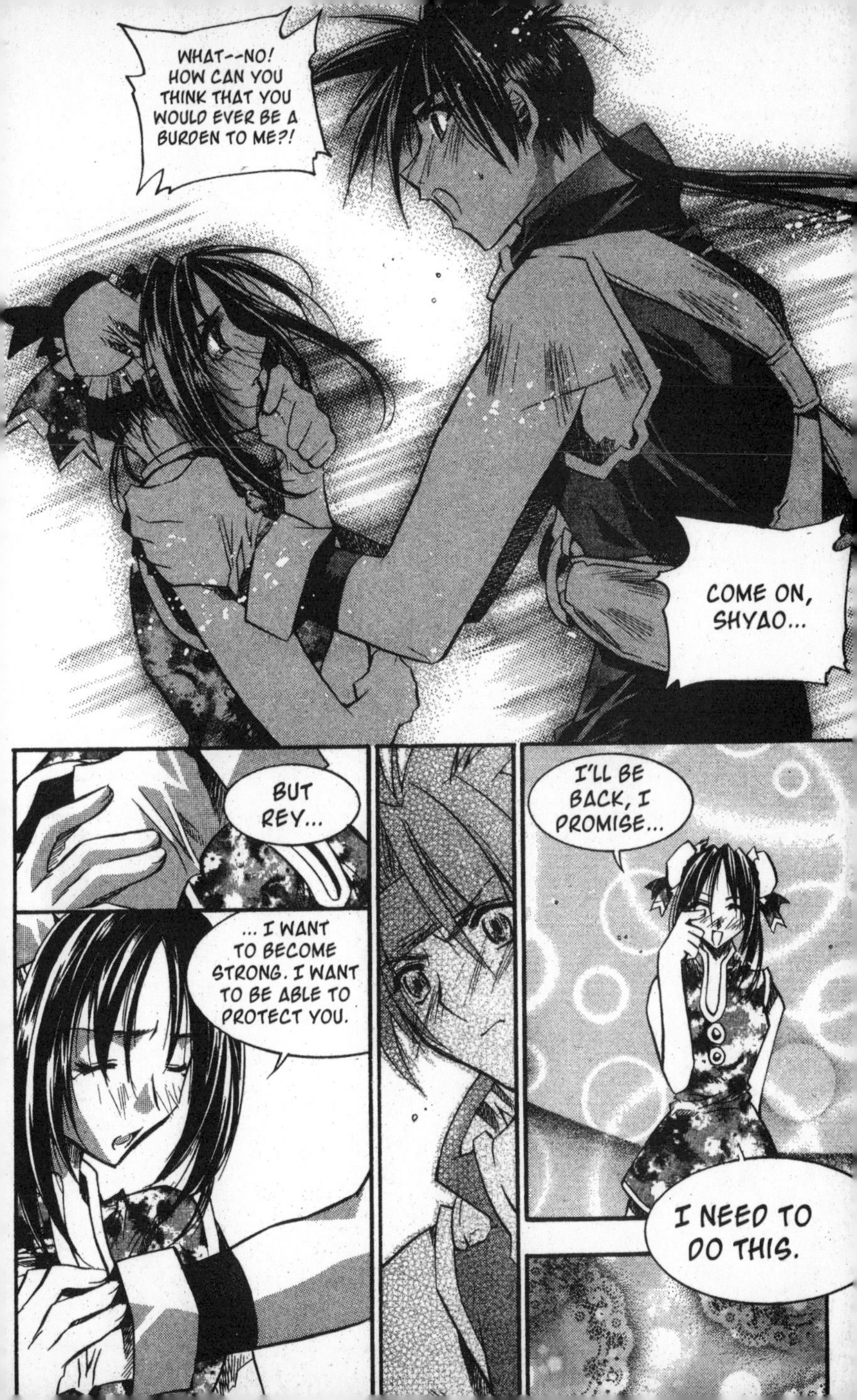
WHAT--NO! HOW CAN YOU THINK THAT YOU WOULD EVER BE A BURDEN TO ME?!
COME ON, SHYAO...
BUT REY...
... I WANT TO BECOME STRONG. I WANT TO BE ABLE TO PROTECT YOU.
I'LL BE BACK, I PROMISE...
I NEED TO DO THIS.

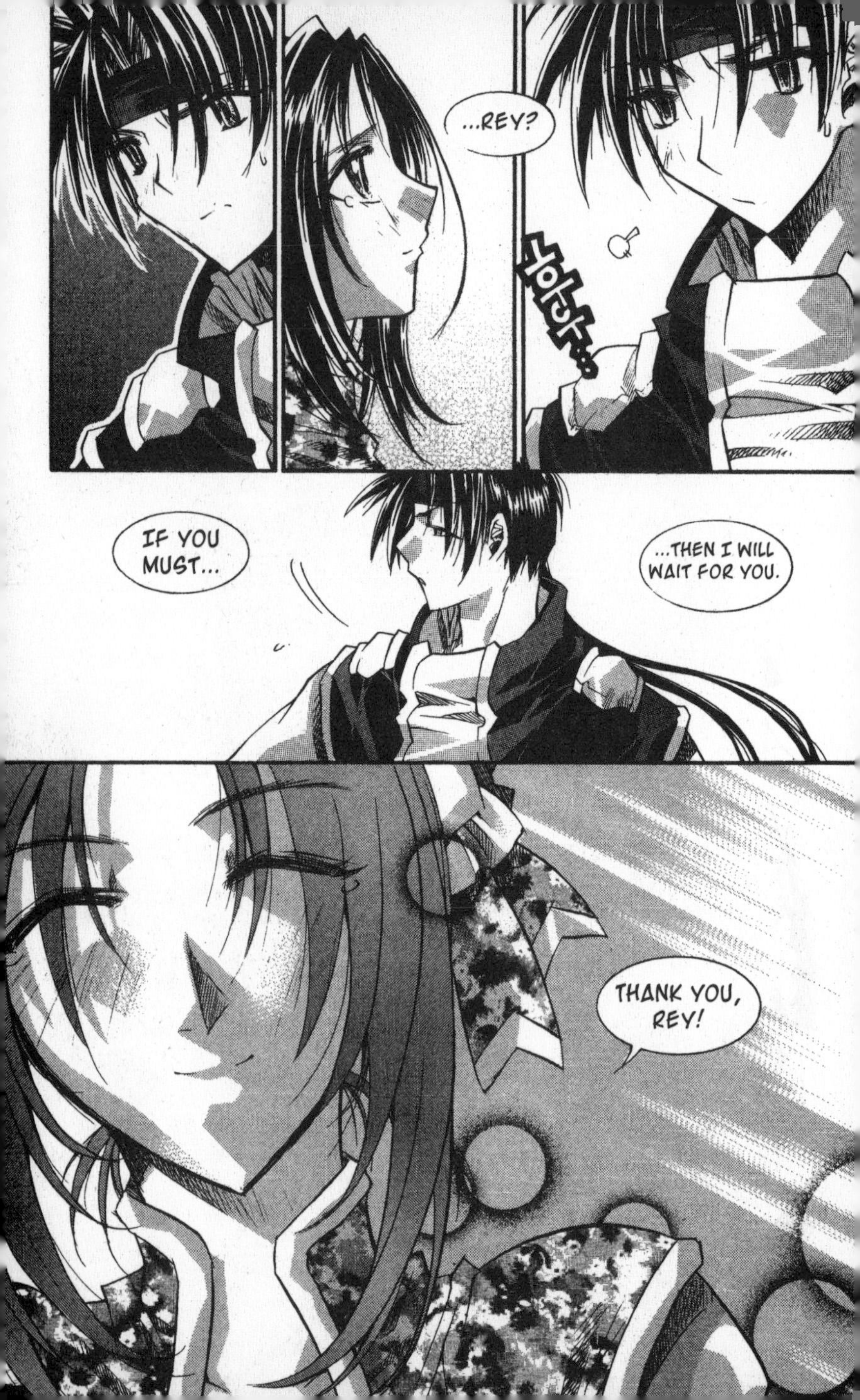
...REY?
YOICK...
IF YOU MUST...
...THEN I WILL WAIT FOR YOU.
THANK YOU, REY!

CHAPTER 22: The Test

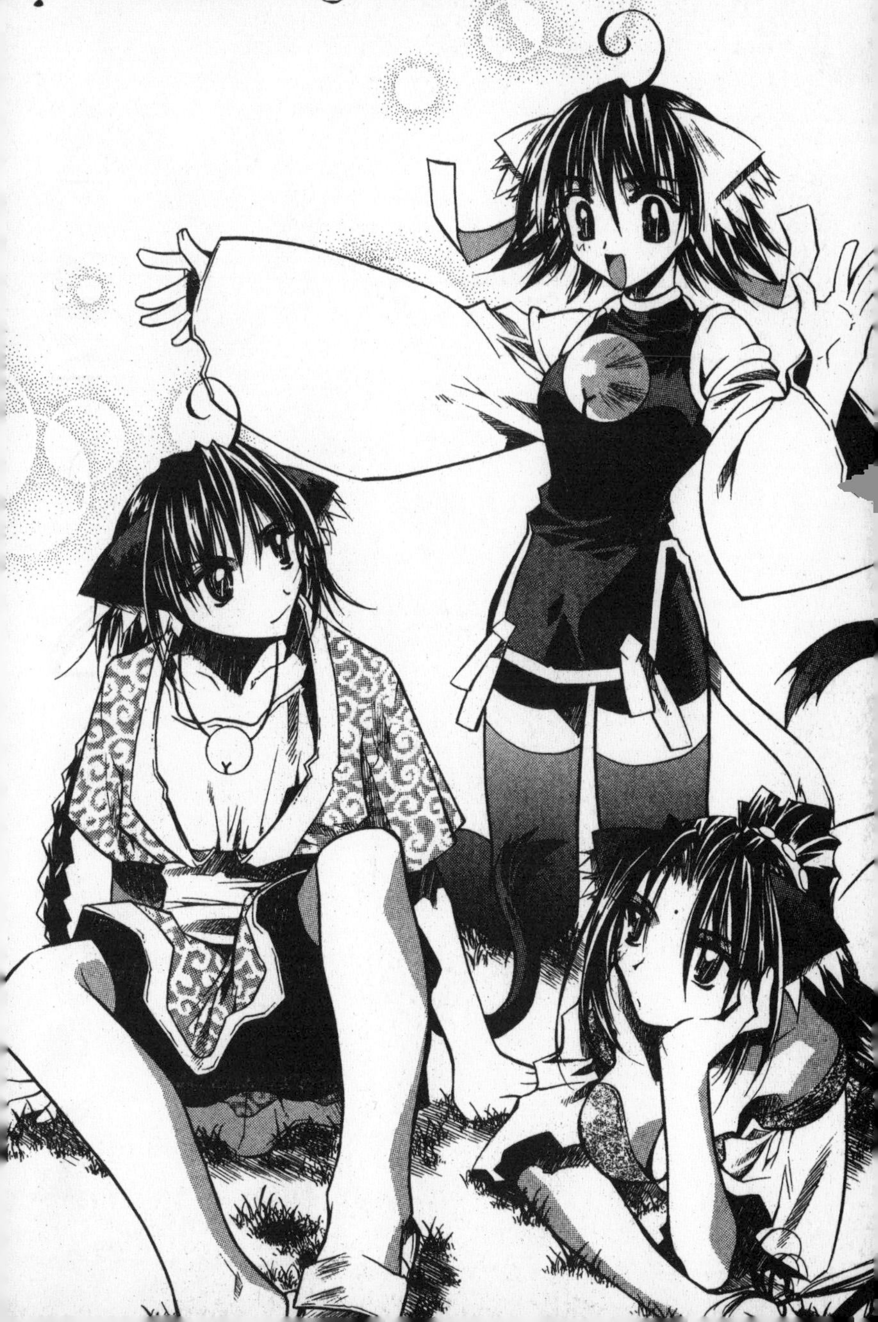

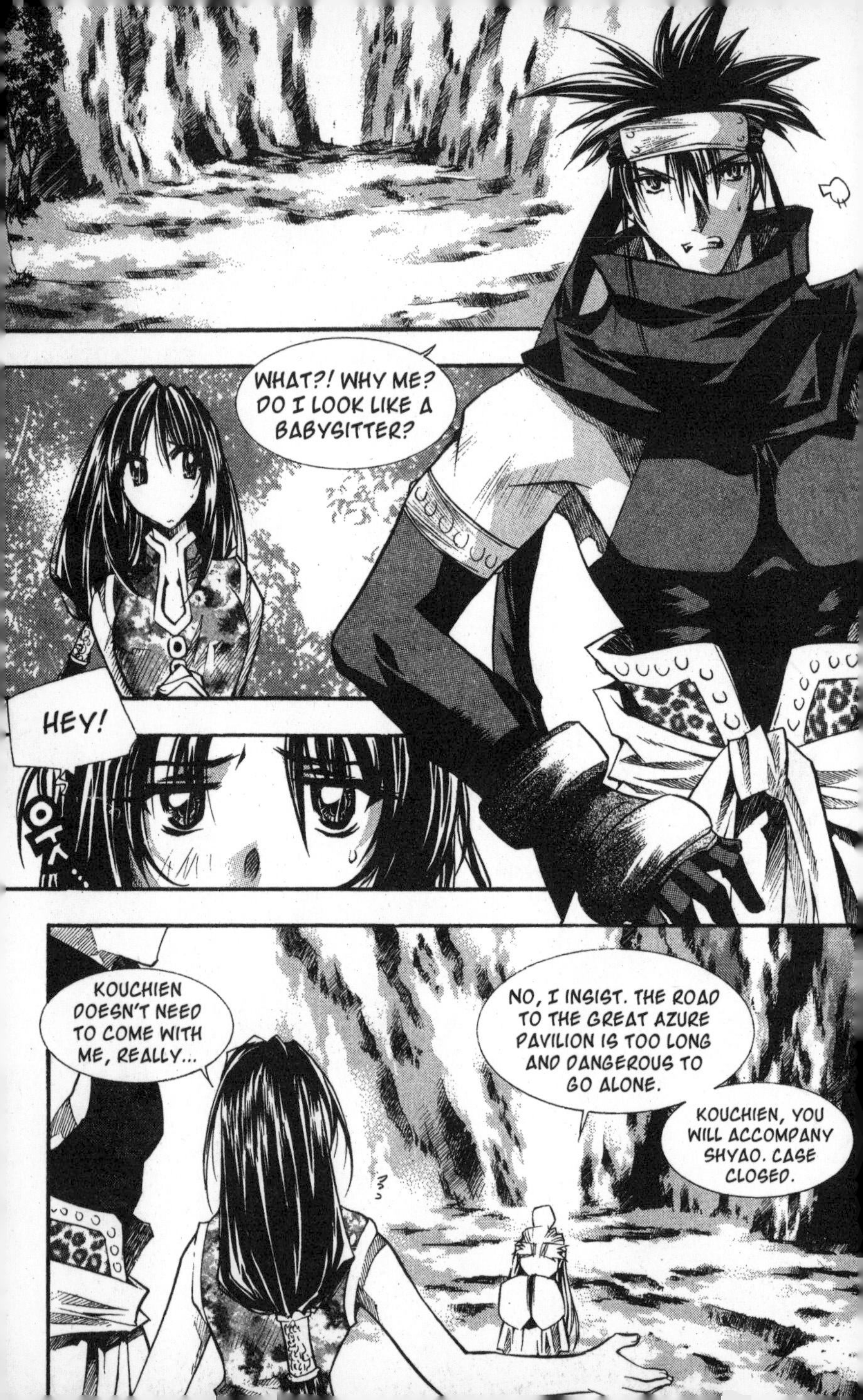
WHAT?! WHY ME? DO I LOOK LIKE A BABYSITTER?
HEY!
OK...
KOUCHIEN DOESN'T NEED TO COME WITH ME, REALLY...
NO, I INSIST. THE ROAD TO THE GREAT AZURE PAVILION IS TOO LONG AND DANGEROUS TO GO ALONE.
KOUCHIEN, YOU WILL ACCOMPANY SHYAO. CASE CLOSED.

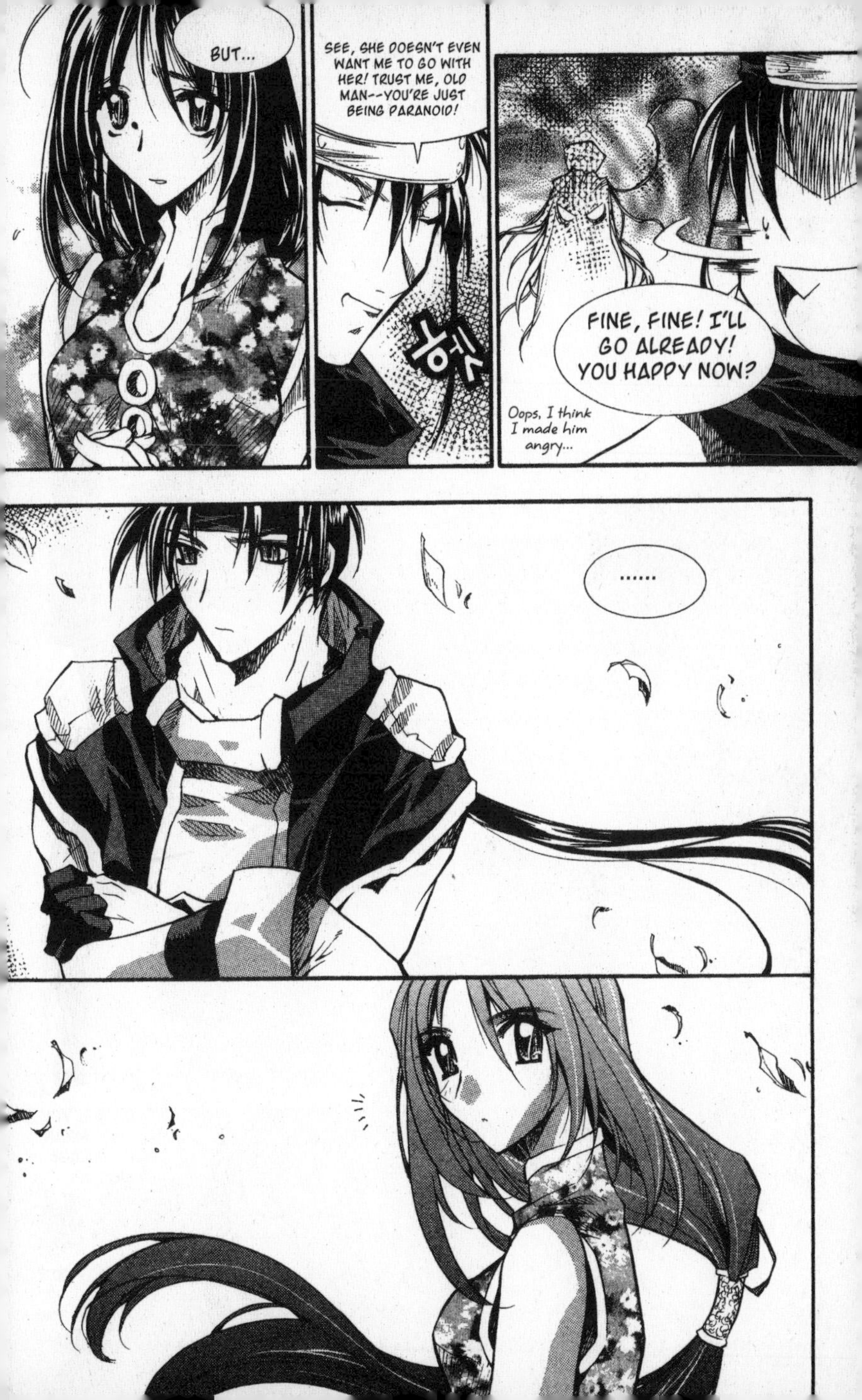
BUT...
SEE, SHE DOESN'T EVEN WANT ME TO GO WITH HER! TRUST ME, OLD MAN--YOU'RE JUST BEING PARANOID!
FINE, FINE! I'LL GO ALREADY! YOU HAPPY NOW?
Oops, I think I made him angry...
......

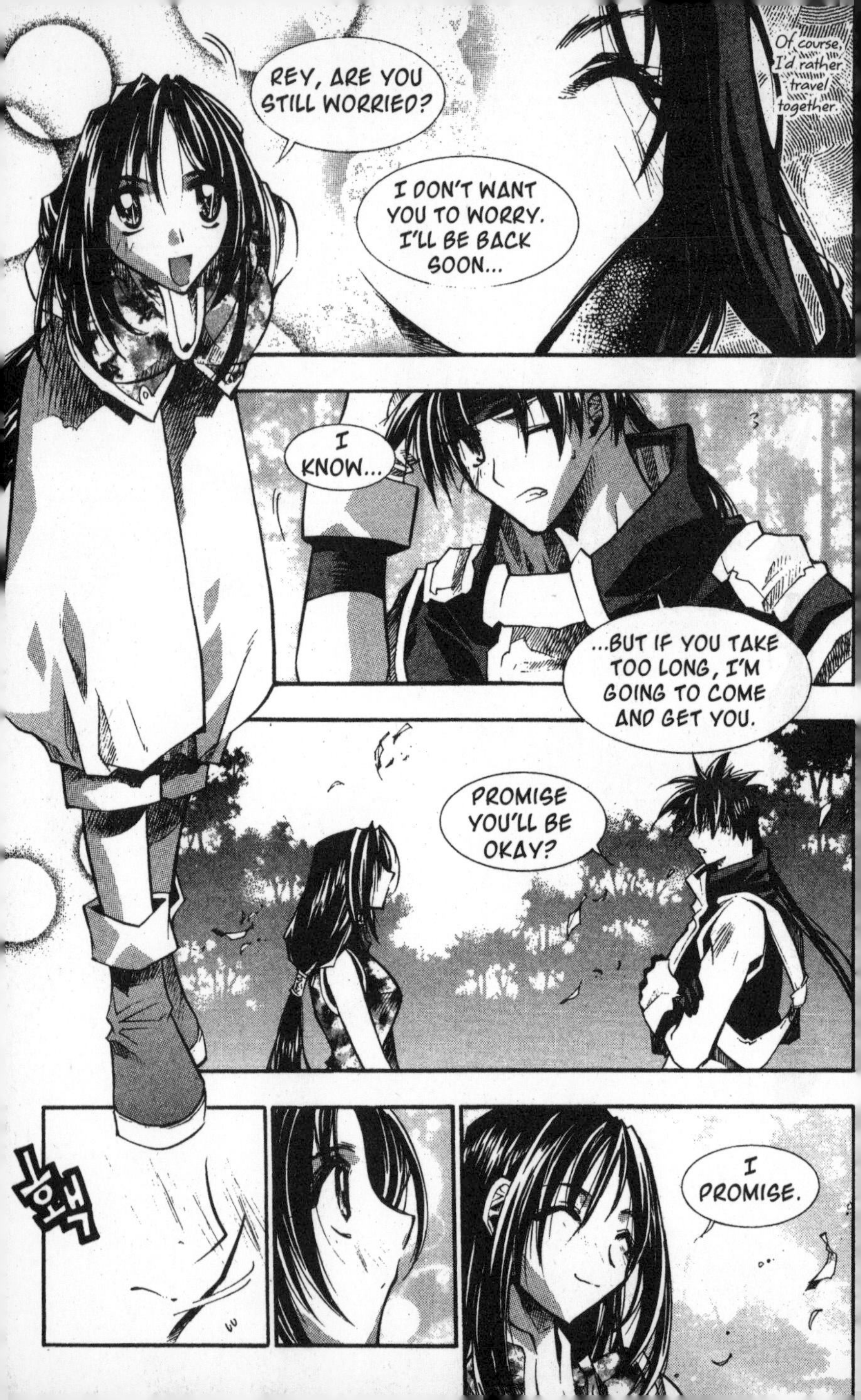
REY, ARE YOU STILL WORRIED?
I DON'T WANT YOU TO WORRY. I'LL BE BACK SOON...
Of course, I'd rather travel together.
I KNOW...
...BUT IF YOU TAKE TOO LONG, I'M GOING TO COME AND GET YOU.
PROMISE YOU'LL BE OKAY?
I PROMISE.

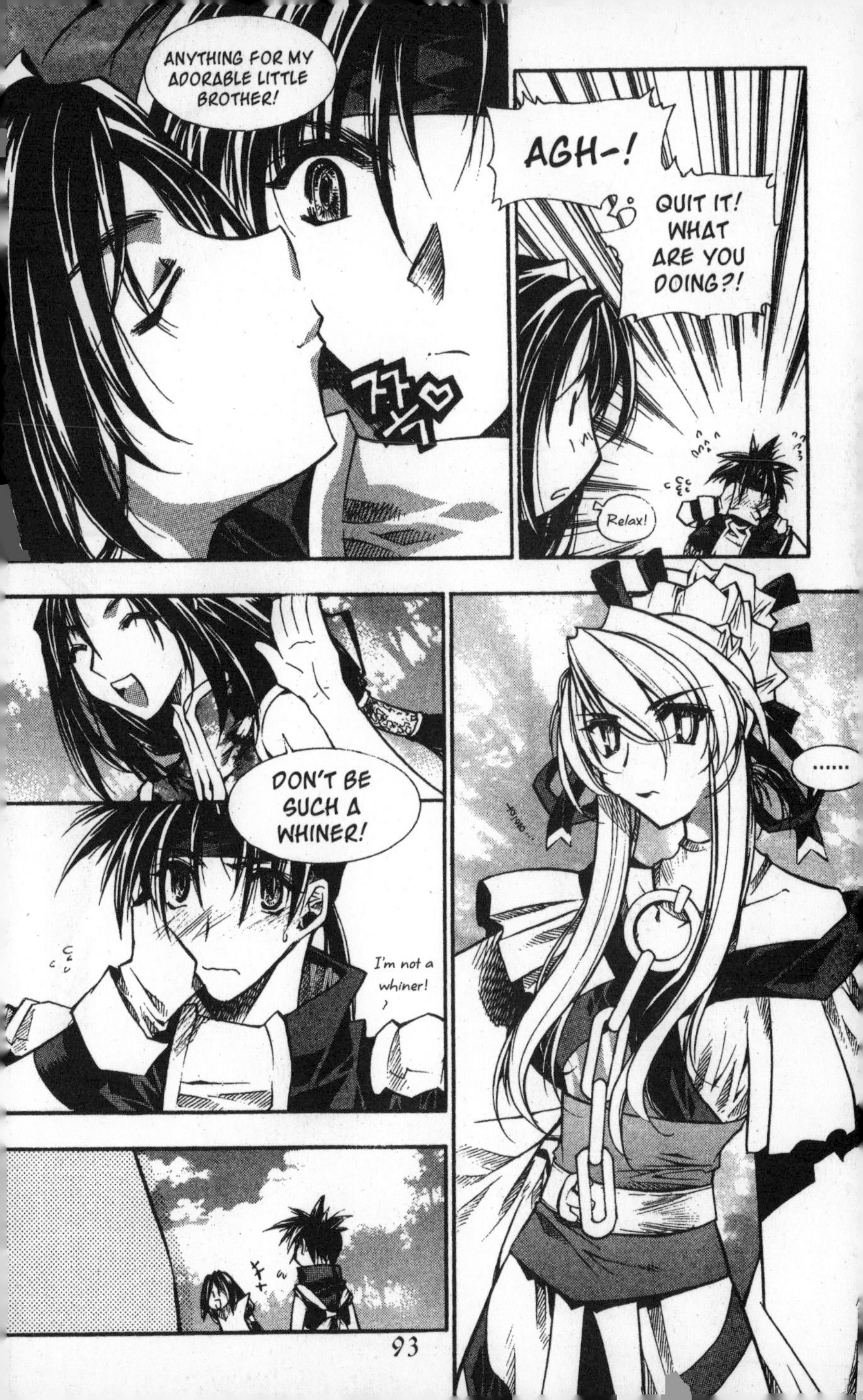
ANYTHING FOR MY ADORABLE LITTLE BROTHER!
AGH-!
QUIT IT! WHAT ARE YOU DOING?!
Relax!
DON'T BE SUCH A WHINER!
I'm not a whiner!
......

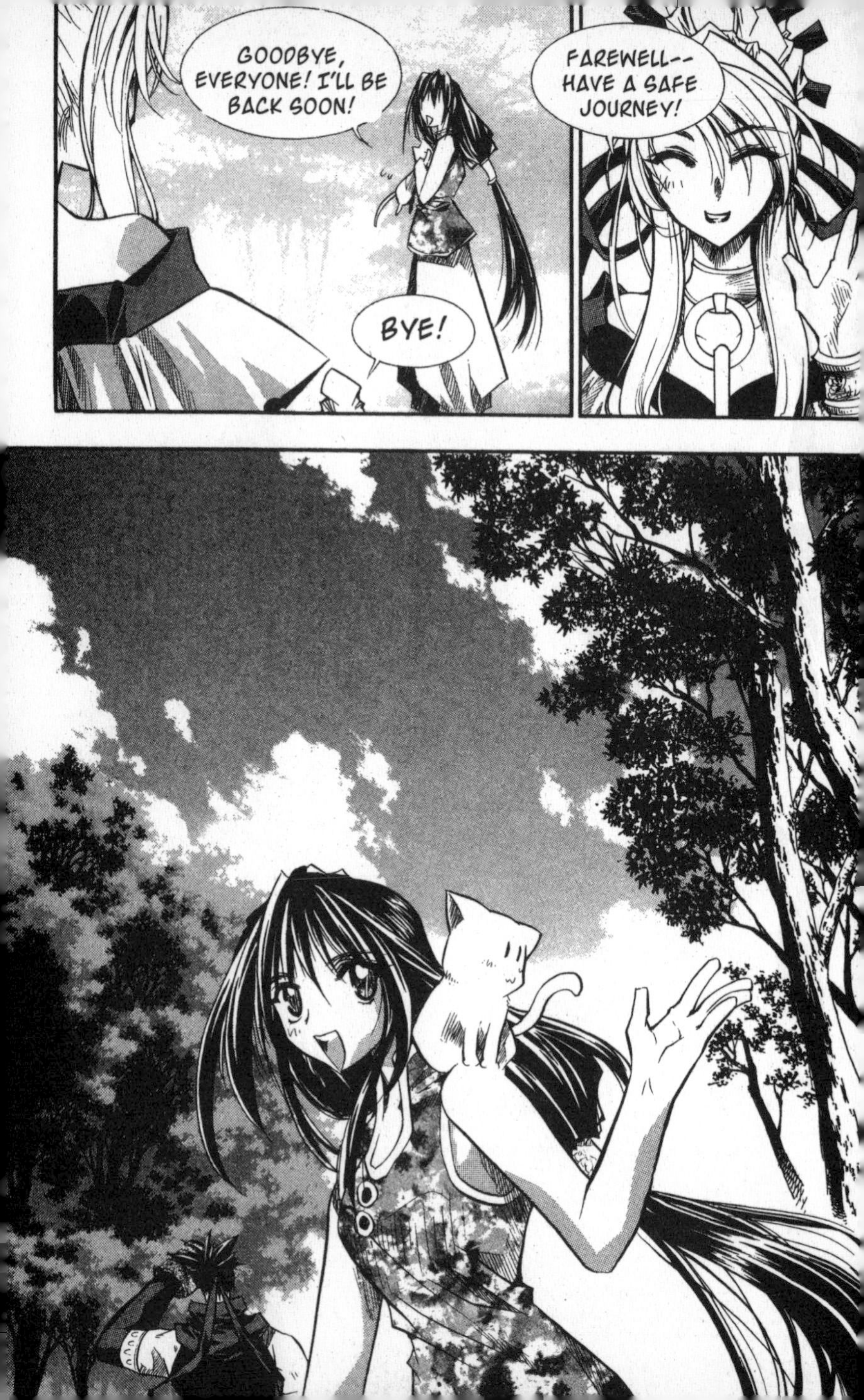
GOODBYE, EVERYONE! I'LL BE BACK SOON!
BYE!
FAREWELL-- HAVE A SAFE JOURNEY!

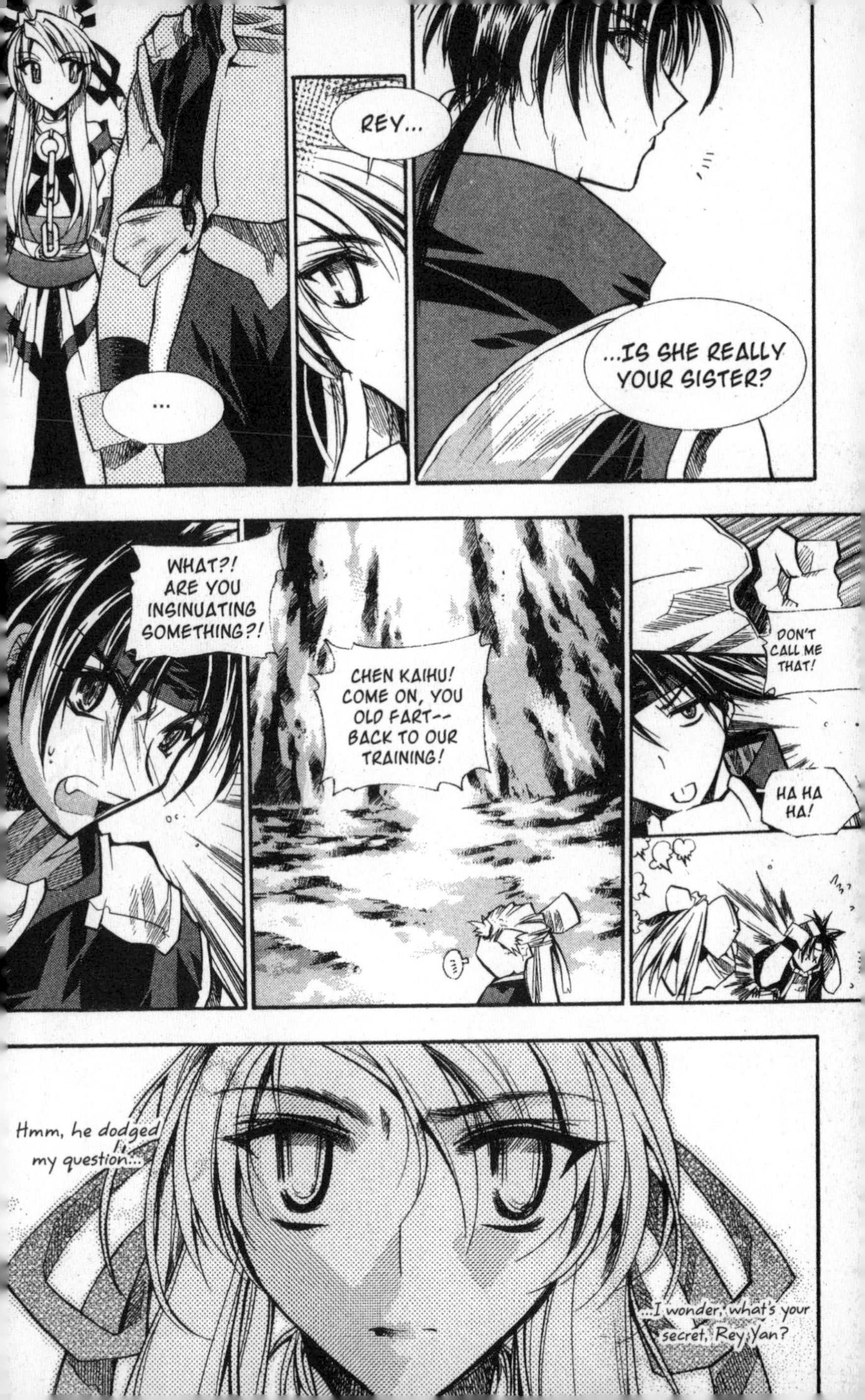
...
REY...
...IS SHE REALLY YOUR SISTER?
WHAT?! ARE YOU INSINUATING SOMETHING?!
CHEN KAIHU! COME ON, YOU OLD FART-- BACK TO OUR TRAINING!
DON'T CALL ME THAT!
HA HA HA!
Hmm, he dodged my question...
...I wonder, what's your secret, Rey Yan?

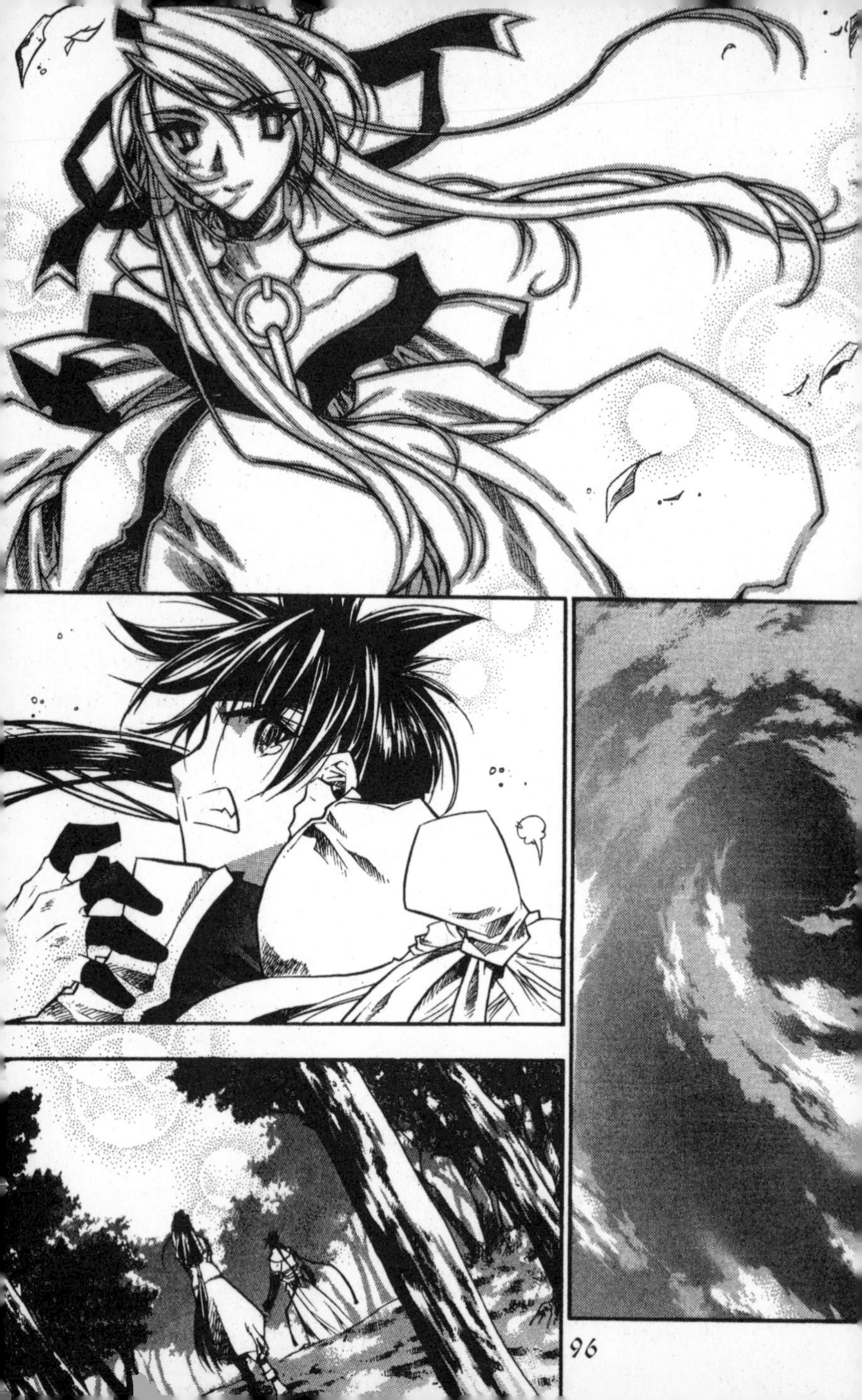

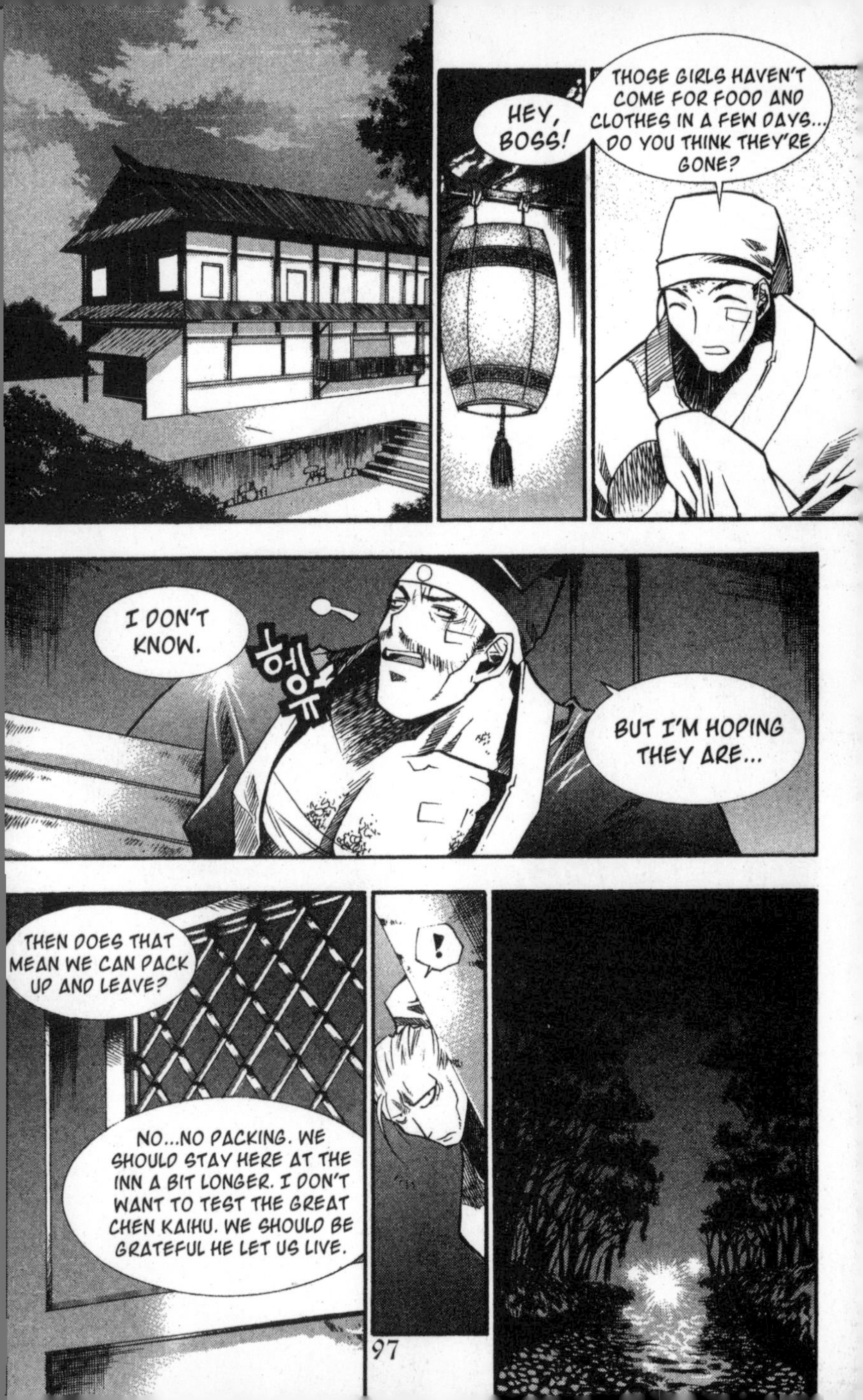
HEY, BOSS!
THOSE GIRLS HAVEN'T COME FOR FOOD AND CLOTHES IN A FEW DAYS... DO YOU THINK THEY'RE GONE?
I DON'T KNOW.
헤유
BUT I'M HOPING THEY ARE...
THEN DOES THAT MEAN WE CAN PACK UP AND LEAVE?
!
NO...NO PACKING. WE SHOULD STAY HERE AT THE INN A BIT LONGER. I DON'T WANT TO TEST THE GREAT CHEN KAIHU. WE SHOULD BE GRATEFUL HE LET US LIVE.

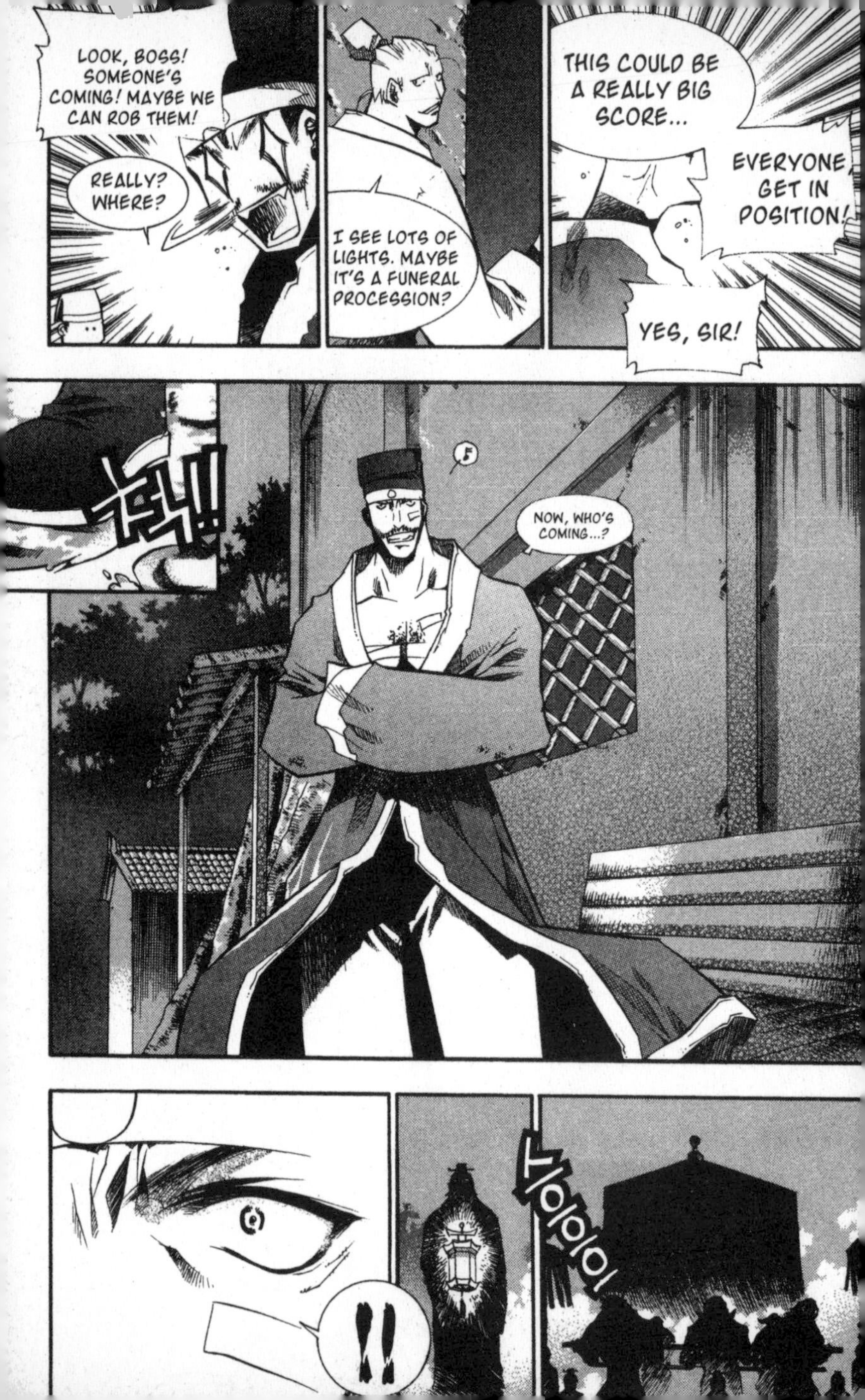
LOOK, BOSS! SOMEONE'S COMING! MAYBE WE CAN ROB THEM!
REALLY? WHERE?
I SEE LOTS OF LIGHTS. MAYBE IT'S A FUNERAL PROCESSION?
THIS COULD BE A REALLY BIG SCORE...
EVERYONE GET IN POSITION!
YES, SIR!
NOW, WHO'S COMING...?
!!

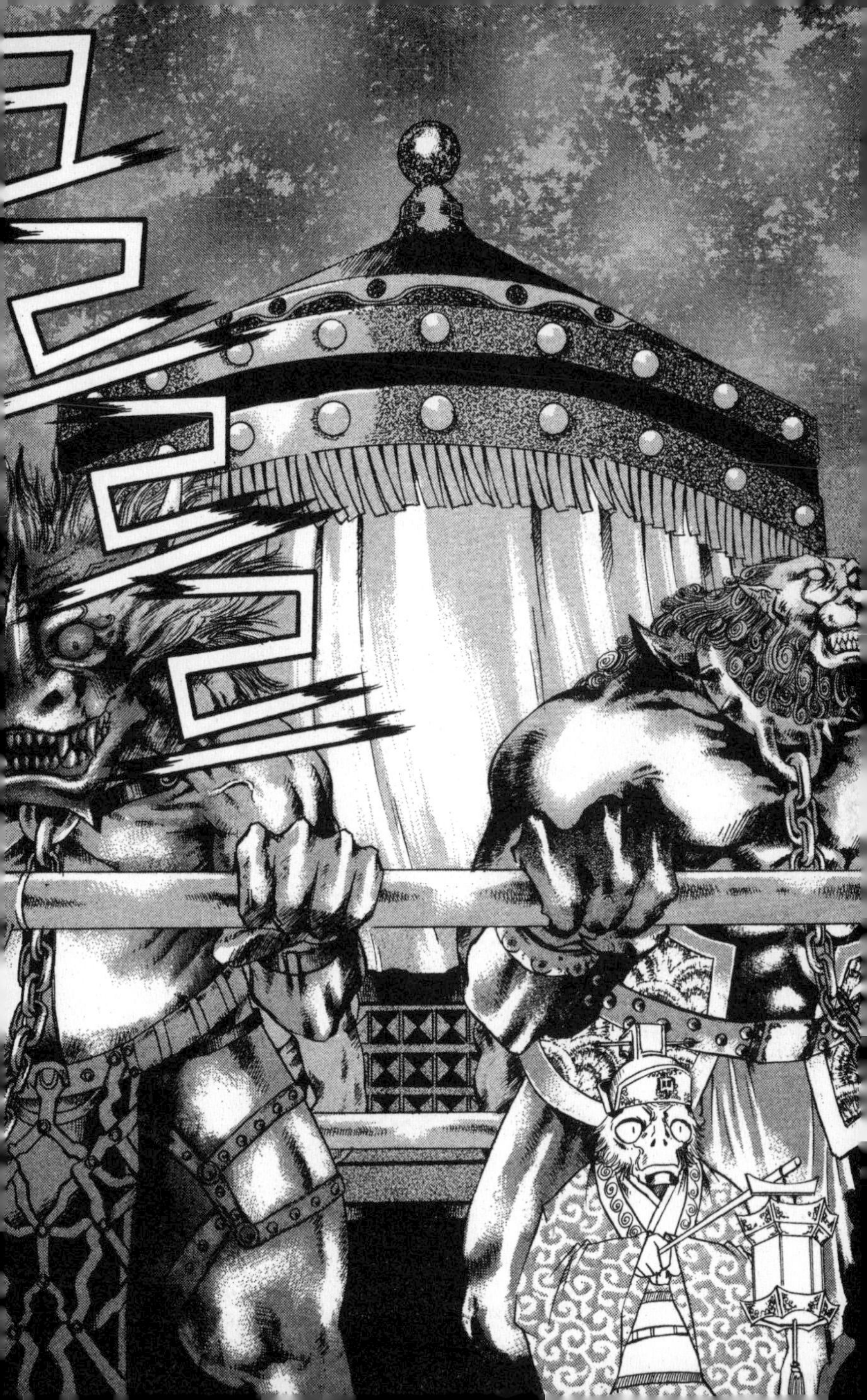

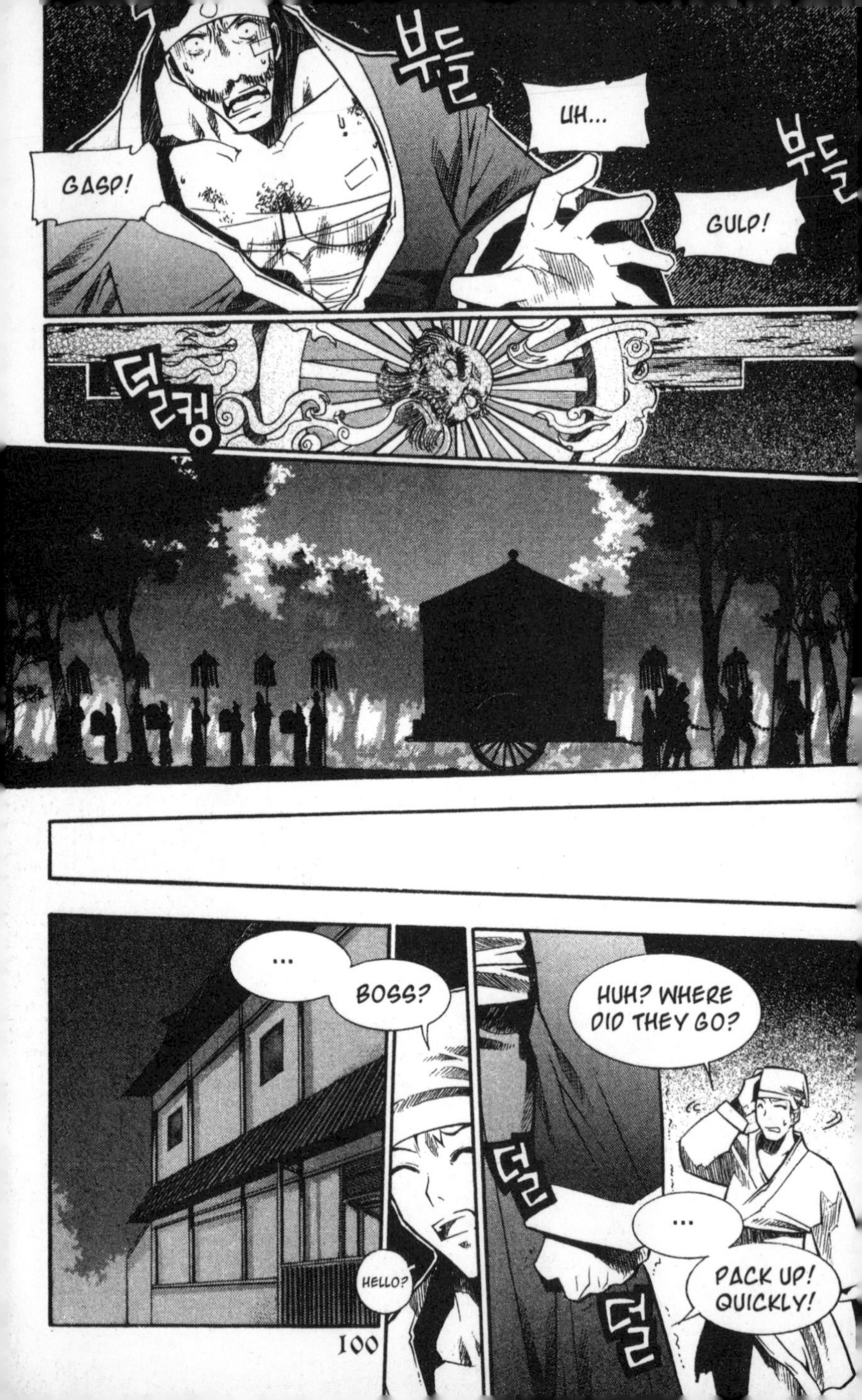
GASP!
부들
UH...
부들
GULP!
덜컹
...
BOSS?
HELLO?
덜
덜
HUH? WHERE DID THEY GO?
...
PACK UP! QUICKLY!

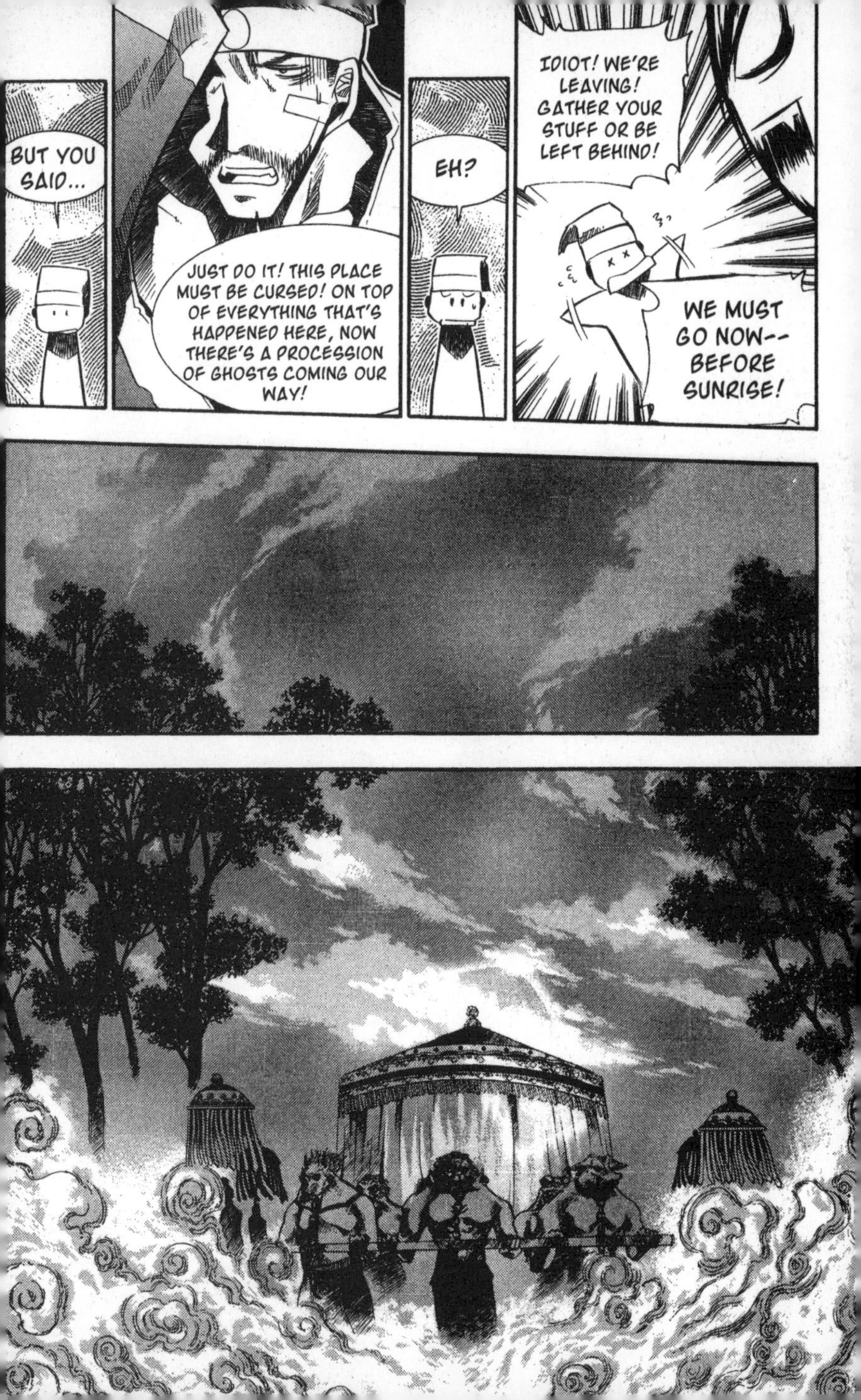
BUT YOU SAID...
JUST DO IT! THIS PLACE MUST BE CURSED! ON TOP OF EVERYTHING THAT'S HAPPENED HERE, NOW THERE'S A PROCESSION OF GHOSTS COMING OUR WAY!
EH?
IDIOT! WE'RE LEAVING! GATHER YOUR STUFF OR BE LEFT BEHIND!
WE MUST GO NOW-- BEFORE SUNRISE!

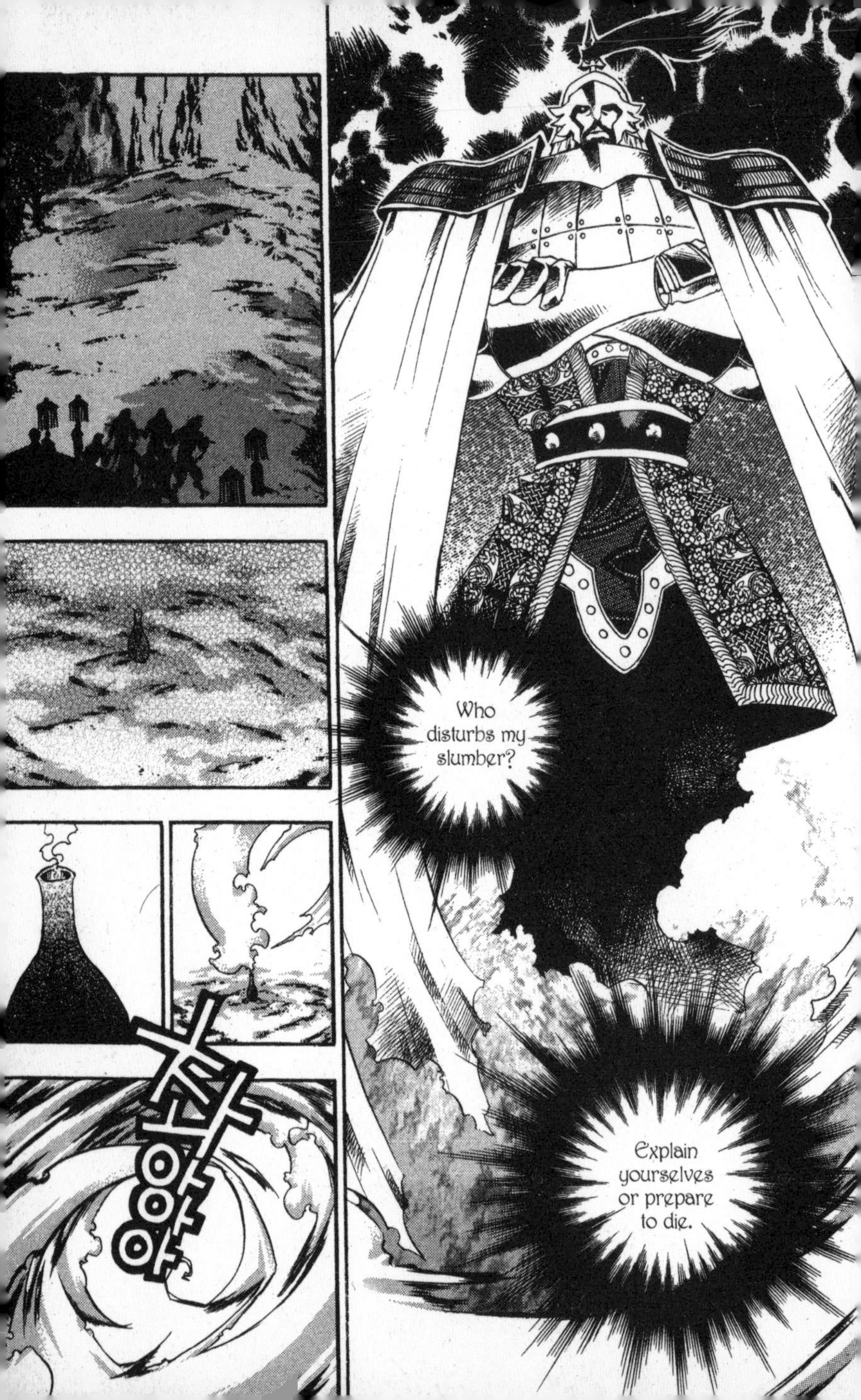
Who disturbs my slumber?
Explain yourselves or prepare to die.

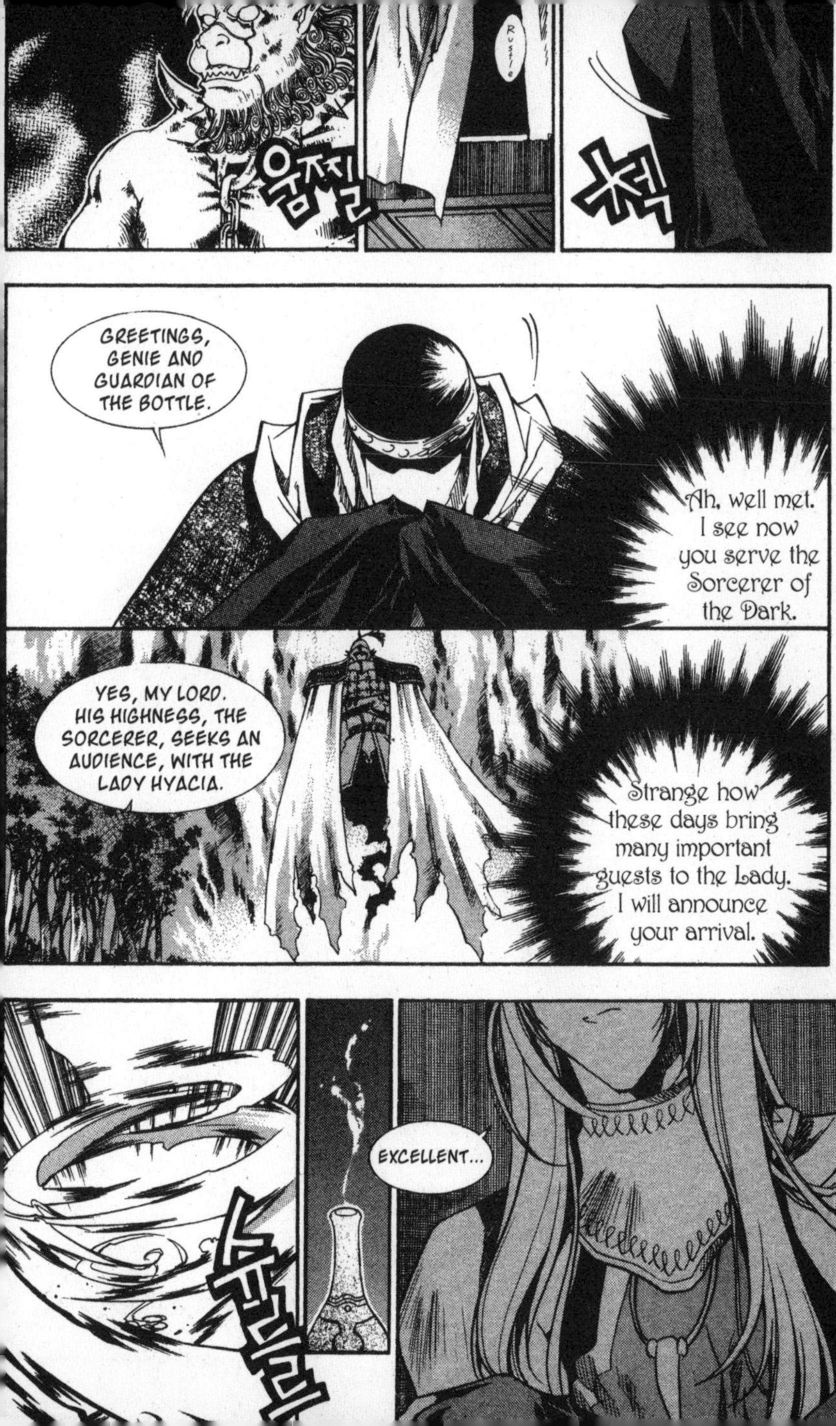
움찔
Rustle
척
GREETINGS, GENIE AND GUARDIAN OF THE BOTTLE.
Ah, well met. I see now you serve the Sorcerer of the Dark.
YES, MY LORD. HIS HIGHNESS, THE SORCERER, SEEKS AN AUDIENCE, WITH THE LADY HYACIA.
Strange how these days bring many important guests to the Lady. I will announce your arrival.
EXCELLENT...

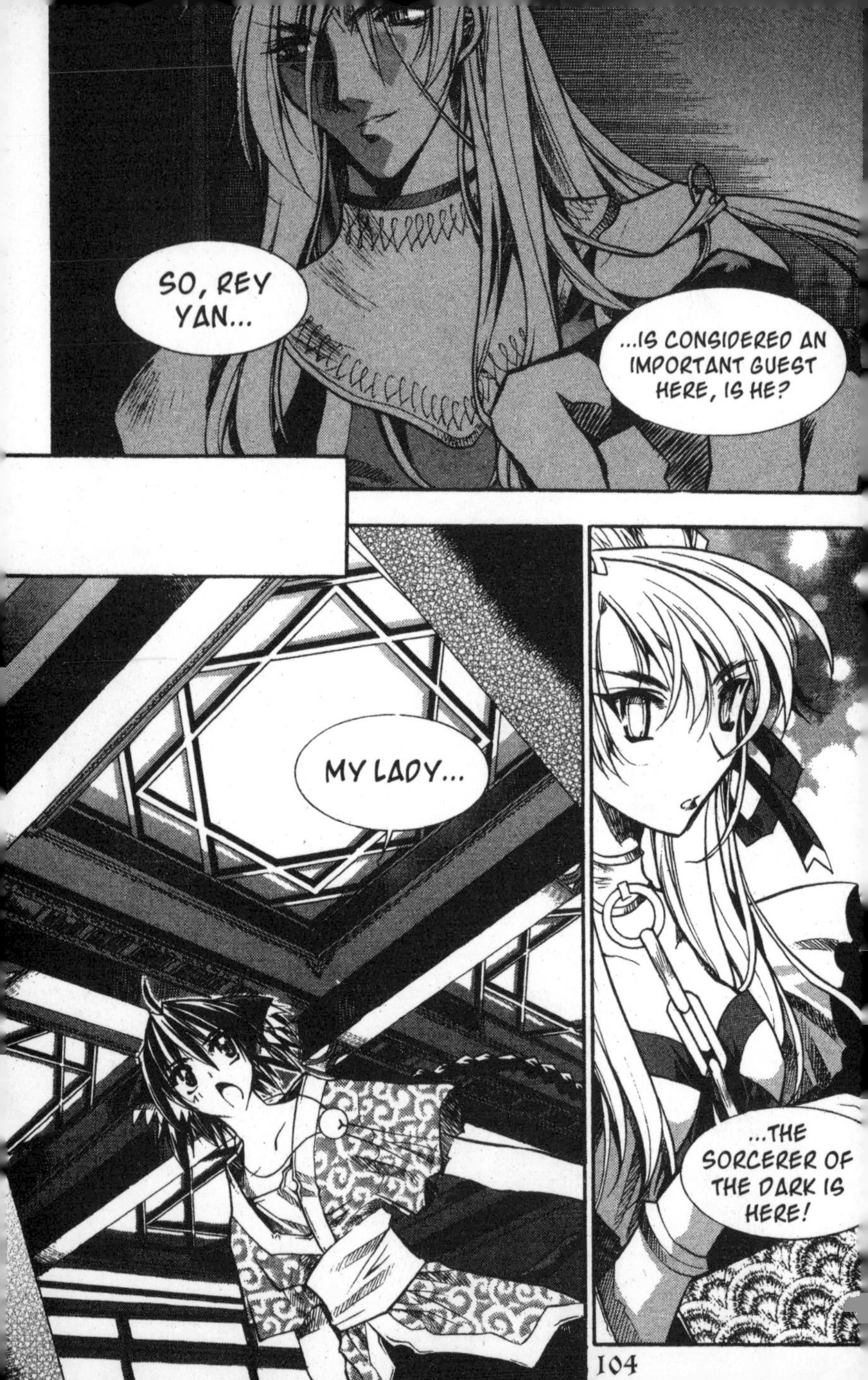
SO, REY YAN...
...IS CONSIDERED AN IMPORTANT GUEST HERE, IS HE?
MY LADY...
...THE SORCERER OF THE DARK IS HERE!

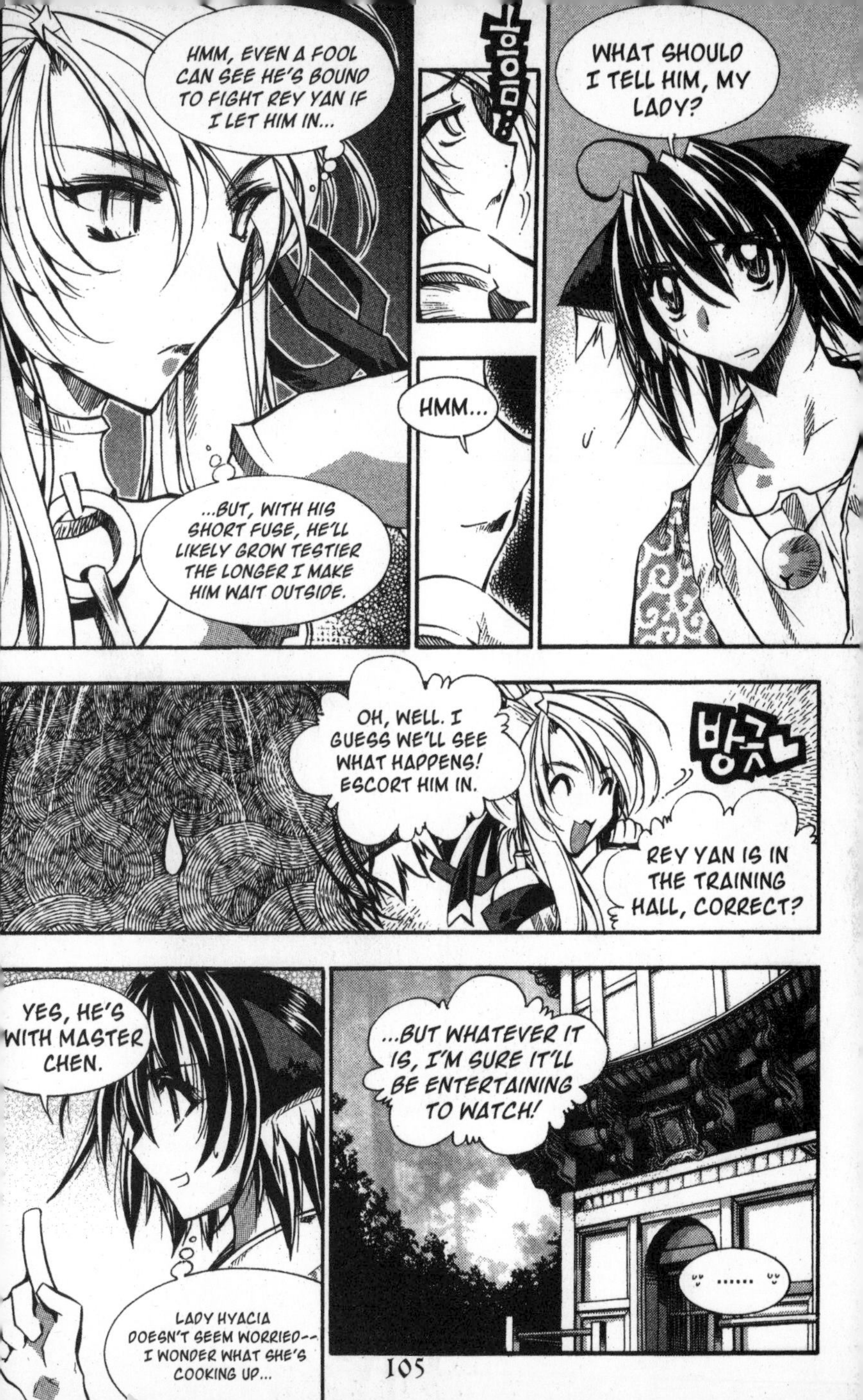
HMM, EVEN A FOOL CAN SEE HE'S BOUND TO FIGHT REY YAN IF I LET HIM IN...
...BUT, WITH HIS SHORT FUSE, HE'LL LIKELY GROW TESTIER THE LONGER I MAKE HIM WAIT OUTSIDE.
HMM...
WHAT SHOULD I TELL HIM, MY LADY?
OH, WELL. I GUESS WE'LL SEE WHAT HAPPENS! ESCORT HIM IN.
REY YAN IS IN THE TRAINING HALL, CORRECT?
YES, HE'S WITH MASTER CHEN.
LADY HYACIA DOESN'T SEEM WORRIED--I WONDER WHAT SHE'S COOKING UP...
...BUT WHATEVER IT IS, I'M SURE IT'LL BE ENTERTAINING TO WATCH!
......

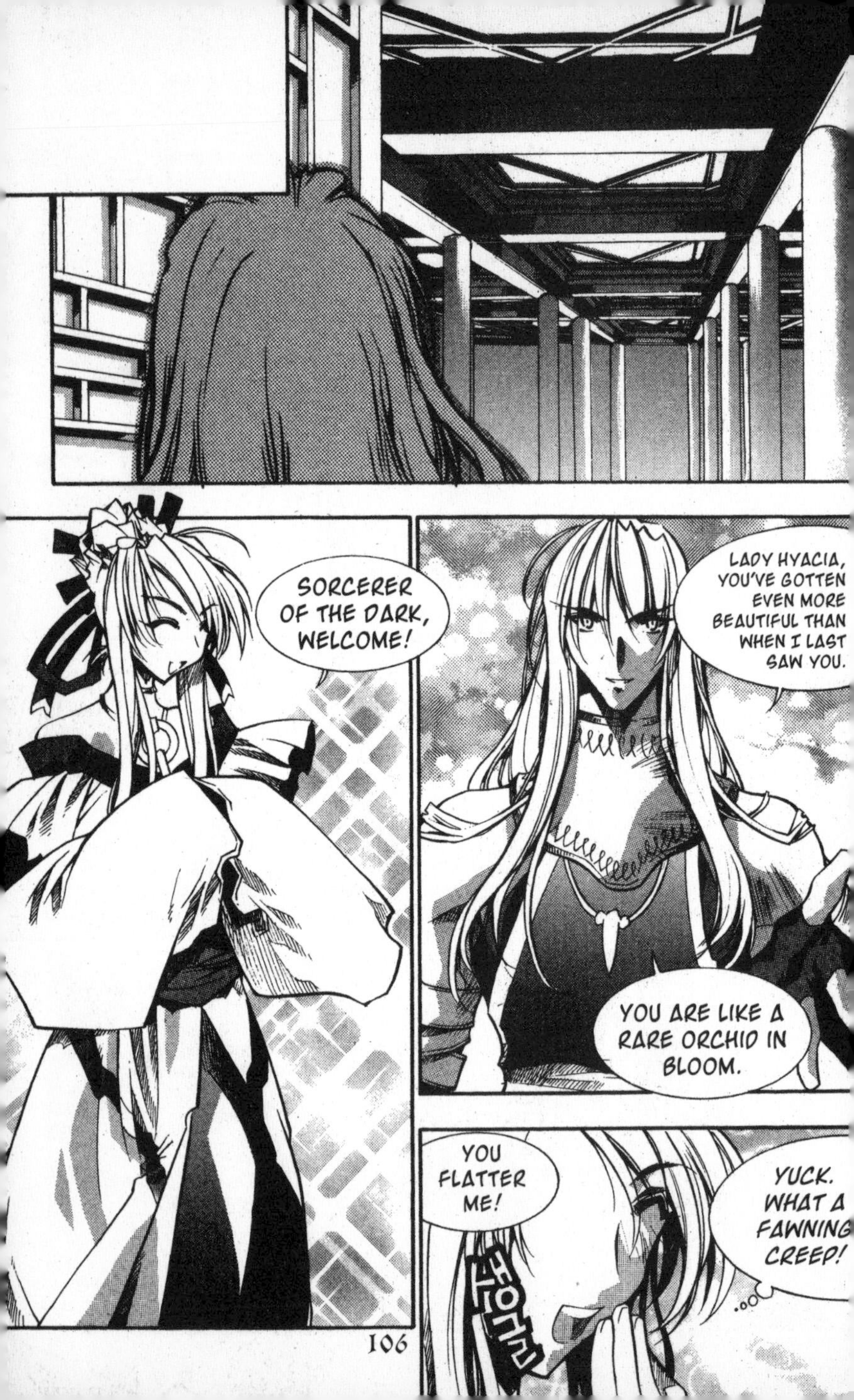
SORCERER OF THE DARK, WELCOME!
LADY HYACIA, YOU'VE GOTTEN EVEN MORE BEAUTIFUL THAN WHEN I LAST SAW YOU.
YOU ARE LIKE A RARE ORCHID IN BLOOM.
YOU FLATTER ME!
싱긋
YUCK. WHAT A FAWNING CREEP!

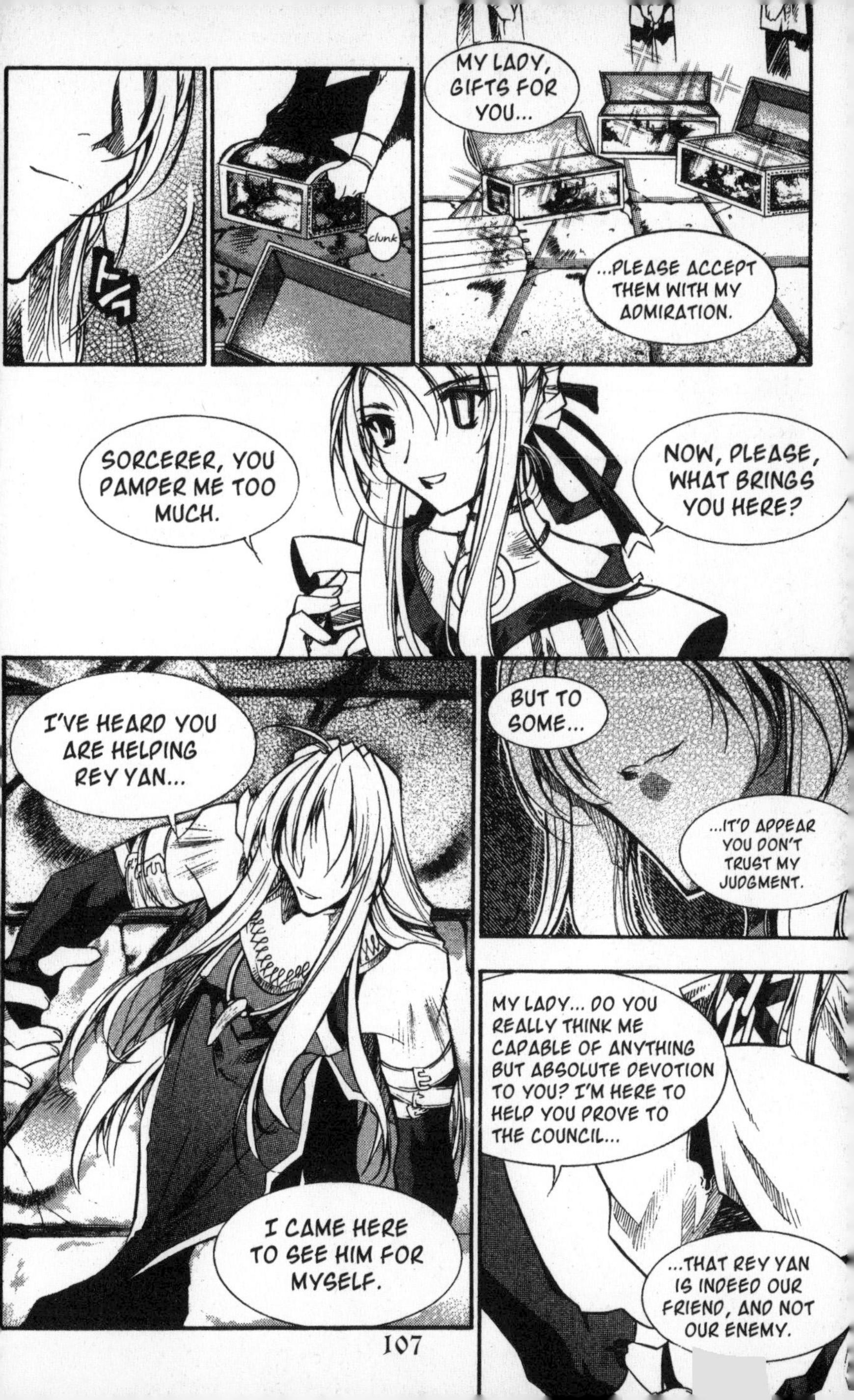
clunk
MY LADY, GIFTS FOR YOU...
...PLEASE ACCEPT THEM WITH MY ADMIRATION.
SORCERER, YOU PAMPER ME TOO MUCH.
NOW, PLEASE, WHAT BRINGS YOU HERE?
I'VE HEARD YOU ARE HELPING REY YAN...
I CAME HERE TO SEE HIM FOR MYSELF.
BUT TO SOME...
...IT'D APPEAR YOU DON'T TRUST MY JUDGMENT.
MY LADY... DO YOU REALLY THINK ME CAPABLE OF ANYTHING BUT ABSOLUTE DEVOTION TO YOU? I'M HERE TO HELP YOU PROVE TO THE COUNCIL...
...THAT REY YAN IS INDEED OUR FRIEND, AND NOT OUR ENEMY.

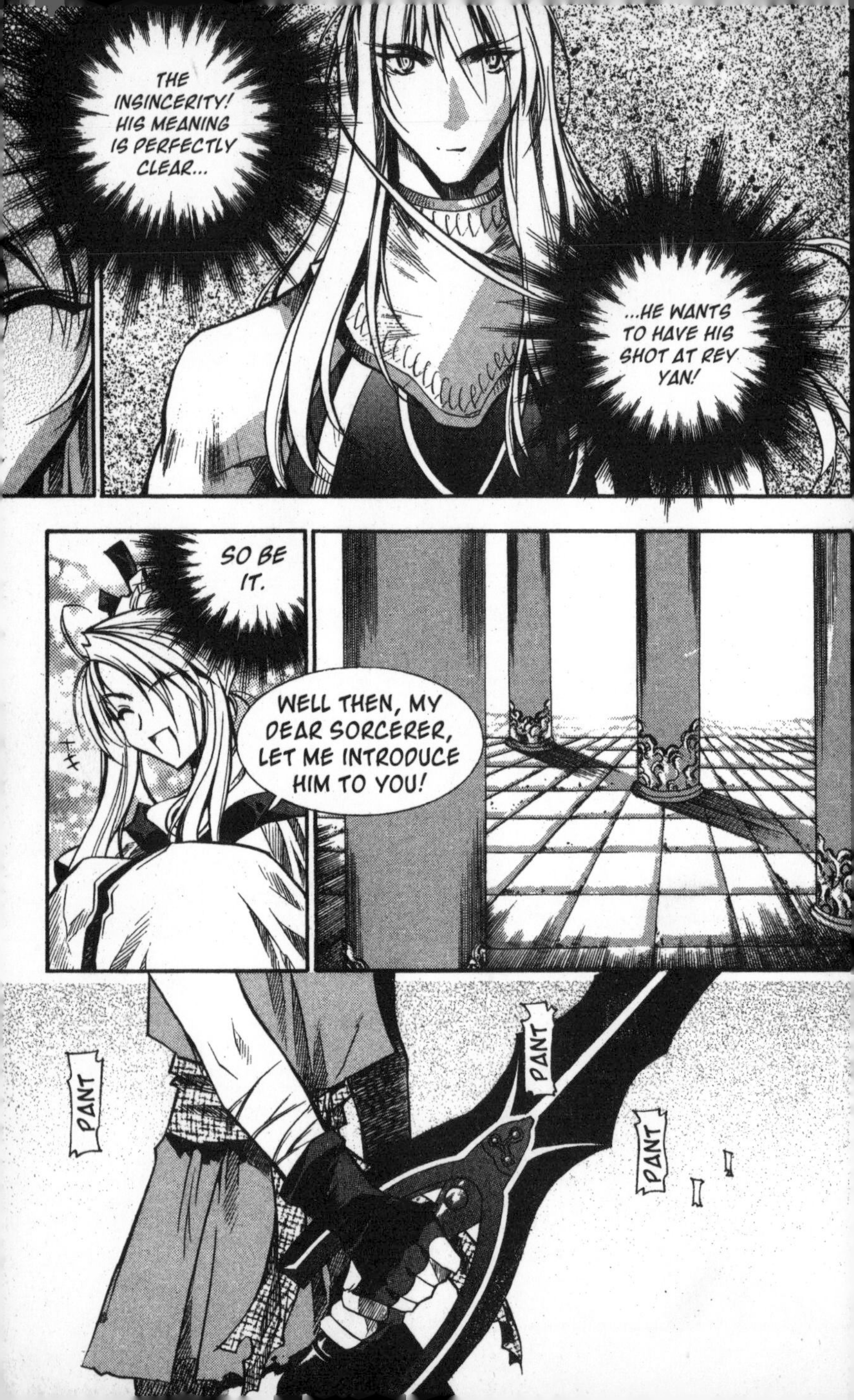
THE INSINCERITY! HIS MEANING IS PERFECTLY CLEAR...
...HE WANTS TO HAVE HIS SHOT AT REY YAN!
SO BE IT.
WELL THEN, MY DEAR SORCERER, LET ME INTRODUCE HIM TO YOU!
PANT
PANT
PANT

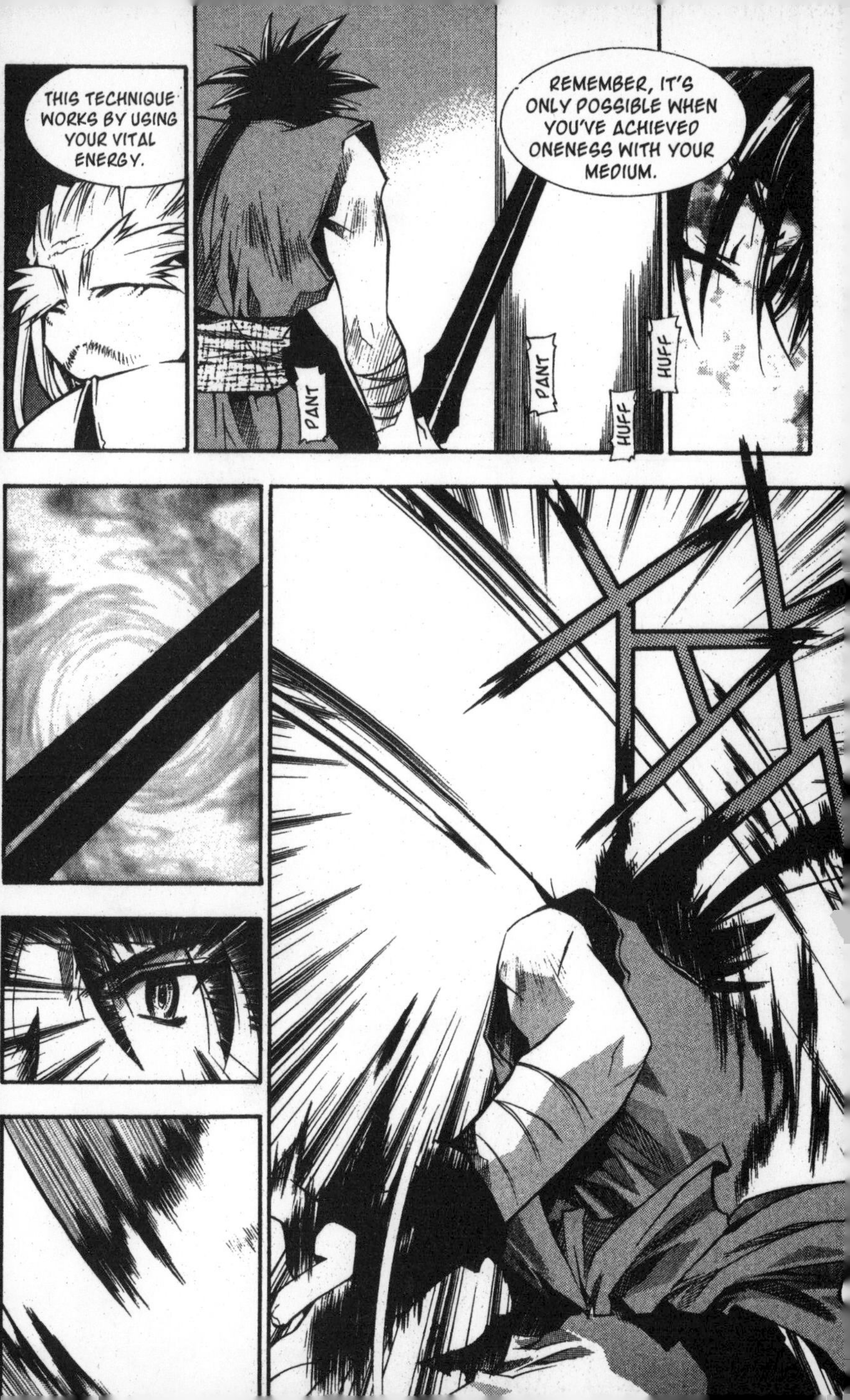
THIS TECHNIQUE WORKS BY USING YOUR VITAL ENERGY.
PANT
REMEMBER, IT'S ONLY POSSIBLE WHEN YOU'VE ACHIEVED ONENESS WITH YOUR MEDIUM.
PANT
HUFF
HUFF

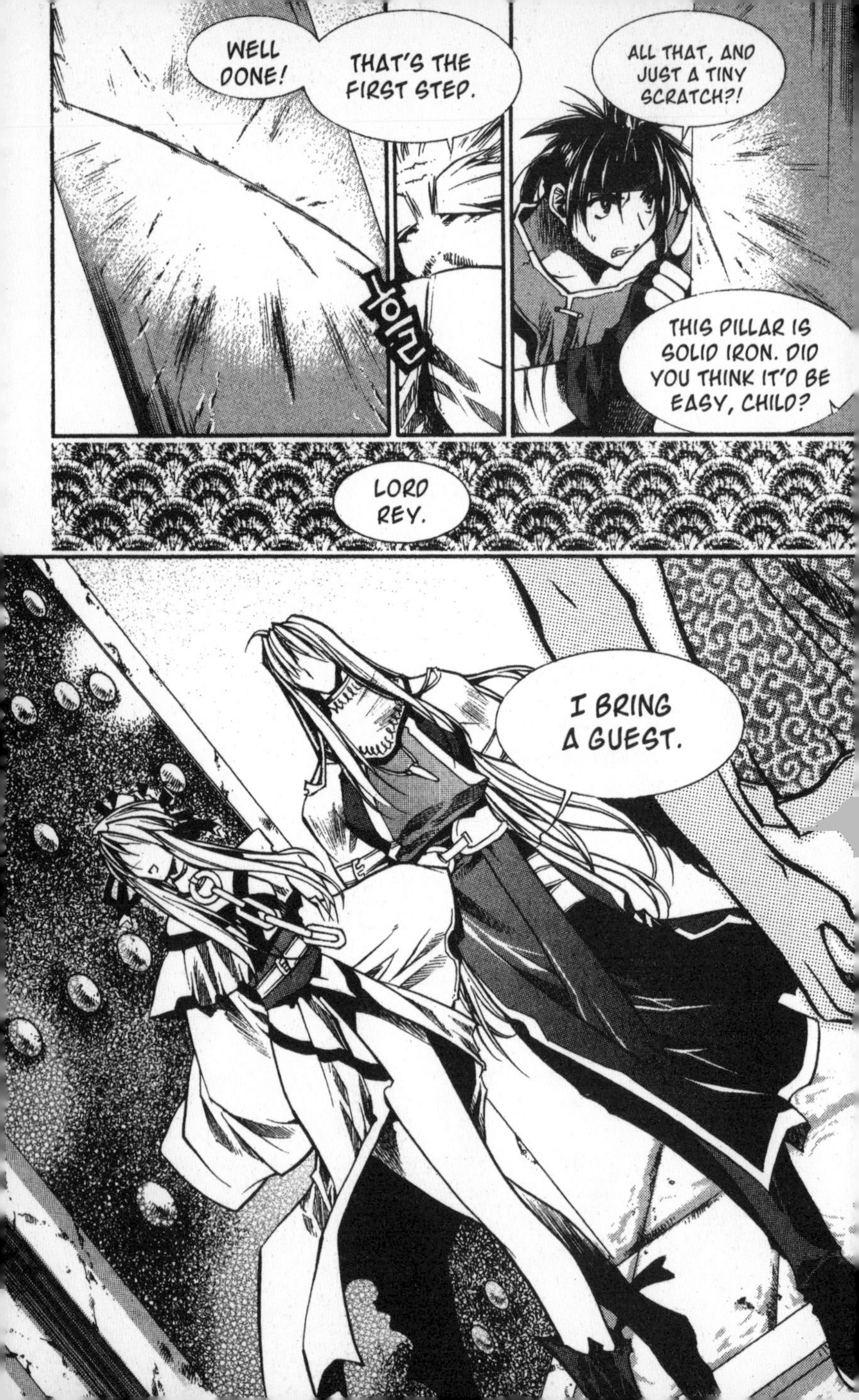
WELL DONE!
THAT'S THE FIRST STEP.
ALL THAT, AND JUST A TINY SCRATCH?!
THIS PILLAR IS SOLID IRON. DID YOU THINK IT'D BE EASY, CHILD?
LORD REY.
I BRING A GUEST.

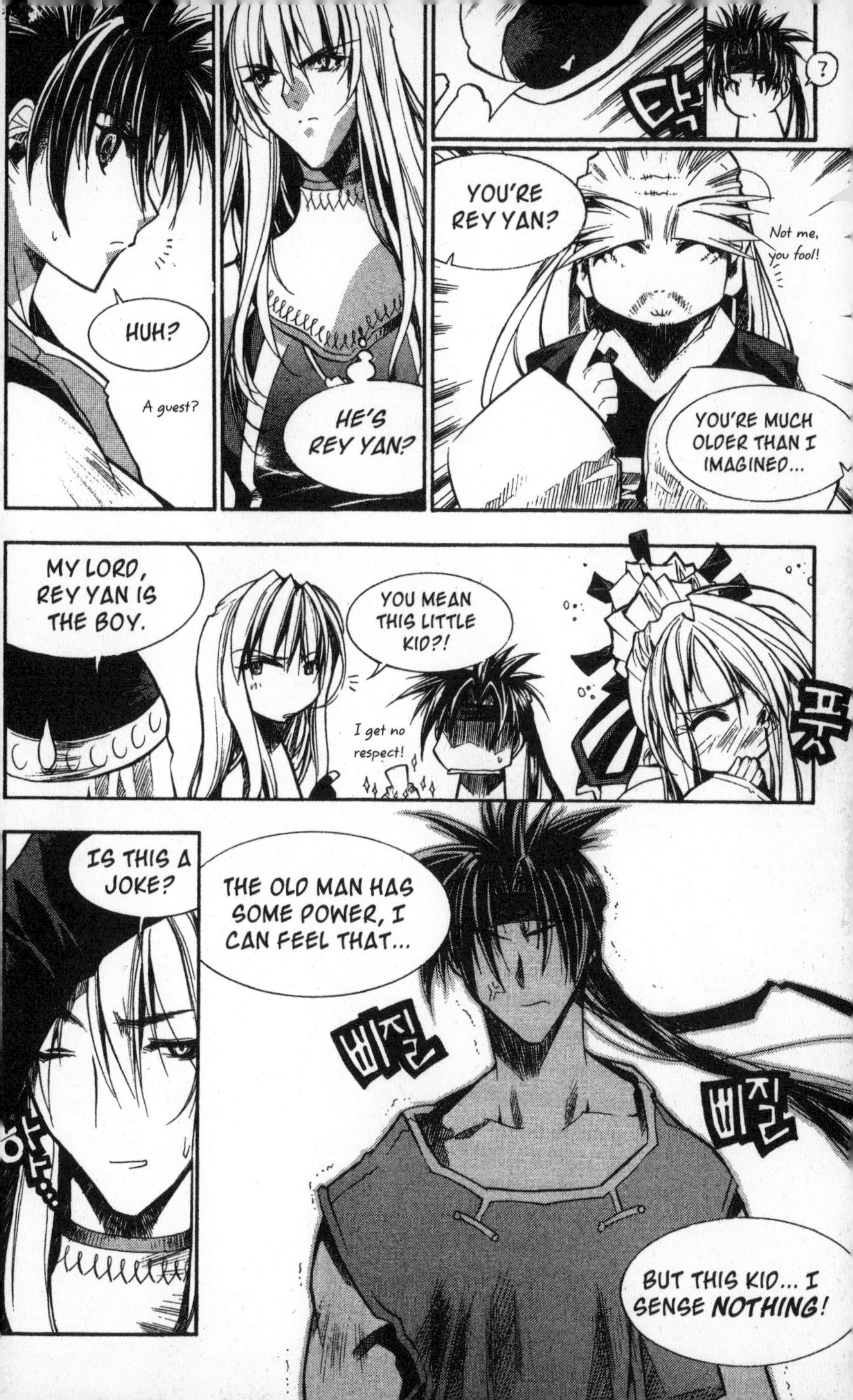
HUH?
A guest?
HE'S REY YAN?
탁
?
YOU'RE REY YAN?
Not me, you fool!
YOU'RE MUCH OLDER THAN I IMAGINED...
MY LORD, REY YAN IS THE BOY.
YOU MEAN THIS LITTLE KID?!
I get no respect!
풋
IS THIS A JOKE?
THE OLD MAN HAS SOME POWER, I CAN FEEL THAT...
삐질
삐질
BUT THIS KID... I SENSE **NOTHING**!

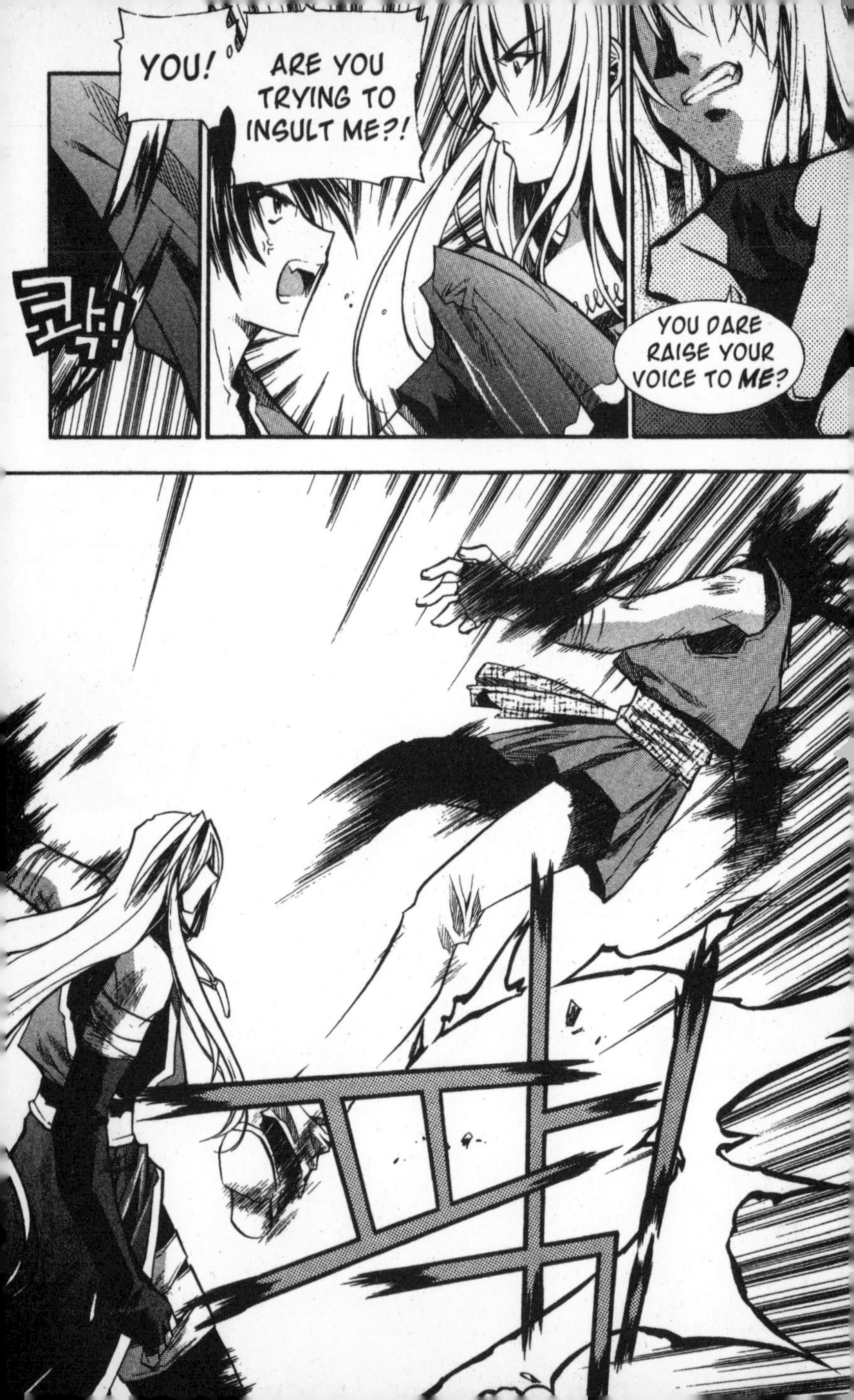
YOU! ARE YOU TRYING TO INSULT ME?!
콱!
YOU DARE RAISE YOUR VOICE TO ME?

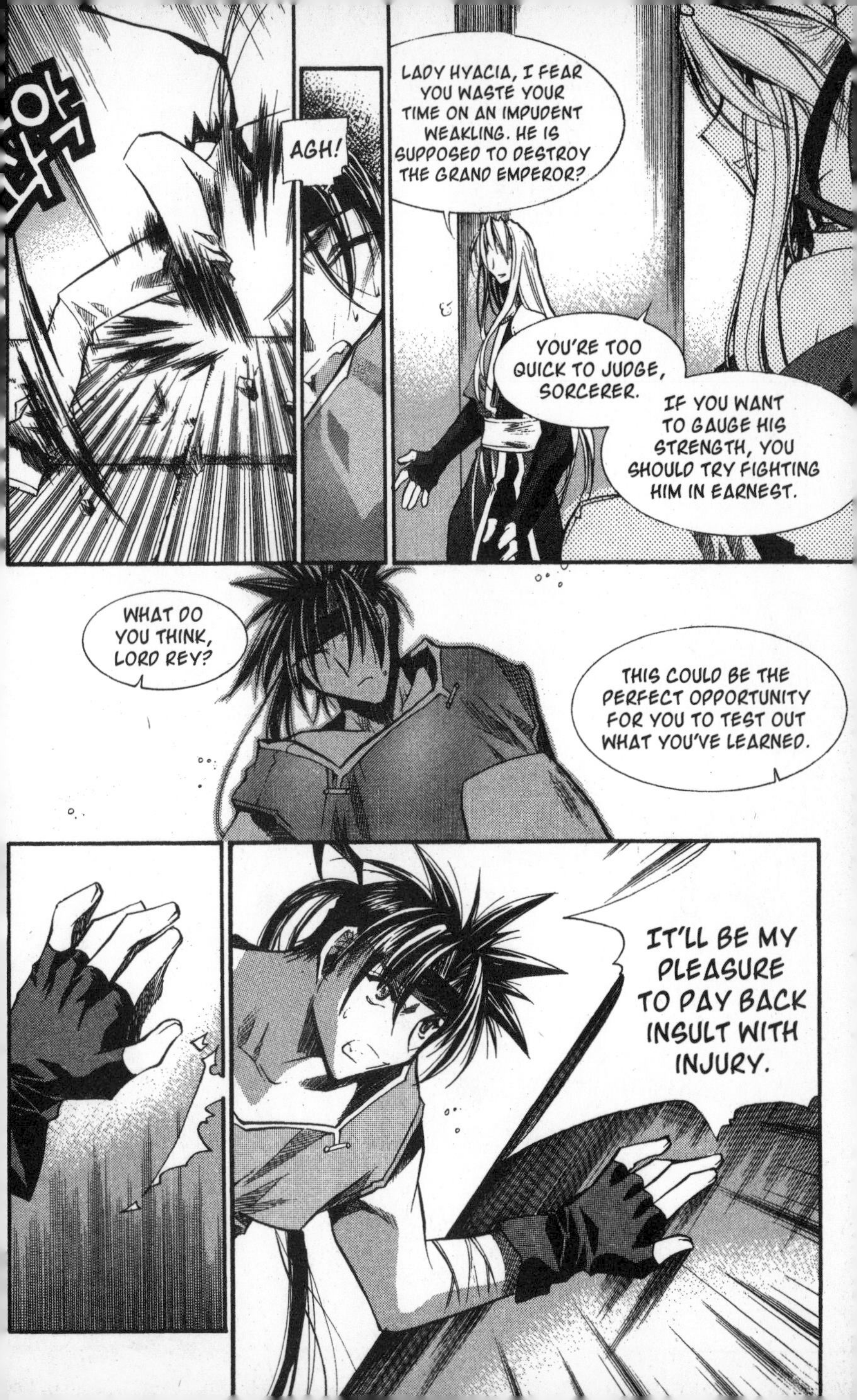
AGH!
LADY HYACIA, I FEAR YOU WASTE YOUR TIME ON AN IMPUDENT WEAKLING. HE IS SUPPOSED TO DESTROY THE GRAND EMPEROR?
YOU'RE TOO QUICK TO JUDGE, SORCERER.
IF YOU WANT TO GAUGE HIS STRENGTH, YOU SHOULD TRY FIGHTING HIM IN EARNEST.
WHAT DO YOU THINK, LORD REY?
THIS COULD BE THE PERFECT OPPORTUNITY FOR YOU TO TEST OUT WHAT YOU'VE LEARNED.
IT'LL BE MY PLEASURE TO PAY BACK INSULT WITH INJURY.

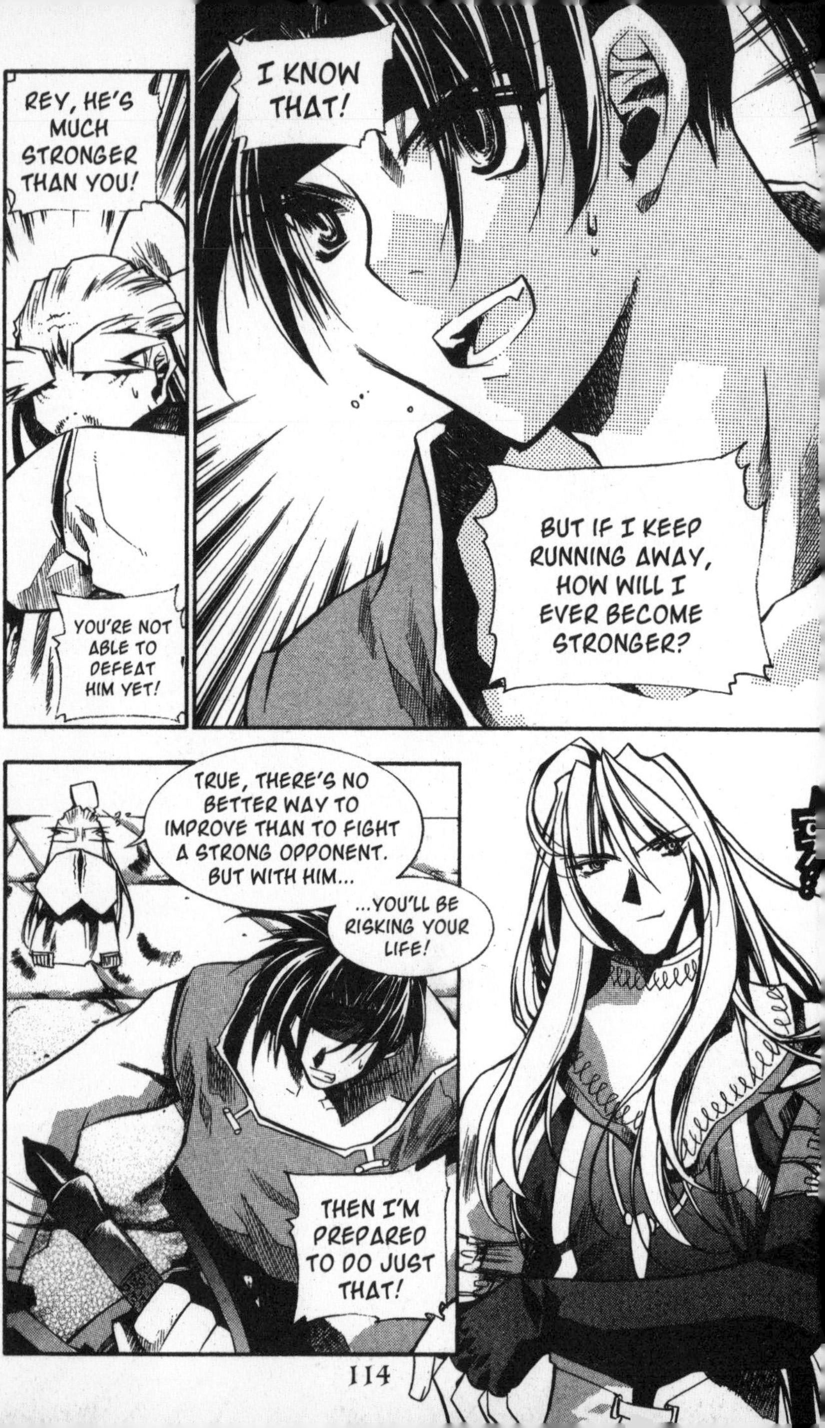
REY, HE'S MUCH STRONGER THAN YOU!
YOU'RE NOT ABLE TO DEFEAT HIM YET!
I KNOW THAT!
BUT IF I KEEP RUNNING AWAY, HOW WILL I EVER BECOME STRONGER?
TRUE, THERE'S NO BETTER WAY TO IMPROVE THAN TO FIGHT A STRONG OPPONENT. BUT WITH HIM...
...YOU'LL BE RISKING YOUR LIFE!
THEN I'M PREPARED TO DO JUST THAT!

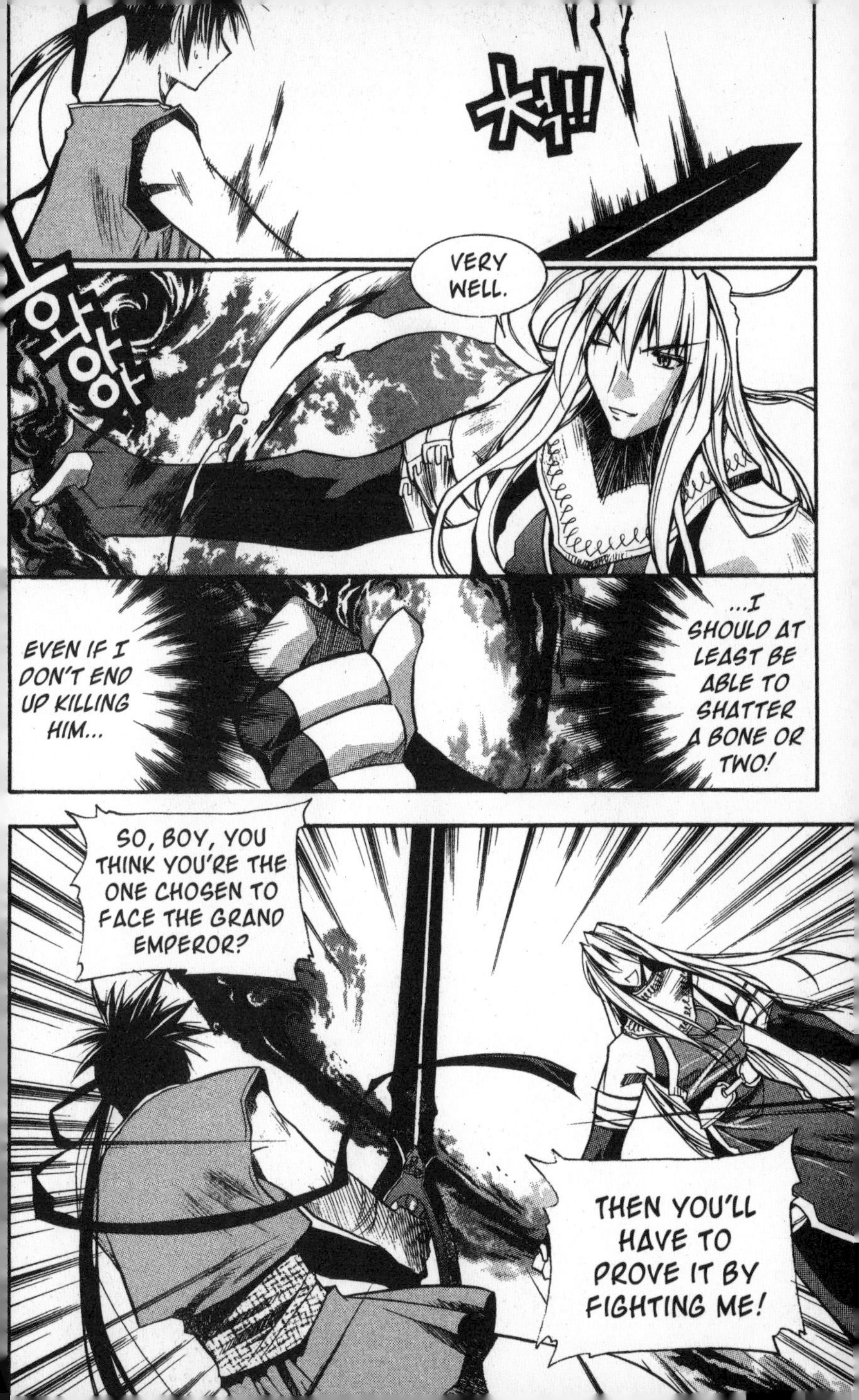
VERY WELL.
EVEN IF I DON'T END UP KILLING HIM...
...I SHOULD AT LEAST BE ABLE TO SHATTER A BONE OR TWO!
SO, BOY, YOU THINK YOU'RE THE ONE CHOSEN TO FACE THE GRAND EMPEROR?
THEN YOU'LL HAVE TO PROVE IT BY FIGHTING ME!

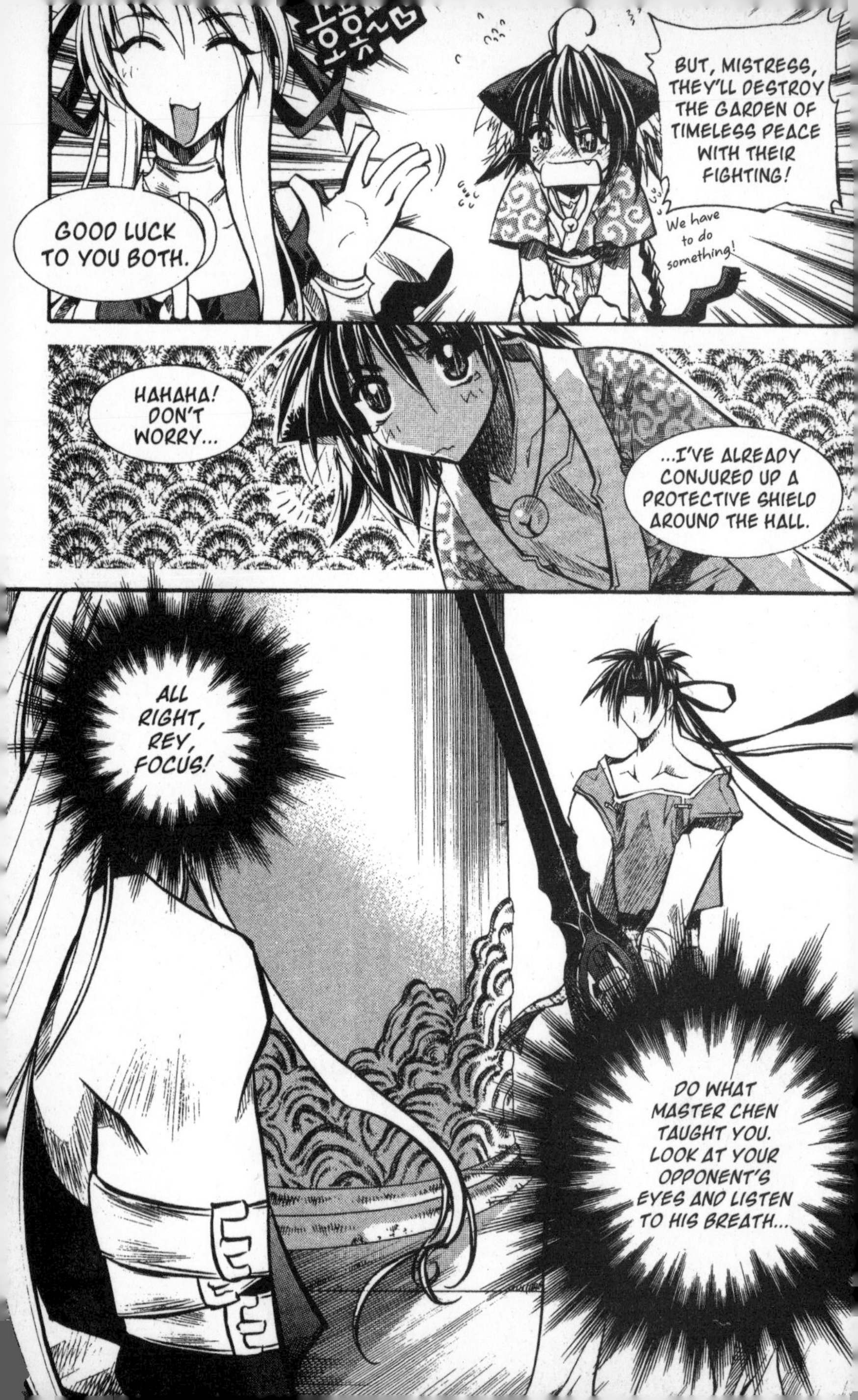
호홋~♥
GOOD LUCK TO YOU BOTH.
BUT, MISTRESS, THEY'LL DESTROY THE GARDEN OF TIMELESS PEACE WITH THEIR FIGHTING!
We have to do something!
HAHAHA! DON'T WORRY...
...I'VE ALREADY CONJURED UP A PROTECTIVE SHIELD AROUND THE HALL.
ALL RIGHT, REY, FOCUS!
DO WHAT MASTER CHEN TAUGHT YOU. LOOK AT YOUR OPPONENT'S EYES AND LISTEN TO HIS BREATH...

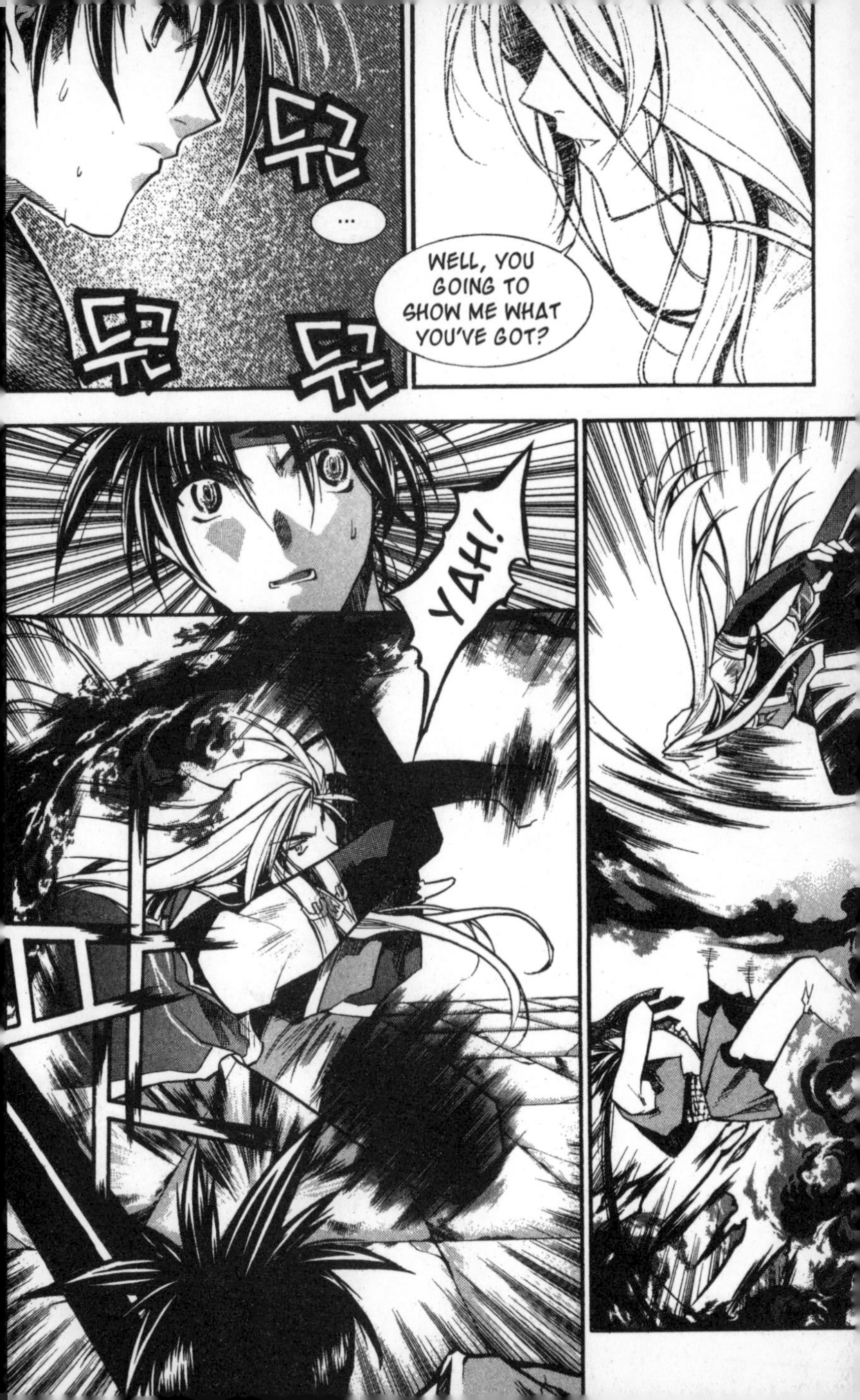
두근
...
두근
두근
WELL, YOU GOING TO SHOW ME WHAT YOU'VE GOT?
YAH!

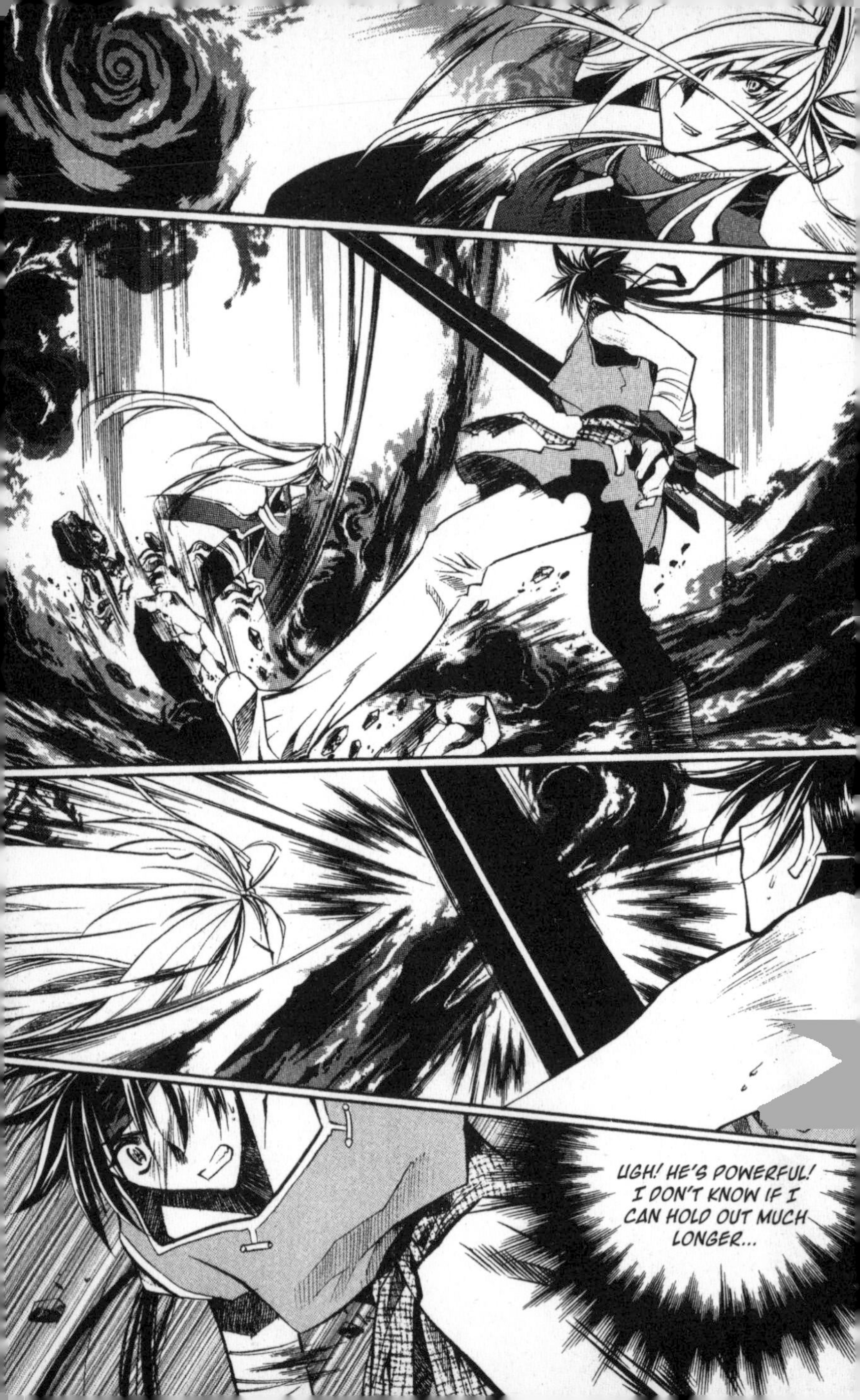
UGH! HE'S POWERFUL! I DON'T KNOW IF I CAN HOLD OUT MUCH LONGER...

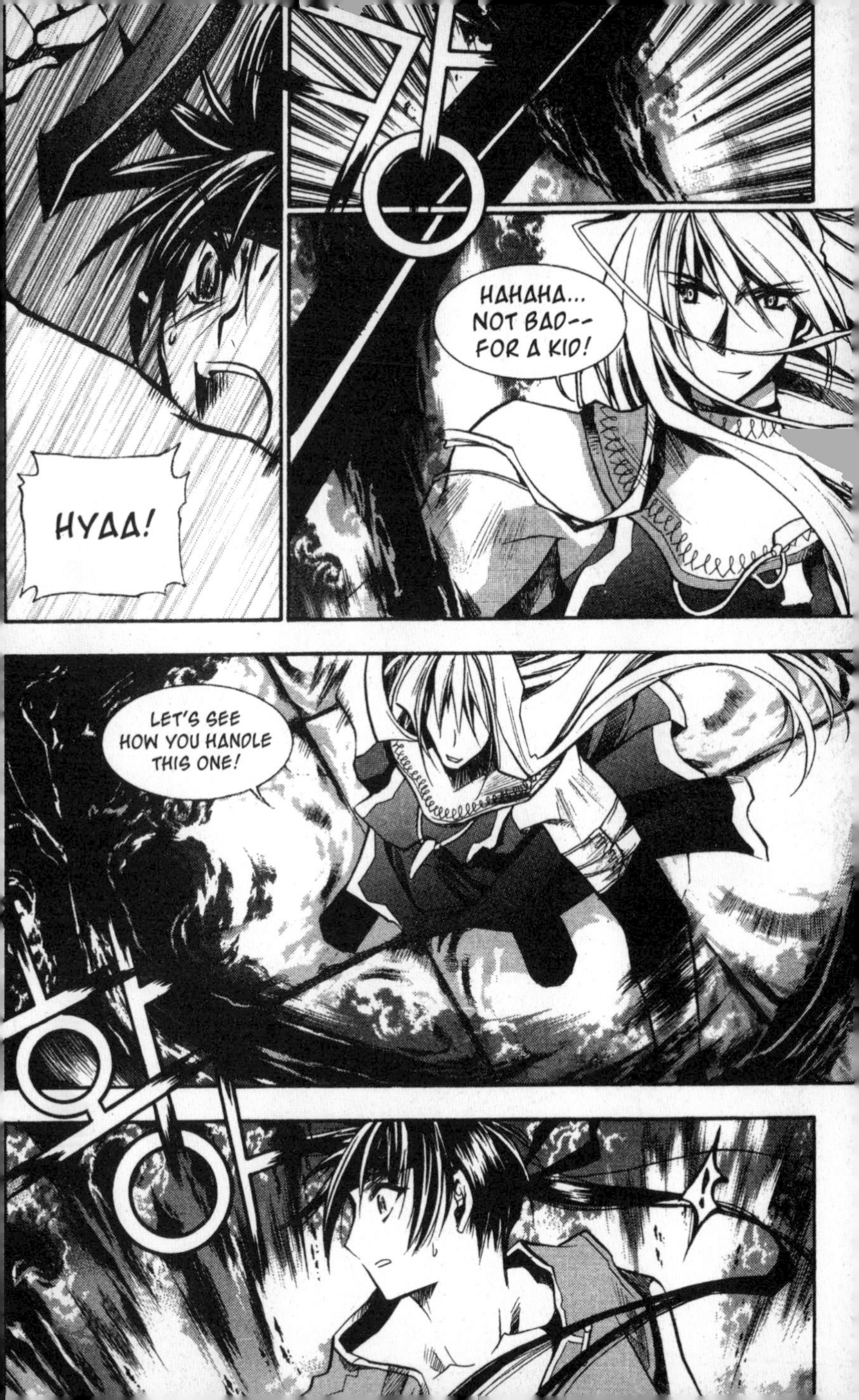
HYAA!
HAHAHA... NOT BAD-- FOR A KID!
LET'S SEE HOW YOU HANDLE THIS ONE!
!

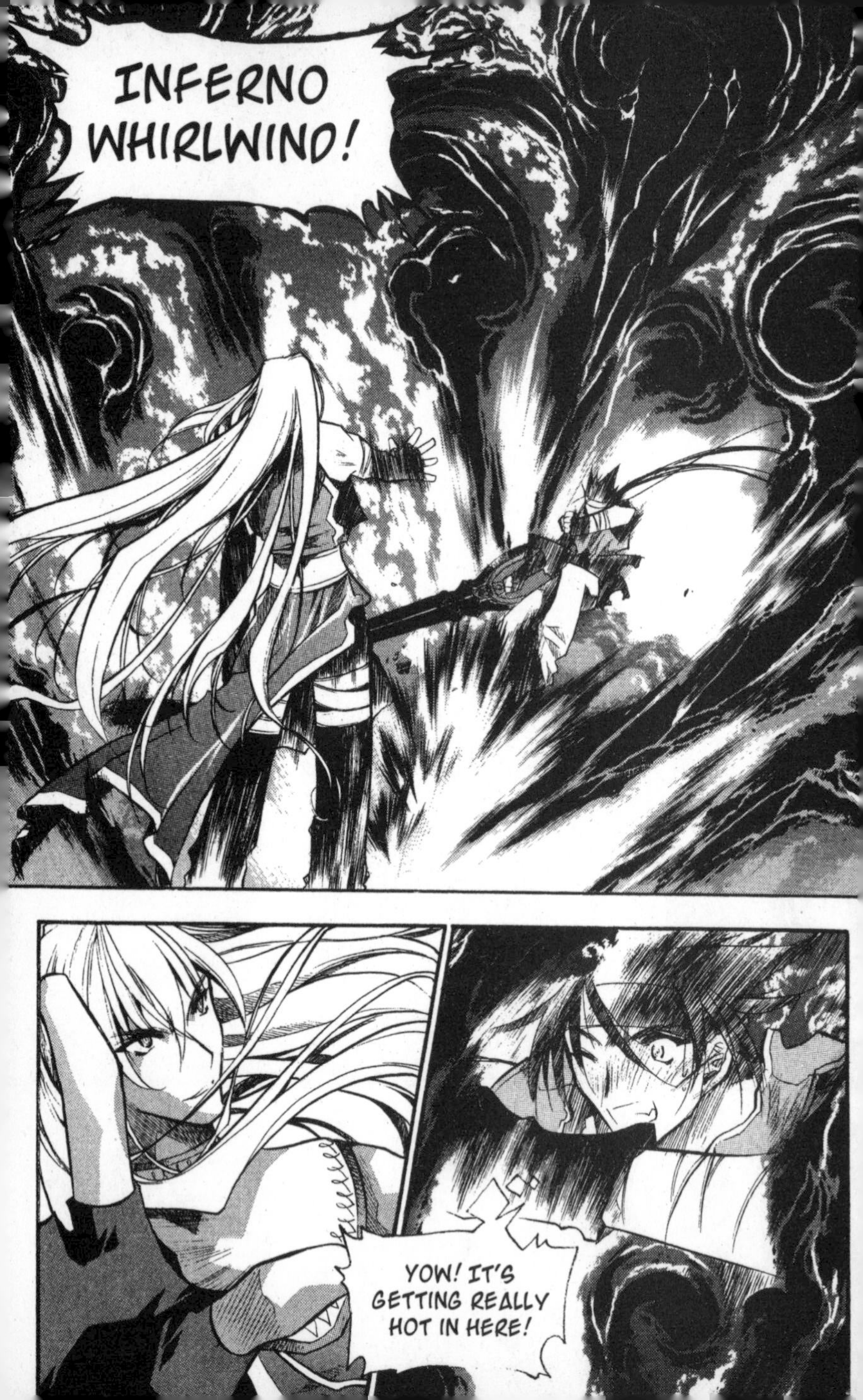
INFERNO WHIRLWIND!
YOW! IT'S GETTING REALLY HOT IN HERE!

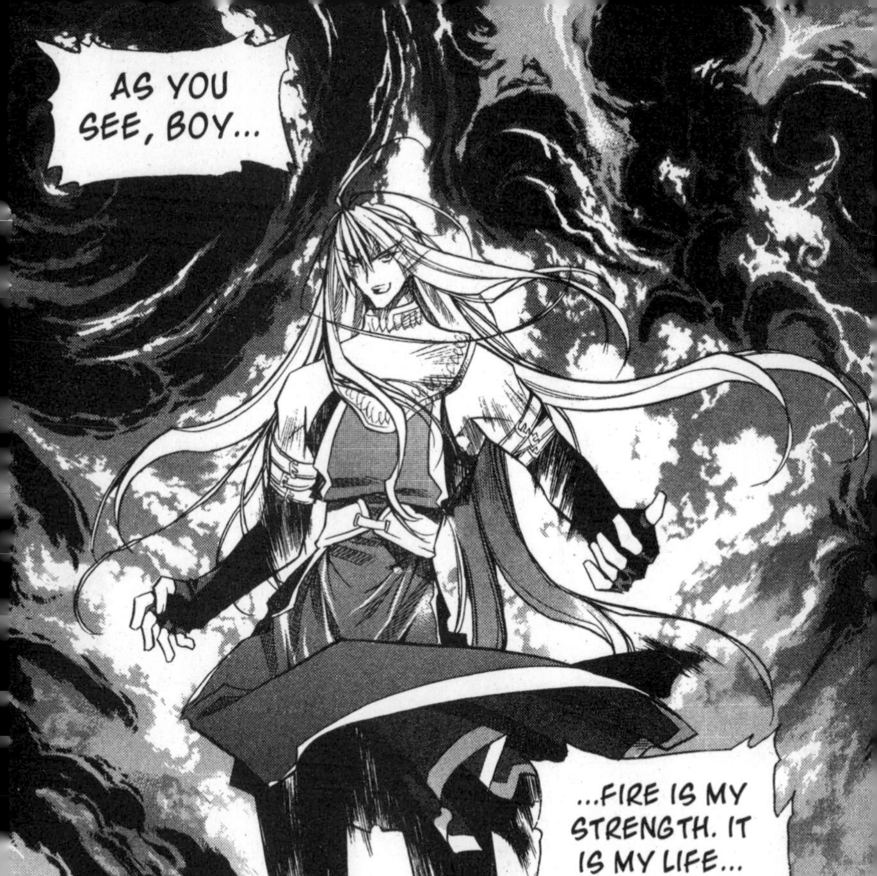
AS YOU SEE, BOY...
...FIRE IS MY STRENGTH. IT IS MY LIFE... MY BLOOD!
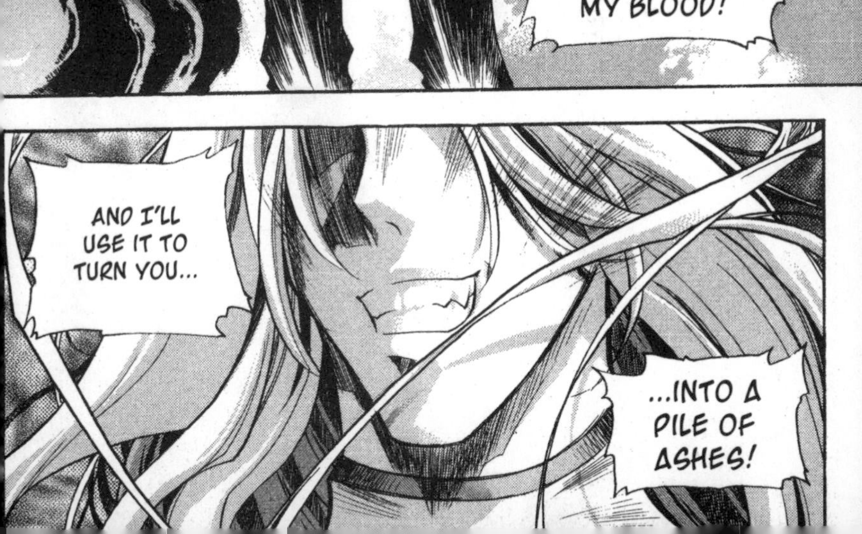
AND I'LL USE IT TO TURN YOU...
...INTO A PILE OF ASHES!

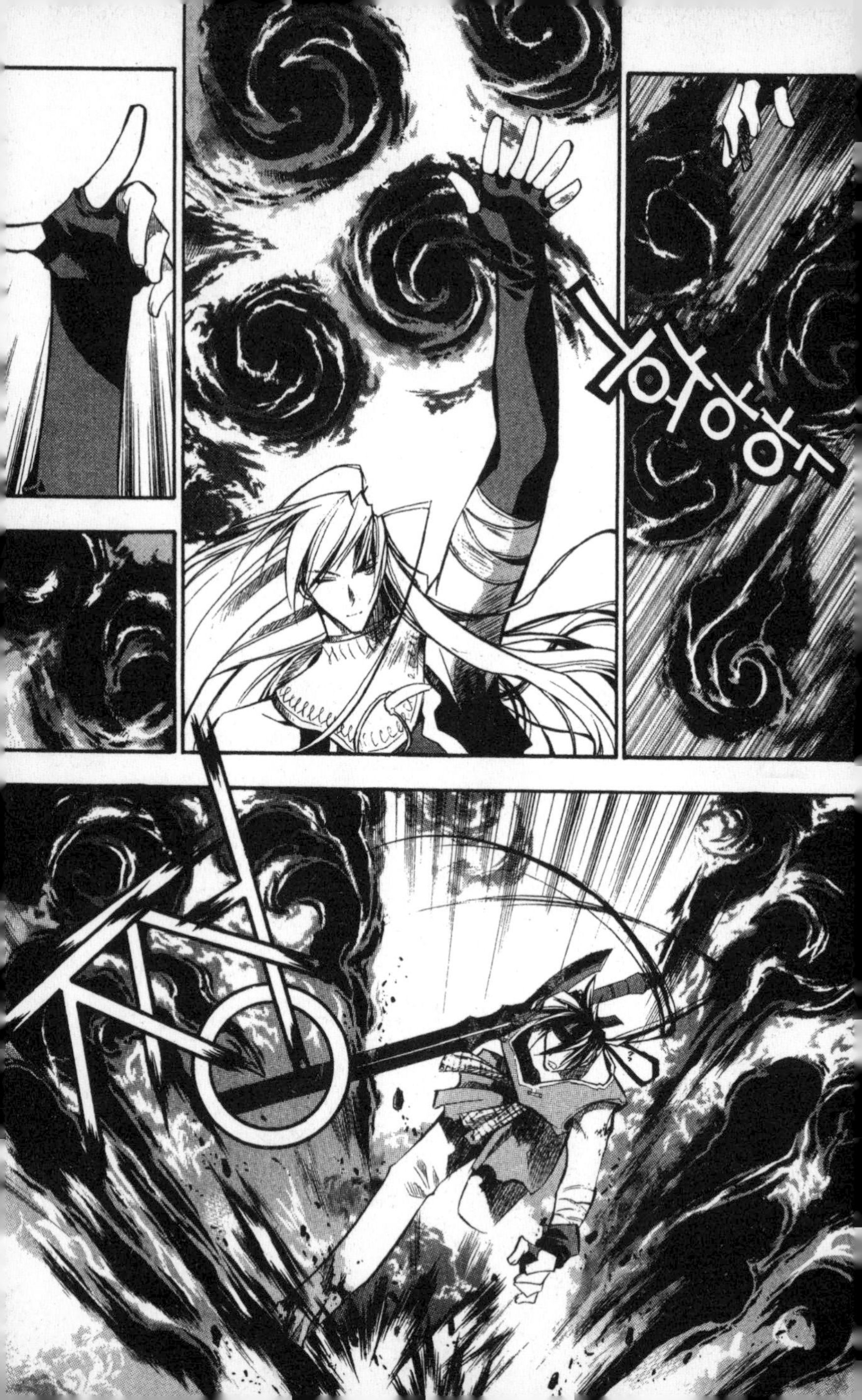

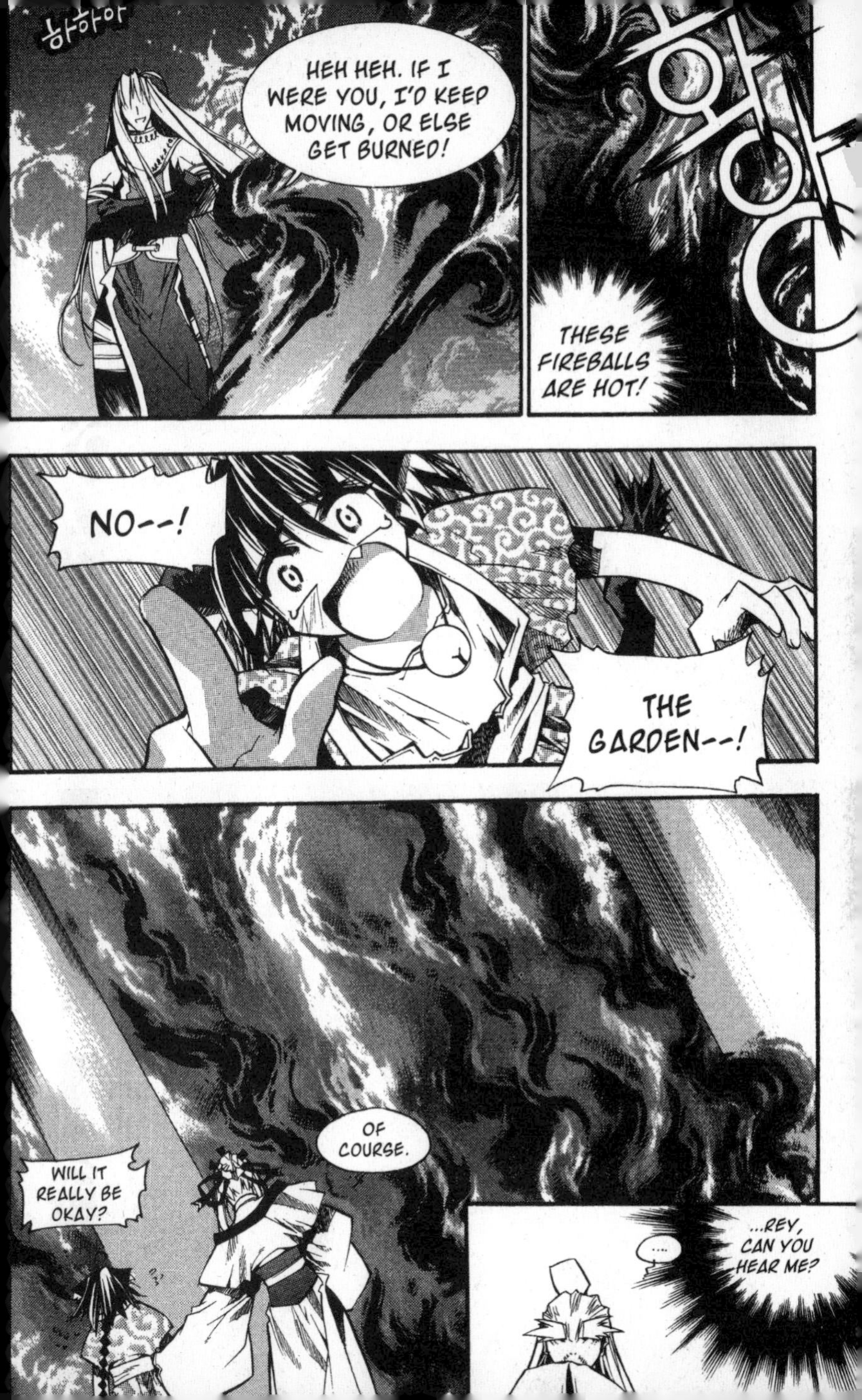
하하아
HEH HEH. IF I WERE YOU, I'D KEEP MOVING, OR ELSE GET BURNED!
THESE FIREBALLS ARE HOT!
NO--!
THE GARDEN--!
WILL IT REALLY BE OKAY?
OF COURSE.
....
...REY, CAN YOU HEAR ME?

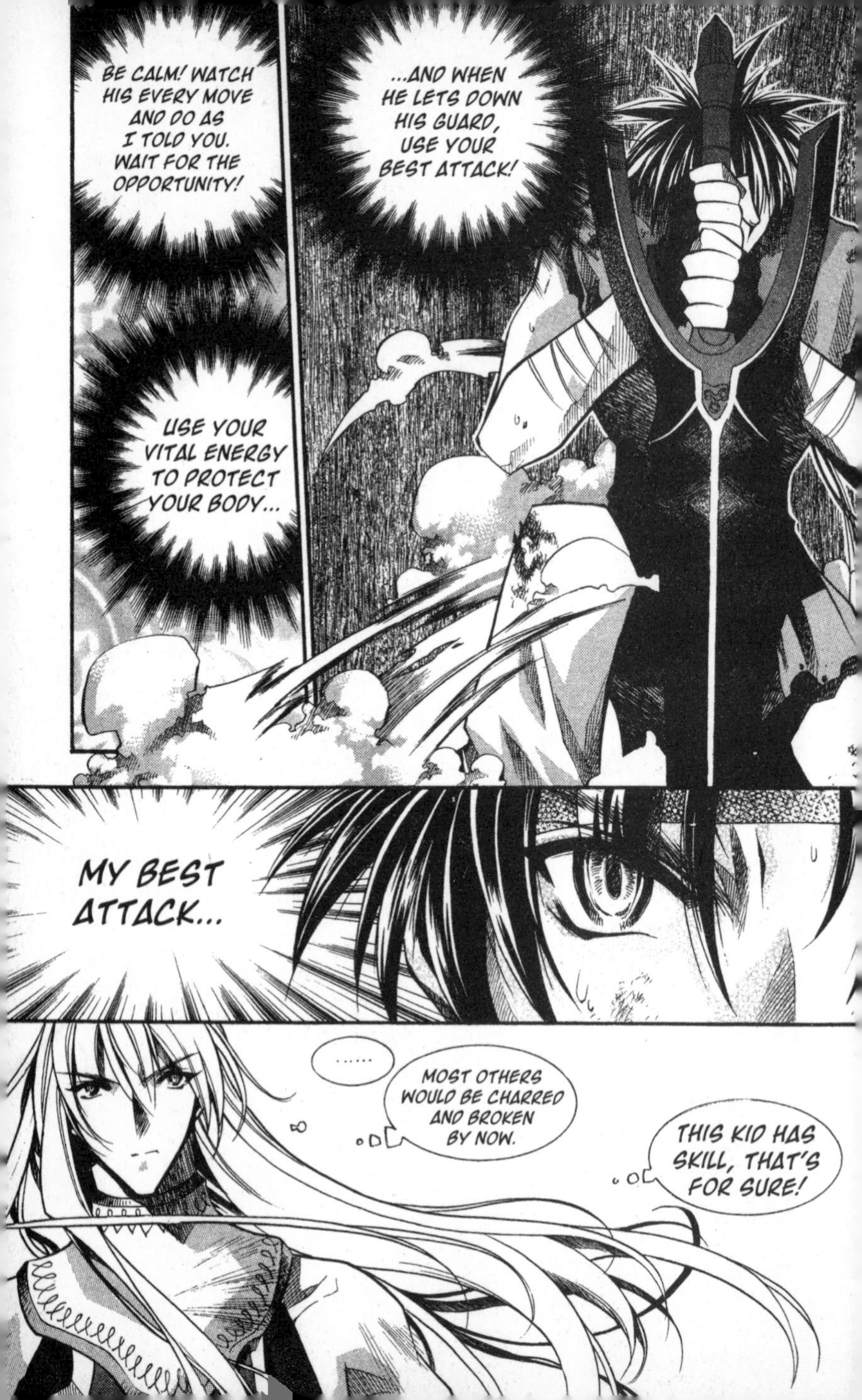
BE CALM! WATCH HIS EVERY MOVE AND DO AS I TOLD YOU. WAIT FOR THE OPPORTUNITY!
...AND WHEN HE LETS DOWN HIS GUARD, USE YOUR BEST ATTACK!
USE YOUR VITAL ENERGY TO PROTECT YOUR BODY...
MY BEST ATTACK...
......
MOST OTHERS WOULD BE CHARRED AND BROKEN BY NOW.
THIS KID HAS SKILL, THAT'S FOR SURE!

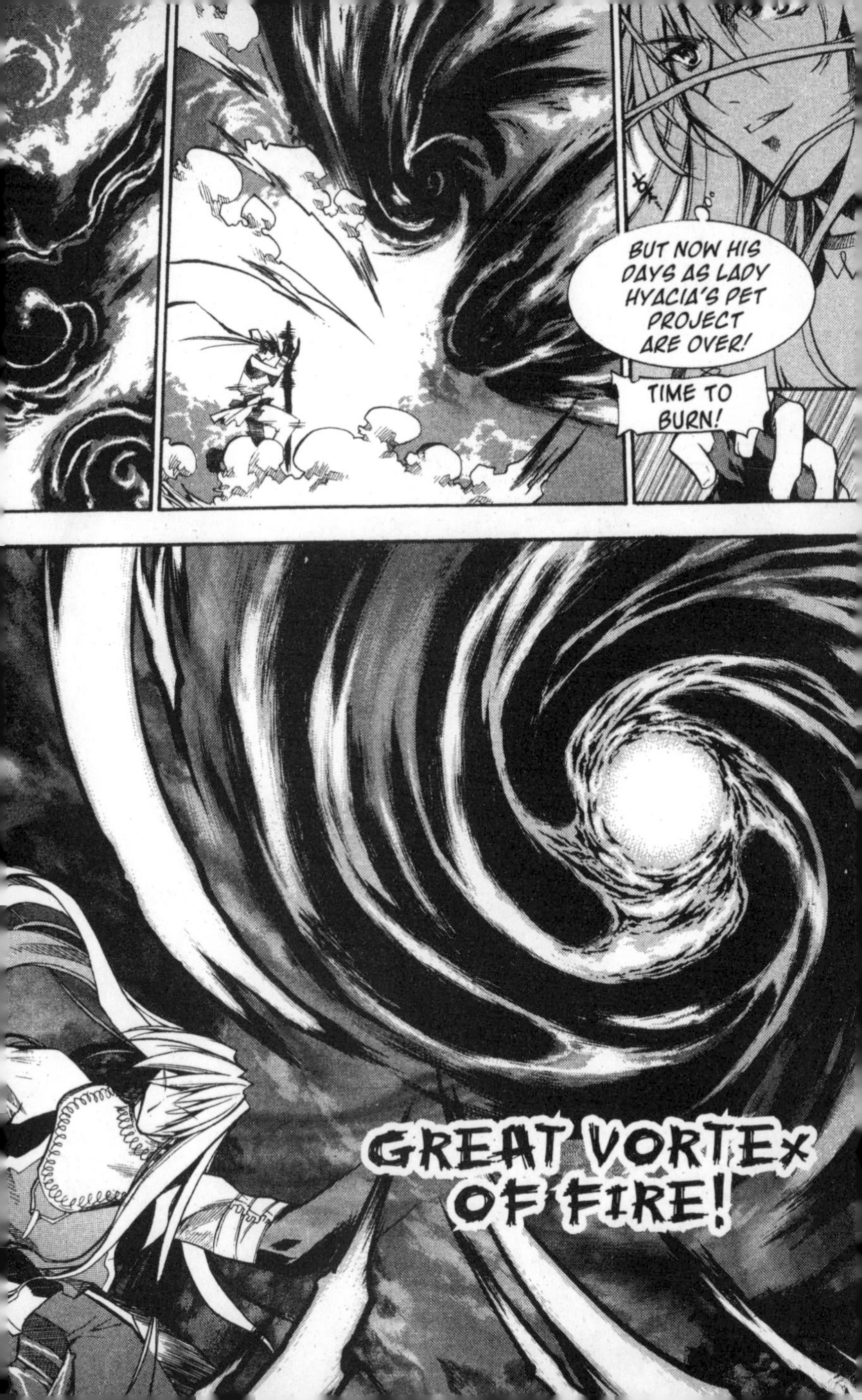
BUT NOW HIS DAYS AS LADY HYACIA'S PET PROJECT ARE OVER!
TIME TO BURN!
GREAT VORTEX OF FIRE!

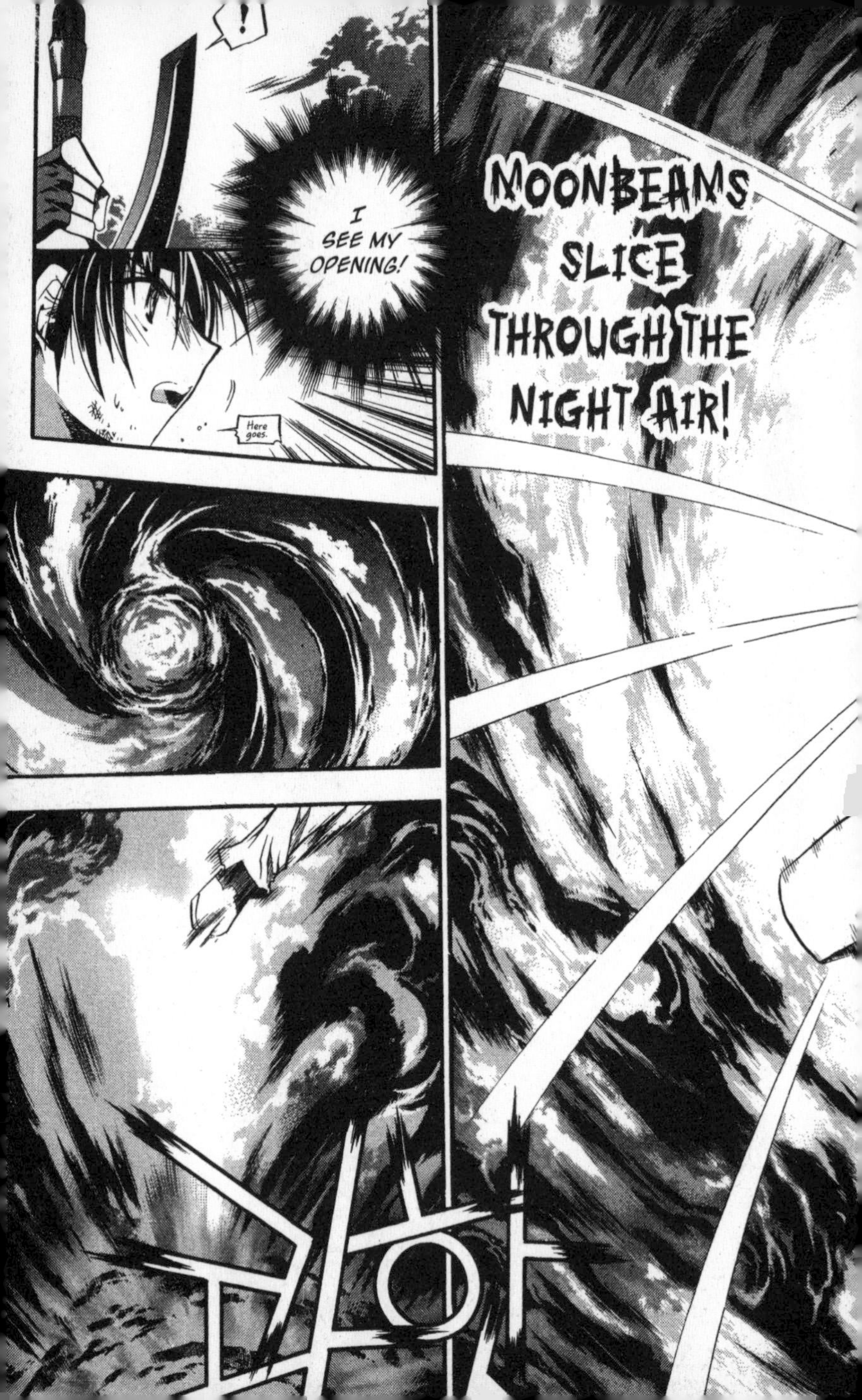
!
I SEE MY OPENING!
Here goes.
MOONBEAMS SLICE THROUGH THE NIGHT AIR!

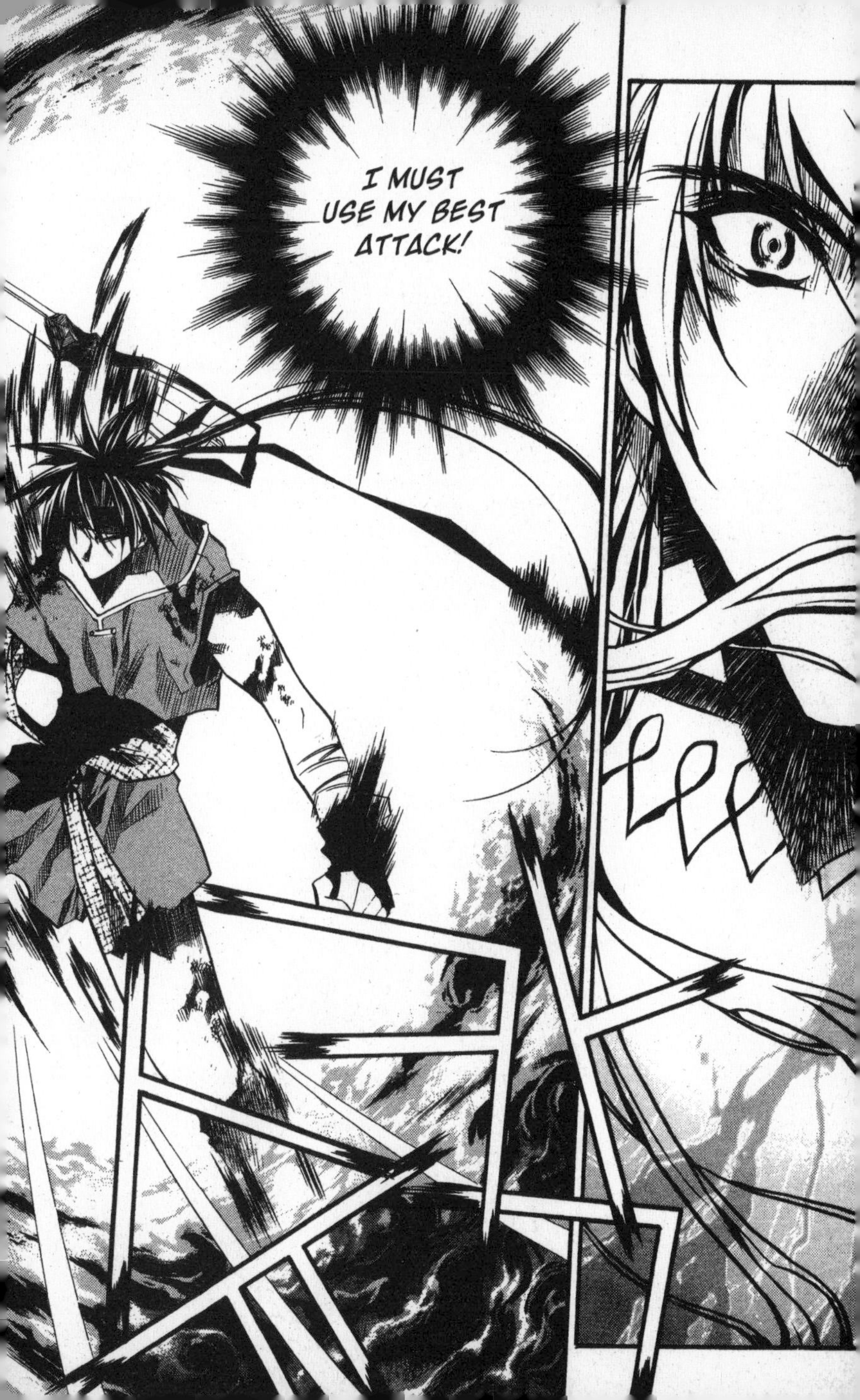
I MUST USE MY BEST ATTACK!

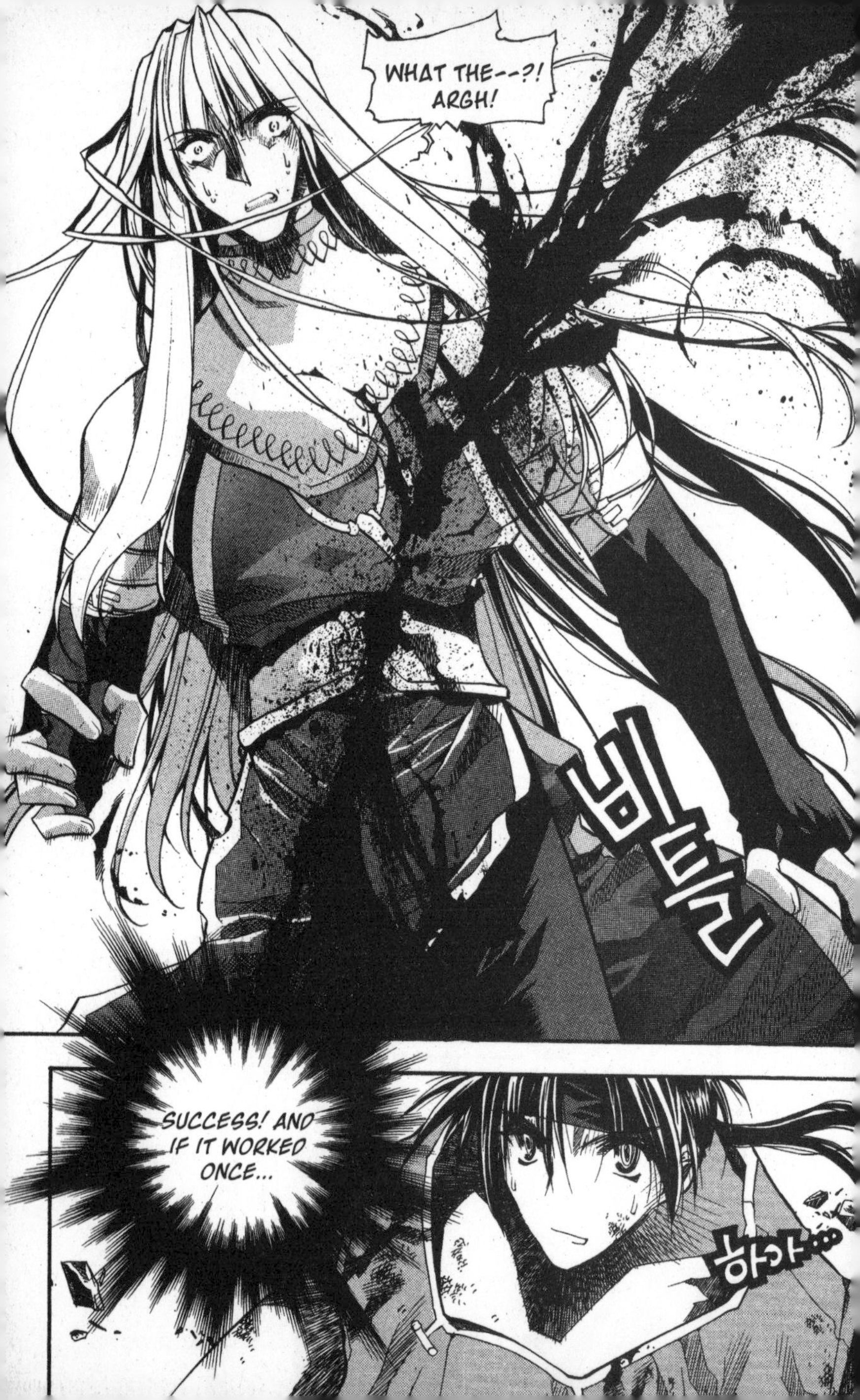
WHAT THE--?! ARGH!
비틀
SUCCESS! AND IF IT WORKED ONCE...

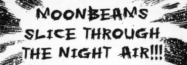

MOONBEAMS
SLICE THROUGH
THE NIGHT AIR!!!

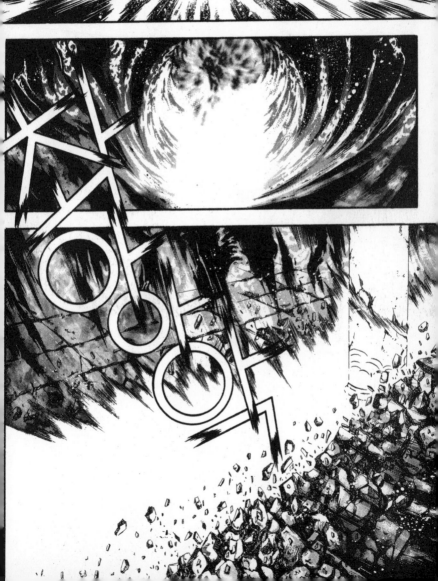

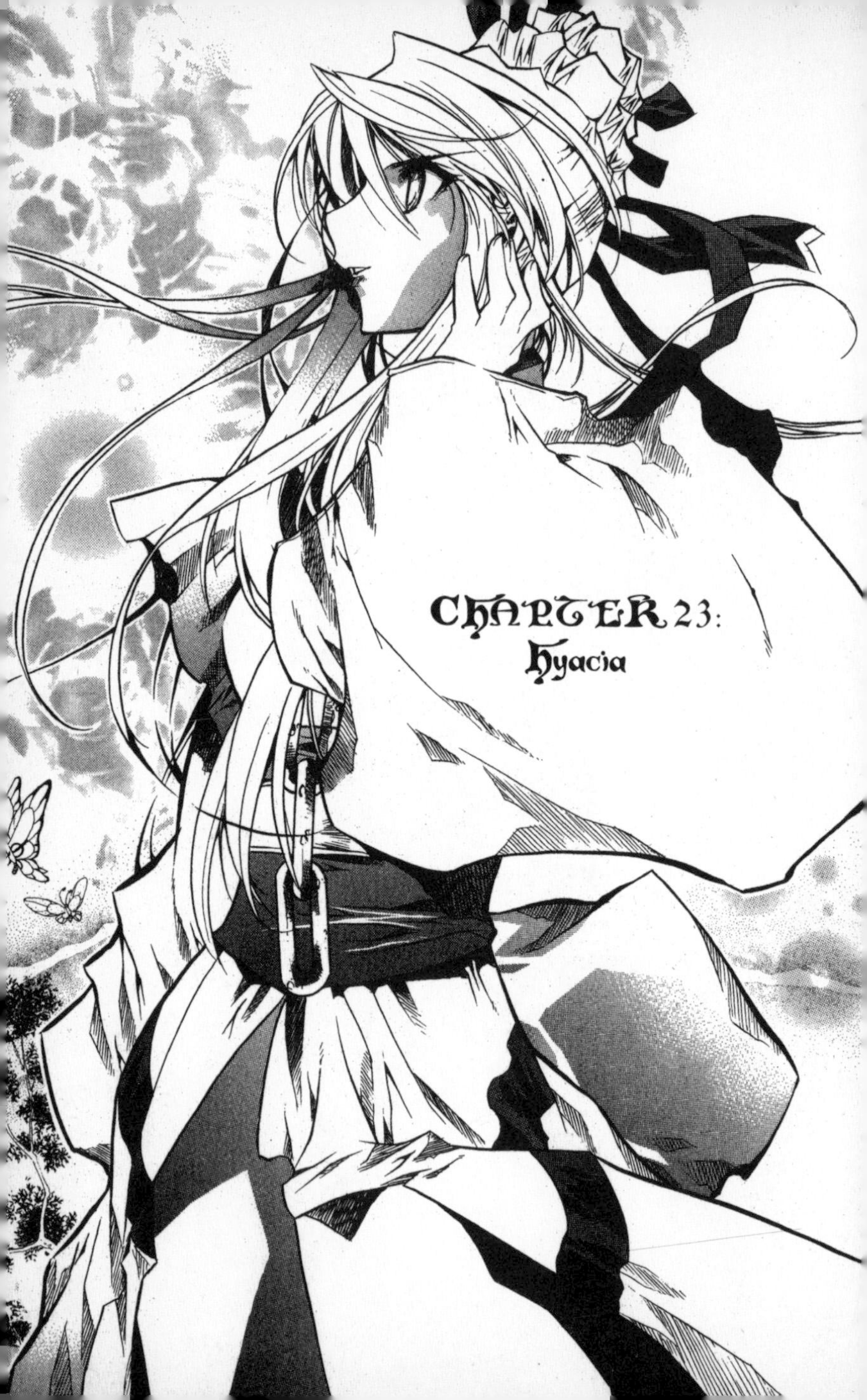
CHAPTER 23:
Hyacia

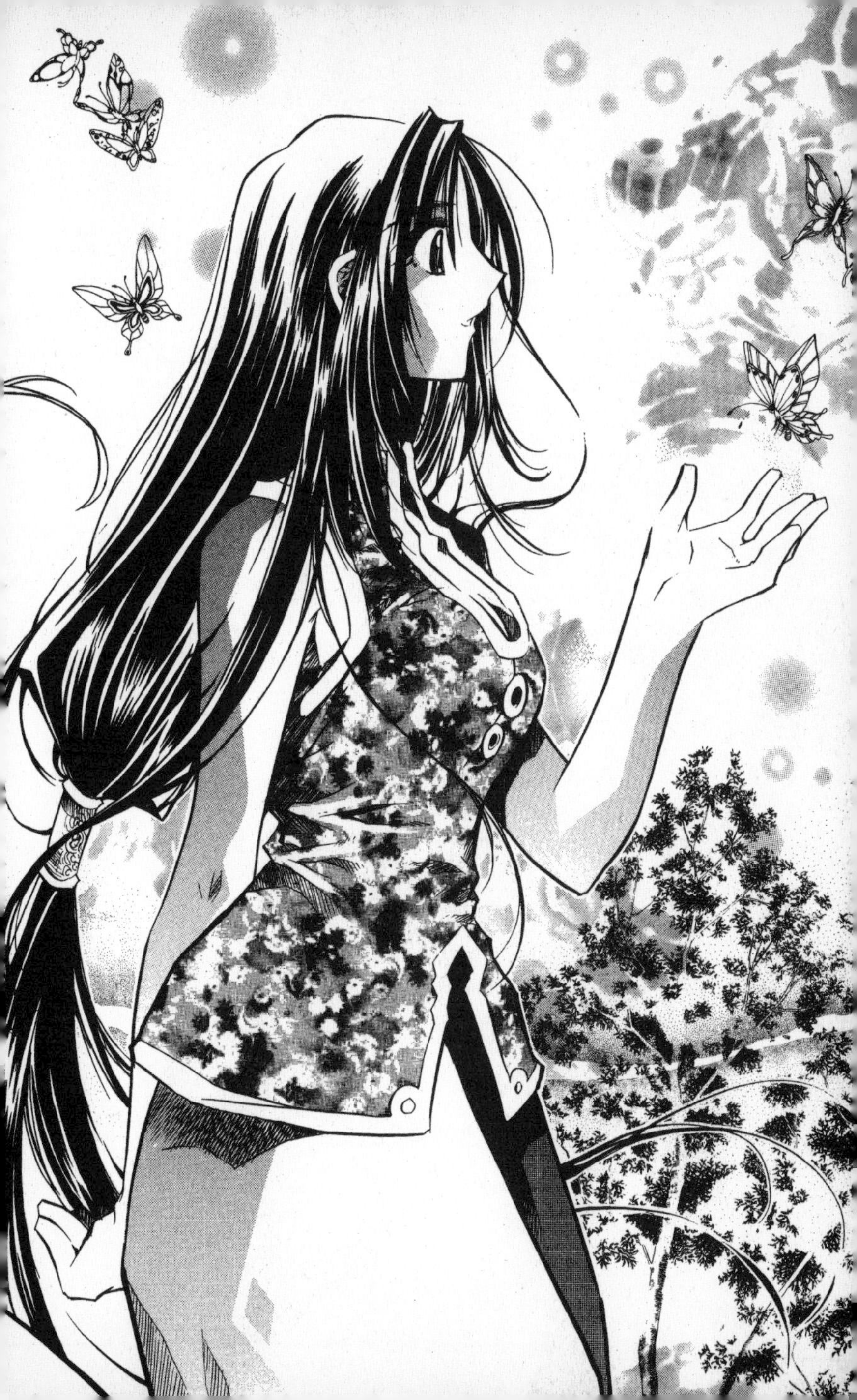

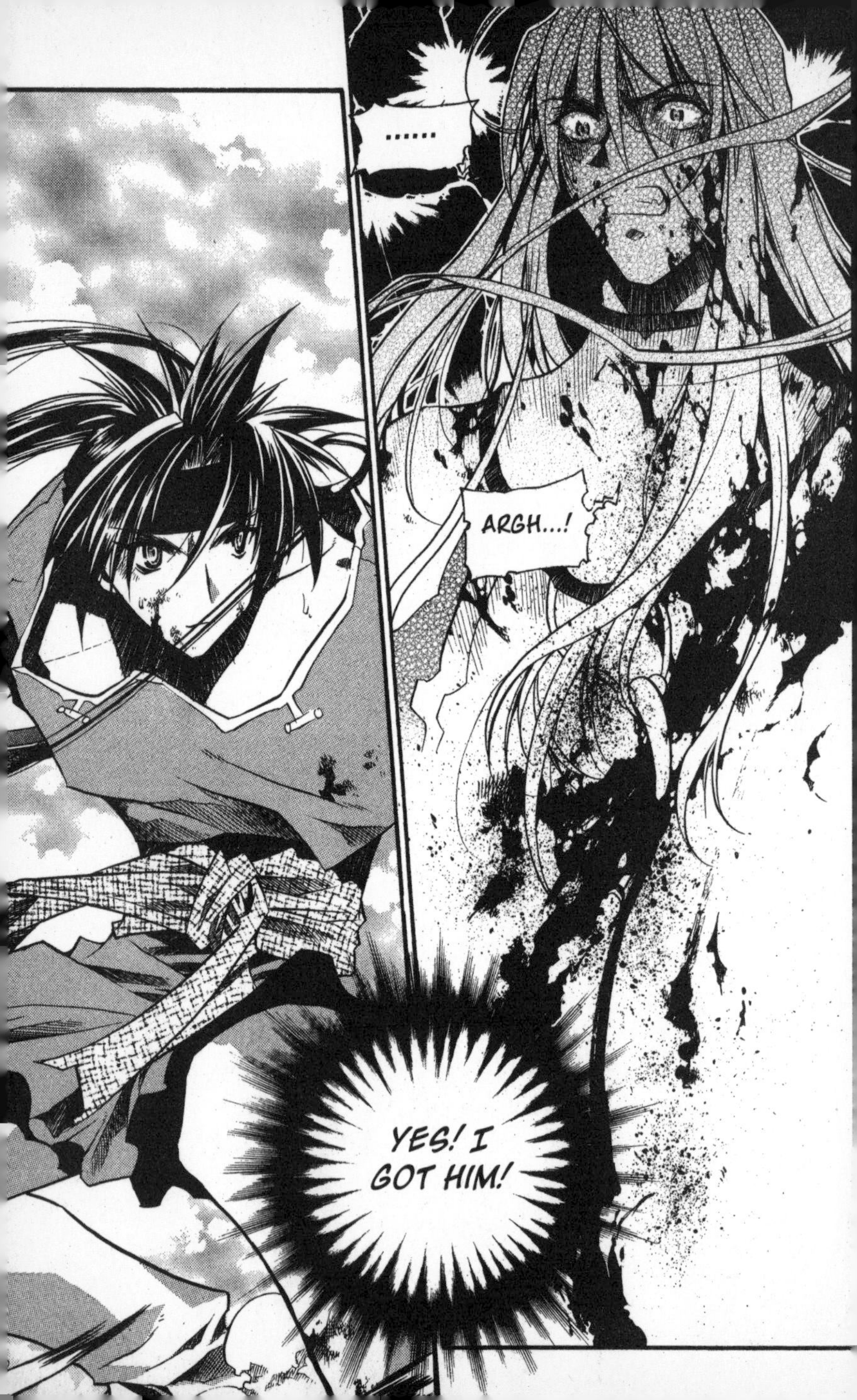
......
ARGH...!
YES! I GOT HIM!

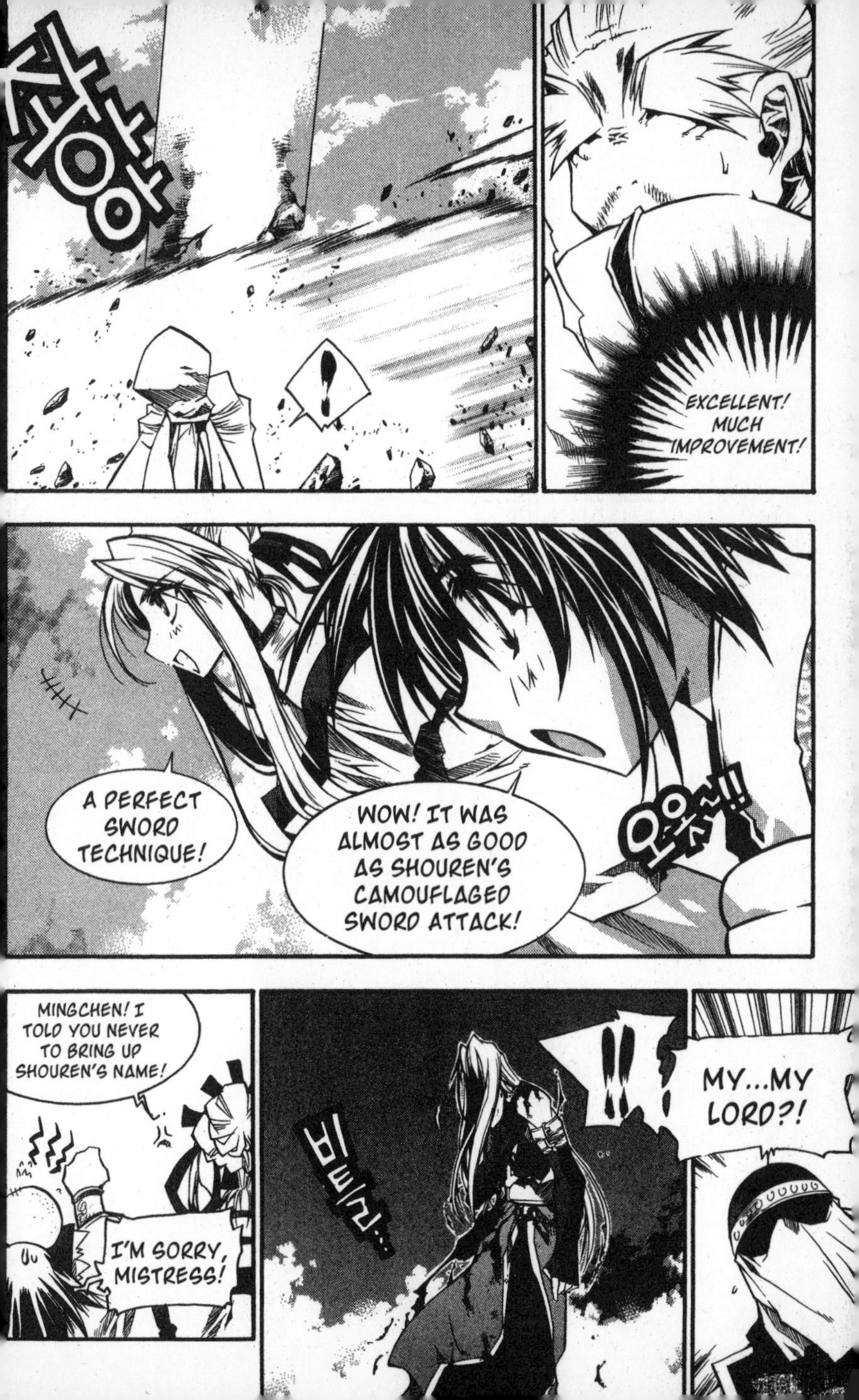
!
EXCELLENT! MUCH IMPROVEMENT!
A PERFECT SWORD TECHNIQUE!
WOW! IT WAS ALMOST AS GOOD AS SHOUREN'S CAMOUFLAGED SWORD ATTACK!
MINGCHEN! I TOLD YOU NEVER TO BRING UP SHOUREN'S NAME!
I'M SORRY, MISTRESS!
!!
MY...MY LORD?!

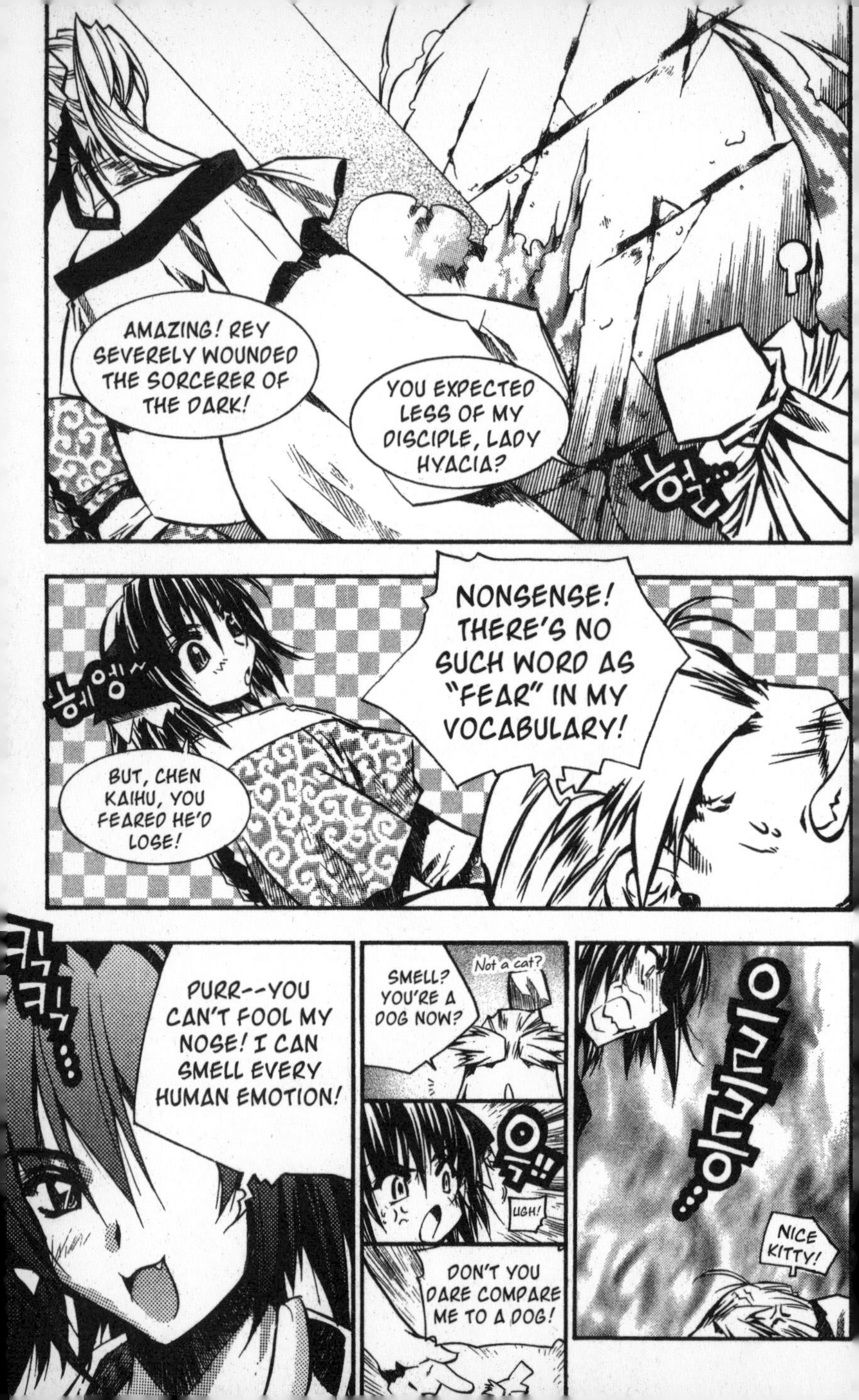
AMAZING! REY SEVERELY WOUNDED THE SORCERER OF THE DARK!
YOU EXPECTED LESS OF MY DISCIPLE, LADY HYACIA?
BUT, CHEN KAIHU, YOU FEARED HE'D LOSE!
NONSENSE! THERE'S NO SUCH WORD AS "FEAR" IN MY VOCABULARY!
PURR--YOU CAN'T FOOL MY NOSE! I CAN SMELL EVERY HUMAN EMOTION!
SMELL? YOU'RE A DOG NOW?
Not a cat?
UGH!
DON'T YOU DARE COMPARE ME TO A DOG!
NICE KITTY!

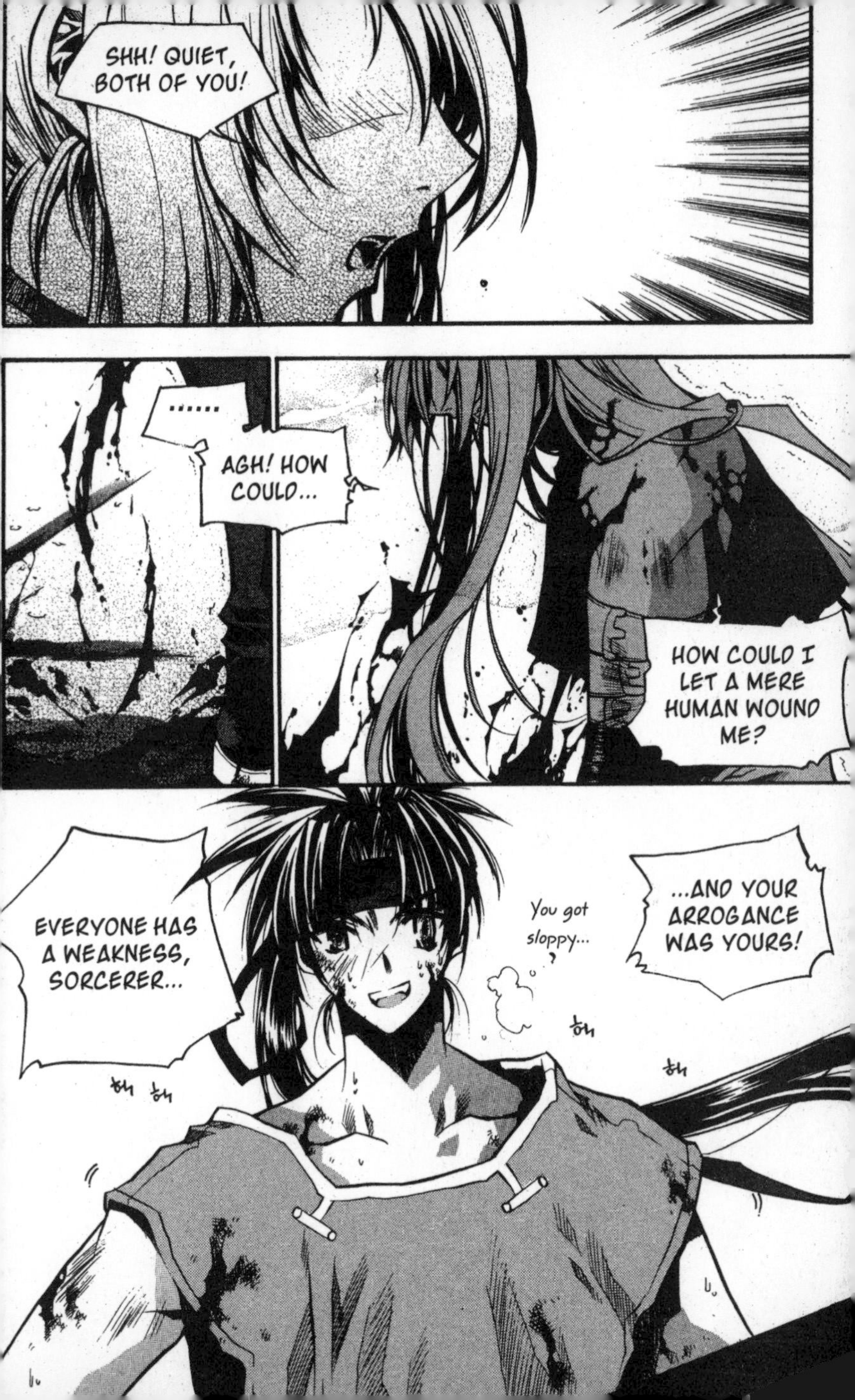
SHH! QUIET, BOTH OF YOU!
......
AGH! HOW COULD...
HOW COULD I LET A MERE HUMAN WOUND ME?
EVERYONE HAS A WEAKNESS, SORCERER...
You got sloppy...
...AND YOUR ARROGANCE WAS YOURS!

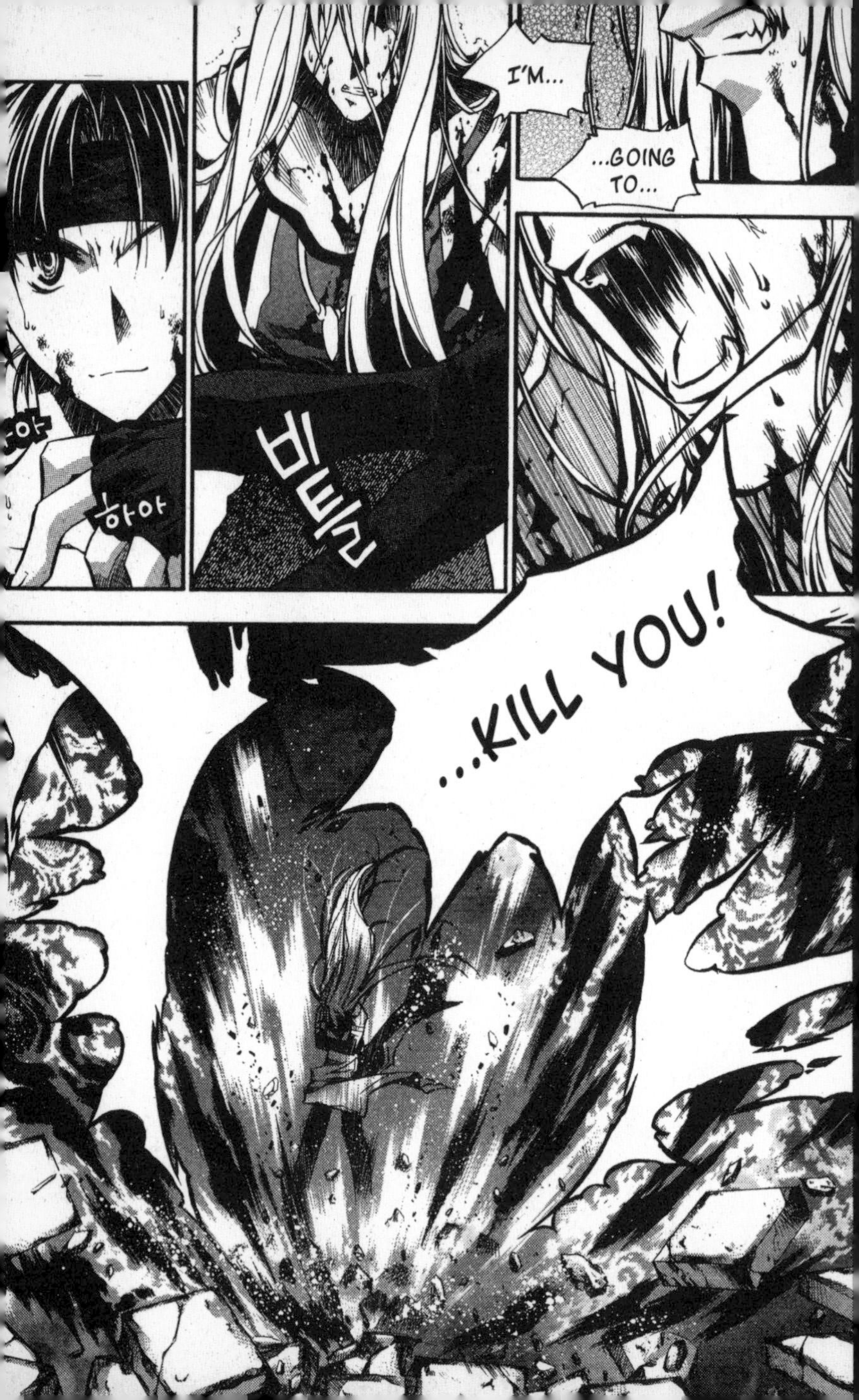
하아
비틀
I'M...
...GOING TO...
...KILL YOU!

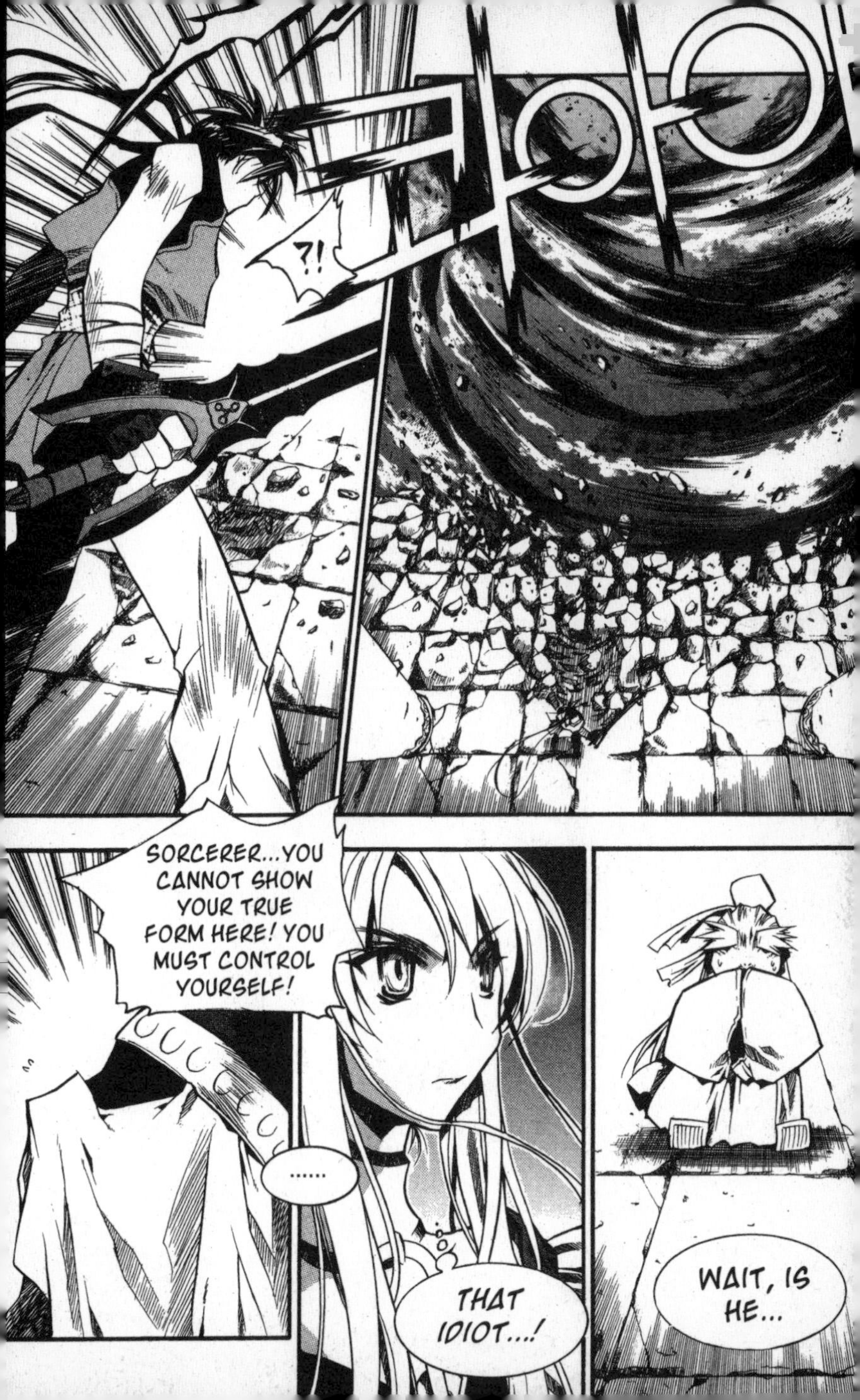
?!
SORCERER...YOU CANNOT SHOW YOUR TRUE FORM HERE! YOU MUST CONTROL YOURSELF!
......
THAT IDIOT...!
WAIT, IS HE...

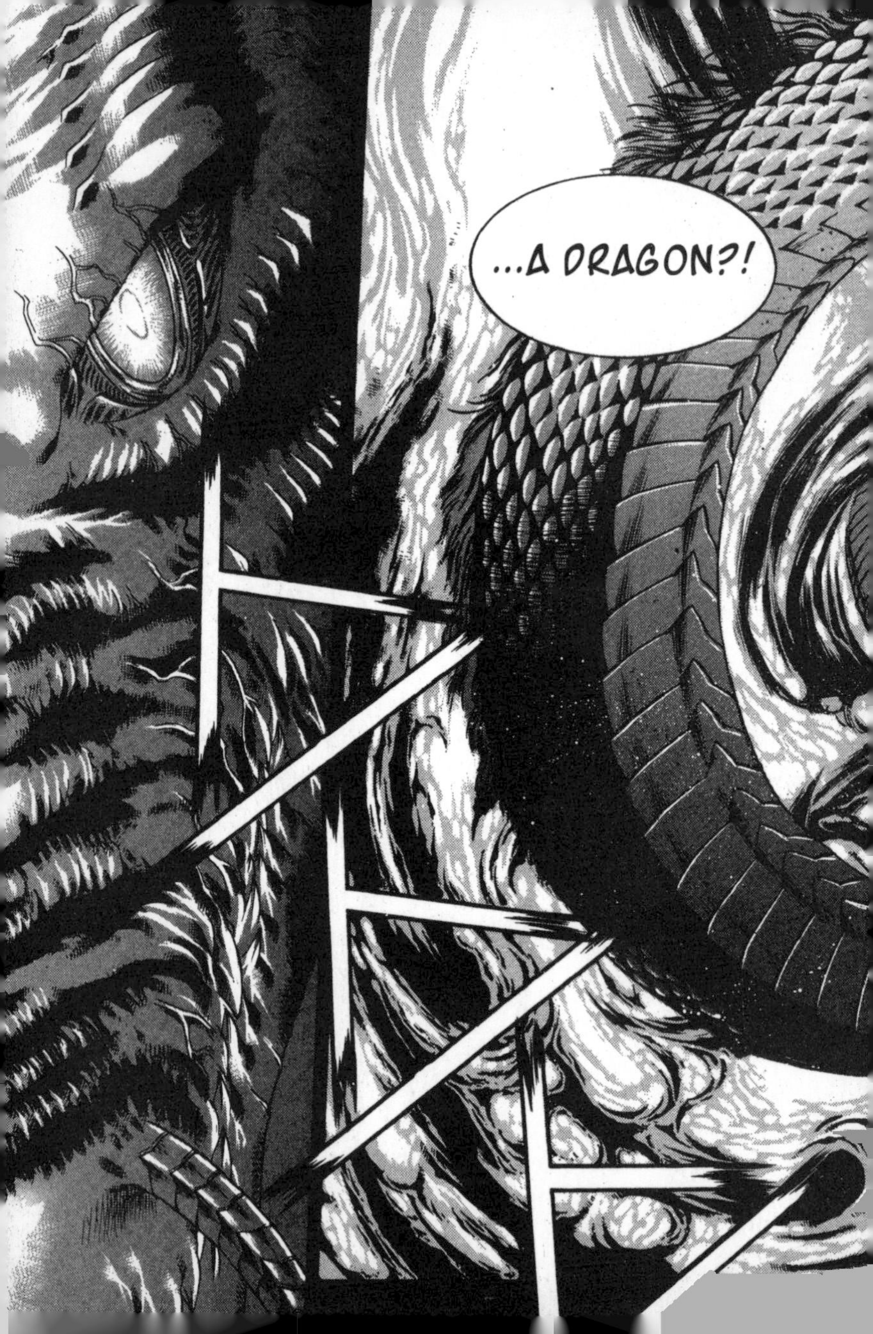
...A DRAGON?!

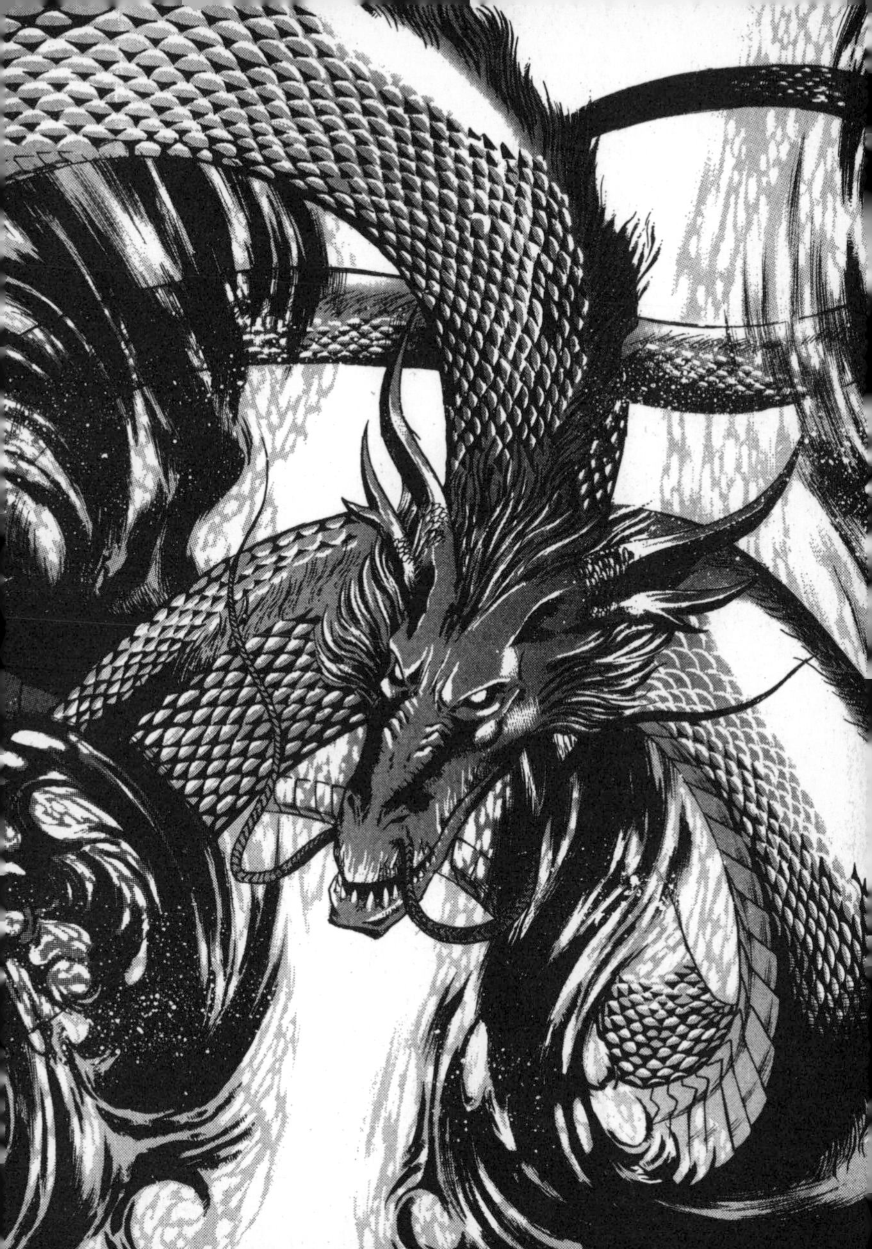

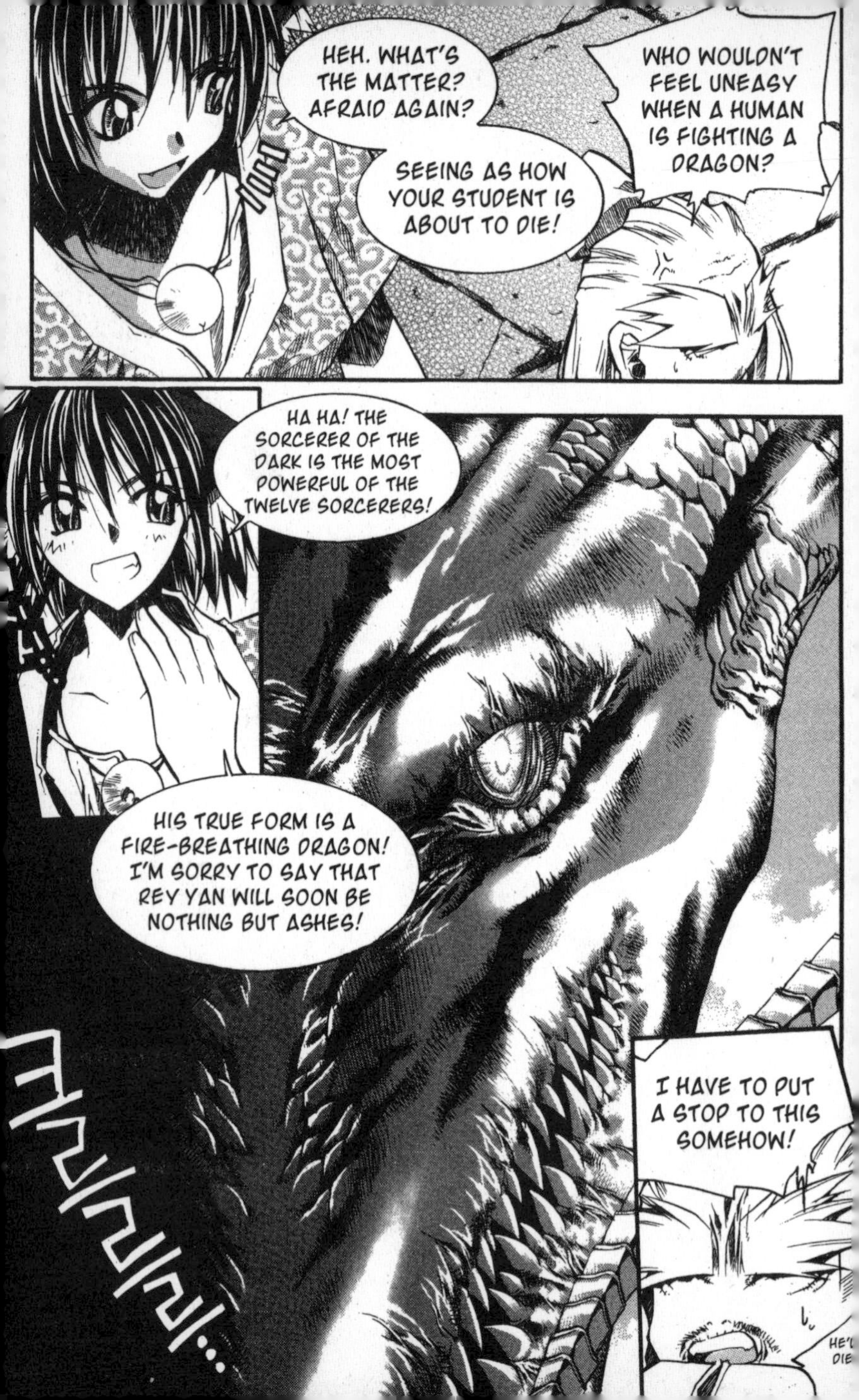
HEH. WHAT'S THE MATTER? AFRAID AGAIN?
SEEING AS HOW YOUR STUDENT IS ABOUT TO DIE!
WHO WOULDN'T FEEL UNEASY WHEN A HUMAN IS FIGHTING A DRAGON?
HA HA! THE SORCERER OF THE DARK IS THE MOST POWERFUL OF THE TWELVE SORCERERS!
HIS TRUE FORM IS A FIRE-BREATHING DRAGON! I'M SORRY TO SAY THAT REY YAN WILL SOON BE NOTHING BUT ASHES!
I HAVE TO PUT A STOP TO THIS SOMEHOW!

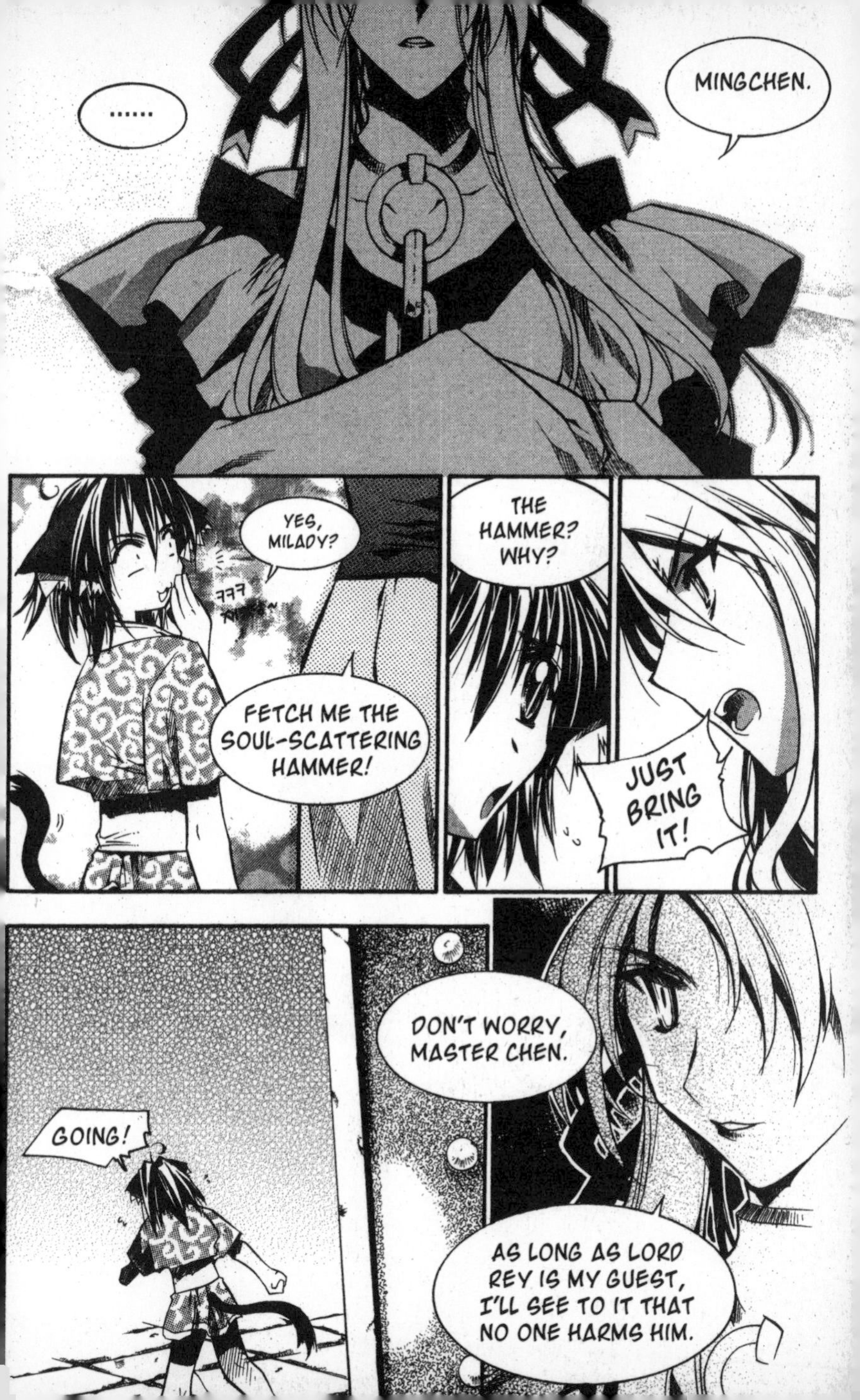
......
MINGCHEN.
YES, MILADY?
FETCH ME THE SOUL-SCATTERING HAMMER!
THE HAMMER? WHY?
JUST BRING IT!
GOING!
DON'T WORRY, MASTER CHEN.
AS LONG AS LORD REY IS MY GUEST, I'LL SEE TO IT THAT NO ONE HARMS HIM.

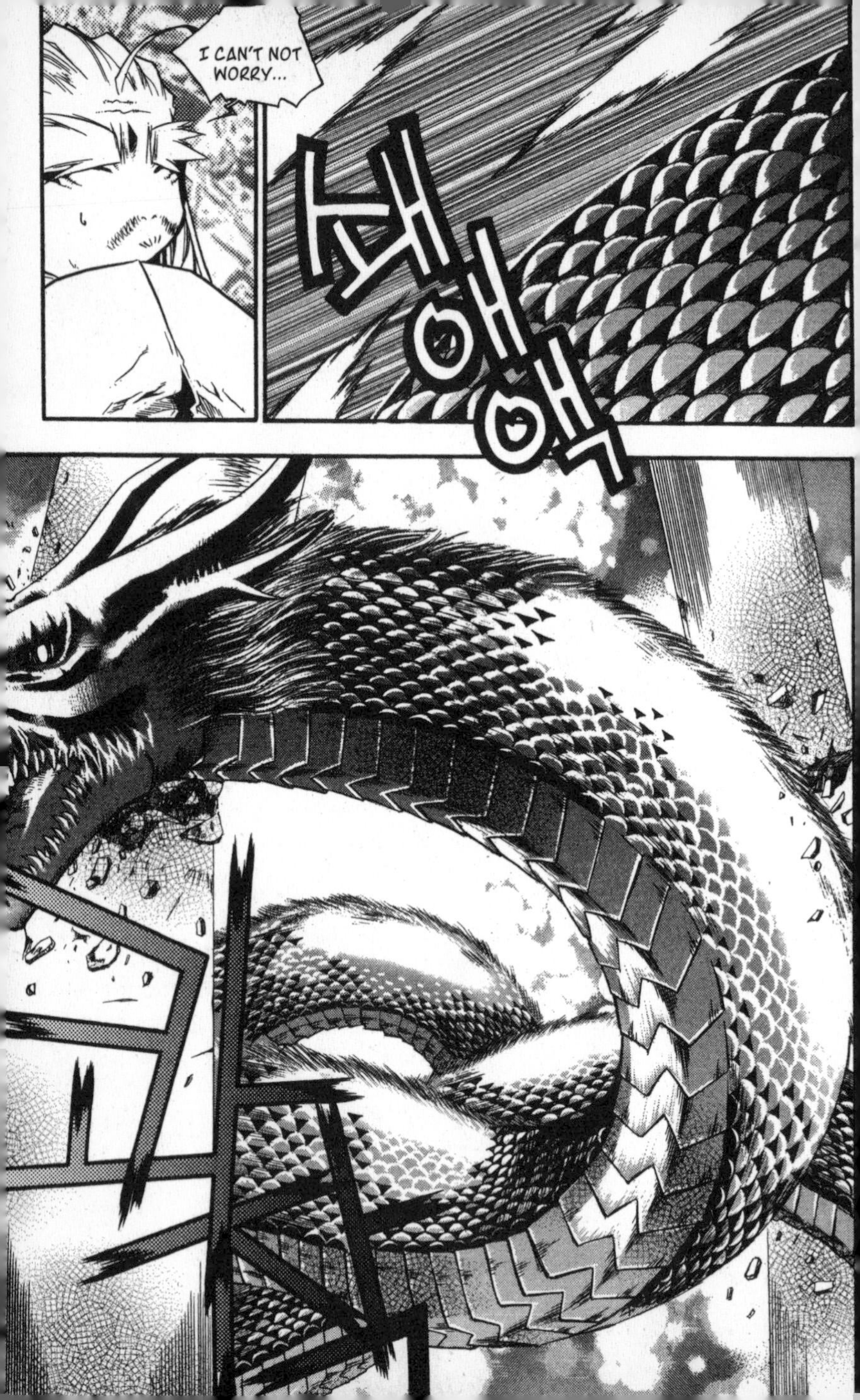
I CAN'T NOT WORRY...

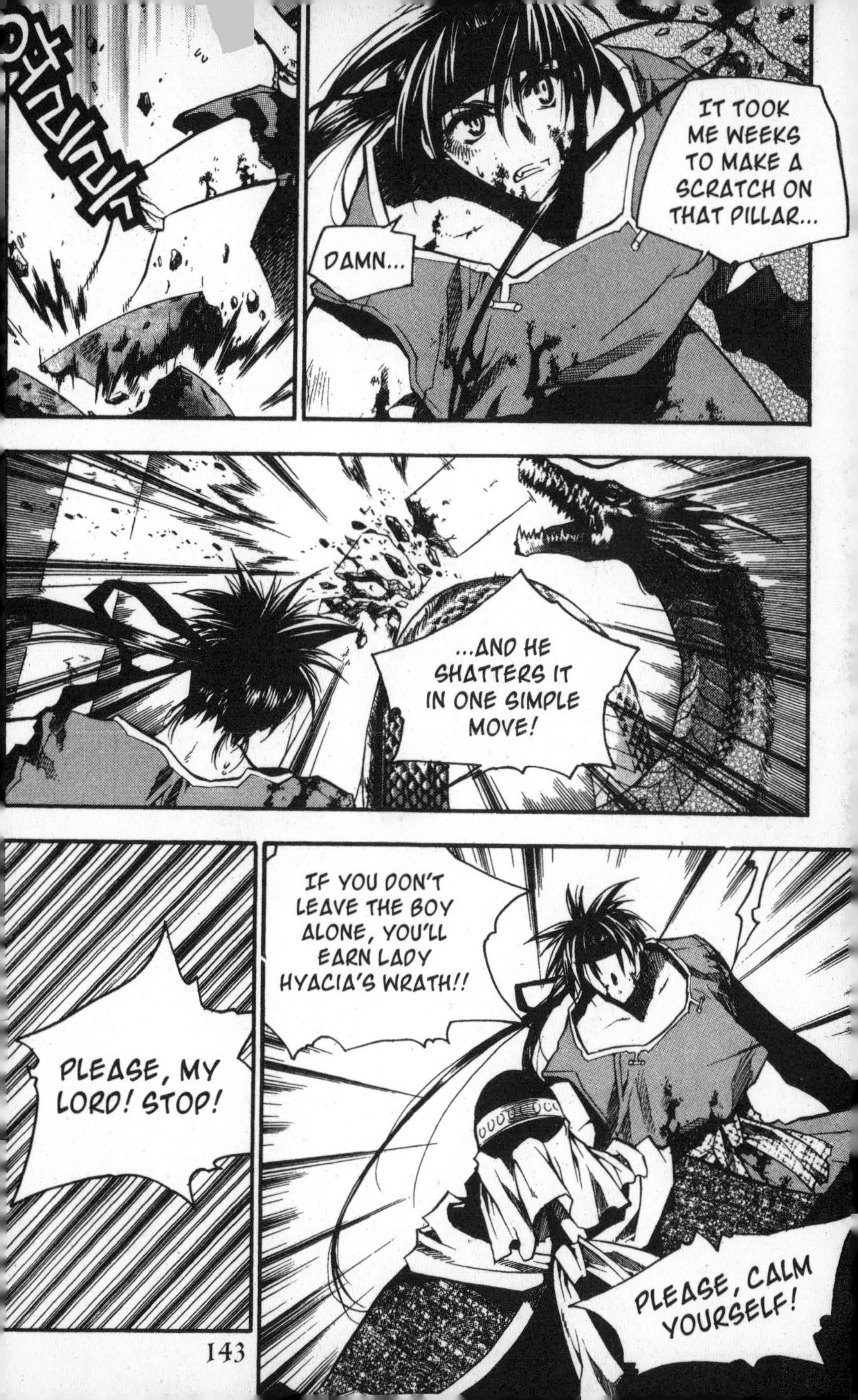
DAMN...
IT TOOK ME WEEKS TO MAKE A SCRATCH ON THAT PILLAR...
...AND HE SHATTERS IT IN ONE SIMPLE MOVE!
PLEASE, MY LORD! STOP!
IF YOU DON'T LEAVE THE BOY ALONE, YOU'LL EARN LADY HYACIA'S WRATH!!
PLEASE, CALM YOURSELF!

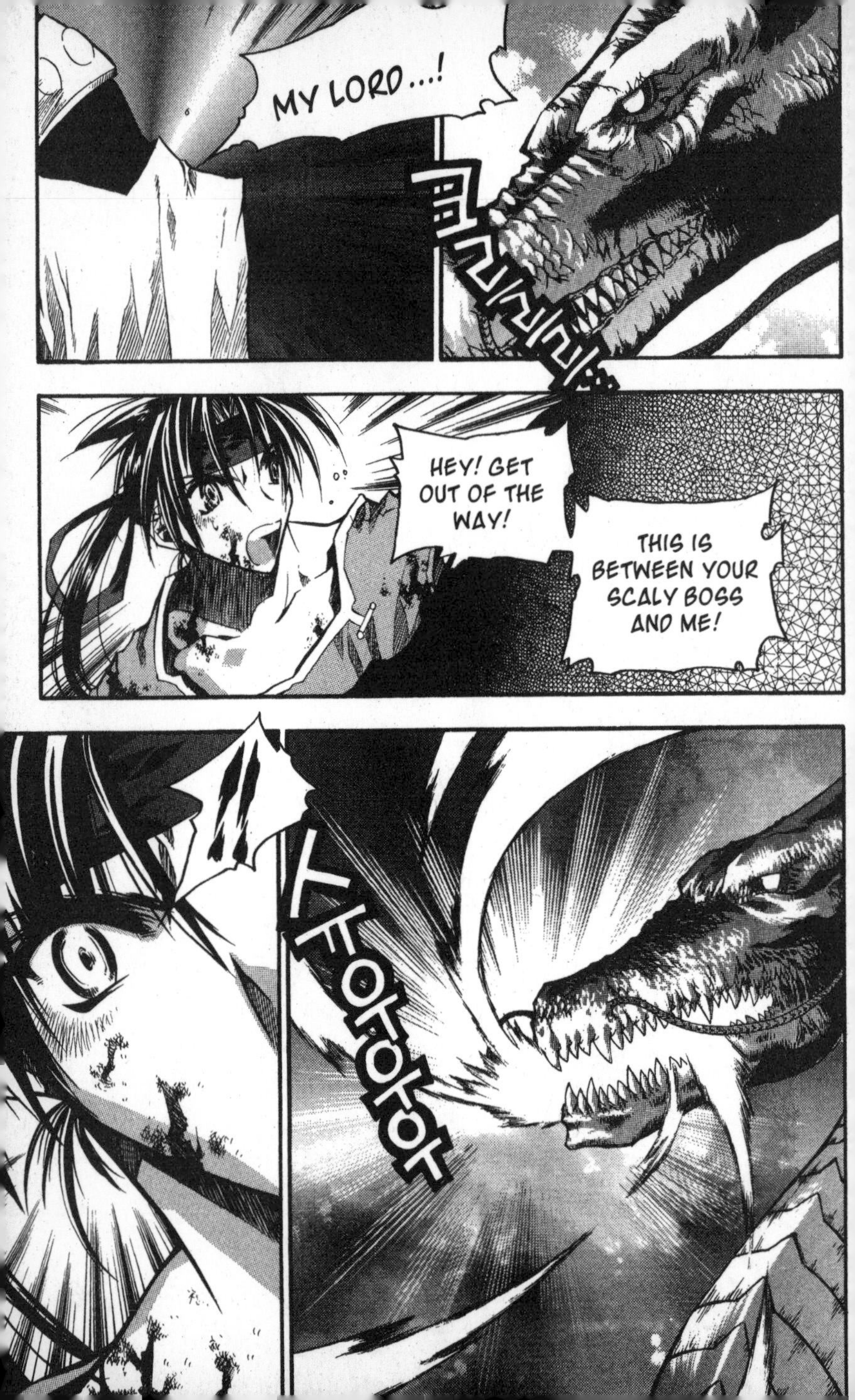
MY LORD...!
HEY! GET OUT OF THE WAY!
THIS IS BETWEEN YOUR SCALY BOSS AND ME!

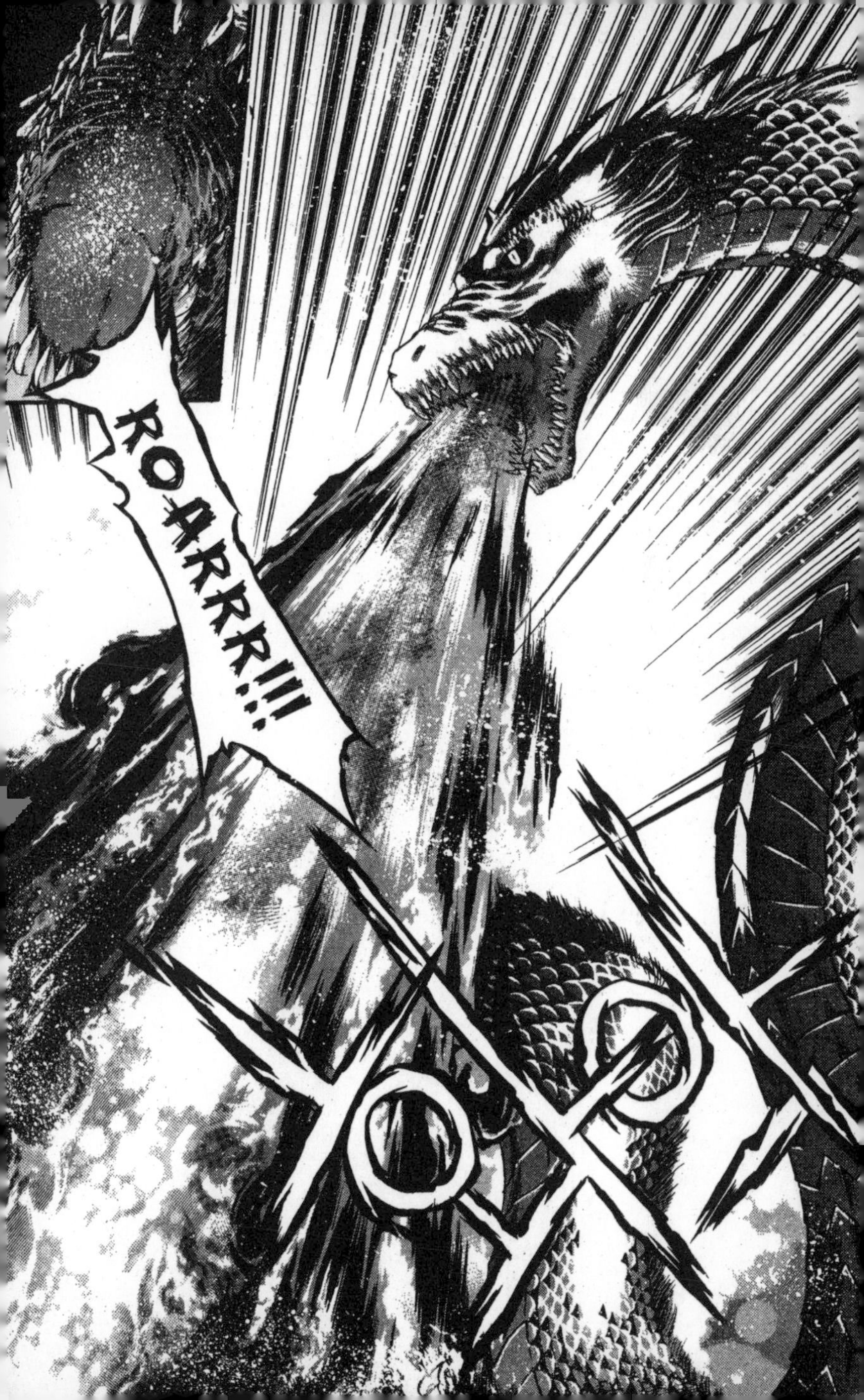
ROARRRR!!!!

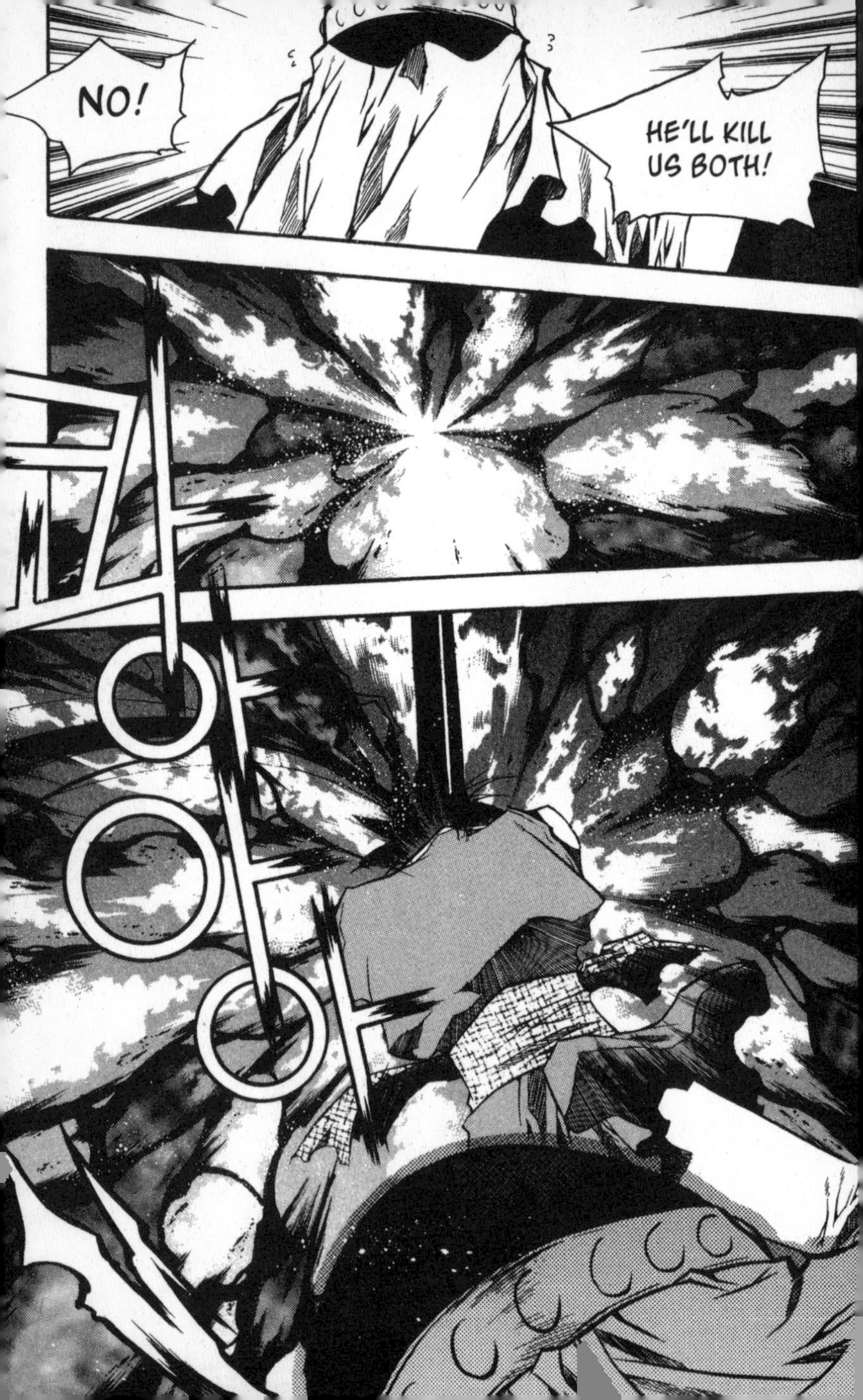
NO!
HE'LL KILL US BOTH!

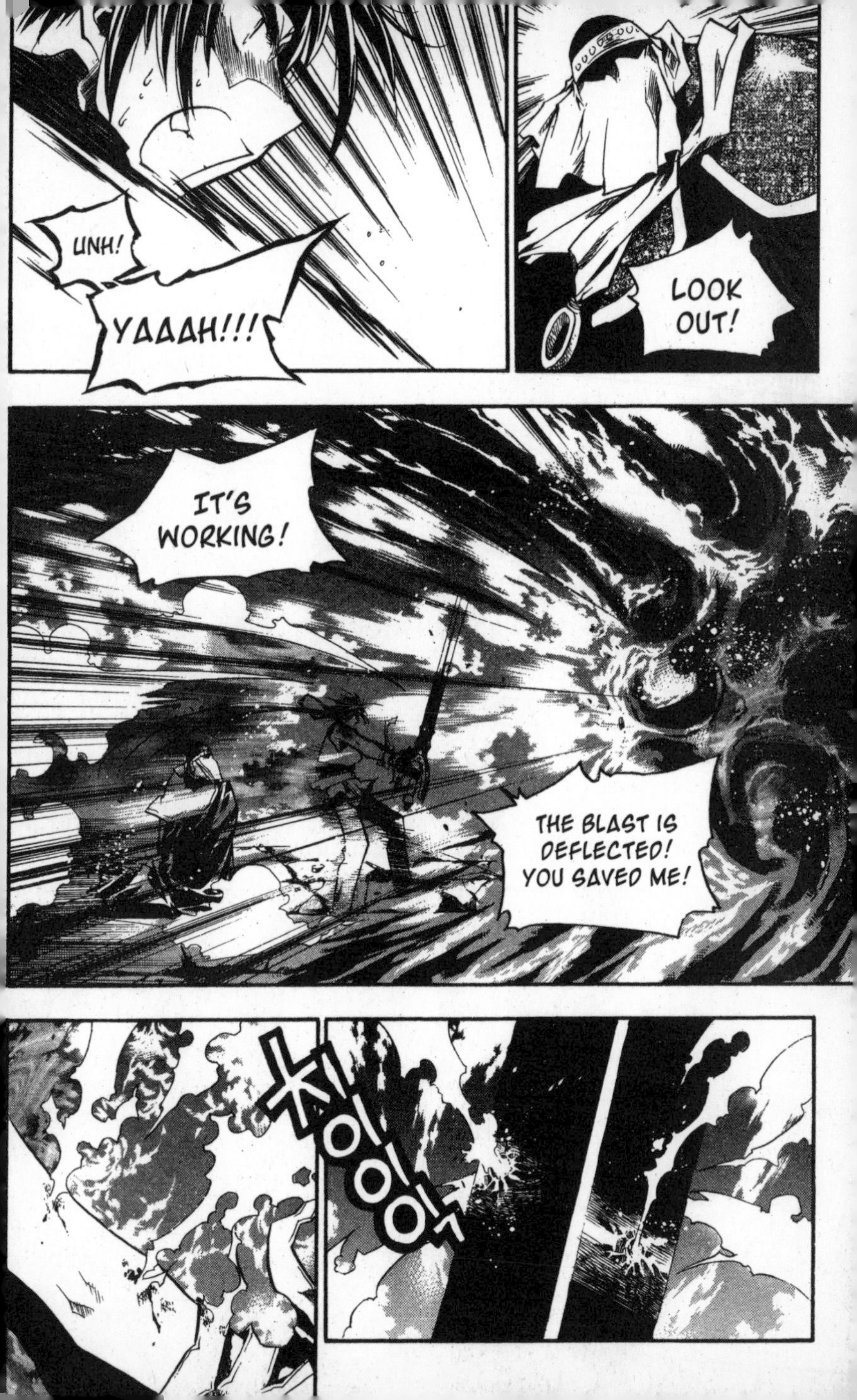
UNH!
YAAAH!!!
LOOK OUT!
IT'S WORKING!
THE BLAST IS DEFLECTED! YOU SAVED ME!

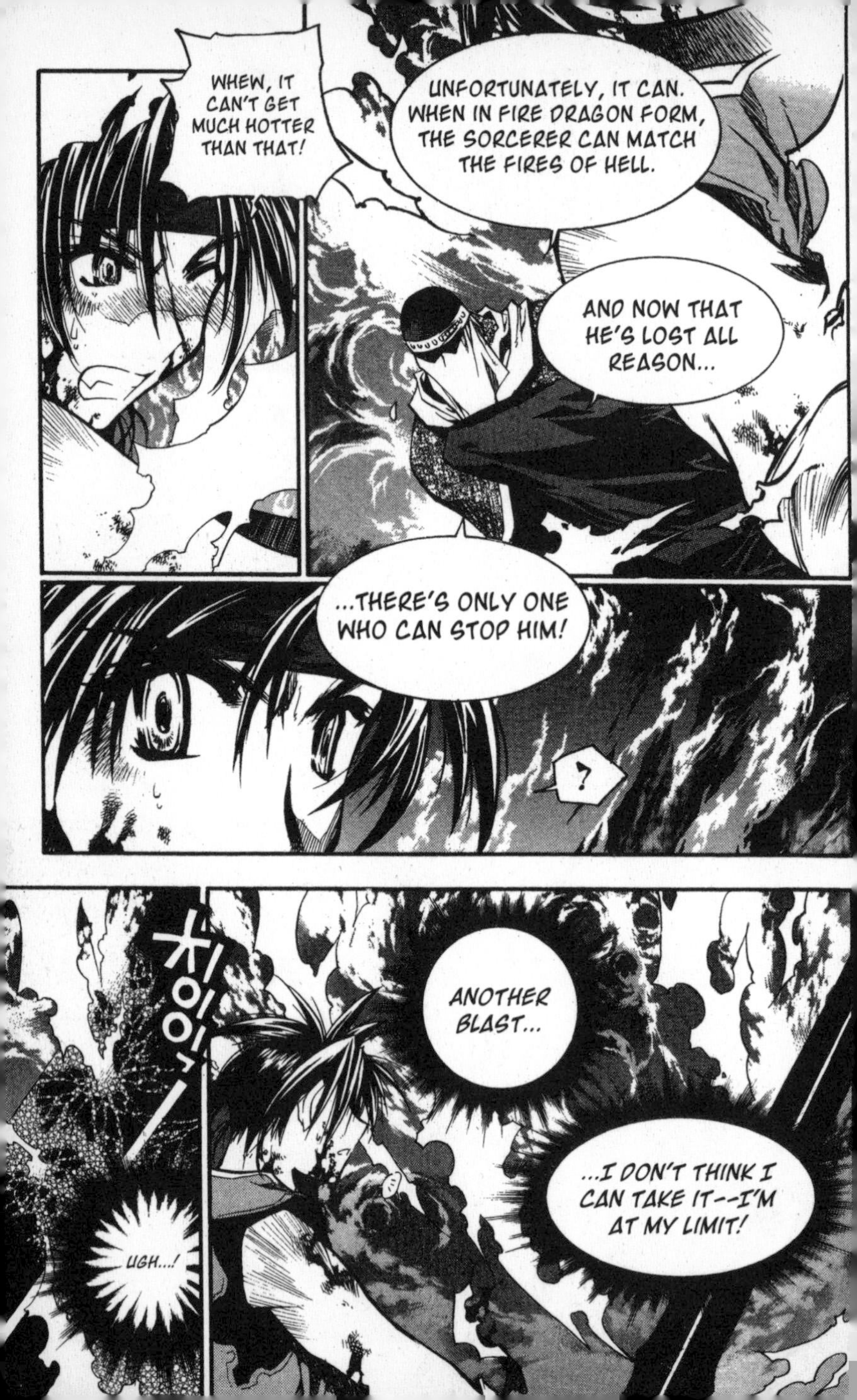
WHEW, IT CAN'T GET MUCH HOTTER THAN THAT!
UNFORTUNATELY, IT CAN. WHEN IN FIRE DRAGON FORM, THE SORCERER CAN MATCH THE FIRES OF HELL.
AND NOW THAT HE'S LOST ALL REASON...
...THERE'S ONLY ONE WHO CAN STOP HIM!
?
UGH...!
ANOTHER BLAST...
...I DON'T THINK I CAN TAKE IT--I'M AT MY LIMIT!

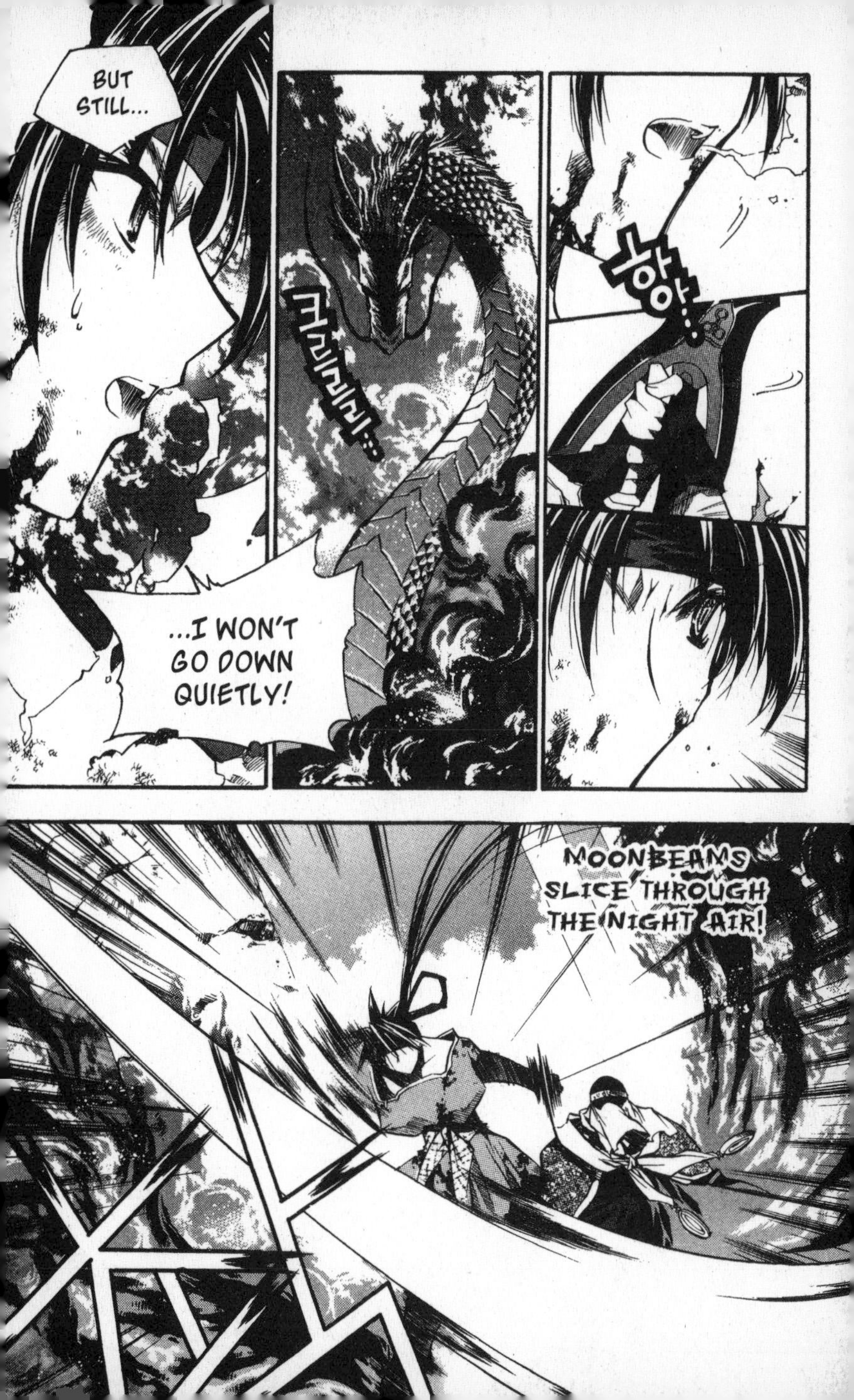
BUT STILL...
...I WON'T GO DOWN QUIETLY!
MOONBEAMS SLICE THROUGH THE NIGHT AIR!

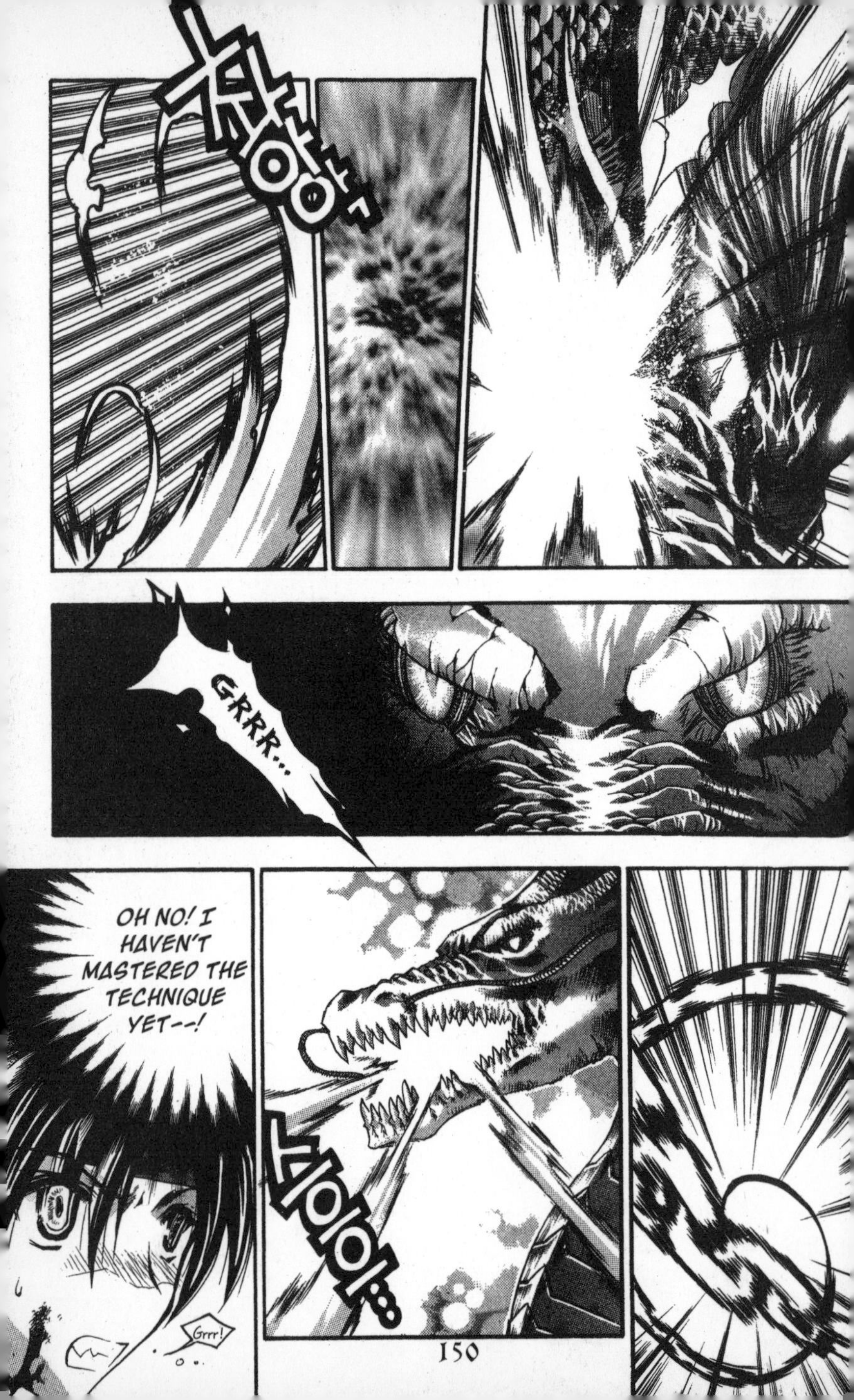
GRRR...
OH NO! I HAVEN'T MASTERED THE TECHNIQUE YET--!
Grrr!

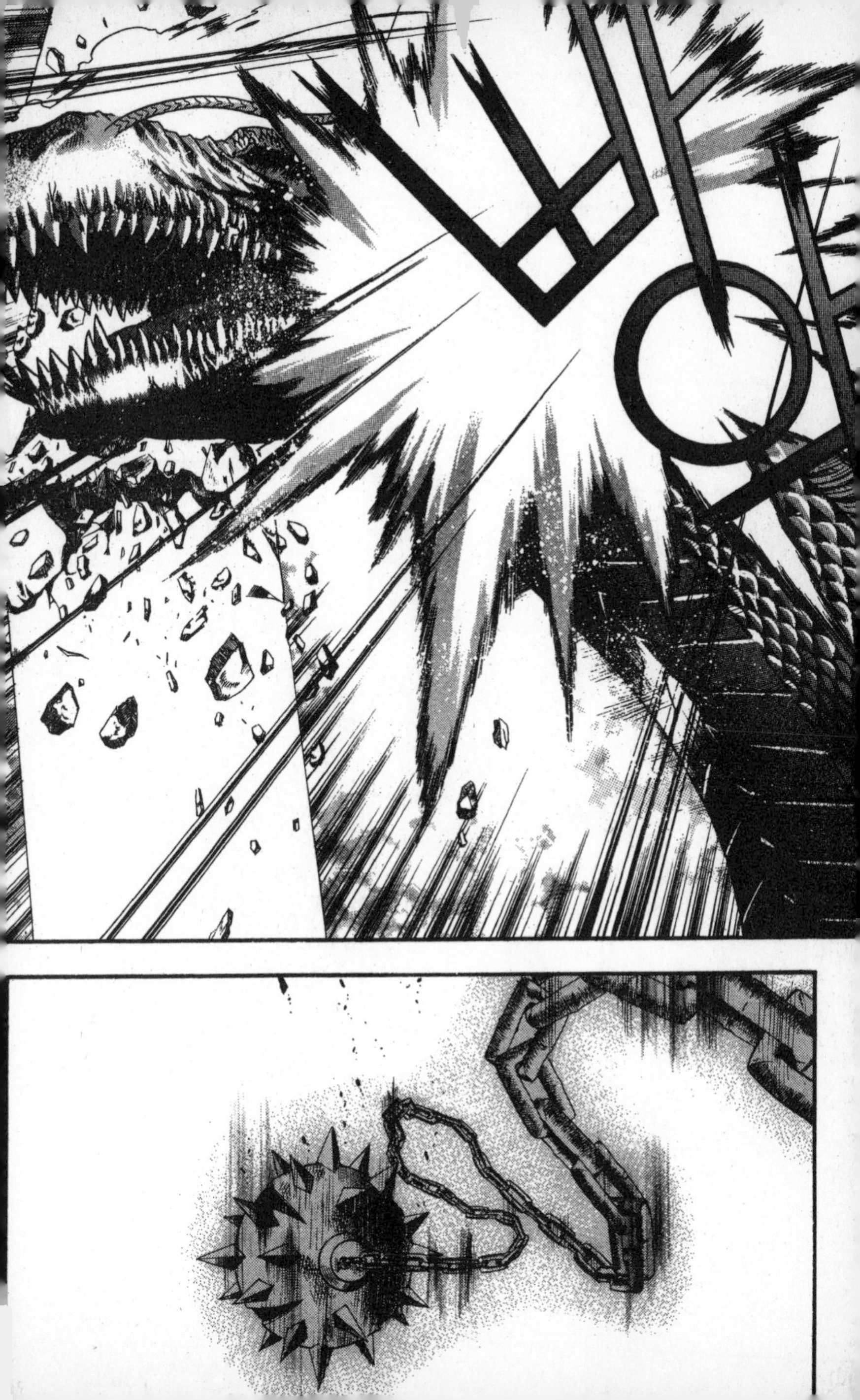

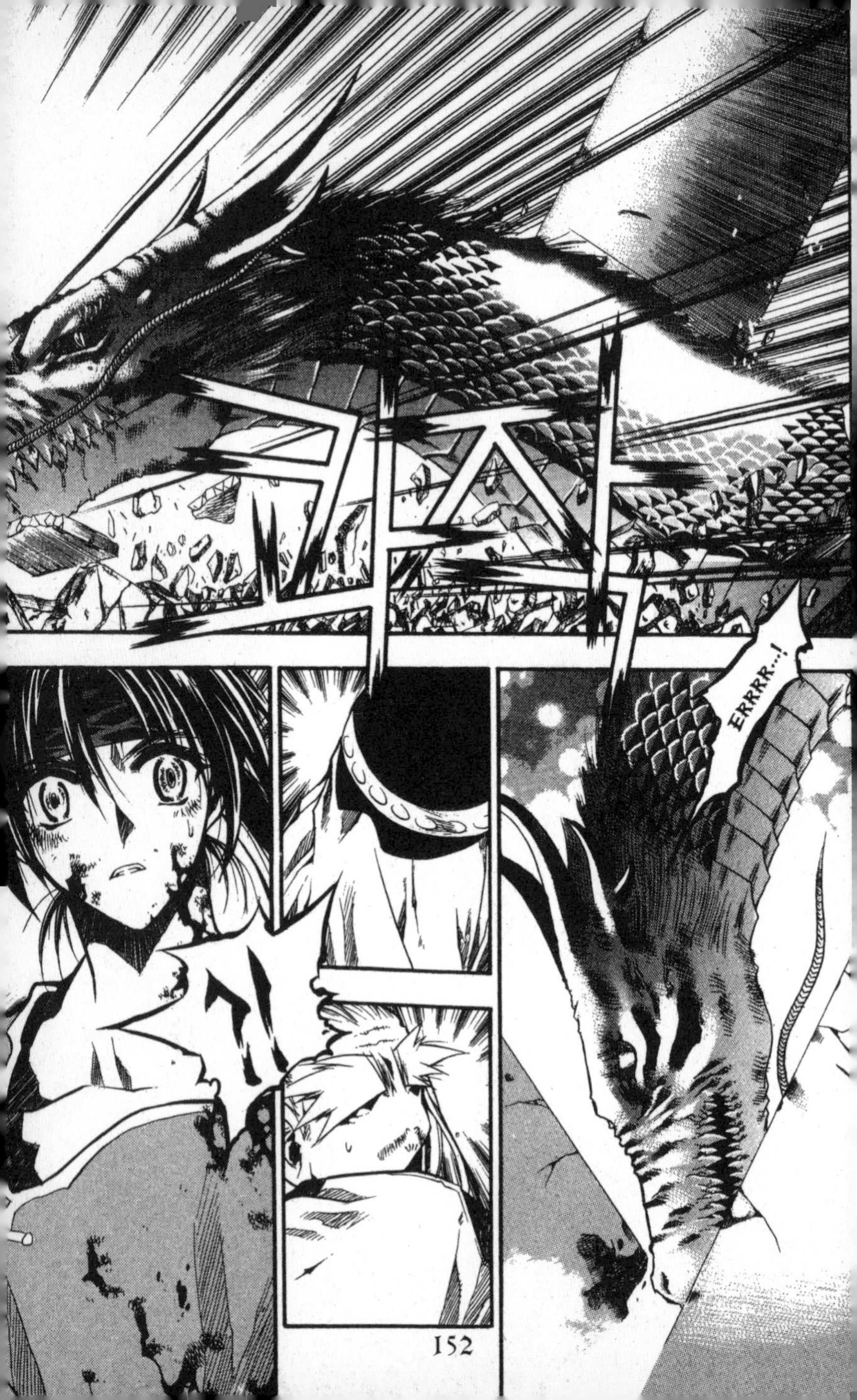
ERRRR...!

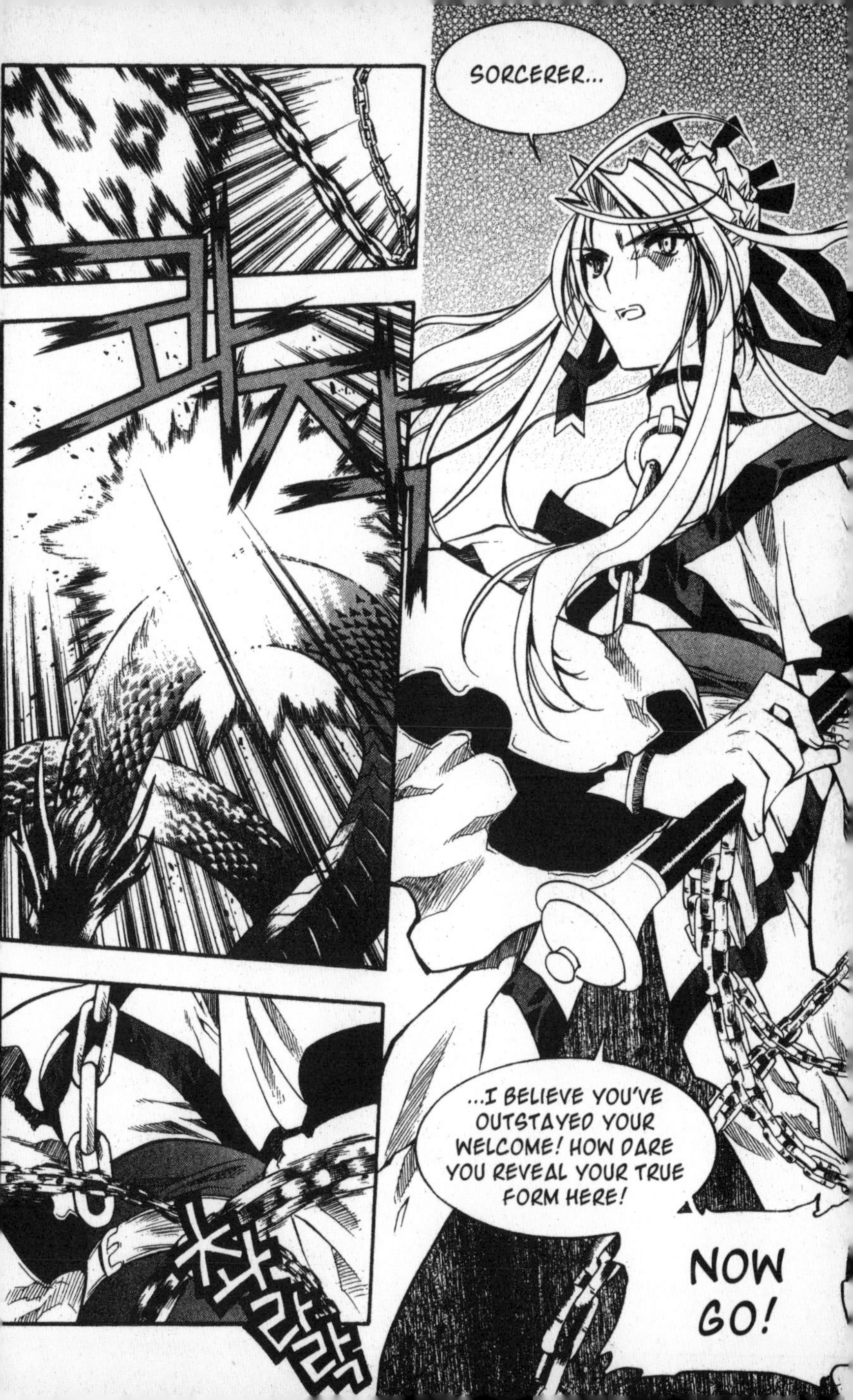
SORCERER...
...I BELIEVE YOU'VE OUTSTAYED YOUR WELCOME! HOW DARE YOU REVEAL YOUR TRUE FORM HERE!
NOW GO!

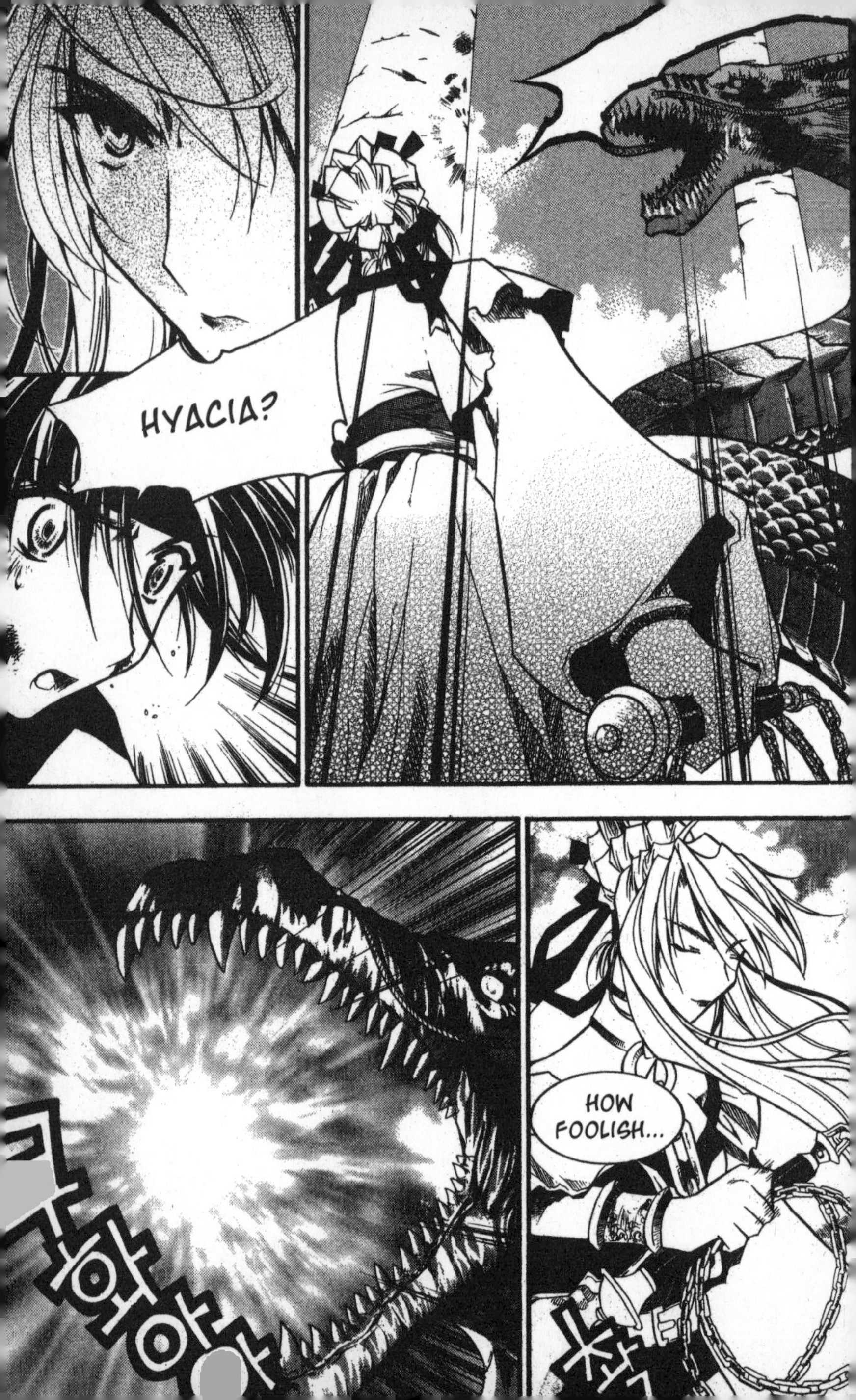

HYACIA?
HOW FOOLISH...

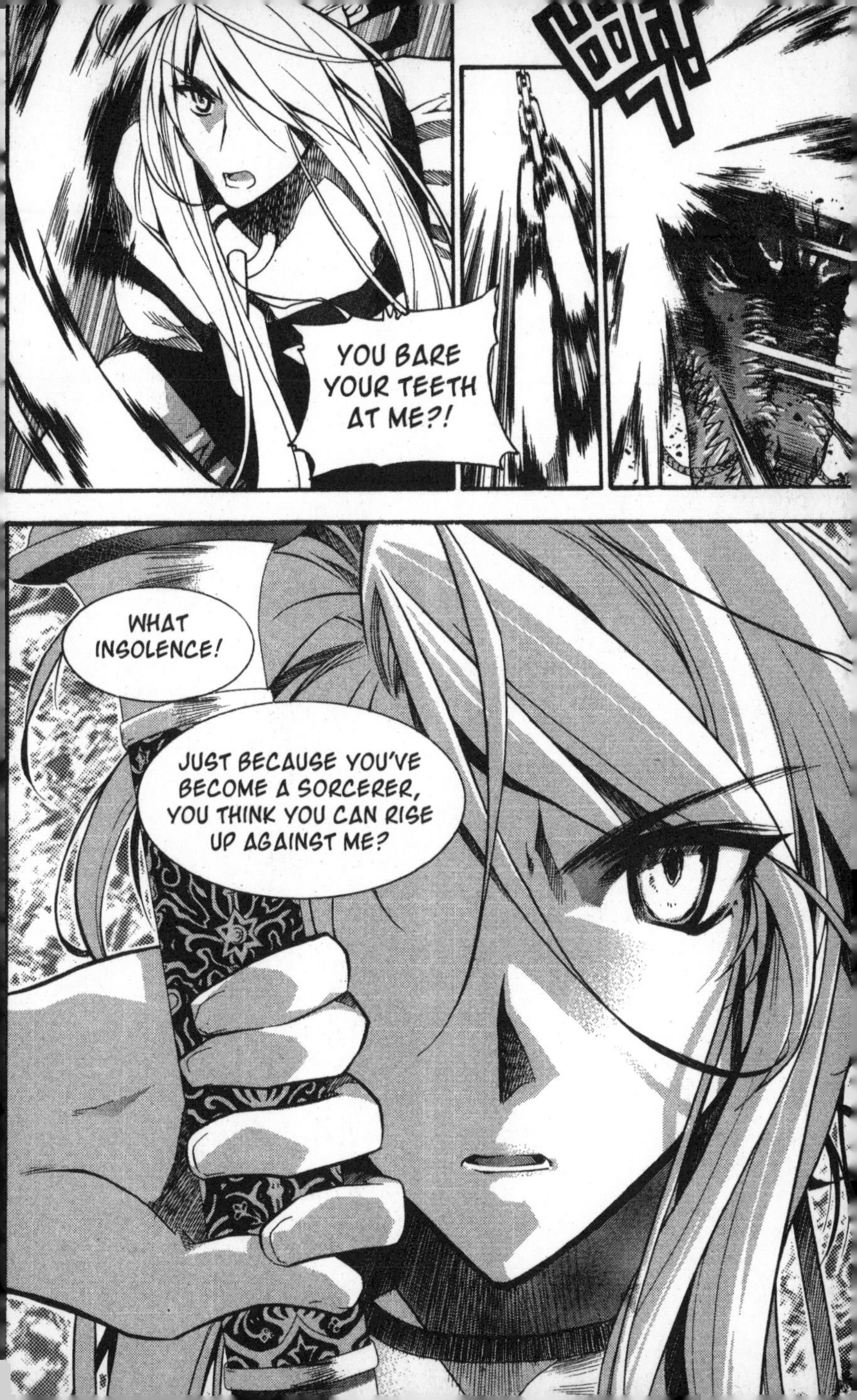
YOU BARE YOUR TEETH AT ME?!
WHAT INSOLENCE!
JUST BECAUSE YOU'VE BECOME A SORCERER, YOU THINK YOU CAN RISE UP AGAINST ME?

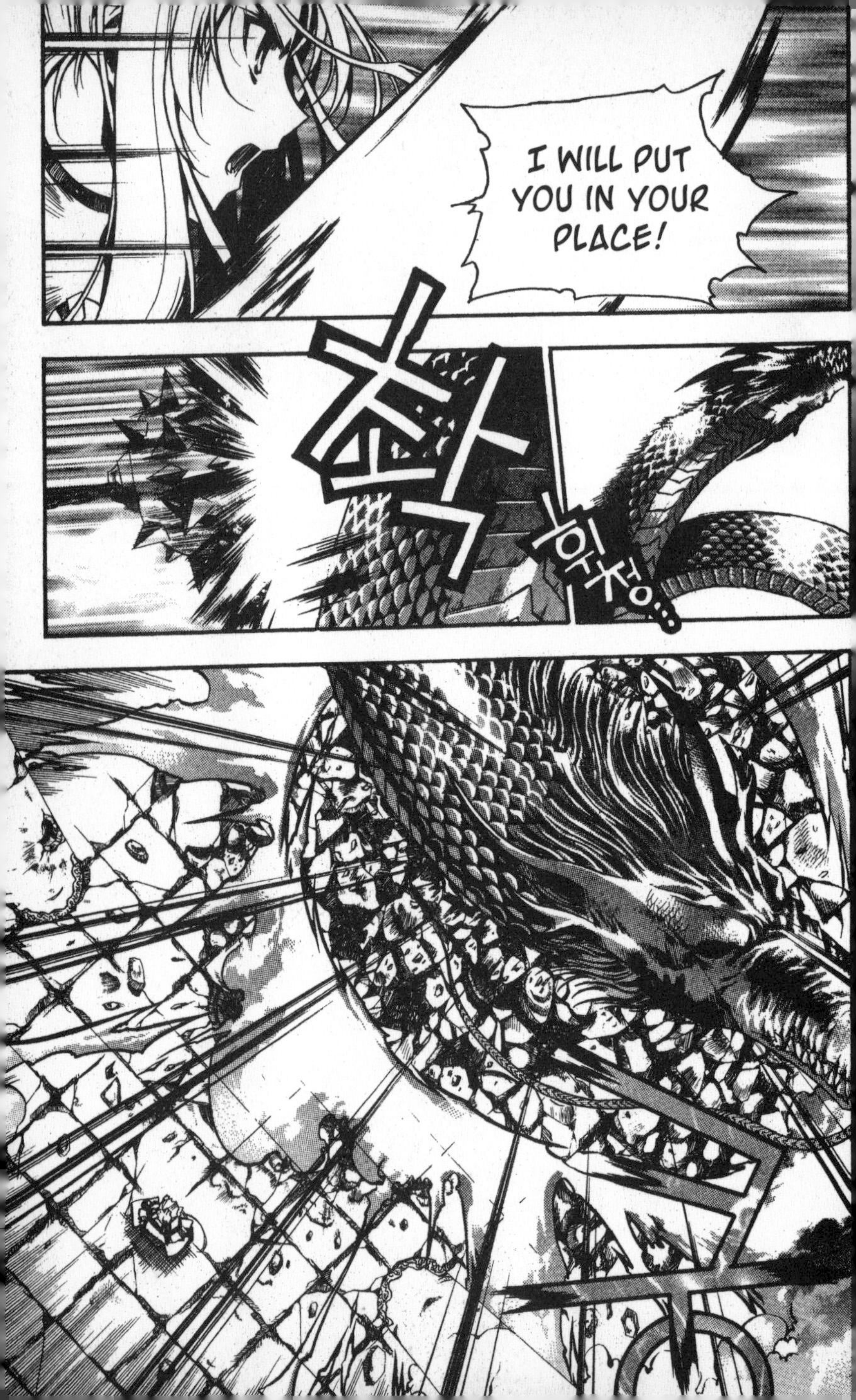
I WILL PUT YOU IN YOUR PLACE!

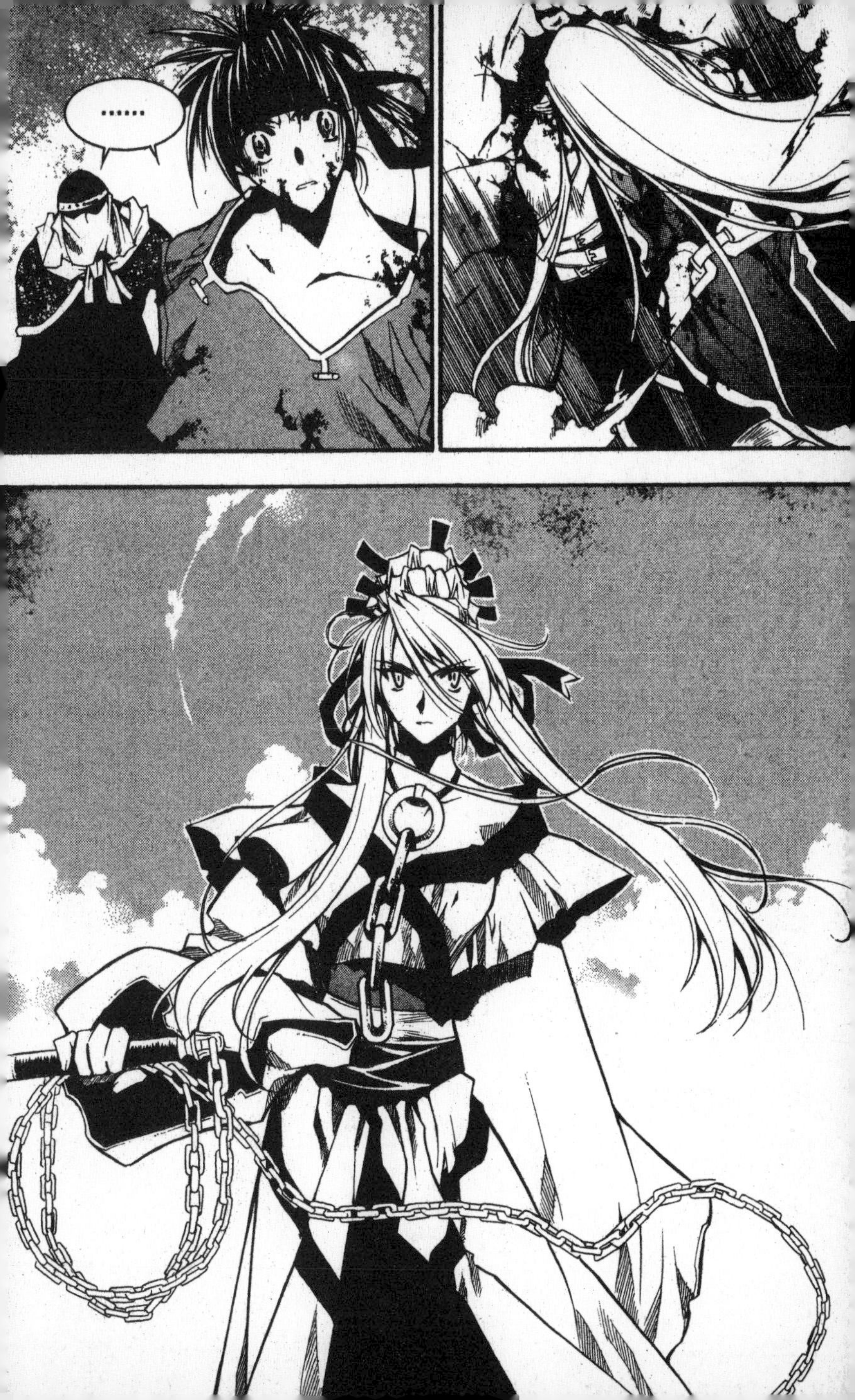
......

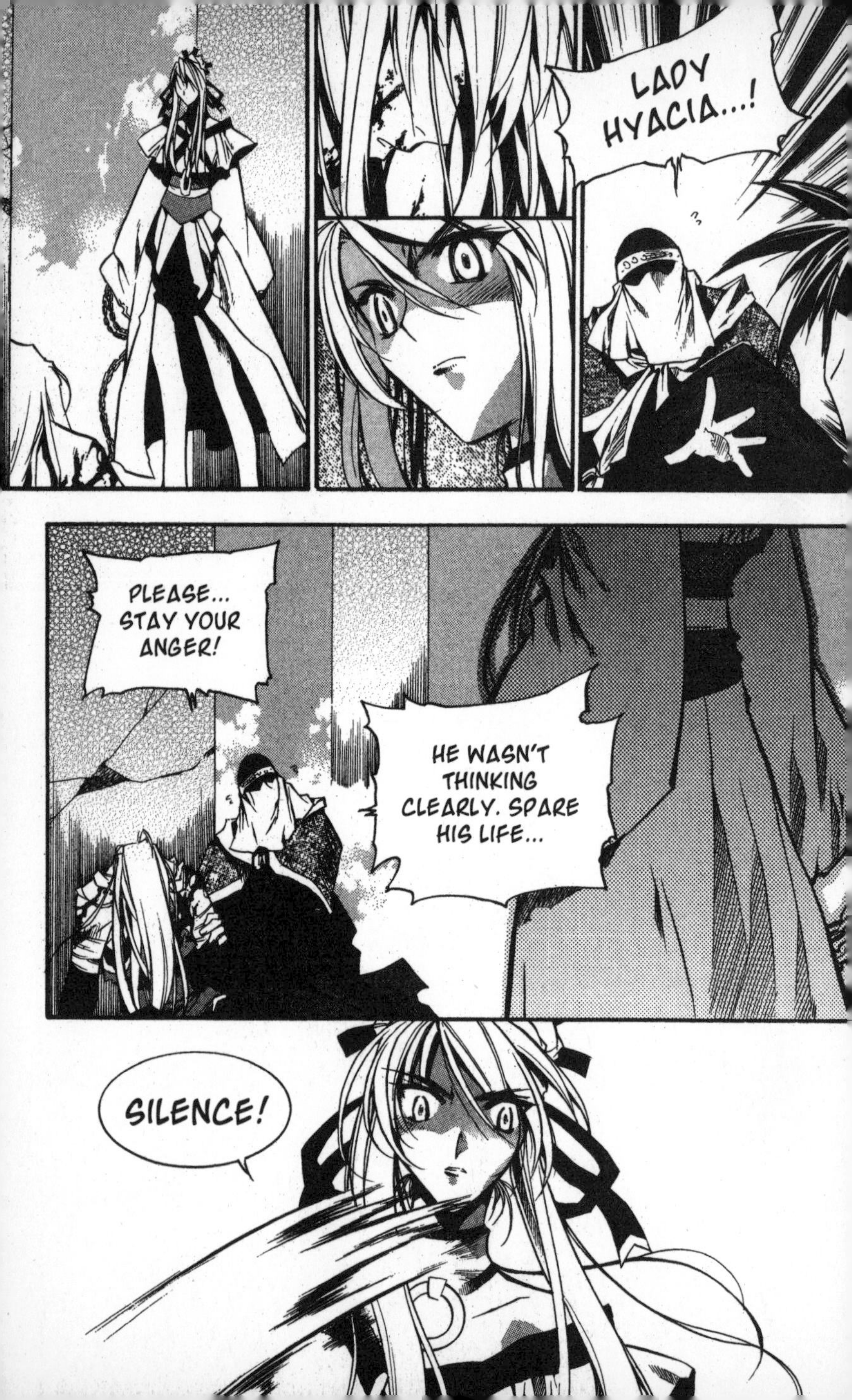
LADY HYACIA...!
PLEASE... STAY YOUR ANGER!
HE WASN'T THINKING CLEARLY. SPARE HIS LIFE...
SILENCE!

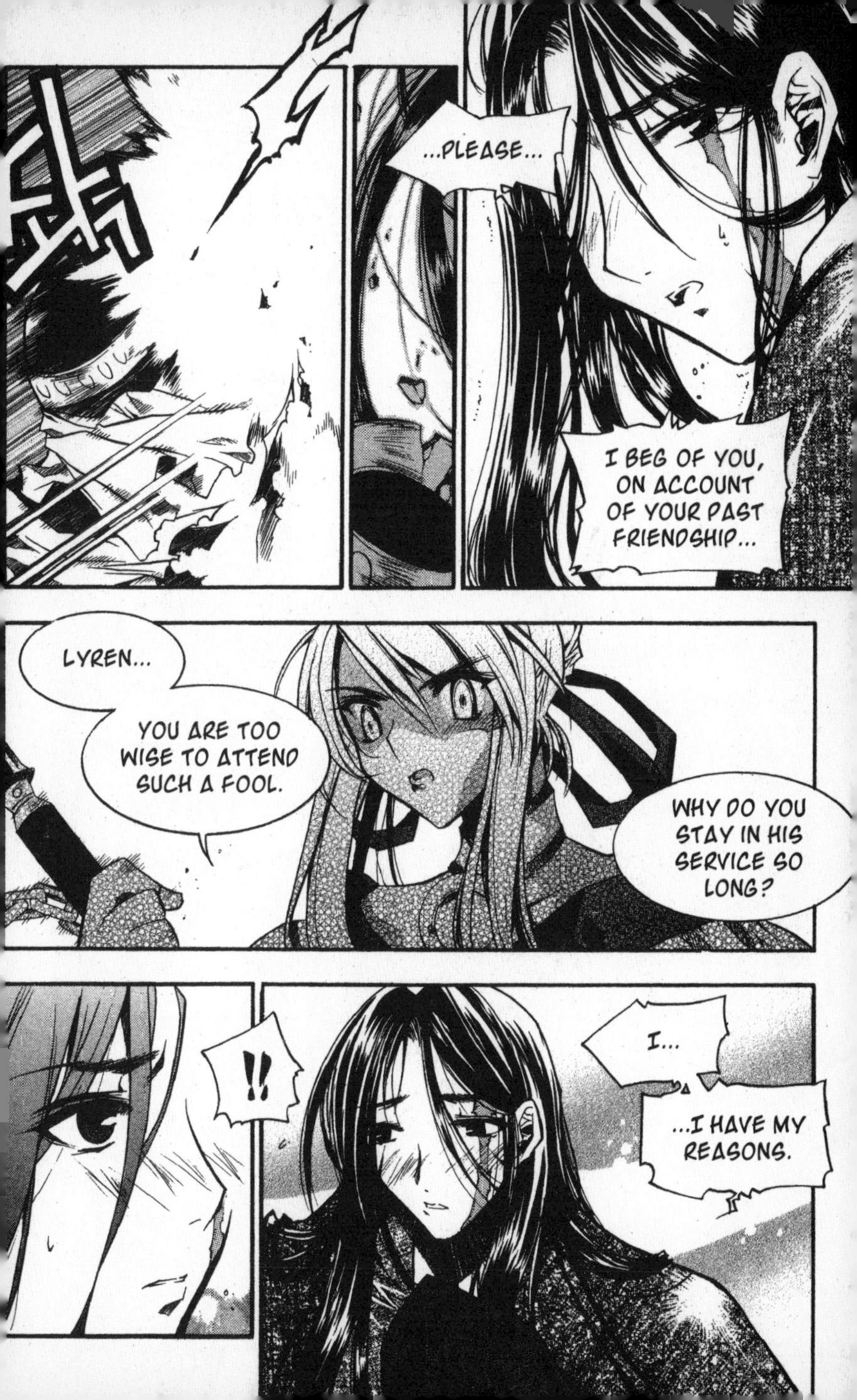
...PLEASE...
I BEG OF YOU, ON ACCOUNT OF YOUR PAST FRIENDSHIP...
LYREN...
YOU ARE TOO WISE TO ATTEND SUCH A FOOL.
WHY DO YOU STAY IN HIS SERVICE SO LONG?
!!
I...
...I HAVE MY REASONS.

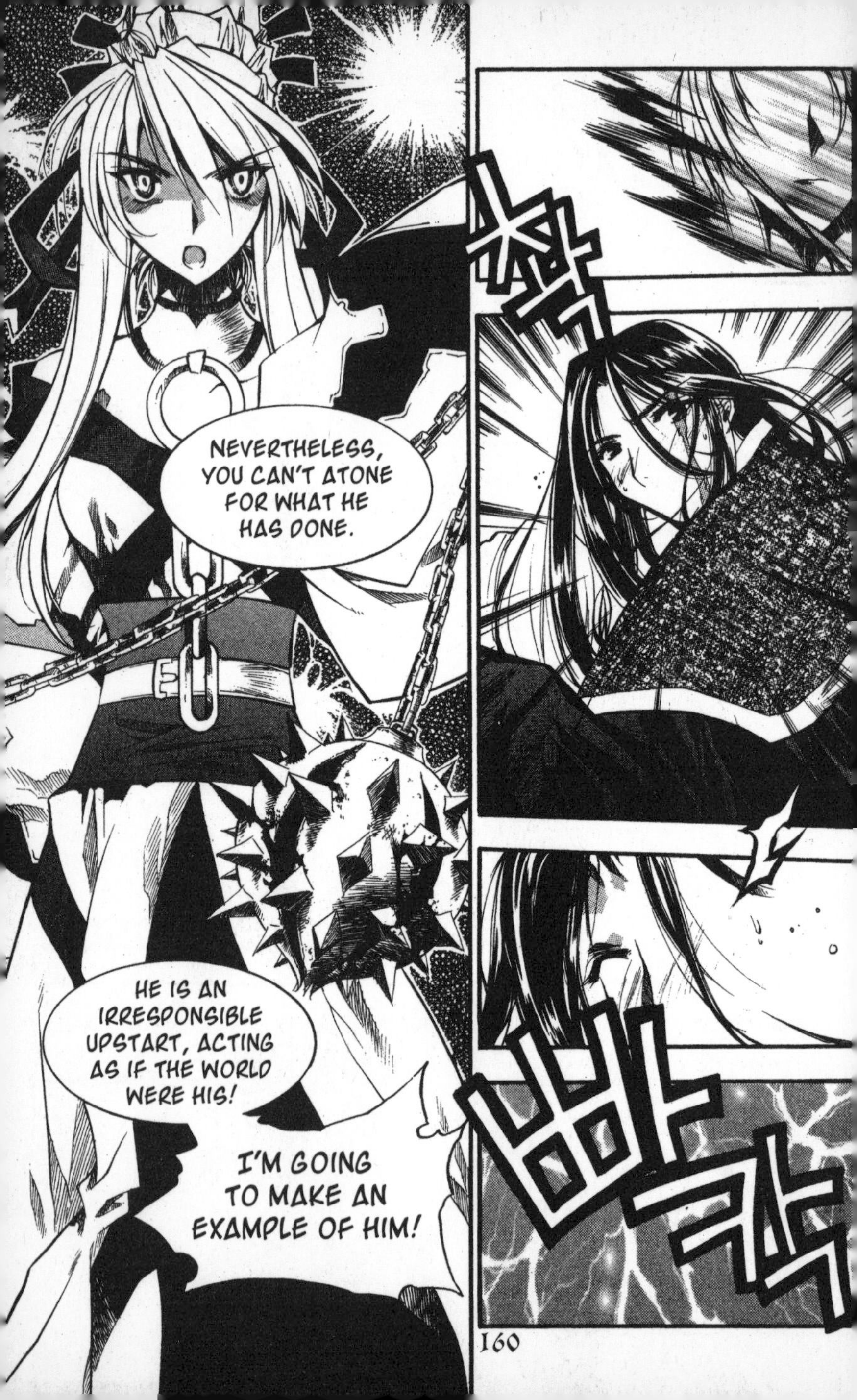
NEVERTHELESS, YOU CAN'T ATONE FOR WHAT HE HAS DONE.
HE IS AN IRRESPONSIBLE UPSTART, ACTING AS IF THE WORLD WERE HIS!
I'M GOING TO MAKE AN EXAMPLE OF HIM!

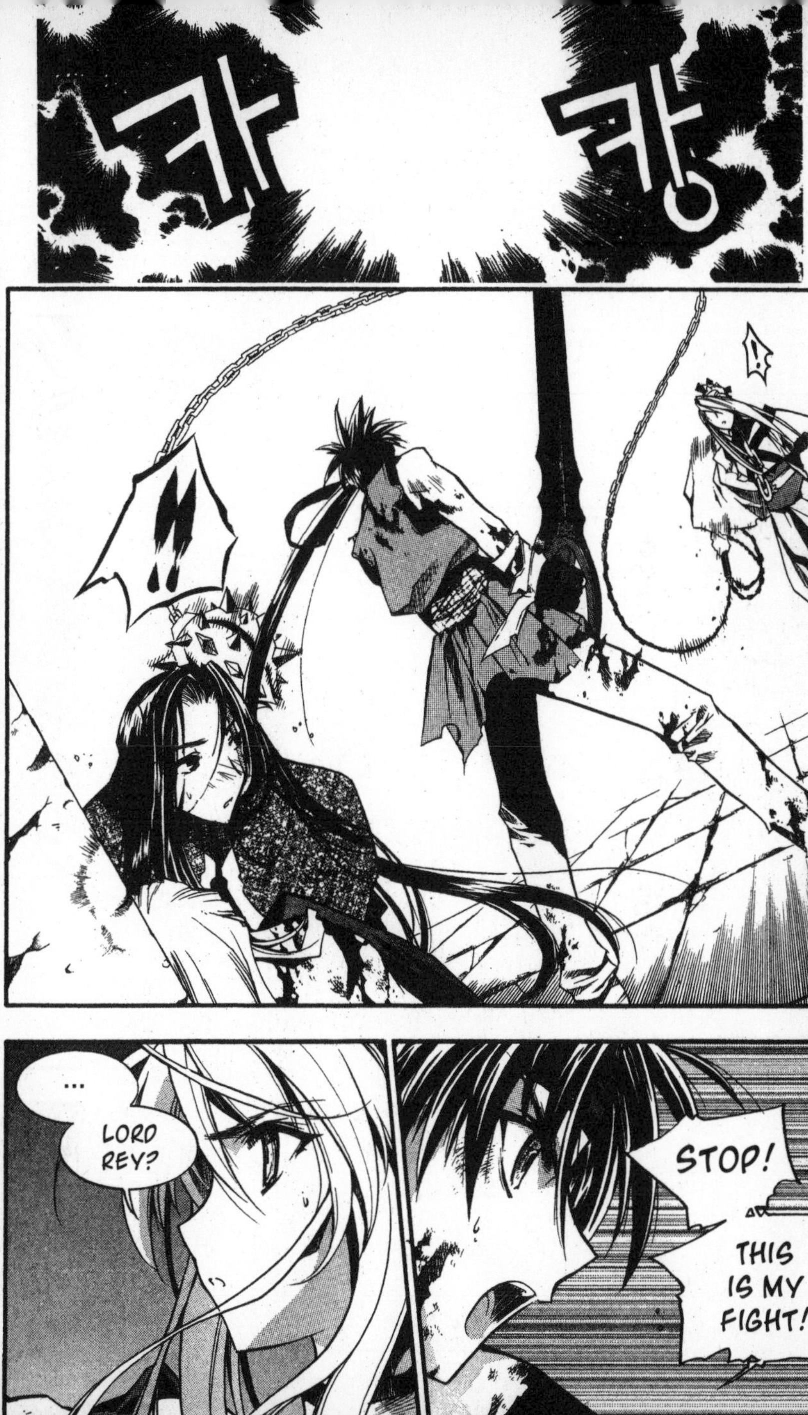
카 캉
!!
!?
...
LORD REY?
STOP!
THIS IS MY FIGHT!

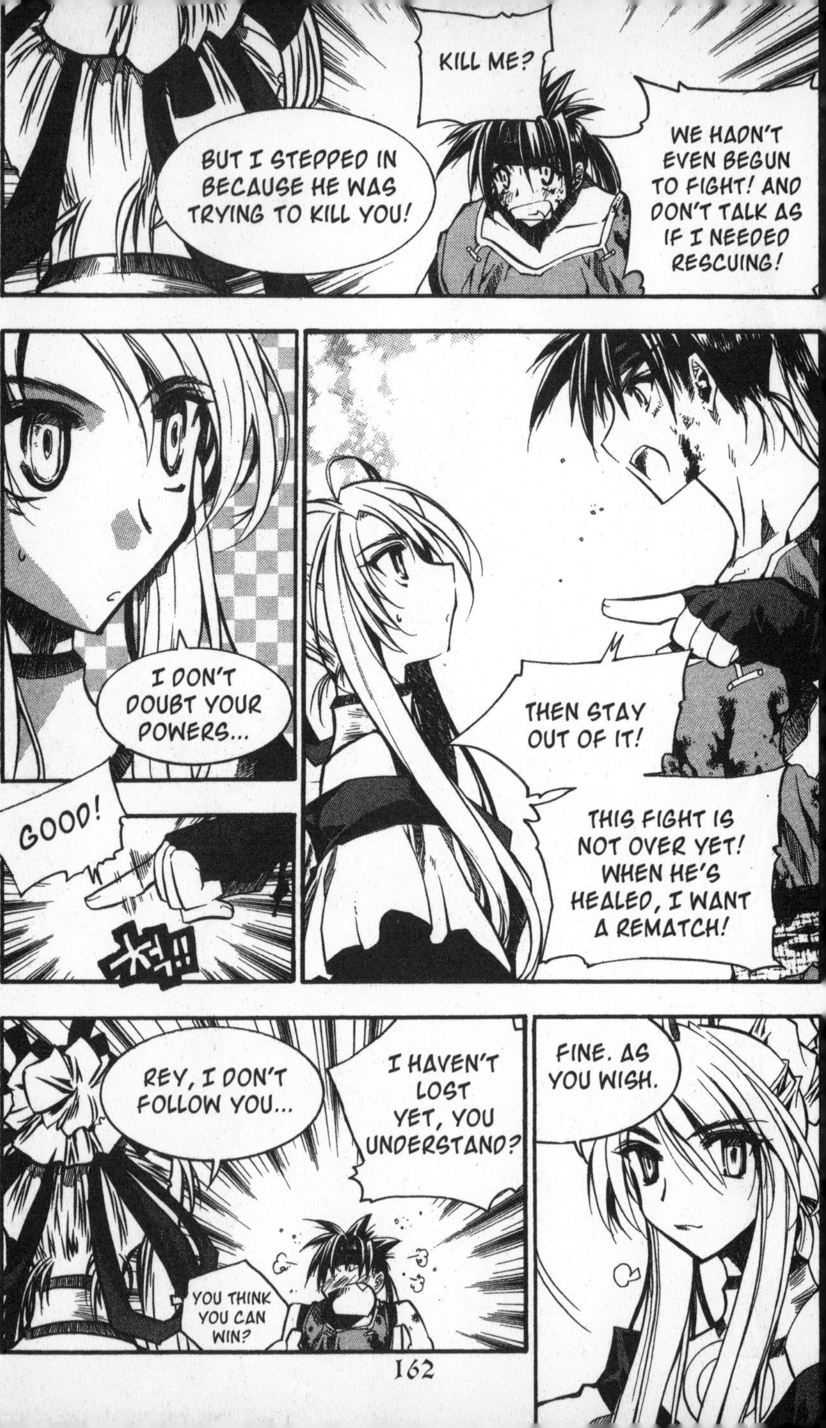
BUT I STEPPED IN BECAUSE HE WAS TRYING TO KILL YOU!
KILL ME?
WE HADN'T EVEN BEGUN TO FIGHT! AND DON'T TALK AS IF I NEEDED RESCUING!
I DON'T DOUBT YOUR POWERS...
GOOD!
THEN STAY OUT OF IT!
THIS FIGHT IS NOT OVER YET! WHEN HE'S HEALED, I WANT A REMATCH!
REY, I DON'T FOLLOW YOU...
I HAVEN'T LOST YET, YOU UNDERSTAND?
YOU THINK YOU CAN WIN?
FINE. AS YOU WISH.

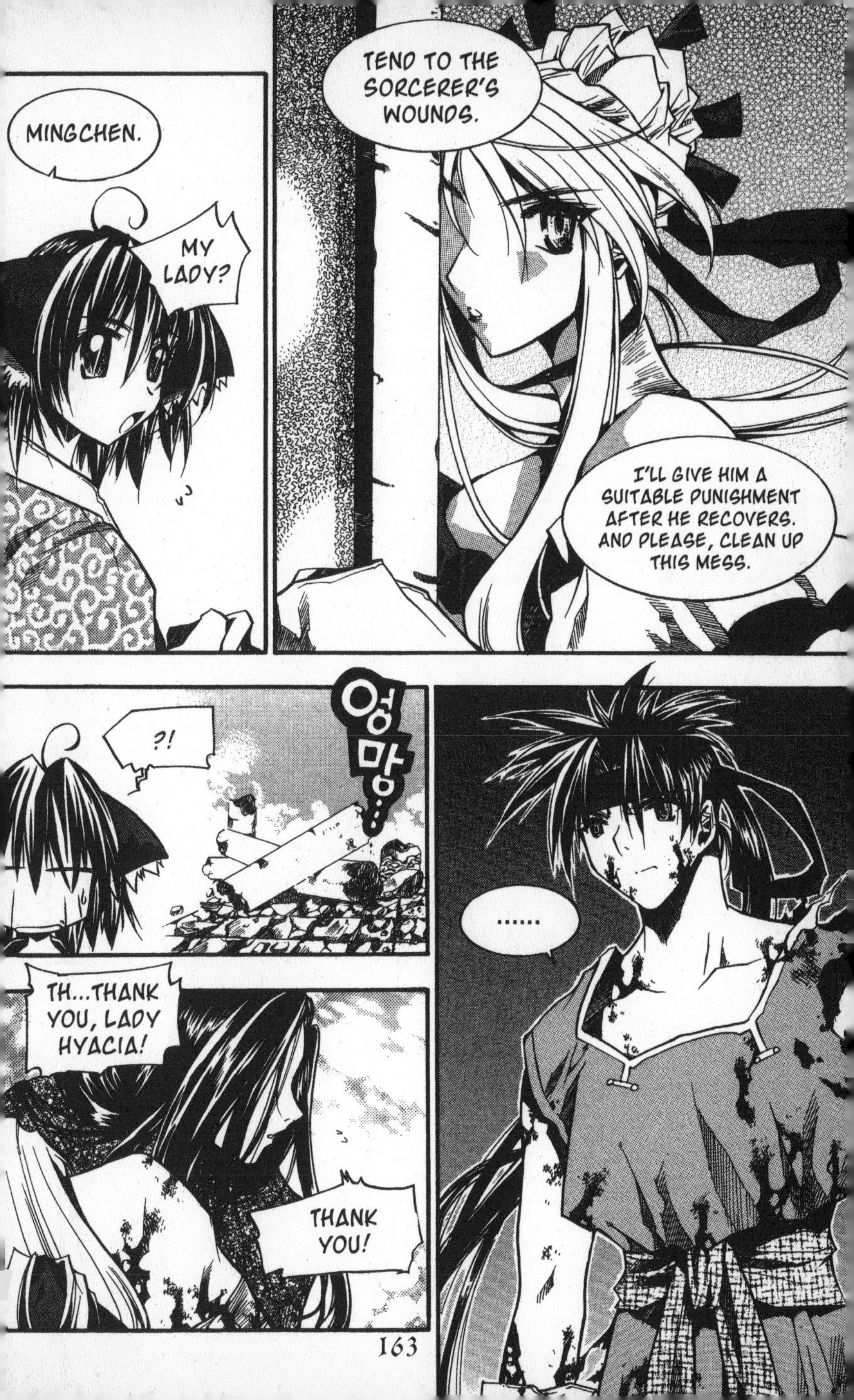
MINGCHEN.
MY LADY?
TEND TO THE SORCERER'S WOUNDS.
I'LL GIVE HIM A SUITABLE PUNISHMENT AFTER HE RECOVERS. AND PLEASE, CLEAN UP THIS MESS.
?!
엉망...
TH...THANK YOU, LADY HYACIA!
THANK YOU!
......

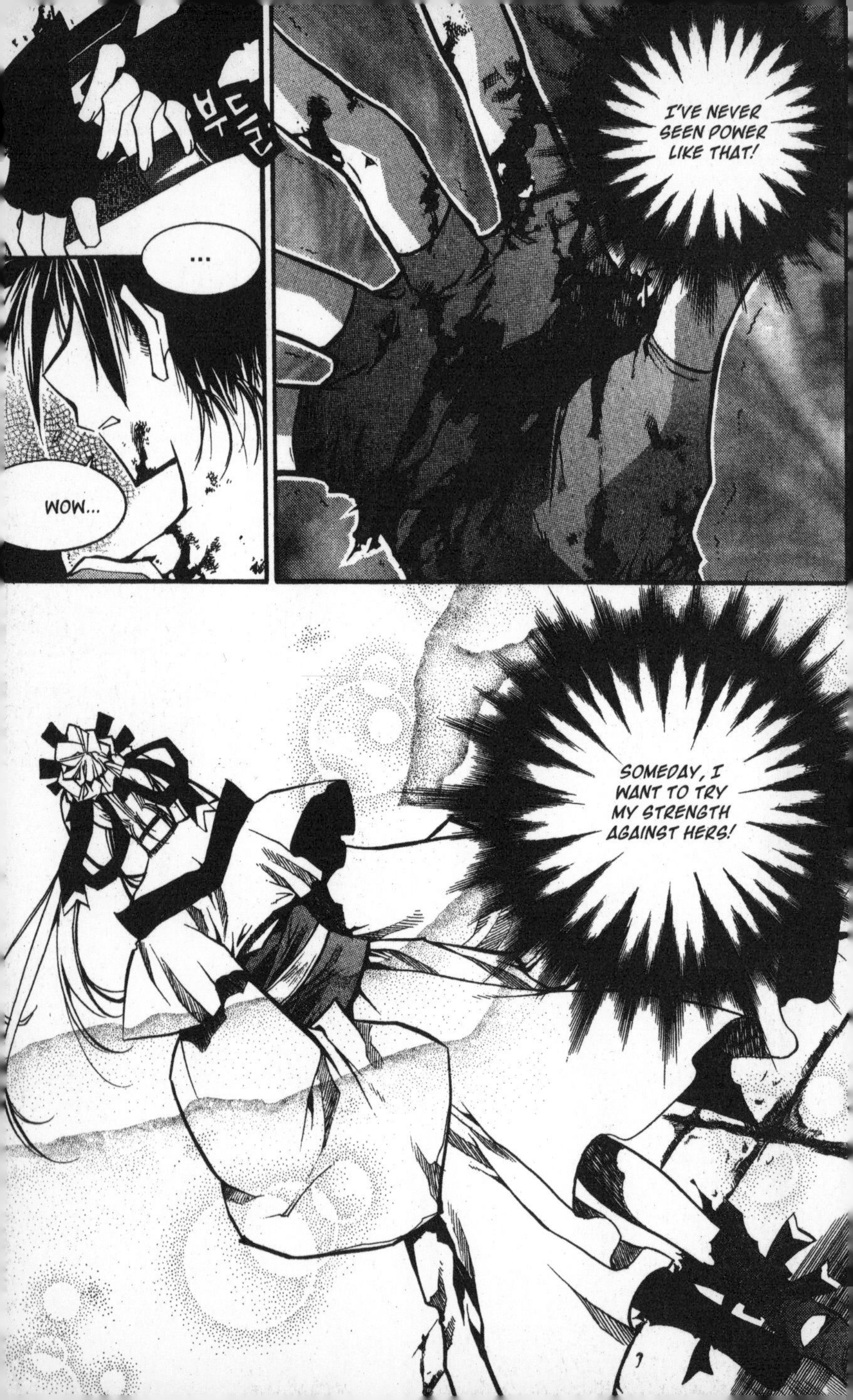
...
WOW...
I'VE NEVER SEEN POWER LIKE THAT!
SOMEDAY, I WANT TO TRY MY STRENGTH AGAINST HERS!

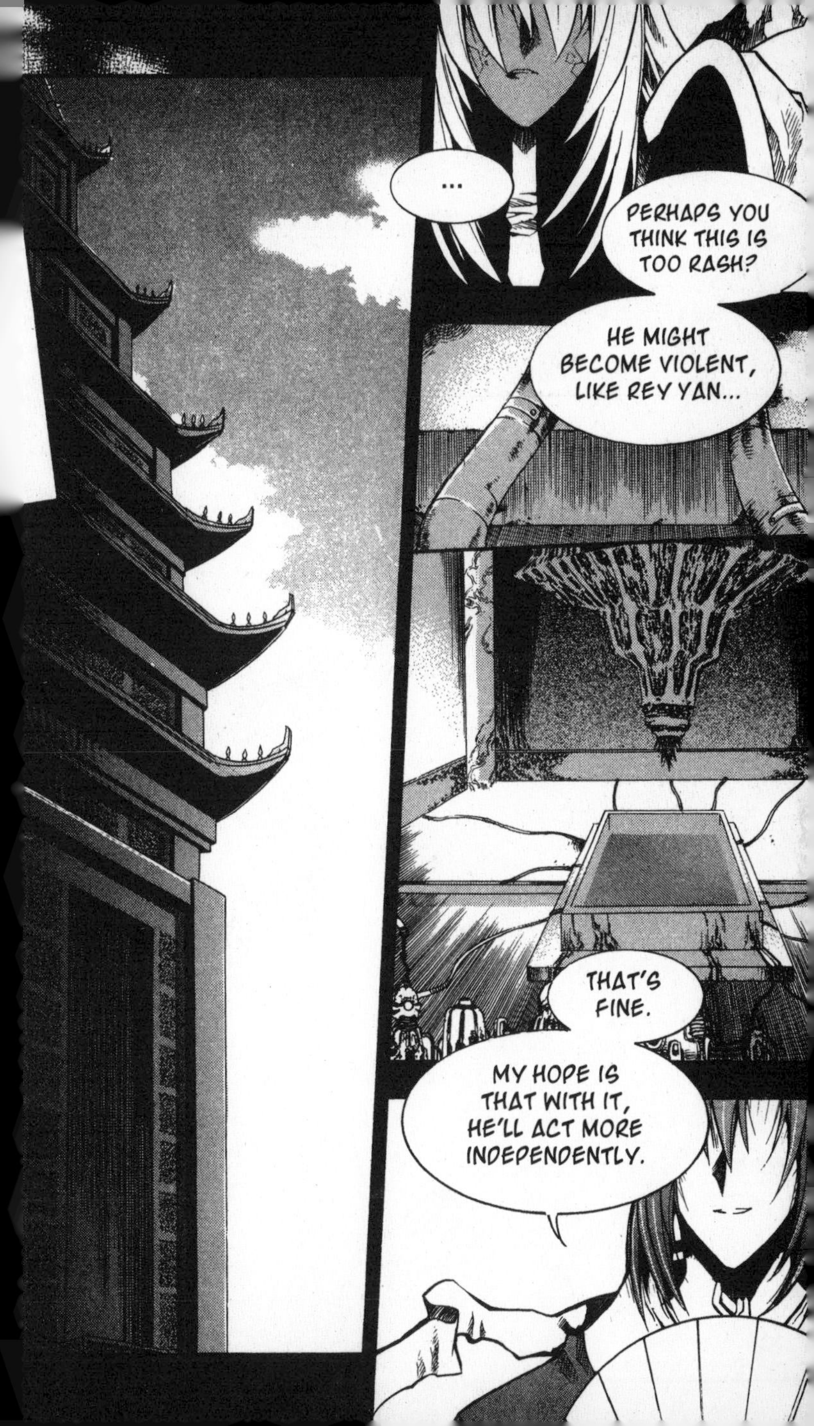
...
PERHAPS YOU THINK THIS IS TOO RASH?
HE MIGHT BECOME VIOLENT, LIKE REY YAN...
THAT'S FINE.
MY HOPE IS THAT WITH IT, HE'LL ACT MORE INDEPENDENTLY.

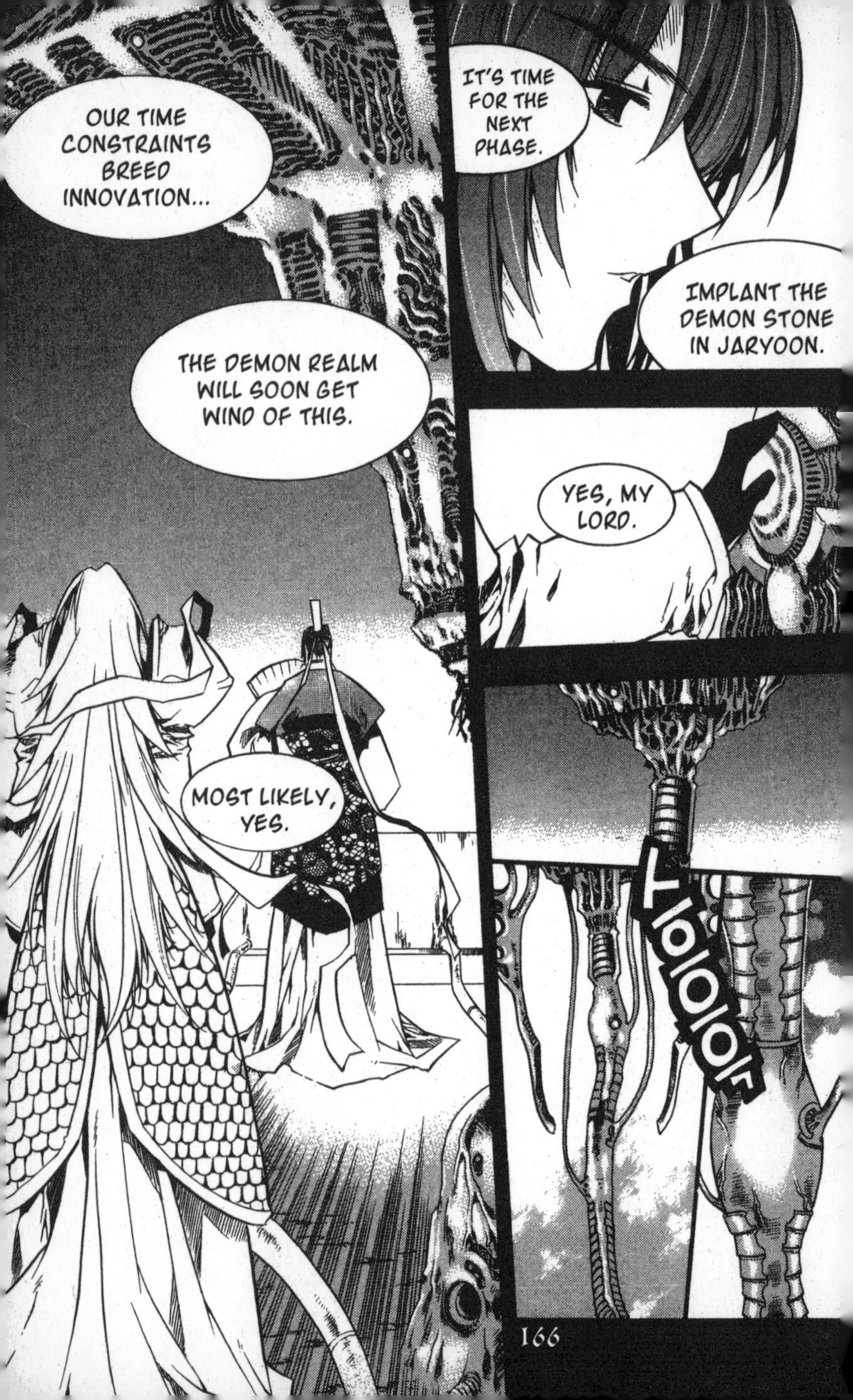
OUR TIME CONSTRAINTS BREED INNOVATION...
THE DEMON REALM WILL SOON GET WIND OF THIS.
MOST LIKELY, YES.
IT'S TIME FOR THE NEXT PHASE.
IMPLANT THE DEMON STONE IN JARYOON.
YES, MY LORD.

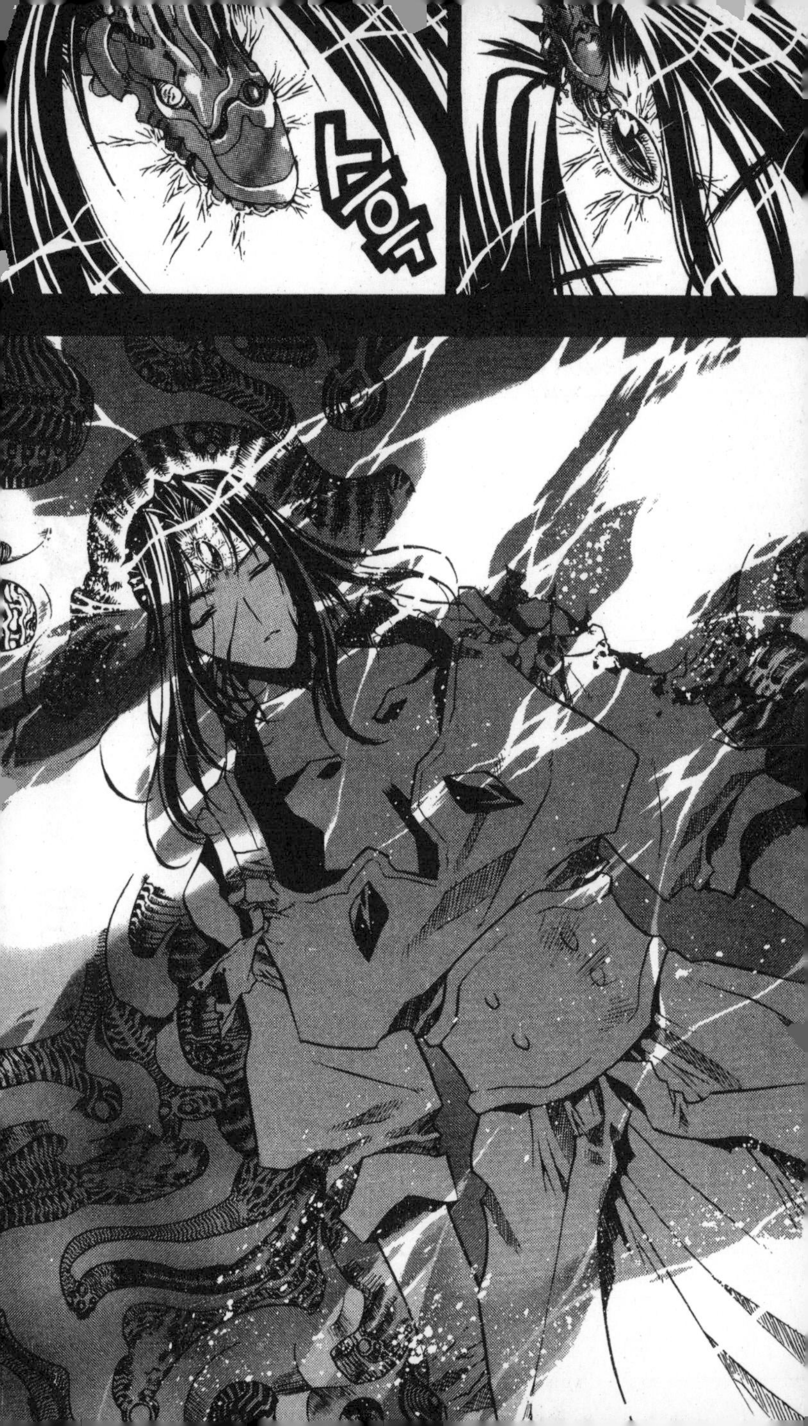

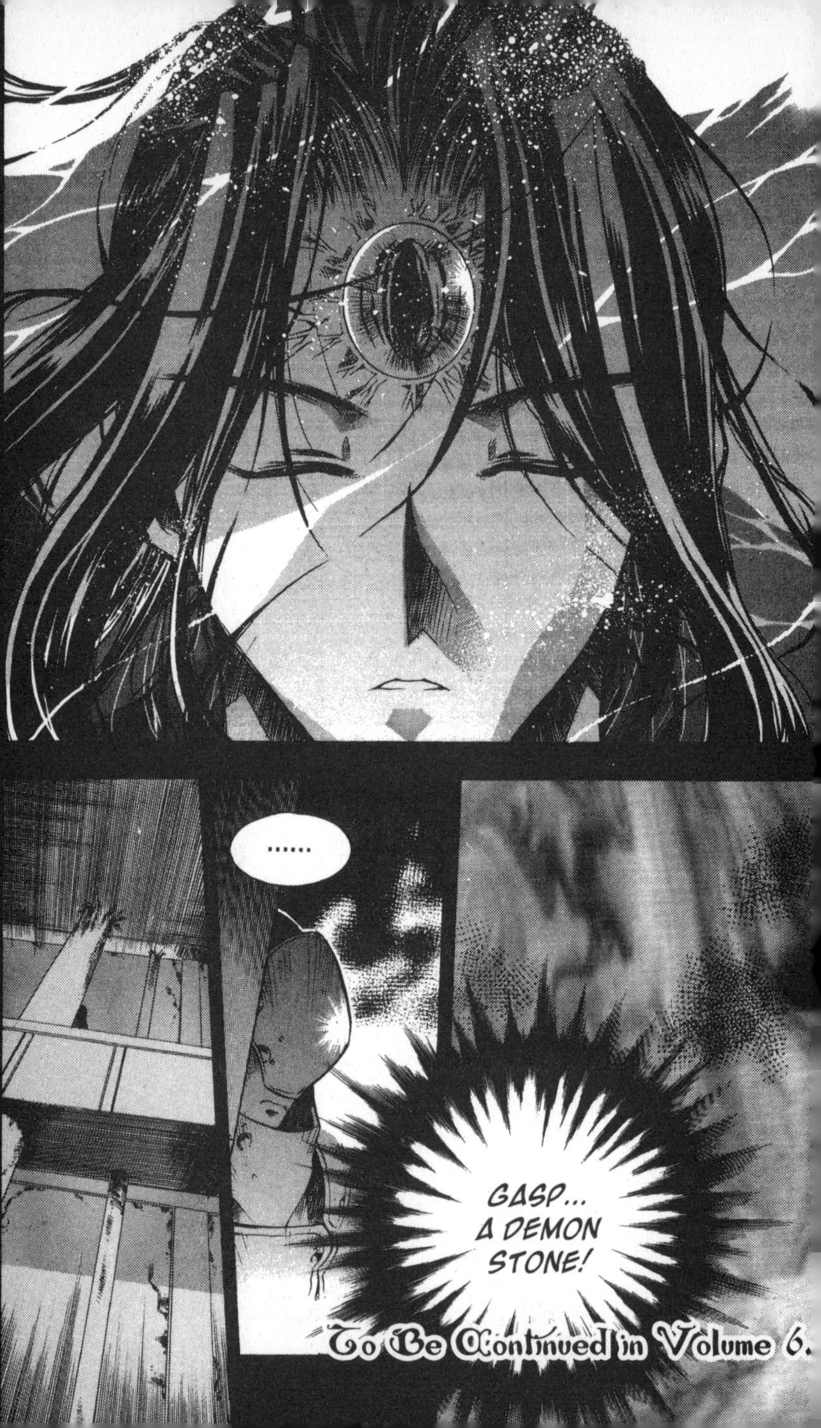
......
GASP... A DEMON STONE!
To Be Continued in Volume 6.

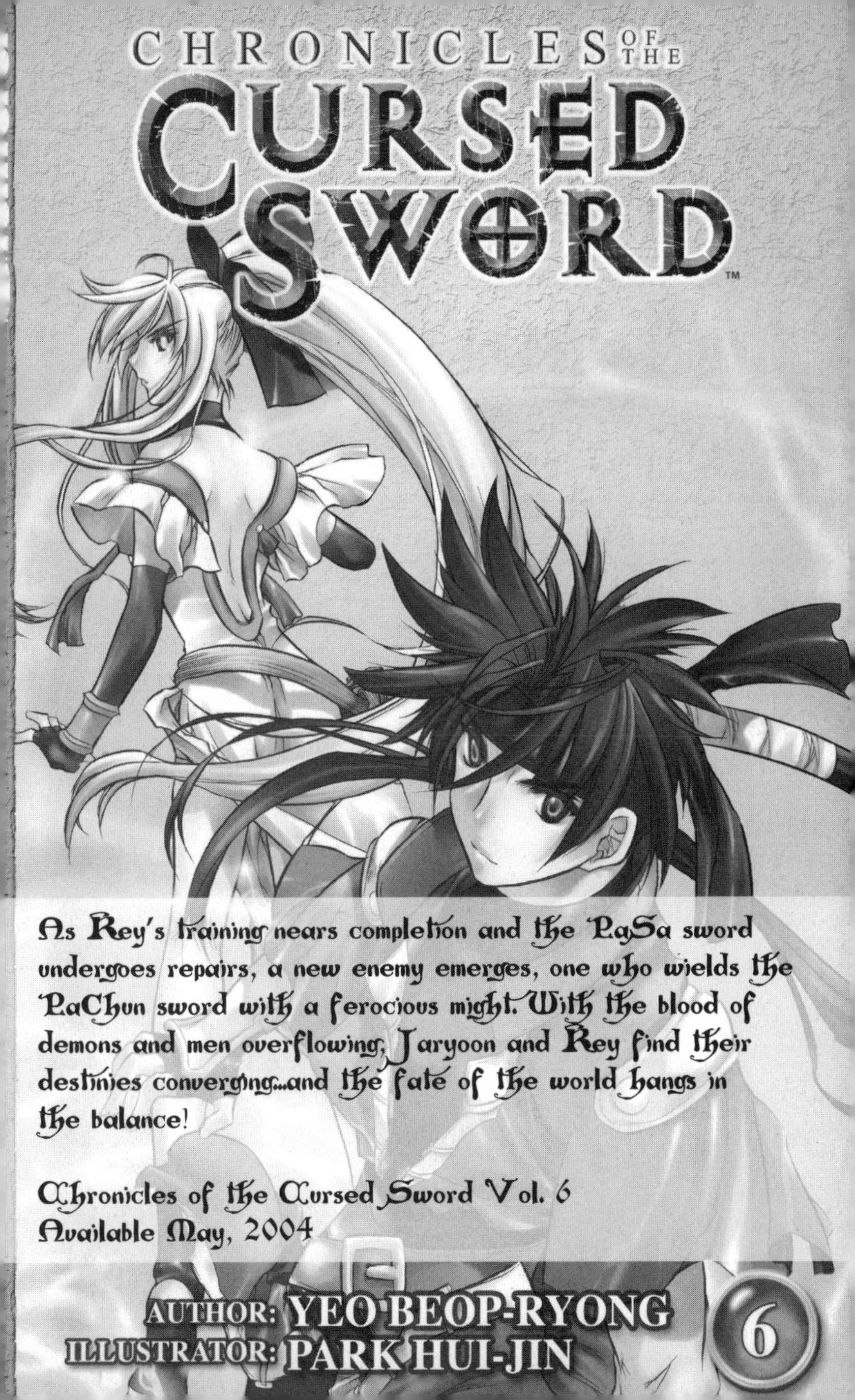
CHRONICLES OF THE CURSED SWORD™
As Rey's training nears completion and the PaSa sword undergoes repairs, a new enemy emerges, one who wields the PaChun sword with a ferocious might. With the blood of demons and men overflowing, Jaryoon and Rey find their destinies converging...and the fate of the world hangs in the balance!
Chronicles of the Cursed Sword Vol. 6
Available May, 2004
AUTHOR: YEO BEOP-RYONG
ILLUSTRATOR: PARK HUI-JIN
6

ALSO AVAILABLE FROM TOKYOPOP®

MANGA

.HACK//LEGEND OF THE TWILIGHT
@LARGE
ABENOBASHI
A.I. LOVE YOU
AI YORI AOSHI
ANGELIC LAYER
ARM OF KANNON
BABY BIRTH
BATTLE ROYALE
BATTLE VIXENS
BRAIN POWERED
BRIGADOON
B'TX
CANDIDATE FOR GODDESS, THE
CARDCAPTOR SAKURA
CARDCAPTOR SAKURA - MASTER OF THE CLOW
CHOBITS
CHRONICLES OF THE CURSED SWORD
CLAMP SCHOOL DETECTIVES
CLOVER
COMIC PARTY
CONFIDENTIAL CONFESSIONS
CORRECTOR YUI
COWBOY BEBOP
COWBOY BEBOP: SHOOTING STAR
CRESCENT MOON
CULDCEPT
CYBORG 009
D.N. ANGEL
DEMON DIARY
DEMON ORORON, THE
DEUS VITAE
DIGIMON
DIGIMON ZERO TWO
DIGIMON TAMERS
DOLL
DRAGON HUNTER
DRAGON KNIGHTS
DREAM SAGA
DUKLYON: CLAMP SCHOOL DEFENDERS
ERICA SAKURAZAWA COLLECTED WORKS
EERIE QUEERIE!
ET CETERA
ETERNITY
EVIL'S RETURN
FAERIES' LANDING
FAKE
FLCL
FORBIDDEN DANCE
FRUITS BASKET
G GUNDAM
GATE KEEPERS

GETBACKERS
GIRL GOT GAME
GRAVITATION
GTO
GUNDAM SEED ASTRAY
GUNDAM WING
GUNDAM WING: BATTLEFIELD OF PACIFISTS
GUNDAM WING: ENDLESS WALTZ
GUNDAM WING: THE LAST OUTPOST (G-UNIT)
HAPPY MANIA
HARLEM BEAT
I.N.V.U.
IMMORTAL RAIN
INITIAL D
ISLAND
JING: KING OF BANDITS
JULINE
KARE KANO
KILL ME, KISS ME
KINDAICHI CASE FILES, THE
KING OF HELL
KODOCHA: SANA'S STAGE
LAMENT OF THE LAMB
LES BIJOUX
LEGEND OF CHUN HYANG, THE
LOVE HINA
LUPIN III
MAGIC KNIGHT RAYEARTH I
MAGIC KNIGHT RAYEARTH II
MAHOROMATIC: AUTOMATIC MAIDEN
MAN OF MANY FACES
MARMALADE BOY
MARS
MINK
MIRACLE GIRLS
MIYUKI-CHAN IN WONDERLAND
MODEL
ONE
PARADISE KISS
PARASYTE
PEACH GIRL
PEACH GIRL: CHANGE OF HEART
PET SHOP OF HORRORS
PITA-TEN
PLANET LADDER
PLANETES
PRIEST
PRINCESS AI
PSYCHIC ACADEMY
RAGNAROK
RAVE MASTER
REALITY CHECK
REBIRTH

01.09.04T

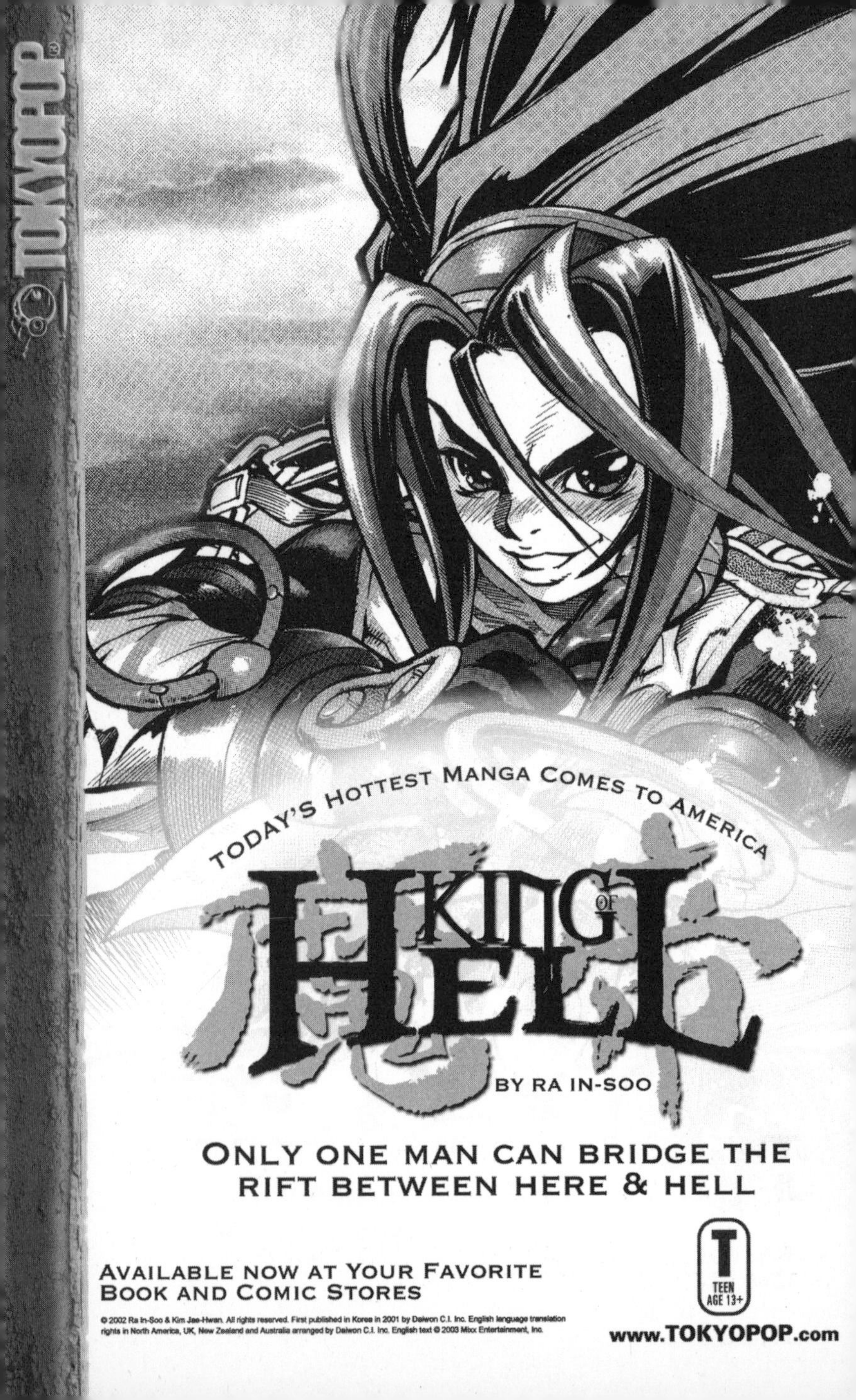
TOKYOPOP
TODAY'S HOTTEST MANGA COMES TO AMERICA
KING OF HELL
BY RA IN-SOO
ONLY ONE MAN CAN BRIDGE THE RIFT BETWEEN HERE & HELL
AVAILABLE NOW AT YOUR FAVORITE BOOK AND COMIC STORES
T
TEEN
AGE 13+
© 2002 Ra In-Soo & Kim Jae-Hwan. All rights reserved. First published in Korea in 2001 by Daiwon C.I. Inc. English language translation rights in North America, UK, New Zealand and Australia arranged by Daiwon C.I. Inc. English text © 2003 Mixx Entertainment, Inc.
www.TOKYOPOP.com

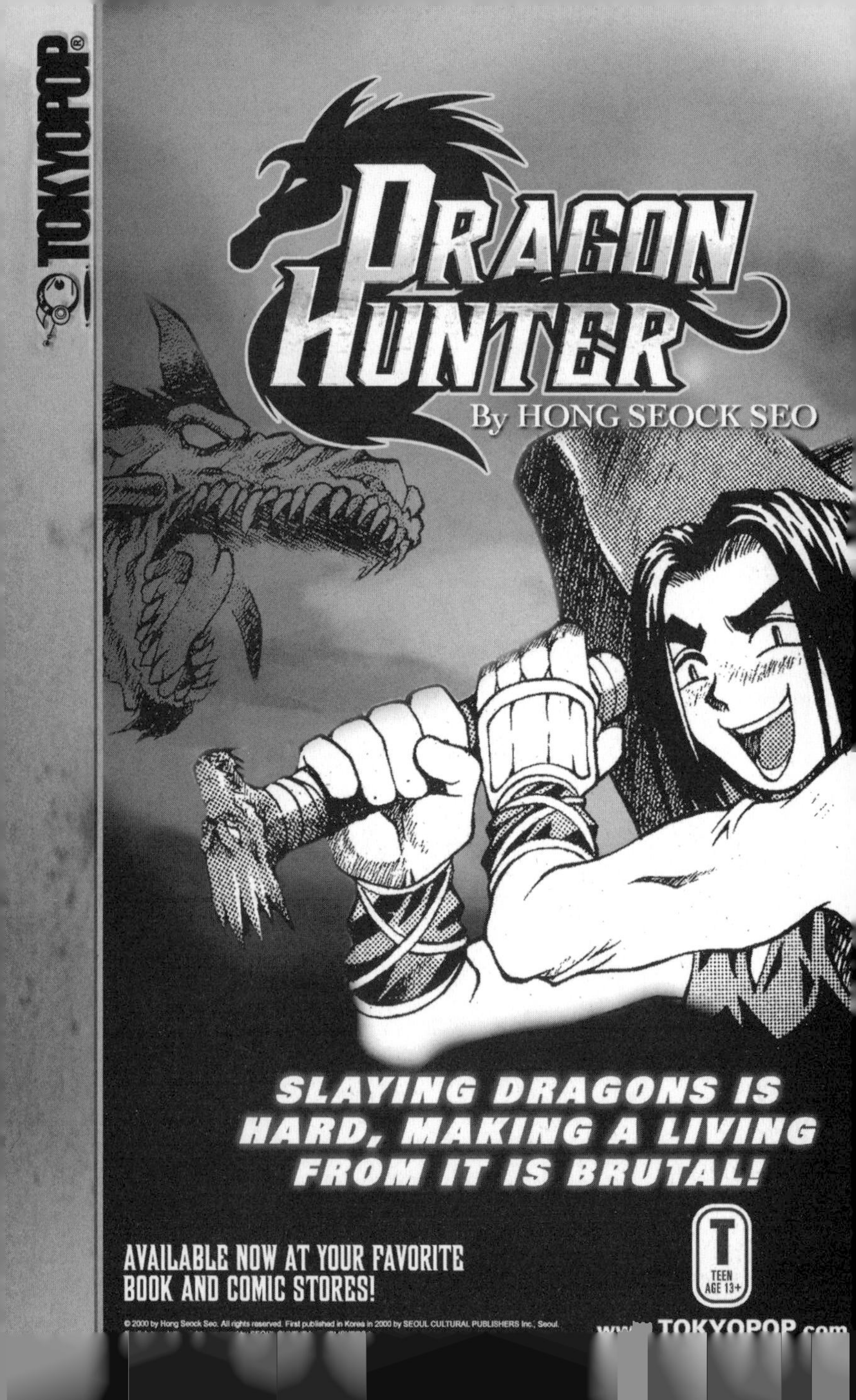
TOKYOPOP®
DRAGON HUNTER
By HONG SEOCK SEO
SLAYING DRAGONS IS HARD, MAKING A LIVING FROM IT IS BRUTAL!
T TEEN AGE 13+
AVAILABLE NOW AT YOUR FAVORITE BOOK AND COMIC STORES!
© 2000 by Hong Seock Seo. All rights reserved. First published in Korea in 2000 by SEOUL CULTURAL PUBLISHERS Inc., Seoul.
TOKYOPOP.com

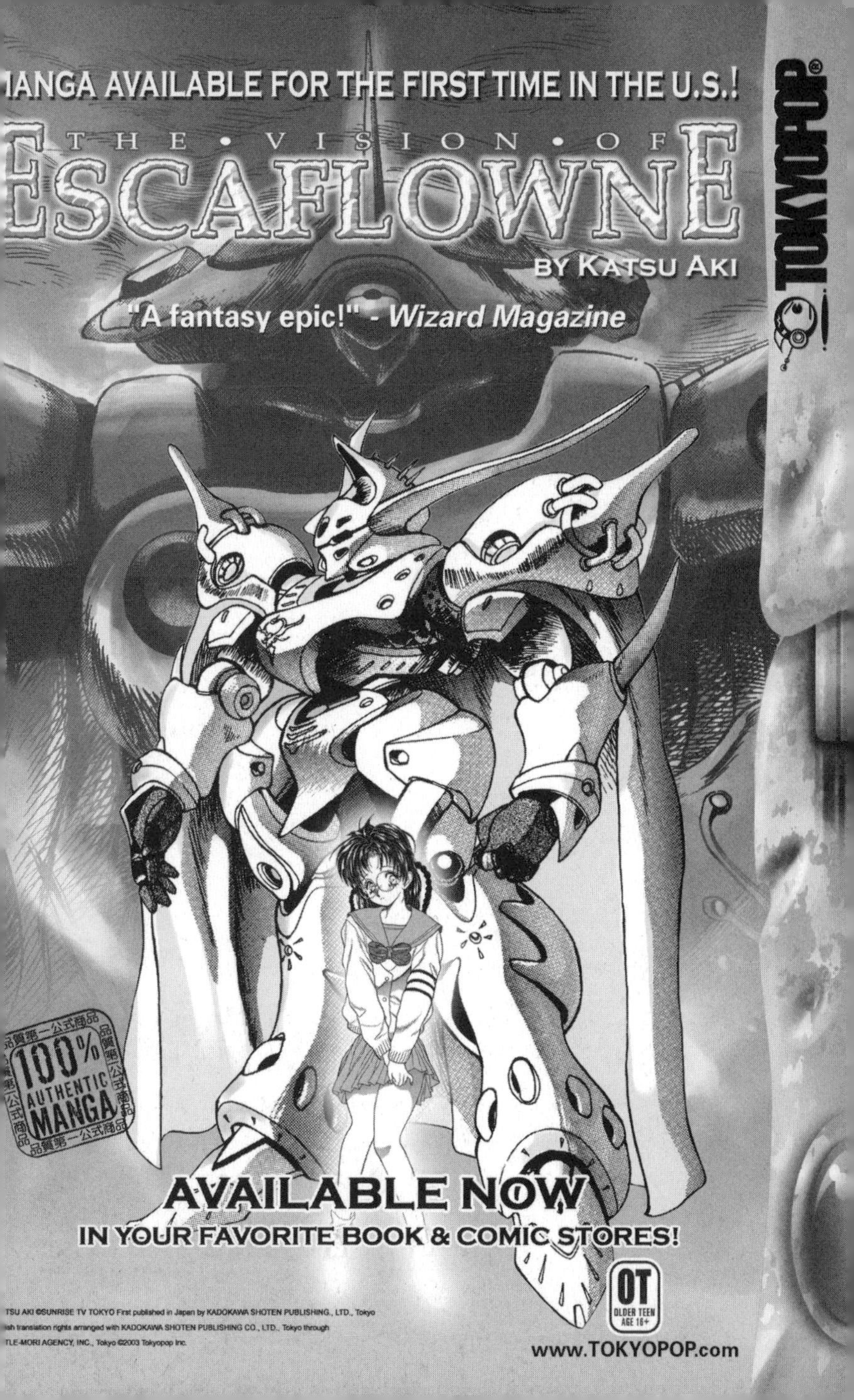

IANGA AVAILABLE FOR THE FIRST TIME IN THE U.S.!
THE • VISION • OF
ESCAFLOWNE
BY KATSU AKI
"A fantasy epic!" - Wizard Magazine
TOKYOPOP®
100% AUTHENTIC MANGA
品質第一公式商品
AVAILABLE NOW
IN YOUR FAVORITE BOOK & COMIC STORES!
OT
OLDER TEEN AGE 16+
TSU AKI ©SUNRISE TV TOKYO First published in Japan by KADOKAWA SHOTEN PUBLISHING., LTD., Tokyo
ish translation rights arranged with KADOKAWA SHOTEN PUBLISHING CO., LTD., Tokyo through
TLE-MORI AGENCY, INC., Tokyo ©2003 Tokyopop Inc.
www.TOKYOPOP.com

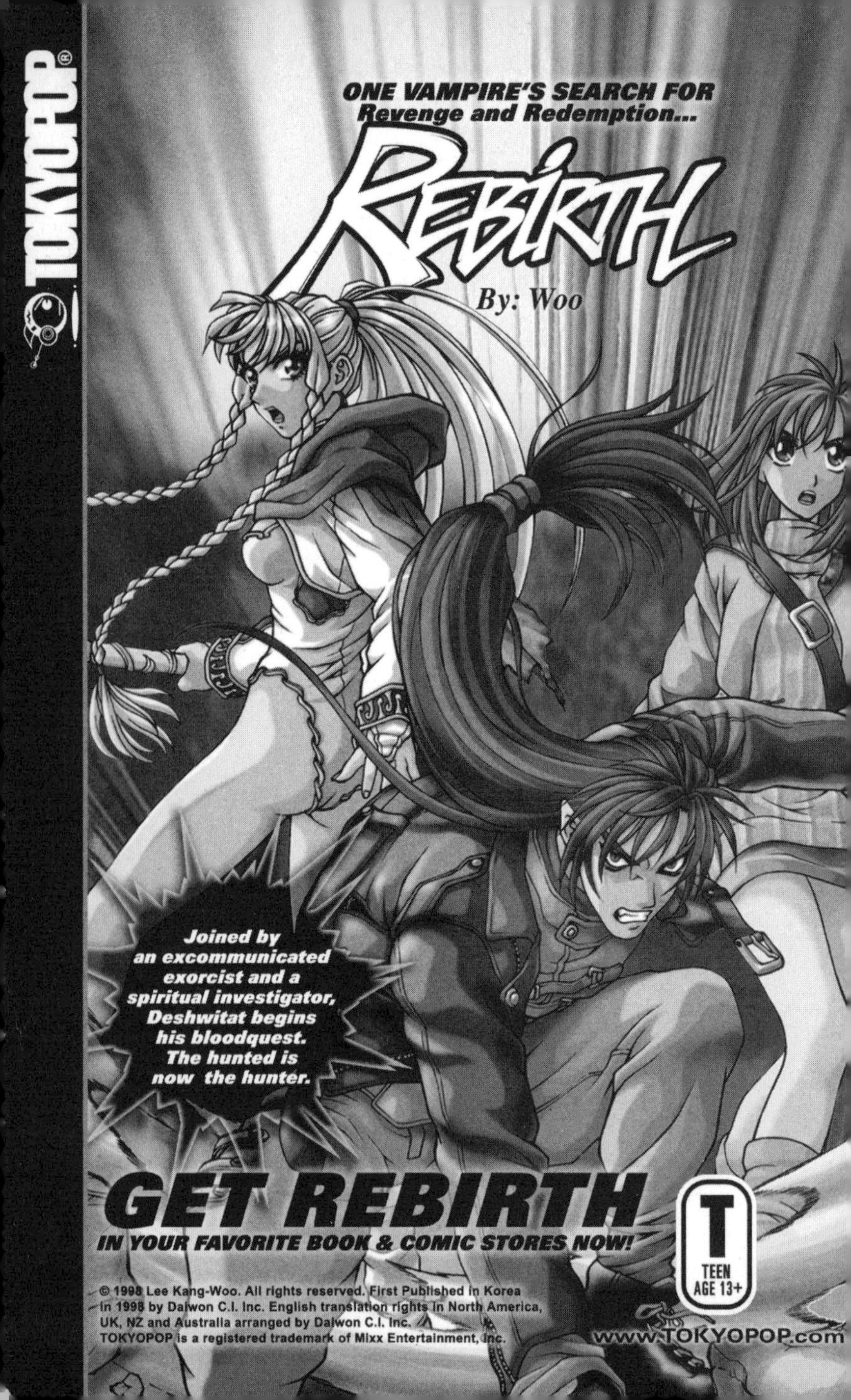

TOKYOPOP®
ONE VAMPIRE'S SEARCH FOR Revenge and Redemption...
REBIRTH
By: Woo
Joined by an excommunicated exorcist and a spiritual investigator, Deshwitat begins his bloodquest. The hunted is now the hunter.
GET REBIRTH
IN YOUR FAVORITE BOOK & COMIC STORES NOW!
T TEEN AGE 13+
© 1998 Lee Kang-Woo. All rights reserved. First Published in Korea in 1998 by Daiwon C.I. Inc. English translation rights in North America, UK, NZ and Australia arranged by Daiwon C.I. Inc. TOKYOPOP is a registered trademark of Mixx Entertainment, Inc.
www.TOKYOPOP.com